ORAGE'S COMMENTARY ON GURDJIEFF'S "BEELZEBUB'S TALES TO HIS GRANDSON"

New York Talks 1926–1930

A. R. Orage
Lawrence Morris
Sherman Manchester

ISBN: 978-0-9572481-0-6

Front cover:
"Bursting with Stars and Black Holes," courtesy NASA.

Acknowledgement is gratefully made to Frank Brück for preparing and revising the text, and to Matthias Buck-Gramcko for reworking the illustrations.

British Library Cataloguing-in-Publication Data.
A catalogue record for this book is available from the British Library.

CONTENTS

CONTENTS

FOREWORD

A. R. Orage's commentaries on *Beelzebub's Tales to His Grandson* are an essential part of the Fourth Way literature. They demonstrate a way of approaching and understanding a work that Orage considered to be literature of the highest kind. As most of us have no experience in reading and understanding this form of literature, Orage's commentaries are of invaluable help. Here, we can find hints on where to look for the keys to understanding *Beelzebub* which, as Gurdjieff once said, are all in the book, but not near their locks. Following these hints we can avoid the fallacy of looking for the keys, like Mullah Nasruddin, only in places where there is "more light."

Orage saw in the intended difficulty of reading *Beelzebub,* not a dirty trick to confuse and belittle the reader, but a conscious measure to shock the intellect whereby emotion is aroused, so that perception is sufficiently expanded to assimilate a thought or idea. Gurdjieff understood perfectly the inadequacy of direct formulation. Hence, Orage tries in his commentaries to illuminate *Beelzebub* from different angles, so that we may approach it, not as a flat plane but as multi-dimensional space. A fine illustration of this can be seen in the film "Contact" with Jodie Foster, where a message from beings in outer space is deciphered by the human recipients only after they add a further dimension to their trials.

When Orage went to Gurdjieff at his Château du Prieuré in 1922, to find God, as he said, he himself lived already with the halo of a wise man. However, Gurdjieff showed no regard to this and Orage had to endure a severe training of body, emotion and intellect. In the beginning of 1924, Orage was sent to New York as Gurdjieff's emissary for America. That summer, Gurdjieff suffered an automobile accident which almost cost him his life, and as a result, his financial situation became drastic. During his recovery, Gurdjieff thought about his situation and realized that the dissemination of his message was no longer possible in the ways he had planned, so he decided to put his whole body of ideas into a series of books, the first of which he entitled *Beelzebub's Tales to His Grandson.* Was it only chance that his deputy in New York, A. R. Orage, was one of the best English literary critics of his time? Gurdjieff's first draft of *Beelzebub,* however, was rejected by Orage as completely unintelligible, but it was not long before a revised version arrived. "This is entirely different," Orage said, "Now I begin to smell something very interesting. . . .

The book will take shape. It is full of ideas. As I see it, it is really an objective work of art, of literature of the highest kind; it is in the category of scripture. It is consciously designed to have a definite effect on everyone who feels drawn to reading it. Anyone who tried to rewrite it would distort it."*

In the following years, Orage rendered one chapter after another into articulate English. Spending several weeks or months of each year at the Château du Prieuré, Orage had the opportunity to discuss the book intensively with Gurdjieff. Often they talked all through the night. Orage was always eager to learn more about the secrets he supposed were hidden by Gurdjieff in the book. Gurdjieff enjoyed Orage's company and was fond of his congenial ability to find the right English formulations to express exactly what he intended. It is no exaggeration to say that none of Gurdjieff's other pupils were so deeply involved in the creation of *Beelzebub* and so near in spirit to the author as Orage.

Back in New York, Orage used each new chapter of *Beelzebub* as teaching material for his groups, masterfully provoking insights and questions from his pupils. For him, the book was, at the least, a device to acquire an impartial perspective of one's life, which is a *sine qua non* for all further steps in personal evolution.

Orage's splendid commentaries on *Beelzebub* would probably never have been known if his New York pupils, especially Lawrence Morris and Sherman Manchester, had not taken notes. A small portion of these notes were edited and published by C. S. Nott.† This present volume is complete and unabridged.

The notes have been edited with an emphasis on readability. Illegible words, missing or wrong punctuation and grammatical errors have been corrected. Missing letters and words have been reconstructed using the context where possible. In cases where no meaning could be deduced, no changes have been made.

Frank Brück
Weyhe near Bremen, June 2013

---

* C. S. Nott, *Teachings of Gurdjieff*, p92-3

† Ibid, Chapter III

29 MARCH 1926

The first form of reason is based entirely on examples from our experience. Similarity of concepts accidentally acquired.

The second presupposed an ability to see an idea or form apart from its contents.

The third form, objective reason, is only possible to "I" and has to do with the nature of things. The epitome of this is the enneagram. The triangle is "I" and the surrounding circle is "it." "I" is under the law of three while the organism is under the law of seven. Only when "I" can begin to think of the whole organism under the law of seven. In the law of seven there are three points: begin at do—then between mi and fa, then from si to do.

Try to think of the triangle as the main spring of the whole. Without its activity nothing will happen. There are three "hands"—one has completed its circle as far as it can go (that is to si)—one has gone do, re, mi—and the third has only just started at do. If we are alert at the note mi, we shall know when to intervene.

Never try to create art or to observe art with feeling. (This is one of the things on the wall of the institute in a script not to be read without the key.)

The story of the bees—merely mechanical—failed, they got no cosmic-consciousness, therefore, they were reduced in size and lived happily after.

A long time for us will be required to learn to know, much longer than to learn to be, much longer to learn to do. This means from an objective standpoint.

[*Orage said regarding writing that he no longer dared at all to write objectively, but has now a glimpse of what objective writing would be.*]

In the matter of writing, it is possible to write sentences such that they will have, if read, a definite foreseen effect no matter what the state of the reader happens to be. These are called "matrices" or magic sentences. If read with the ear, the rhythm affects you; if read with the eye, the arrangement of the letters affect you; if read with the understanding, the meaning will affect you.

There is expected of each of you, a certain work. That work we do not yet understand, and of course, still less are we able to undertake this work at this stage. Every "I" that has some possibility to self-realization has as its duty to carry the organic kingdoms over the note si, i.e. 2,000 million organisms waiting through numberless recurrences for a shock to carry them over the missing half-steps.

When you have established the separability of "I" so that you can non-identify at will—a different sort of instruction will be available. When "I" is born, then there will be someone to care for it—just any new form. It is not best to make the way to the prenatal growth smooth and too easy, lest "I" shall be born a weakling. Despair is a divine fire that purifies—burns up impurities. Nobody who brings to birth "I" will be left.

"As if" you were a reasonable person deputed to act as a reasonable person would act. Situations in which we find ourselves from which we cannot escape. Take it as if you were placed in that situation to find out what a reasonable person would do in that situation. Then, "as if" you had to proscribe what is best to be done every changing moment. Then the aspect to one's state is real. We are only ghosts, really. These illusions are caused by sense imaginations. Try to see what your organism has been from conception to the present, and then see the whole of your life. Imagination based on sense impressions produces negative emotions. In this state, it is not possible to act reasonably, but real perception will enable you to think and act reasonably.

A mother crying over (to us) a repulsive criminal is enslaved by an earlier actualization. But we are enslaved with the present actualization. Ceasing to hate a person who arouses negative emotions is one step—learning to love such a person would be another. Generally speaking any negative state can be used for self-observation, then participation, then experiment. These are exercises for "I."

Ceasing to hate means no longer wasting energy. Learning to love is developing positive emotion. But to do this we must have a positive reason for so doing—i.e. a neutralizing force. (What would one be?)

If you would say to yourself: "I have a body" and realize it, you would have arrived at our object of self-consciousness, self-realization with non-identification, by the direct method.

We must discover that here is finally and forever "I" and "it." We will then be at do of the intellectual. So long as my relations with Orage are very friendly so long will "I" be identified with "it."

The case of the Russian—cliff, boulder, rope = do, i.e. self-realization ("easy way").

One loses all fear of death. Fear is merely an elementary crude form of clairvoyance.

Are you desperate? "I am a desperate man" (in a certain tone of voice the man means it, essence is always calm).

As I understand it one can only be or do reasonably by doing.

Recite dialogue with regard to objective morality—maintenance and improvement—with regard to experiment, and being indifferent to results.

Common sense is always king.

When the intellectual is a function of the emotional, this is rationalizing. When the emotional is a function of the intellectual this is reason. In this work we sacrifice the lesser for the better. Emotions: do-re-mi—equanimity but no la, sol, si—active.

If you go to sleep observing yourself with non-identification you will find that you resume upon awakening—"Hello, it is waking up!" Each of the centers is dreaming all the time. Dreaming is an absolutely continuous process. (Reverie is emotional center.) In Roget's thesaurus you can take all the states between thinking and feeling and classify them according to center.

It is probable that never before has anyone of us observed ourselves, therefore we probably will never recur to this identical recurrence. We will leave a shell to which perhaps someone may be "promoted" from a lower note in the scale. If we discover the pattern we have discovered a "new line," and it will be easier in subsequent next recurrence to step out of the present line. To the extent of our power to observe with non-identification we have the power to step out of our present line.

Three Degrees of development of "I":

1. Individuality.
2. Consciousness.
3. Will.

Ahoum—widest possible to closed lips—not a consonant, must be thought—positive absolute and negative absolute. A to M. The consonants are points on the circle.

"I" is, or can be rather, eternal. The emotional center of "I" is a certain part of the heart.

When the method is really commenced a change in the magnetic currents will probably take place. Try to stand it, if it is disagreeable. It is nothing serious. If you will to continue to observe the symptoms, nothing else matters. Your feelings don't matter.

The myth of the Medusa, the hero could look at her only in a mirror—so you can only look upon emotions in the physical symptoms. Try to comprehend that this method is only to observe and to understand the mechanism of behaviors, continuously and simultaneously.

Nothing else matters. Literally and absolutely—nothing else matters. A complete knowledge and acceptance of the theory would be of absolutely no value. Only proving it counts. Proving facts on a state of being. And that state of being rests on a new and peculiar doing—this method. A new faculty will be developed to be aware of oneself continuously and simultaneously.

One might ask as the old lady did in a lecture she attended in London—"What is this Einstein theory of mathematics?" Of course, since she knew hardly any elementary mathematics it was impossible to explain it to her.

One should have a professional attitude toward this work.

[*Edna Kenton asked Orage: "Do you mean 'as if?'" "No," he roared. "But an attitude comparable to that held toward your writings."*]

Sphinx:

Lion—no fear.

Bull—strength.

Woman—love.

Wings—aspiration.

Mr. Gurdjieff said that we are full of fears of things that are absurd to fear—and of no fears of the things we should fear.

Intellectual state.

Emotional attitude.

Instinctive behavior.

The emotional center is the natural engine for controlling behavior. Emotional attitude is determined by images held in the intellectual center. The emotions sit in a dark cave. But through the images we see, and through the unconscious images which the emotions see and we don't, the emotions are dictated. "I do not like thee Dr. Fell, the reason why I cannot tell." The emotions see far more than we consciously see.

[*Orage said that in the institute he said often to himself—"My God, I awake in a lunatic asylum! I must get out!"*]

And so when I had found this happening again and again I wrote a declaration. "I have been logically convinced that self-observation and non-identification are the methods, therefore lose no time in this attitude but get to work. So perhaps at three o'clock that day I would be wholly back to the task.

Sin—remorse.

Forgiveness—restitution.

Sin is: That we still identify purely with the mechanism.

Chief feature is in "I's" relation to the body. It's discovery will induce shame. Chief feature has no relation to higher emotions.

The lowest form of animal life lives for, say, three seconds. But in his own sight it has lived what to us might be sixty years—been young, adolescent, mature, old aged.

We have never lived before—yet, we have lived many, many times—fourth dimension.

There are whole scales, psychically, between each center. (This is your experience (Zaza's) of leaving the body.)

Observation that does not carry with it the idea that all of behavior is the behavior of "it" (the organism) will tie us even more closely to "it."

Keep saying it, it, it, it. I am not it. I am not Orage. I will observe the behavior of it—Orage.

But self-identification without non-identification is not futile. It is a step. The next step will be non-identification.

You could completely realize that I am not "it," intellectually, but you have not let go emotionally.

I know that I am not familiar with myself. I do not even know in the sense of being aware even of my body's activities—muscular movements even. I am ignorant of it and its behavior. I certainly wish to know about it. Therefore—

Moon—do, re, mi—going down.

Sun—sol, la, si—up.

Two streams, up and down—there is a bridge—effort within the method.

All emotional attitudes one held toward this work are of no account.

The Gospels tell us nothing of what happened to Jesus between the ages of twelve and thirty. And then, after a blank of eighteen years, he reappears, and in the role of a teacher, lives three years. During these eighteen years he was put in school, that is, he went out into, and became a man of the world. The claim was that he started like anyone of us; that he broke down the middle wall, that he then recovered the consciousness of his mission and performed it.

The prodigal son went into a far country. He found himself living on husks (passive impressions) and feeding swine (moons!) then he went back to his father and received the robe of loveliness—i.e. mental body.

TESTS

Can one say I have a body = observation? I do not care what its activities or experiences may happen to be. I will observe them scientifically, i.e. without either approval or disapproval.

12 APRIL 1926

The interval between mi and fa requires an outside aid or shock, but between si and do, a shock is required, but this can be supplied by oneself from inside.

There are in nature only three notes: do, re, mi, for sol sounds like a new do when fa is struck.

This formula was originally a physical and chemical formula, but later it was adopted as the musical scale.

At six, we now have passive impressions, but these may become active impressions.

Ordinary food = 768. Air = 192. Passive impressions = 24.

These would be, if air were fully digested, a double 24 and a double 12—relatively higher and lower emotions and high and low sex. And then, eventually a third 24 and a third 12. In the case of sex, there may or can be positive and negative and neutralizing. When do begins to be active, the first experience is higher emotions.

Sex power of the three times sort is creative, not procreative.

All drugs (hashish) tend to throw out the magnetic currents. Gurdjieff said no one should be allowed to commence work in these groups who had taken drugs. They apparently become insane—during a rearrangement of magnetic currents, they will be out of balance.

Insanity is complete identification with fantasy, perhaps a role. Perhaps half criminal, half monstrous.

[*Note: Jessie talked a great deal, chiefly about insanity.*]

Movement is circular from top to bottom, and the reverse.

Our desires determine our movement, i.e. up or down.

Try to play a role superior to ourselves—up playing a role superior ourselves = down consciously playing any role = up.

Some people develop an unusual amount of magnetism (animal magnetism). Powers of sexual attraction. Powers of persuasion. Powers of "getting things over."

Gurdjieff, when over here, offered to produce any phenomena ever produced before.

[*Orage personally made this offer at Harvard. They said that they would attend, but would supply neither the materials nor the means.*]

Tricks, half-tricks and phenomena. Science has arrived at mi.

In playing roles one will find the resistance in oneself (mechanism) against playing certain roles.

12 APRIL 1926

Essence in recurrence will act in each in accordance with the experiences in former recurrences.

PEOPLE ARE SHELLS

JESSIE: Is our interest in this work due to an accumulation of active impressions?

ORAGE: Essence depends on what elements following conception affect us. Mother has a great effect on us because essence is so near the surface. So, in prenatal, and for a short time afterward, essence is easily affected. But, soon a layer of impressions is accumulated and afterward, because of the layer of convention (passive impressions etc.) it is difficult, almost impossible, to get an impression through them to essence.

If we can observe our behavior, it will change from opaque to transparent and we can then observe essence.

Oriental education is directed to the development of essence but only in the emotional. Occidental education is directed toward personalities. In the East they like the development of types—here of informity. Even guilds of robbers. Even at the expense of the fabric of society, they prefer the development of types.

Watson admits the existence of many potentialities never yet actualized. The idea is to begin to exercise potentialities not brought into play by our environment.

Jessie re-stated her question. "C"-science (facts so called) are from every ordinary thing in life. (Have certain weight.)

"B" (Moonshine) certain diluted occult knowledge—theosophy, fairy stories, religion etc.

"A"-impressions are and must be received only from a person who is capable of originating "B"-impressions. "A"-impressions are of pure and direct esoteric nature.

No one who has not had "B" can contact successfully with "A." Easterners have "B" but not "C."

[*Sherm has no "C" (Sherm said this himself).*]

In science, there is no interest in significance—only in mechanics. The Oriental tries to satisfy his emotions, the Occidental tries to satisfy his mind.

"A" recognizes other "A's" and "B's," and "C's."

"B" recognizes other "B's" and "C's." Always thinks "A's" are "B's" and perhaps thinks another "B" is an "A." "C" recognizes only other "C's."

Tell the story of Geomancy to a "B" person of the Order of the Golden Dawn. I asked: "Which degree?" "I am number seven." "Oh," I said, "I've passed that long ago." "Tell me then one thing please: what does Pee Bee Pee mean?" "Oh," I said, straight off the bat, "that really means a very high degree." "Yes," he said, "but what does it really mean?"

"Pro Bono Publico," I whispered. "Oh," he said, "that puts me on the scent"—"B" perceiving another "B."

An "A" only occasionally comes into the world. His fishing, so to speak, is always among "B's." It is accident if we are "B" and again accident if we contact with an "A." "A" always comes into the world for some specific reason—chivalry, a new religion, science, an institute or the like. (Gothic Cathedral.) "B's" who are really helping "A's" will become "A's."

Motives:

"C"—individual advantage, spiritual, psychological etc.

"B"—something related to the welfare of the group he is related with.

"A"—the idea for which the whole thing exists. In this case the establishment exists. In this case, it is the establishment of an institute—the prospect of which only exists at present, and will never be actualized unless there are enough "B's" to accomplish this.

10 JANUARY 1927

PREFACE OF BEELZEBUB

This preface is to the book what an overture is to the opera. The ideas to be developed are indicated lightly. The expression is not by direct statement but entirely by parable. Compare Swift's Tale of a Tub. The preface is called a Warning.

"When commencing a new venture, it is customary everywhere and always to recite in the name of the Father, the Son, and also in the name of that Holy Ghost, said to be known only to the priest and a few of the learned beings."

Father is the intellectual center.

Son is the instinctive center.

Holy Ghost is the emotional center.

The "higher" emotional center, i.e. the "heart," i.e. the capacity for emotional understanding of things as they are: reverence, awe, real love etc. is the Holy Ghost.

The book thus opens with an invocation to all three centers. Wholeness—but with special attention to the Holy Ghost. That is, this book is to be read from the real heart. It is true that it is not customary everywhere and always to recite such words, at least in our experience, but Gurdjieff wishes to suggest at the outset that beings living normally would undertake all ventures in this attitude of wholeness, and that in all the rest of the universe, such in fact, is the case. But in our little corner, due to local conditions, we never undertake anything in this attitude.

"Therefore, placing my hand on my heart" (but in parenthesis), he adds, "which is well known to be below the stomach," i.e. we mistake our solar plexus for our heart, we have no real emotional understanding developed, no Holy Ghost, no neutralizing force. He says, "I have no wish to write this book." He is compelled to write by will, which is indifferent to personal inclination.

The attitude of the preface is the attitude of Beelzebub and the attitude in which self-observation must be undertaken by each one of us.

Important considerations lead him to write a book. What is a book? (See later.) Further, will begin with a preface because other books do, i.e., will follow conventional methods so long as useful. But the preface will be a warning. Art (see later) consists of conscious variations from the usual. And the art we know ordinarily is as natural as the song or the nest of a bird. The nest of the oriole seems to us more perfect than the nest of the snipe, but we attribute no value. Similarly, Shakespeare or Michelangelo. He will not be a creature of custom; but will use customary form and add something not merely different, but better and thus fulfill two purposes.

He will address his readers. Notice his tone. This is the attitude and distance we will take in addressing our object of observation—"my dear, honorable and doubtless very patient"—i.e. will not take it very seriously, non-identified. Amused, but not unkind . . . "with God's help and of course, with the permission of the local authorities" . . . all the conventions and rules of this planet, that is the worldly body. The word "local" in the book means of this planet. We are squalid villagers in the cosmos. He will not use the language of the intelligentsia, i.e. our local dialect of thought; will not write in the language of grammarians, not grammarians of words but of logic. In short, ideas in this book will not be presented in our habitual thought patterns.

Our intellectual life is based on chance associations. Only when our habitual associations are broken up can we begin to think freely. Our associations are mechanical; a whole mood can be destroyed, for example, by the use of one word with a different group of associations. (In midst of a serious discussion, introduce a vulgar word.)

In what language shall he write, he has begun in Russian but cannot go on because he is going to treat of philosophical themes? Russian is a mixture of essence and personality. Russians will philosophize for a short time and then drop into gossip and yarns. Russian is excellent for stories in the steam bath. (This refers not really to the Russian language, but to the Russian psychology.)

Also English is useful for practical matters, but inadequate for abstract thinking of the whole. This also is of the English psychology and not of words. It is of the way of thought. There is no language in English for speech about self, "I" and "you" are excluded. Russian and English are like a soup which contains everything except "you" and "I." English cannot confess. In an English or Russian psychological state, we cannot tell the truth about ourselves.

The English are the psychological, that is, sociological not biological descendants of the ancient Romans; the Germans of the Greeks.

He is familiar with two languages, Russian and Armenian, the Armenian of thirty or forty years ago (i.e. development of every person from essence to the covering of personality.) English is personality; Russian, half-and-half; Armenian is essence, pure. But in Armenian one cannot express modern ideas, because modern ideas are not about the essence he was familiar with in childhood. We all are Armenian essentially, but as we grow up, we "learn Russian and English," i.e. take on sociological influences. Armenian used to be pure (essential), but in thirty or forty years has acquired neighboring words, i.e. psychologically has grown impure to be interpreted as the history of man.

Native Greek was his first form of speech, infantile (posture, gesture etc.), but unfortunately he cannot use Greek. In case of a conscious person, behavior is a language. Jesus said, "Watch what I do," because somebody would have to translate, i.e. explain his behavior.

How to get out of this language mess? Heigh ho! Will get over the difficulty.

Gurdjieff never uses the word "life" in the book. He merely asserts that we exist, but says we can live. Life consists in voluntarily getting over voluntarily imposed difficulties. Arrangement of ideas etc. will be behavior: native Greek.

Every style indicates the psychology from which it is written. There are tubercular, cancerous, syphilitic styles. The latter is disintegrated, glittering short sentences, epigrams etc. It is very seldom we find a book or work of art which is not symptomatic of pathologic disturbance. But in this book, Gurdjieff is not writing from impulse, wish, etc. He is constructing this book as an implement to bring about a given effect. He has disliked the language of the intelligentsia since childhood because he is a black sheep. Suppose there is one sheep in a flock who realizes the two things which we consider especial to sheep: mutton and wool. If he continues to develop this realization, it will alter his attitude from other sheep; he will become the black sheep.

He suspected that our bodies are mutton and wool, i.e. that our bodies are stations for transferring energy up and down regardless of our own purposes; and we fail to realize that our intellection is mechanical reaction.

While a "teacher of dancing," (that is of movements, teaching our bodies to make non-habitual movements) he learned that man has two modes of speech (thought):

1. Words.
2. Form.

When speaking or writing you often use words for which you have no personal experience. If you ask yourself, "Have I a personal context for this?" you will realize the difference. There is often nothing but literary associations. Veterans speaking of front trenches and journalists who stayed at home speak of front trenches on two different planes of psychology.

Animals have only real experience; human beings have both, can pretend, and often get away with it.

Can you, as a literary critic tell the difference between a style which is only words and style which is words plus content? (Song of Deborah in the Old Testament.) It still is not art even if written out of the fullness of a heart because its content depends on accidental associations. This book destroys existing values in art and is devastating to a sincere person.

He will write in a manner befitting a teacher of dancing, i.e. a person who is directing his movements. He warns you; you may find cacophonies which will be disagreeable and will make you not want your daily meal, i.e. your habitual associations.

You may think I'm young. I'm not young. I have lived long enough to have "eaten dog," i.e., swallowed my pride, endured disagreeable sensations; fatigue; made an effort; swallowed negative emotions.

"I stand on my own feet." Beelzebub has hoofs (individuality). Boots are sociological aids.

The compulsion for writing the book is a realization of logical need. "I propose to allocate certain sums to those who return the book after beginning" i.e., if you listen to these ideas a little you pick up an increased psychological agility, very useful in ordinary pursuits . . . but if you go on! . . .

Fable of the Resolute Kurd who bought a freshly gathered, i.e. (from someone practicing the method) red pepper, which looked beautiful but made the tears pour from his eyes and his face burn. The wily bookseller will urge you not to return (A. R. Orage); but if the book is digested it will be for your health and the health of those near you.

The book will be like the red pepper, disagreeable to our mental and emotional association and to our inertia.

Beelzebub has:

Hoofs: individuality, ability to stand on his own feet.

Tail: consciousness which can be furled and unfurled.

Horns: will. Explanation of use of this symbol comes later.

Beelzebub is an "I" who has developed individuality, consciousness and will. He is speaking to Hassein, who is any little "I," who has begun self-observation and is by way of developing these three functions.

We have Beelzebub in us, undeveloped. The book may help us develop him. Wish is always for or against, i.e. polarized. When freed from polarization it becomes will. It still contains its double potentiality but contains the two in one and is directed by reason. Hence the symbol of the two horns sprouting from the head which is the seat of the mind or reason. Finally he is a "teacher of dancing" of the movements, also one who directs the three streams of movement, instinctive, emotional, and intellectual. All is nonsense but is right so long as things that don't exist, exist. This is a dig at those who console themselves over the realization of the non-existence of things, by falling back on one of them.

"I have spent the night writing this. Now I shall sleep and you go about preparing a meal of first food." He has prepared us a meal of third food. Go on stirring to make it thick with water. (A nourishing soup—water, our usual associations.)

Terrifying suggestion that all our thought depends on chance associations; for I realize that I have been using these ideas for two years, hoping to assimilate them into my old set of values and enrich these latter without giving them up. Thought the new ideas would widen the scope, extend the perspective and give variety to the content. Now, I feel the actual framework becoming valueless. Will I go far enough to lose the old values which gave incentives and then perhaps not be able to go on to new ones of a different order?

10 JANUARY 1927

The process of thought is an attempt to establish a relation between things.

We wish to cut off the tail of our observation—we wish to make our observation manx.

Now, we won't quarrel over the mixing up of awareness and thought for we are judging then, not reporting.

We hypnotize ourselves into all sorts of diseases—for example the air is coming in through the window at an unusual rate—the suggestion is to say: "I feel a cold draft" etc., and so assign to it a malicious content—and us hypnotizing ourselves into almost anything.

We have three forms of consciousness in us now: mental-thought, emotional-feeling and instinctive-sensing.

But we wish to discover if there is another process of real experienceable consciousness. Awareness is another, inclusive, another sort of consciousness. I am aware of physical symptoms—not of emotions etc. Our feelings don't matter and our thoughts even less. What does matter is what our miserable carcass does. If we become aware of this last, however, we will then indirectly (Perseus and the Medusa) become aware of our genuine thoughts and feelings.

Every fruitful discussion proceeds according to the law of the scale—but at a certain point when it has gone do, re, mi—

[*So now Miss —— asks about her appendix.*]

Consciousness is exactly comparable to electricity:

Intellectual—light.

Emotional—heat.

Instinctive—power.

(The three brains.)

The first prime and possibly the only element of consciousness is awareness. So we begin to try to be aware, objectively, impartially, non-critically of our bodies, respectively each of us. We propose to get back to this background of original or primal consciousness, awareness within which is now only successively apprehended in one of three systems.

We establish a separation between I and the body and when the body falls off "I" will remain. Try to distinguish between the potential and the actual. Compare a seed of a cabbage—by evidence. We know that only a cabbage will grow from it, if anything—not a rabbit. It has definitely characteristic potentialities which may be or not be actualized. We each of us have brought into this room definite characteristic potentialities. I am speaking in a voice which is within the potentialities of Orage. If I say I can listen to my voice but that I do not—I designate a potentiality.

I cannot think—the body does
I cannot feel—the body does
I cannot move—the body does

So I can only look or be aware of them—and only at first should it be possible to be accurately aware of the body as a physical machine, registering.

I have a body
and
I am a soul

If I, as a person, am conditioned to believe behaviorism or spiritualism or what not—I will believe on the flimsiest pretext of evidence. Community of consciousness is not possible, i.e. awareness of another's inner state. A man very inflammable politically was taken into a furious political meeting, seated apart with his eyes completely blindfolded and hearing completely muffled. He was not affected but then he was released as to sight and hearing and in five minutes he was a raving lunatic along with the rest of the political meeting.

As to immortality we should believe nothing. It is not a foolish question to propose but at the present moment we cannot reach anything other than a foolish answer. We have not the equipment. But we can become aware of gestures, postures, tones of voice and facial egressions—this is new—there is the seed. We ought to know ourselves as well as our neighbors, oughtn't we?

One said: "But we know our own thoughts?" "No!" said Orage. "We imagine we are Christians or interested in art or what not—but suddenly we find that this is not true."

The number of perceptions that we are receiving is 30,000 per second. Ten intellectual, ten emotional, ten instinctive. These determine our content in our three centers, but from birth we have been aware of only a fraction of one percent.

Of what are we certainly usually unconscious—our physical movements, so our first effort will be to bring up from the subconscious and make conscious this bit of unused area in our potential consciousness.

Bertrand Russell will take one day of our lives—any ordinary day—and from this will interpret us in exactly the same way that Freud will interpret us from a sleeping dream.

But since there is no significance in mechanical behavior either in a dream or in this existence, there will be no significance in the interpretation. If you tumble out onto the floor a box of letter blocks and it spells the word "pig," is it significant?

We depend on three forces of food for our life: food, air and impressions. Stop one of them and our psychic life stops. If you change any one of them—feed me different food for a month and I will be a different person, or air, or impressions—all within the potentialities of Orage.

The peristaltic movement of the physical and visceral systems produces dreams. Laughter is a movement of muscles—a visceral movement. In my solar plexus which has no senses and which derive impressions only indirectly—i.e. through the spinal and cerebral system which show the solar plexus an image and it reacts mechanically, thus laughter or sobs or whatever your possibilities of reaction necessitates.

Enumerating the symptoms of a negative emotional state will—far too quickly for a complete report—dissipate the emotion and then the symptoms, of course.

At the present moment most of our energy is poured out in the sink of our emotional—i.e. visceral system. It should go to our cerebral and spinal systems—and if we employ this method it is stated that less and less of this energy will be so wasted (poured into the sink) and more and more will be properly employed.

Space and time make it impossible for any two individuals to be alike. You for instance are now in another part of the room and your impressions will inevitably be different. Then time for us is different, food, etc.

(My, Sherman's, intellectual center wakes first—that is why I do not get up. Then I must use this as a lever.)

If you have a decision to make that worries you, commence to observe your physical manifestations and by the time you have finished this, you will have decided the question—why in the world were you worrying?

10 JANUARY 1927

It goes without saying after the discussions you have heard last year that the sponsor of these ideas is, in European terminology, not naive. So in this book there is nothing naive. But it is a device to induce a sort of thinking that is a little unusual.

Plato went from dialectical to myth. But the myth was obscure. "Imaginatively logical," i.e. the book.

There is in existence in the human mind a potential logic that is as different from ordinary logic as memory is from mathematics.

The proper reading of this book requires a kind of reading of which none of us is at present at all capable, for we lack the form of logic necessary. The exact sequence of ideas, even words, is necessary—as they appear in the book.

The preface is to the book what the overture is to an opera. Though frankly I did not and you probably will not understand this at all, yet you cannot afford to miss it.

The entire book is a parable, and a series of parables. The "sower," etc. in the Bible obviously does not refer to agriculture.

I ask for adjectives at the end of the reading—what will you say? Satirical? Plain? Or what? We later discuss the author, that is to say, Beelzebub. For we have in each of us a Beelzebub.

Title: "Warning." (Why not "preface"?) It may strike you as a piece of impertinence—it is that, but not only that.

It should put you on your guard that it is not easily to be understood. You must be prepared to read with emotions and intellect. You must try to understand and at the same time to feel.

When beginning a new venture, it is usual always and everywhere to commence with these words: In the name of the Father and the Son and the Holy Ghost, known only to priests and to some scholars. This is as if we went into a squalid village and say: "Before dinner, it is customary to say grace." But they would say: "No, we don't know such a custom!" But here we are introduced to a custom from the great world not on earth. We live in a squalid village—earth. This book is written in the name of the Holy Ghost.

Every enterprise of the nature of the book must be begun in this spirit. (Obviously this is not customary here.)

And having pronounced these words, I have begun according to all the rules, and probably my new business will now proceed with good fortune. I place my hand on my heart. (Here is a diagram—hand on solar plexus. An indication to the reader that we must look some other place for our hearts.)

I can say candidly I have no wish to write. (Here we must distinguish between "wish" = solar plexus and "will" = heart. One can do a number of times as much by "will" as by "wish." That is, by being concerned only with the process.)

God, the Father—intellectual center.

God, the Son—instinctive center.

God, the Holy Ghost—emotional center.

We have no Holy Ghost, only a solar plexus. It is obviously proposed to write this book from the heart. He avows in this invocation: "I have no wish" but propose to write from the heart—from will.

Very important consideration impels me to write. A book, but what a book it is we will come to later.

It may be a definite thought-form and may continue to exist even though the printing or writing may be destroyed. It may be only a talisman by means of which we can see what Gurdjieff's thought is. He has spent many hours over each part of this book.

Many pathological writings are really only writings of "books that exist" as thought forms.

If it is regarded as a sort of telescope the book will be understood. Gurdjieff proposes as far as possible to use the conventional forms. But he says: As I have always all my life done nothing as others it shall begin with a "Warning."

Art consists of conscious variations from ordinary rules. All the art we see ordinarily in the world is just reproduction of nature as we see it. The nightingale etc. Michelangelo and Shakespeare are only nightingales.

Uniqueness is no merit. Consciously unique is uniqueness according to art—not according to nature. We must make in art something more beautiful than nature. Conscious uniqueness will evoke conscious uniqueness.

I will so begin my mission here but with a very great politeness. My dear honored and doubtless very patient Sirs. (So you should address yourselves to your personality—"My dear honorable and doubtless patient Orage, you are—." So if you can pitch the tone of your observation thus, you will have the spirit that is necessary and proper.) And my dear, adorable, kind and impartial ladies. Not "I'm a lady" but as above, a woman should pitch her attitude! So, if you can pitch your own observation in the key—very good.

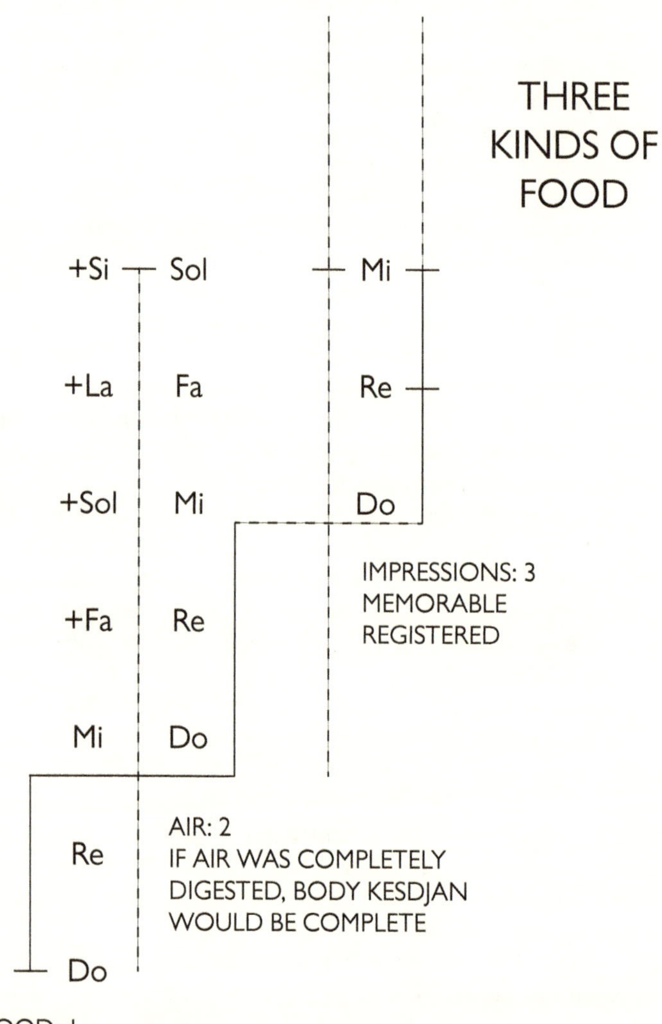
THREE
KINDS OF
FOOD
+Si
Sol
Mi
+La
Fa
Re
+Sol
Mi
Do
+Fa
Re
IMPRESSIONS: 3
MEMORABLE
REGISTERED
Mi
Do
Re
AIR: 2
IF AIR WAS COMPLETELY
DIGESTED, BODY KESDJAN
WOULD BE COMPLETE
Do
FOOD: 1

With God's help and of course with the permission of the local planetary authorities. (Whenever the word "local" appears it means conventional earth.)

Although I have been taught the language of intelligentsia (mode of thought) I have always refused to use it.

I shall not write this book in the language of the grammarians. (Not ordinary grammar but he means modes of thought in use on this planet. Mechanical thought—we have an intellectual life based on accidental associations and on chance impressions.)

He will use words that (may—will, but should not) destroy the mood or meaning. Rude words—but we must definitely break up our present associations.

"What is the aim of this book?" I asked Gurdjieff.

"To make free thought possible," he said, i.e. thought without planetary accidental associations. If this were done, further breaking or freeing would still be necessary.

It seems that I have not decided in what language to write. I cannot write very long in Russian. (A mixture of personality and essence.) I have begun in the Russian language but as I intend to write upon philosophical subjects I cannot go very far with Russian. (This book is also a history of the institute—or of this group.)

Russian, (Gurdjieff says in effect) is an excellent language but only for smoking room anecdotes. Russian in this respect is like English. It is good for discussing Australian mutton, the Indian question and smoking room anecdotes.

What is the English attitude? If he is drunk he is religious for a moment—if angry he becomes philosophical—for a moment or two.

How shall he, the English, enter into the Kingdom of a higher understanding?

Italians are biological descendants of the Ancient Romans. The English are psychological descendants of the Romans.

The Greeks are biological descendants of the Ancient Greeks. The Germans are psychological descendants of the Ancient Greeks.

The English and Russian languages are like "Solianka"—Russian soup—into which everything goes but you and me. (I.e. neither English nor Russian ever questions themselves.)

MORRIS FRANK: Don't the English say it is immodest?

ORAGE: Yes, a defense.

FRANK: Well—what do the Russians think?

ORAGE: Oh, (in disgust) they don't think.

10 JANUARY 1927

English—personality.
Russian—half personality, half essence.
Armenian—essence.

11 JANUARY 1927

A "NEW GROUP"

Certain statements I made in last week's meeting no doubt rankled. What have you to say or ask? What effect have these statements had?

[*No answer.*]

There is no one who ever thinks or does or says or feels anything except mechanically. How were these statements digested? What would you say if you had the courage?

[*No answer!*]

We begin by saying all the things we already know but never realize—for instance "in one hundred years everyone here will be dead."

In my early youth I used to be very fond of Armenian for it had nothing in common with the neighbors, i.e. it had a psychology of its own. (As children we spoke essentially.)

I observe that during the past thirty or forty years this language has become just an admixture of neighboring tongues. (Gurdjieff is Greek.) We must return to Greek—a first form of speech—gesture, posture, facial expression, etc.—the language of infancy.

The behavior of a conscious being is as much a language as any other can be.

It is all (i.e. behavior) Greek to us, and will remain so until we recall the language of ancient Greece. A native language, i.e. behavior. Gurdjieff refers to his own "native language," i.e. Greek.

But suppose you should take modern behavior to an ancient Greek who understood the language of behavior, he would not understand a line or word of it.

As like a requiem as a nail.

I have gotten over so many difficulties that it has become quite a habit with me and I remain full of hope.

ORAGE: He never uses the word "life"—only existence. Voluntarily overcoming difficulties created in life.

Somehow I will find a way out of these difficulties.

(If my hand aches I quit for a time for fear it will go out of commission. I only quit for thirty seconds though.)

In literature there are quite specifically "conservative styles," "cancer styles," "syphilitic styles," (etc. styles). The last named, brilliant, disintegrated, etc. Every form of art is indicative of a state—usually pathological.

In the case of this book there is no such indicative—it is from "will" not "wish." This book cannot be psychoanalyzed. When I say "pathological" I mean indicative of a certain state, but not necessarily a bad state.

I do not know why I have always disliked the language of the intelligentsia but I have. Perhaps because from childhood I have always been a black sheep. (Which you are whenever you start self-observation and non-identification.) That is, each of us is from that moment (to commencing self-observing and non-identification) a "black sheep." That is the sheep that knows or suspects "mutton and wool." We transfer up and down, chemical substances.

From the very bone and sinew to my right side and little by little in my mind I hated the language of the intelligentsia and began to discover the law of association, i.e. mechanical intellection. Since the time when I was a teacher of dancing, i.e. from the time when I began to try to change my habits of walking etc.—experimenting. I very clearly realized that human beings have two modes of thought:

1. Words
2. Personal experience. (Common to human beings and animals.)

Sublimity, awe, etc. mean nothing to me—except sound. "Front trenches" means to a man who has been through something very different from that which means to the man who stayed home and wrote about it.

Every time you use a word denoting an actual experience you return and in some measure go through that experience again.

How can you discriminate between a writer whose words are full from those whose words are empty?

But Gurdjieff says he is not going to write in either (1) or (2). Since all art is from accidental personal experience, we cannot produce art.

"An objective criticism of the life of man as it exists"—is the subtitle of the book.

Your writing will be from your personal experiences—chance—accidental.

Namely, to write, in a manner appropriate to a small teacher of dancing. "I warn you, i.e. to say the warning, that the cacophonous character of this book may put you off your appetite. I.e. the young in this work always avoid —— and bitterness of failure, i.e. eating negative emotions, but not to avoid nor endure them but to eat them.

He says in effect that he is not young in this work for he has eaten dog, and the young always avoid that in this work.

Wishes to obtain or to avoid are simply a petty form of necessity. Gurdjieff says that not because of this is he writing this book.

Gurdjieff warns that anyone really reading this is warned that he may get shocks. A writer, for example, may realize that he may (shall) never become the great writer. The ultimate conclusion is that nothing I can do is any good—and therefore I will do my best.

There are certain members of the London groups who attended two or three meetings, who picked up enough new ideas (by-products)—very valuable—to be an entertaining dinner guest, a more successful psychologist, play writers, etc. But if you go further, you will perhaps . . .

"But if you go only a little way you will get your money back."

I remember the story of the man from a little village who went to town, saw a beautiful fruit, bit into it and found it was a pepper!—all the same he continued to eat it. A man came along and said "What are you doing?! Stop that!" (So your friends say "stop, you fool, bad!") The man said: "Haven't I spent my last groat? I shall continue to eat though my soul should depart from my body."

(People taste this method—find pepper—say "ptou!" and go get their money back.)

A good appetite and with my whole soul I hope that you may digest all that you read, not only for your own health but for that of all those near you. It will be hot like that pepper. (I.e. to our inertias.)

A whole hog including the postage (you know the story). There may be purely extraneous difficulties in connection with self-observation—which may be regarded as "postage." (If you are drunk you'll pay.)

My grandmother said: "Never do as others do—go to school or just do nothing, but not the same." Grandmother is chief feature, I suggest. I.e. have a reason for doing anything—not doing anything just because others do it.

I take for the theme of my book events that occur on earth but I do not propose to cramp myself only to this planetary existence. (I.e. to man's planetary existence or "it"; i.e. Adam Kadmon's body of 2,000 million cells. The mechanical part of us will certainly be written about only in that proportion that "it" really deserves.)

The mood attitude of "I" when observing "it" is the Beelzebub attitude.

I (consciousness) Beelzebub (individuality) have developed (will).

Beelzebub, a developed "I," is speaking to a little "I" (Hassein), attempting to grow. The book may be a mediator between "I" developed and "I" undeveloped.

You must not joke if you undertake a vow otherwise you will pay a year's rent for a house only occupied three months.

Seriously—I was called in youth "Black Greek," in middle age "Tiger of Turkestan"; later Monsieur Gurdjieff, finally simply "Teacher of Dancing." I.e. teacher of motion—i.e. how to manage the three streams of forces running through us. We cannot dance—so we cannot make "it" dance. How to get control of oneself.

"All the world is nonsense always provided that Mullah Nasruddin the cross-eyed bobtailed dog of the President to the USA and Prince are all right. (But they don't exist therefore cannot be alright.)

There are three forms of foods: food, air and impressions. Impressions are the form of food that alone will make possible further development of the second food—air.

Stir water until it is thick—stir it until you make of hope a thick and nourishing soup.

Divine reason, impartial intellection, objective reason; Gurdjieff uses various terms for the same thing.

Try to sell these ideas to a hundred people—you will find a psychological problem. And for very shame you could not talk about these ideas unless you used them.

This preface is to create if only for a moment or two the attitude to the observer—"I."

The next chapter is called "Why Beelzebub was on this solar system."

[*End of meeting—midnight.*]

If anyone realized this, every moment of his time would be occupied. Not one of us can guarantee that he will be alive tomorrow. We know it but we never realize. But the realization of this we cannot achieve by ourselves. We are taking part in events about which we know but cannot realize, we behave mechanically—i.e. without realizing what we know. Although we exist somnambulistically we cannot wake ourselves up and there is unfortunately no one to wake us up. If you continue to attend these groups you will not only be told how to wake up—but you will receive an occasional shake. What we know about ourselves, or rather about others, for we do not or rarely apply this knowledge to ourselves—is that we are the result of heredity and environment. How can we realize this? Only by doing something of which we are not ordinarily accustomed. But there is a shorter way, i.e. the beginning of this method. Just watch yourself. When you get up in the morning—watch the habitual way of your behavior.

The way of catching rabbits, those of you who have lived in the country know, they always run in a field in the same runs—place a trap there. . . We invite you to prove that all our external behavior is determined by outward circumstances—and cannot be changed. You think perhaps that you can think at will what you choose—you cannot, any more than you can change your physical habits and behavior. Observe yourselves—watch your own behavior and if you cannot perceive anything else than automatic behavior, as I am sure you will, then you will realize what you know.

It is possible to induce a change by another means than by any of our habitual means. He constantly reasserts that he has repeated or "as I said last time" or "as I think I have told you."

Convicts familiar in convict settlements in Australia through generations concealed from themselves and their descendants that they were convicts. In the same way over a period of thousands of years, we have become mechanical. If you realize your state, you will at once say "I must have a way out of this terrible state."

We are not even "higher animals"—we are only more complicated animals. We are in this state because our forefathers concealed the fact that they were deteriorating. By the time of the Greeks, people were almost mechanical. They only had myths of real life—but once, men in Egypt or Atlantis were free men. If this realization comes, then this method will carry you fast and far. But just a wish to improve will accomplish little. However, if done from a sense of shame then much will be accomplished.

I cannot have told you things that are disgraceful—"you are only a tree, a vegetable"—without you having been insulted.

[*Sherm said this to Sherm—I have within me a cell corresponding to each man being on earth—observe them and myself simultaneously.*]

(For instance—six puppies, one is given to a hunter, another to a circus.)

So, a business man can talk intelligently to an artist. We are an abnormal sort of monster, developed into something so disgraceful that a realization would shame us into doing something about it.

"But" asked a lady—"why should we be ashamed of something over which have no control?"

ORAGE: If my father died a disgraceful drunken death, I am ashamed, though I have no control over this.

"But you should not be," she said.

ORAGE: I am not saying that you should be, only that we are so constituted that we are ashamed of certain things over which we have no control. We propose to utilize the only means that exists in us. We act only from our feelings—and there is a certain element in our feelings which we can use.

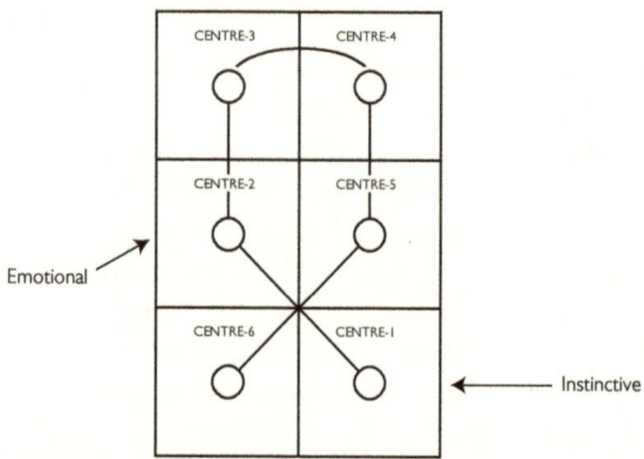

We are capable of sensation and movement. We can feel pleasure and pain. Generally speaking we wish from these states to do certain things. Where in your body do you feel disgust, fear, anger? You say: "It made you sick to your stomach"—solar plexus. Which center makes us move?

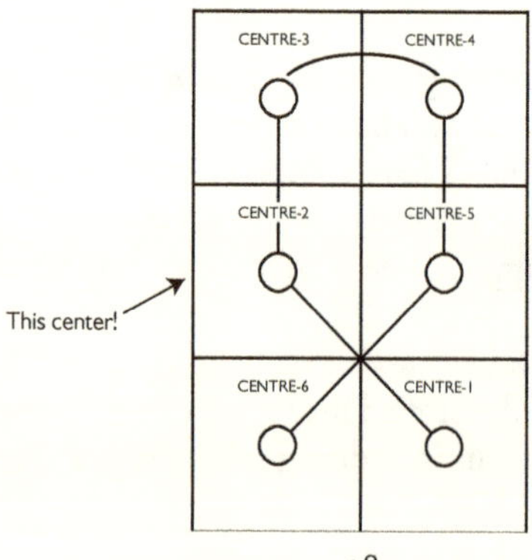

My hand has no likes or dislikes—it has only sensations. But I like and dislike—this I don't know why—and my body must do "what I like."

ORAGE: I thought and I came to only the conclusions to do this—"But my dear fellow" we say, "You would have done that without thinking for you were already disposed to do it by your likes and dislikes."

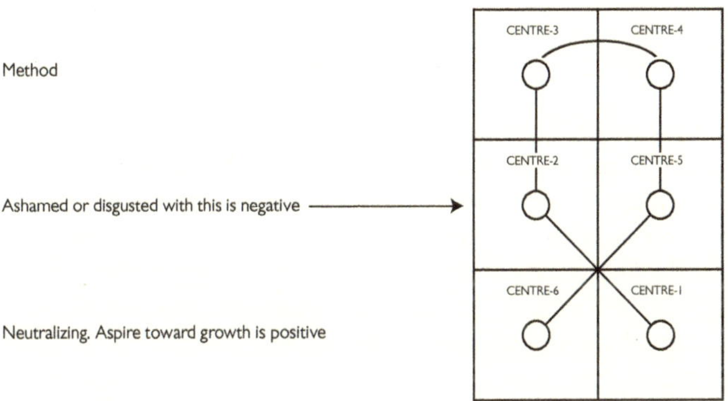

If we can take a wish not to be as we are plus a will to be something else and attach it to a proper method we will have the strongest possible arrangement for growth. Then the program will go:

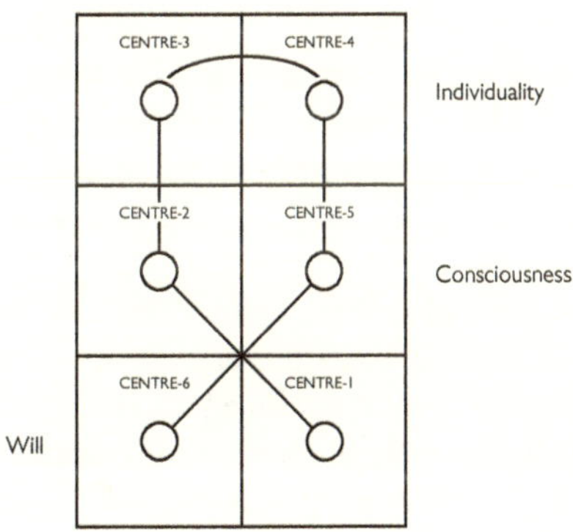

Abnormal:

—3

—2

—1

The whole method is to develop (4, 5, 6) and at the same time to make normal (1, 2, 3).

There is at the back of the head an area that is never used. Actually it is there now. So at the back of our trunk there is an organ about which we know, even talk about. We say: "I feel with my heart," but it is not so.

Certain poets have had real emotions—has any of the modern poets had an experience of "awe"—Milton did when he had a vision of paradise.

[*Sherm's interjection—I find in myself a certain smugness of attitude, dear fellow.*]

At the base of the spine at six is sex. The real function of sex is not procreation but something associated with the highest concept you can attach to the word "will." This method is a true use of sex. It can only be brought about through individuality, consciousness, and will.

It is the *finale* of the development of a complete human being.

Well I could go into it. Interesting from our point of view, as details as to why evolution goes on in this way:

Why first instinctive?

Why second emotion?

Why third thoughts?

Why nature takes these steps so far and cannot take us further?

Why can we by this method take ourselves further?

You are a walking figure, an incarnation of the figure.

You should begin to feel as you walk about this world:

"Is a lifetime enough?" We say a week is long enough—a day.

I say, quite truthfully, that you can develop thus in a week. If you can for one week be continuously aware of your physical movements of your body, you will be then an *individual* with consciousness and will.

It is not concentration—we cannot use any word we have never used before—at any rate in its present meaning. So, if you introduce the word concentrate you introduce its association. What does a camera do when it registers light waves? Concentrate? *No,* we say it simply registers. This is simply a psychological registration—we call this *awareness.*

Be aware of yourself speaking, moving, tone of your voice, etc. You see me walking now, but I am aware that I am not ordinarily aware of what my body is doing.

But if for one week you can be aware of this you will have completed this development.

Hetero-consciousness is what we ordinarily call "self-consciousness." But this method will entirely cure "self-consciousness," as we ordinarily use that term.

Nothing we have ever done will have the slightest effect upon our ability to do this work. For if it did, obviously, it could not be a new function. Take a plane—we might say if we extend the plane far enough we will reach another dimension—but it won't, will it?

QUESTION: How does this differ from observing others?

ORAGE: Try it.

QUESTIONER: I have—no difference.

ORAGE: But there is—try listening to the tones of your voice, etc. The difference is as great psychologically as the difference between actually running and sitting. If I listen to the tone of your voice it is as easy as sitting. But I have to run to keep up with hearing the tone of my own voice. There is really as great a psychological difference. Now there is an iron filing falling between magnets—etc.

He is thinking of absolute freedom (i.e. of something that cannot be thought of). There is no such thing. There is only possible a greater choice of potentialities.

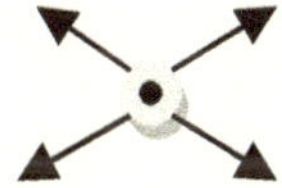

This dot is, let us say, a being, call it what you like. When you reach a crisis you are in fact in a certain chemical state—we call it a state of doubt.

Say you can go to Europe—you have the money etc. But you have an invitation to go to California. And your business is in a certain state. Your family is likewise. Your brother needs a vacation but if you go he cannot, etc.

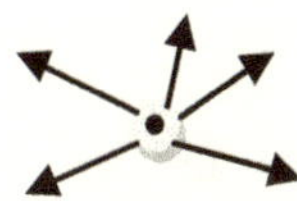

The pulls varied, but not determining. Finally something happens and you say "that decided me"—indeed it did; chemically. But sooner or later you find yourself in Paris.

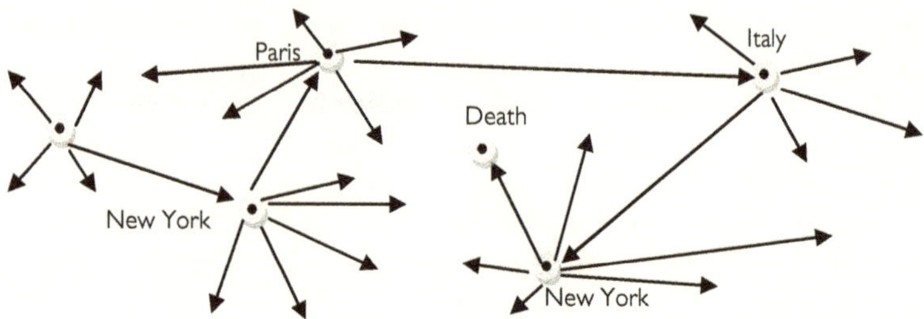

And again a number—a definitely limited number—not an infinite number of potentialities appear until you reach death.

But suppose you had developed individuality, consciousness and will, i.e. you were free—then the line would be:

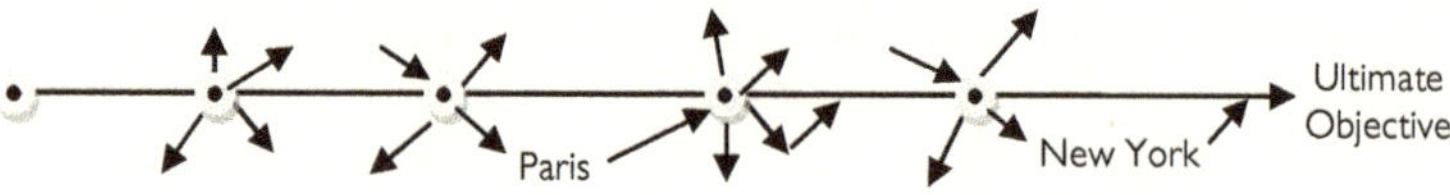

Though it might involve exactly the same movements—New York—Paris—Italy—New York—etc. Yet they would all bear on your ultimate objective, and so you would be free.

A conscious man—he will go through all the same exterior behavior as the businessman, for example, yet he will be undiscoverable. Yet he is not doing it as a businessman will—for money power etc. Suppose when you are dead you find yourself exactly as you are—but without a body—you will know exactly what to have observed.

Facial expressions—only a limited number.

Tone of voice—limited number.

Postures we fall into mechanically and habitually.

Movements—walking, running etc.

Gestures—we have certain number.

Sensations—heat, cold, touch.

How to produce a substantial and permanent change in the character of the human species? He prepared himself to be able to be impartial. He then set about formulating the existing conditions. The human race had gone too far in subjectivity to be able to appeal by any genuine feeling of either faith, hope or love. So he chose something either deeper or more accessible—objective conscience. The representative of God in the essence. Not dead, only dormant.

Objective conscience would serve an individual as an infallible guide for himself—so that he will voluntarily participate in the function of the universe proper to him. Slave to Son.

He gave them teaching exercises—the threefold form of self-observation to realize one's place in the universe and what is necessary for one to do.

Objective morality:

1. The satisfaction of the planetary body. Satisfy, not gratify. Fulfill the needs of the planetary body just as one would have to do for a dog one was training. Not over-eating or under-eating—over-drinking or under-drinking. A maximum of fitness—i.e. health.

2. To improve one's being.

A dog has being—it cannot be defined in terms of understanding or of ability or of planetary body. Essential being is the kernel of the nut—i.e. what we are. Have you any fear of being alone? Would you fear to go to China on a secret mission? Have you any "gut"? Are you manly or womanly enough? No one who shirks or loses his head? A good person to go tiger shooing with? This state of being is the only part of us that never changes. One's inside is independent of the organism. All that St. Paul affirmed of love can be equally affirmed of being. What sort of being have I? Pigeon-hearted or strength?

Being effort is the only method of developing. You are aware when you have made effort—when you have done something that you are aware required effort.

Every successful effort adds—every failure subtracts. An effort that involves ample reward is no good. It must be gratuitous. St. Paul said always to be running in the great race. Gurdjieff says "always be in a huff." Every effort creates energy and at the same time intrinsic strength.

1. Attainment of health.

2. Attainment of strength.

3. The aim always to know more and more of the world and the laws of its creation and maintenance.

This is the formal aim of philosophy—the understanding of life. This is one of the functions of a normal human being. The dignity of man does not require that he arrive at conclusions—but just that he be so occupied. Curiously questioning one's experiences. The attainment of understanding and wisdom. Everything developed by exercise. Pondering exercises the whole mind.

There are many areas of knowledge that must be eliminated from the field of wisdom. By pondering on "God created the universe as a defense against time"—you may never understand this, yet by so pondering you may understand many other things.

You work physically until you drop—then beyond this you are using being effort. Every one lives on his "first wind"—create or find the conditions wherein you voluntarily proceed to your second wind, (Gertrude first wind only, except in the Movements), try to discover when you have reached the second wind, then within the realms of common sense repeat this.

4. To pay one's debt in order to be free to serve.

The Western conception of the word "duty"—the stern sister of the voice of God—the recognition or performance of justice. We must pay for our birthright and our favorable environment, but most of us are content to childishly enjoy it, i.e. earning your living can be done by gracious effort. Or by the obligation to spend $1,000 with strictest ——. From the standpoint of nature's bookkeeping men are debits—no being—no real accomplishments resulting from their own efforts.

5. The attainment of, and performance of duty.

6. Helping others to attain individuality.

By gratifying instead of satisfying, pleasing instead of serving—we serve only kundabuffer.

Ouspensky never gave an exercise which he did not perform—or do something more difficult.

What is instrumental to the end of the first four is service—that which is not instrumental is either nothing or a disservice.

These five functions comprise the reason of a normal man. "Huff" is a passionate wish without heat.

You can reach a point where I (anyone) cannot let you down—and I (anyone) where I (anyone) would not.

A leaf surrenders back to the tree sap—life, recurrence—but seed takes life with it. The leaf is "recoated"—recurrence. Seeds do not recur—men become men and gods. Extract from the universe this substance prana and crystallize within—then can reincarnate.

We are recurrent leaves—but can become recurrent seed. Detached. Plane—tree, we—leaves etc.

11 JANUARY 1927

VOLUNTARY SUFFERING

When a being makes himself able to endure the manifestations of other beings when these are disagreeable. But Buddha's disciples soon forsook this procedure, by retiring to remote places out of touch with other beings—monasteries etc. The foundation of the all embracing is to be found in various coatings for different beings on various planets. Three-centered beings are able to obtain for themselves, by means of the holy prana, the conscious use in themselves of the laws of three and seven. But unless, at the time when crystallizations of the most sacred prana begins, a being by voluntary suffering and conscious labor continues to perfect in himself the laws of three and seven to the sacred degree required. It will appear and re-appear in great travail in successive coatings and ——.

Automatic elaboration of energy proceeded in jungle animals during the night and not as in three-centered beings during the day. We kept fires burning of which these jungle beings are afraid. Therefore we traveled during the day—and camped and guarded ourselves at night, when these animals were abroad and ferocious.

These monks inured in boxes could not have secured prana because it was very far from where they lived and the pass to this spot was already almost impossible to manipulate.

("His Conformity" the archangel Looisos.) The ship (Beelzebub's) "Occasion." Beings on the planet Mars use for their first food only vegetables. (One brain is in the spinal column.)

"THE DESCENT OF MAN"

The cause of every anomaly can be found in woman.

1. Science of studying astronomy
2. Mathematics and algebra
3. All manifestations of three-centered beings
4. All manifestations of three-centered and other beings on the planet earth.

THE ILL STARRED PLANET "EARTH"

Conscience—allegorical and symbolic figures at Atlantis.

1. Head—virgin breasts of female (pure love) attached with amber—non-identification.

2. Trunk of a bull—indefatigable labor.

3. Legs of a lion—without fear.

4. Wings of an eagle—must contemplate only those matters that do not include being work.

For a release of the properties of kundabuffer you must possess these qualities. On Mars were erected tubes outside the observatory instead of a telescope in the center of the pyramid. (Pyramid = three-centered organism.)

17 JANUARY 1927

WHY BEELZEBUB WAS ON THIS SOLAR SYSTEM

I won't cross examine you on last week but say that the purpose of the preface was to describe the attitude which in the new form of thought would be possible. Two modes of thought. Two modes of consciousness. So Gurdjieff hints by way of preface to a third mode of thought and consciousness.

Three forms of food.

Three forms of bodies.

1. Instinctive body.
2. Spirited body (rather than the hackneyed spiritual body).
3. Mental body.

Thus you see our physical body is complete. And there is a beginning of a spirited (spiritual, but I prefer to avoid the old term) body.

If the air we take in were completely digested, we should have a second body which we would have the right to call our astral body.

There are necessary shocks in the course of food digestion. One can be given from outside, but the other sort can only be given by ourselves—by an act of will. The particular act is the positive taking in of impressions. So that every time you observe yourself you are taking one little spoonful of food that will enable you to grow.

Observation is mental food. A complete air body means self-consciousness and this means a possibility of cosmic-consciousness.

Last year no exact exercises were imposed. When you observed, you observed with something "not yet I."

1. Observation.
2. Exercises, "as if."
3. Real experiment—playing roles.

You probably think you can do more with these than you have done, but you cannot. You have done all you can—without another shock—which is precisely this: "An effort at a new kind of thought." For example:

1. Try to set down in black and white what you really think others would write about you.
2. Pondering the book.
3. Pondering "Lady Into Fox."

[*Morris Frank talks all the time.*]

FRANK: Is not humility necessary?

ORAGE: No

FRANK: But . . .

ORAGE: No! Neither humility nor pride. This new kind of thought is not verbal.

The ability to think in form—say of a play—is the highest form of thought now possible. But we cannot now define the next form of thought for it has nothing to do with words or form.

How do you imagine yourself in another form—cat, camel, etc.? Define this. How do you define your attitude when someone else is speaking of you? This form of thought requires a process which we cannot describe.

DALY KING: How does this differ from ordinary imagination?

ORAGE: How does ordinary imagination differ from the attempt to imagine how someone else feels about you?

[*M. Frank blurbs again "Pfa"—he is drunk again.*]

When you find that you can go no further in the method there remains the possibility of a shock. In this case it is precisely an attempt to understand the reasonability of all things in life.

1. The world is an intelligible phenomenon.

2. Human beings have a certain place in the great game of life that is being played.

3. Trying to understand the mind of a creator.

If the individual will undertake to become reasonable, he will come into contact with the reason of the universe.

WHY BEELZEBUB WAS ON OUR SOLAR SYSTEM

It was in the year 223 objective time after the creation of the world.

What do we mean by objective time? Our time is measured by our rotation around the sun. But on our sun a year would be measured by the duration of its rotation around another sun. Such a rotation might conceivably be called "a year." Say it takes four million of our years for one rotation—spring would be a million years long, etc. On the moon "a year" is a month here, so every week is for them a season.

So as every epic opens with a statement of ——.

Through the space of the solar system flew the ship Karnak. Somewhere in space—this is the spot from which an impartial observation can be made. How remote are you when you observe? In the case of Beelzebub who is doing for the universe what we must do for ourselves, he is in space—a ship with an observer on board.

The ship was flying from Karatas toward the pole star solar system. Beelzebub with his kinsmen on his way to a planet for a conference at the request of some old friends. For all I know Beelzebub may be one of your unrealized "I's."

Man has the potentiality of developing into a being that would cooperate with the reason of the great world—of developing from mutton and wool to shepherds—to Buddha—to regulators of food material.

Reluctantly from the fact that he had returned to his own planet Karatas (an old being) from which he had sprung. (Gurdjieff is an old being now. The book is perhaps the last great work he can do on earth. If he could have now his youth what could he do?) Lucifer is our present power of reason—cannot, except by enormous effort, recover its original state. He (Gurdjieff) proposes in the book to show the steps by which he has recovered his own reason. Experiences had made him different. He had in his youth been taken into the service of the Lord God on the Sun Absolute. (Remember how these ideas first struck you?) If we had been able to remain in that state—but we immediately re-identified ourselves with emotional center, instinctive center, etc.—but we had been on Sun Absolute but couldn't stay there.

Owing to his youthful intellection, Beelzebub found what seemed to be some irrational aspects and interfered with what was not for the moment his business. (So we observe and then attempt to interfere—to correct something we think wrong.) So His Endlessness had to banish him to a remote solar system. So we are identified with our solar plexus. Can an Englishman do without his head? Certainly. But the one part none of us could do without is the solar plexus. The whole man is "I"—but we identify ourselves with the solar plexus. The arrangement of nerves in the solar plexus would correspond in an interesting way to the planets, sun, etc. in our solar system.

Beelzebub was therefore exiled and assigned to planet Mars. Each of the planets is an emotional mood. In us our normal mood is that of earth—and determined by earth considerations. Beelzebub was however identified chiefly with the mood of Mars—"will to overcome." Others may have the mood of Venus, Mercury, etc.

Among the people who were exiled along with Beelzebub were associates and all their goods and chattels.

Last year I spoke of magnetic center—mechanically imposed by fairy-tales, by occult knowledge, etc.—it is isolated, it formed a little tract where these ideas could more easily be received. (So in us.)

Chemical composition of Mars is different than that of earth. Mars is the agent of wars but not the author. Certain rays from the sun pass more readily through Mars than through earth.

Although this solar system was totally neglected and in a remote corner of the universe (who are we to think that our solar system is either totally neglected or the center of the universe?) during the following year either voluntarily or in response to needs of a general public character, they adapted themselves on Mars and some came to the planet earth. (Why was the continent of America populated? Partly voluntarily and partly needs of a general public character.)

Beelzebub remained on Mars and amused himself with an observatory which afterwards became always and everywhere famous—so that all points of the universe became, through this, visible. Although this solar system had been hitherto neglected. (Our solar system is body.)

[*Hugh: Do you see how we were last year at Lindsay's hearing the book? Just deaf, dumb and blind, that's all.*]

It was of one of these planets, earth, which Jesus Christ was assigned and Beelzebub performed a necessary part of his work. (The "assumed" trained Jesus Christ in Egypt.) Beelzebub furnished a method for Christianity—this method is not anti-Christian. "Take no thought for yourself" (love), but Beelzebub says: "Take thought for yourself" (knowledge), so he is called diabolical.

When Jesus Christ had completed his mission and realized the service Beelzebub had rendered him, he pleaded with His Endlessness for the forgiveness of Beelzebub. (He begged for the readmission of Beelzebub into reason.) Taking into account Jesus Christ's request and the modes and conascent life (a coined word meaning "living for understanding.") His Endlessness pardoned Beelzebub.

Christ = love. Beelzebub = understanding (and wisdom is both)—hence it is that Beelzebub once more finds himself in the center of the universe (i.e. center of gravity). Whatever mistakes you make in the pursuit of the method, if you continue to pursue the method further you will be found to be very valuable. So he (Beelzebub) returns "enriched" by the experiences he has had on the solar system Ors.

It was in consequence of this that his friends had invited him to the conference. There is a very —— chapter later that shows how much further he might have gotten if only he could have found an observatory already constructed.

He (Gurdjieff) went to monasteries, endured untold hardships and labor, etc., etc. He checked up on Madam Blavatsky—went to all sorts of countries and found there was nothing in it. She wrote many things (sleep writing) that were true, but also many untrue things. He later became an assistant of the great Lama; later, lecturer on Buddha (i.e. of priests) etc. and came to the conclusion that the method itself has never been adequately set down. Gurdjieff said: "I would gladly spare any human being the fruitless efforts that I have gone through."

The passengers on ship, Beelzebub's kinsmen, crew, etc., all were engaged in various being activities. ("Being activities" are the sum of what we can simultaneously think, feel and do.) All the people on the ship were true beings. Among all those passengers on the ship Karnak (Armenian word meaning "our body as it is put into the grave") a very handsome boy stood out—Hassein, son of Beelzebub's favorite son, Tooloof.

(Hassein is that part of you that is open to the suggestions of another part of you, not yet actualized.)

The "stop exercise" shows one cannot oneself stop oneself in an unusual posture—for one would inevitably stop oneself in an habitual posture. But Gurdjieff could not stop you. You hear and transmit yourself the command. The whole book is composed of words that can be appropriated to oneself and by that magnetic center (Hassein) given to oneself so as to enable one to become reasonable.

Hassein—More radiant than the sun, purer than the snow, subtler than the ether is the self, the spirit within the heart. I am that self. That self am I.

[*Hugh: Orage gave this as a sort of mantra for repeating to oneself. That's beauty.*]

So Beelzebub undertook the education of Hassein, i.e. I undertake the education of that part of myself that is worthy and eager and Hassein on his side was always with him and eagerly devoured everything that he was told. So when you were a child—constant interest, search on the part of whatever is interested in this work is Hassein.

Psychological interest is also a chemical process that brings about a change in what we call our understanding.

Hassein is always on hand accumulating material and heating it in a crucible, i.e. "pondering."

Beelzebub with Hassein and Ahoon, an old servant who accompanies him everywhere (that is, Ahoon was his body) spoke of Tooloof, father of Hassein.

[*Tooloof, Beelzebub's favorite son, was Gurdjieff in the case of Orage, and it follows, of course, Orage is Tooloof to you and me.*]

They were seated on the topmost deck underneath the dome (name denoting—"through which can be seen the heavens"—i.e. the intellectual center.) From there they could survey the boundless cosmic panorama (i.e. never forget that you can survey the great cosmic plan . . . through yourself.)

He was speaking of the planet Venus. Very characteristic of us.

(The word "philosophy" means either "love of wisdom" or "wisdom of love.")

The captain came in to ask for Beelzebub's advice and said: I foresee that in the line of our progress a comet has passed. If we pursue our line of progress we will run into its path and into the gas left there which is always injurious to our bodies. That is, the captain (always common sense) says if this discussion goes on (about Venus) it will injure Hassein. So Beelzebub says we can either stop or detour. But if we take the detour it will mean wear on the ship. So we will stop and think and instruct Hassein. You go and give the necessary orders and come back. I wish to know from you about ships—that means a communication between centers, methods and vehicles for psychological changes. There is a third sort of ship between solar systems—i.e. between self- and cosmic-consciousness.

I might say for instance that trans-solar ships, in my youth, spent nearly half their energy in carrying supplies and fuel. (I.e. monks etc. in Gurdjieff's youth spent their energy in locomotion. The type of ship that Buddha designed was immediately superseded by an inferior ship.) Whereas this ship is so simple that we might think we were on one of the planets (i.e. behaviorism, for example, might appear to be similar to this method, it might be mistaken for a planetary method, a mood, religion or what have you.)

Beelzebub says to Hassein ask me anything you like (what would you ask?) Hassein says: You have told me so much about that solar system upon which you once were, that I am very curious. Tell me, are there beings there?

Beelzebub says: Yes, there are beings who have the potentiality of possessing or becoming souls. Of course the external form differs on the various planets. I.e. evolution has determined our particular form—there is a certain chemistry on this planet as on no other planet and therefore we differ. If you were on a different planet you might find yourself in a really different form. I mean planet quite realistically.

Hassein is looking at a map of himself but Beelzebub is looking at a cosmic map. So when Beelzebub says "solar system and planets" Hassein thinks of "solar plexus and moods." For instance, on Mars beings are coated (note) in the form of a corona, i.e. large trunk, two large wings, two legs, eyes so bright that they can light up the dark and wings so strong that they can take them even beyond the atmosphere of their own planet. Wings; imagination, eyes; to see—understanding.

To incarnate—a neutralizing form supplied by a mother is coated on a three-centered essence.

There is also a small planet in this solar system called moon—of second order. I watched it from my observatory. (What is moon in yourself?) The beings there have very strong spirit and very weak bodies. The air is so cold that breath is immediately congealed and the next day so hot that you can cook eggs on a rock. Immediately behind it is a planet called earth. On this planet there are also beings called men closely resembling our own selves only their skin is a little slimier. They have no tail, no horns, no hooves, they have invented boots but they are no good—(i.e. horns = will, tail = consciousness, hooves = individuality). But we invented shoes, boots = personality. Our individuality is touchy, shows tenderness. If their exterior is so unattractive you can imagine their psychological condition. This is due to external conditions existing only there. Nowhere else in the whole universe are the conditions as miserable as on this planet earth.

[*Next meeting—24 E. 40th, second floor.*]

17 JANUARY 1927

The preface defined the attitude. Also mentioned a form of thought corresponding to two forms of consciousness. Will now discuss the third form.

There are three kinds of food. To digest, we need two shocks, one at "mi" of air digestion. This shock must be conscious and from within. It is given by conscious impressions, taken by self-observation. Each self-observation is a spoonful of food to build the astral body.

Bodies and corresponding states of consciousness:

1. Food—body—waking and sleeping consciousness.
2. Air—spirit or astral body—self-consciousness.
3. Mental—for cosmic-consciousness. We have no fact of this yet and have no mental body at all.

The three stages of self-observation:

1. Self-observation.
2. Participation.
3. Experimentation.

At first it is not "I" who observes. The above three takes us to "mi" of the air exercise. Then we must have exercises for "thought."

For example:

1. Imagine ourselves in a different body. (Lady into Fox.)
2. Write down what somebody really thinks of you; and you will find it requires unusual processes.

In the book we will find graded exercises in this kind of thought. It is not verbal thought nor thought in forms (i.e. so much of astral mechanical thought as we possess) but is a different sort.

Ordinary imagination consists in assembling known images into new patterns.

Objective thought is an attempt to understand the nature of things as reasonably exhibited. To understand the reason in the mind of the creator. Start on the assumption that the whole is intelligible, a process being played through; man with a function; but not yet intelligible in terms of our reason as so far developed.

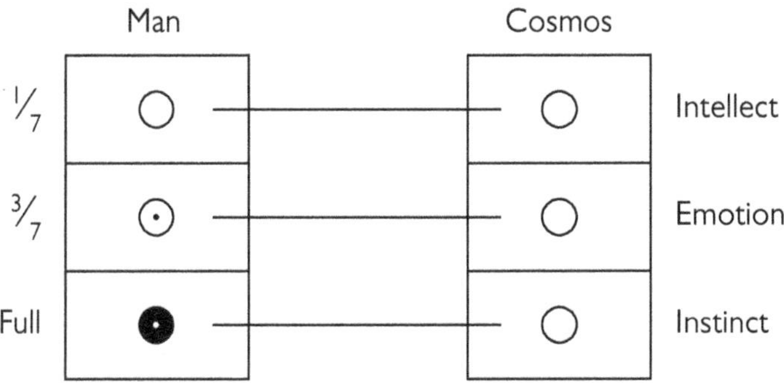

We can understand only what we have chemicals for. Number 1 is only a word, number 2 emotion only three-sevenths understood (such words as sin, sacrifice, purgatory). If an individual can develop reason he will come in contact with number 1 and will put content into the word he now knows.

WHY BEELZEBUB WAS ON OUR SOLAR SYSTEM

It was the year 223 in objective time, after the creation of the world (1923). It was on the ship Karnak in space, between the solar systems. This means in complete detachment; from here impartial observation may be made. The ship was passing from the milky way to the pole star. He was on his way to a conference. The implication being that the universe is reasonably and intelligently conducted and that there are many details to be taken care of. There is a suggestion that beings may develop from unconscious agents, "mutton and wool," to reasonable agents.

Beelzebub was reluctant to go on this journey, because he had just returned, an old being, to his planet Caritas, after long exile. What has been exiled? The "I," objective reasoning. Beelzebub has returned by great effort, later will show how. He is marked by his experiences and has aged.

In youth he had been taken into service on the Sun Absolute, in attendance on His Endlessness; that is, he had obtained a moment of non-identified observation. After the first moment of observation; he had dropped back to the emotional or instinctive center. This is comparable to having been on the Sun Absolute and then exiled.

Beelzebub then, was young and thought he detected something

irrational and he interfered, that is in a moment of illuminated self-observation, he tried to correct something he saw wrong. He was banished to a remote corner of the universe, solar system Ors. We try to correct Ors from solar plexus. We are all identified with the solar plexus. But our solar plexus is a disconnected and disorganized center. One result of continued self-observation would be the knitting up of the solar plexus with one emotion toward a situation instead of struggle.

Beelzebub was sent to Mars (planets are emotional moods). Our moods are determined by earth, the instinctive center. We live on the earth. But Mars' mood is the mood of overcoming. More frequent in some people than others there is a Venus mood, Mercurial mood, etc.

Beelzebub was with his associates (early ideas of fairy tales, occult ideas put in different cells than scientific ideas, forming a magnetic center.) These are the associates of Beelzebub. The magnetic center makes reception of these ideas easier. Ors had been neglected; solar plexus Beelzebub and his associates were sent to Mars. Some of his associates migrated to other planets either voluntarily or because of general needs. Beelzebub stayed on Mars and organized an observatory to observe remote corners of the universe. This is the first reference to the method. Afterward this observatory became famous but not until after many improvements had been made.

General application: Must practice self-observation a long time and make many discoveries before developing reason.

Personal: Gurdjieff worked thirty years before he was able to publish the method.

Ors was neglected but occasionally messengers were sent. Jesus Christ trained among the Essenes, an Egyptian sect. Beelzebub played a necessary part. This does not refer to the temptation on the mountain. His observatory was also Egyptian, that is he added a practical method to Christ's message addressed to the solar plexus.

The first objection often made to the method is that it is selfish. Christ says: take no thought for yourself and Beelzebub says: take thought only for yourself because only then will it be possible to take thought for others. The Gnostics introduced the method into Christianity. But the early Christians expelled the Gnostics.

Jesus recognized the value of the method and pleaded with His Endlessness to restore Beelzebub. Although Jesus' own followers denied the method. His Endlessness pardoned Beelzebub on account of his cognizance, i.e. his living for understanding—life. *We live for understanding*.

So Beelzebub is back in the center of the megalocosmos, that is, he was identified with his true center, his real "I." His prestige was not spoiled by his errors and identification, for mistaken identifications enrich the final one with the true center. So Beelzebub and his attendants were with the crew on the ship Karnak. Each was busy with his duties or his being-intellection. Most of what we do is done mechanically; but when we do something, putting into it all of our three actualized functions, thinking, feeling, doing, this is a being act, although still mechanical.

Karnak is an Armenian word, meaning our body as put into the grave. The ship is our body, travels on the planet, the planets and the systems.

Beelzebub has his grandson Hassein. Who is Hassein? Hassein is capable of listening to Beelzebub or the magnetic center. Open to suggestion from the undeveloped "I." (Compare the "stop exercises," where the suggestion is given from without and must be reissued from within.)

Hassein listens and what he takes in he will apply. The book is of words uttered by "I," what is understood will be acted on. Nothing I have not known and yet nothing which I ordinarily realize. The book is to provoke my own understanding.

"More radiant than the sun, purer than the snow, subtler than the ether, is the self, the spirit within my heart. I am that self, that self am I." Hassein is representative of the self in us.

Beelzebub undertakes the education of Hassein; and Hassein was always with him and eagerly devoured all that he heard. "Interest" is a chemical process, heating the crucible. (Light, heat, weight, psychological attitude must precede qualities we attribute to objects.)

Hassein is stirred emotionally by being with Beelzebub and accumulating raw material of thought, combining the two, he actively ponders.

Ahoon, Beelzebub's faithful servant, is his body, which he always takes with him.

He is seated in the topmost cabin under a dome (the head) surveying the universe (mind). Beelzebub is speaking of the solar system Ors (solar plexus), of experiences we all have. He was talking of Venus (discussing love).

Interrupted by the captain (captain is common sense) of the ship who asks Beelzebub's advice: "If we continue, we will run into 'gas'" (if we keep on with this discussion of love we will come into an aspect of the situation which will be poisonous to young Hassein). Beelzebub says either we detour (hedge, finesse, evade the issue) or stop and think (Venus, love, Christianity). The line of love will end in distaste, causes and provides a neutralizing force.

We will stop and talk about ships (ships are means of communication between centers i.e. methods—method of self-observation is a ship). Ships, when he began the method, were very clumsy, that is, Gurdjieff spent years of effort and travel searching for a method. All those he found were wasteful of most of their energy in clumsy approximations.

Beelzebub finds this present ship so simple that one might think himself on a planet, i.e. this method seems to be a natural and logical conclusion of behaviorism, yet is not contained in it. He sends the captain off and offers to talk to Hassein about anything he wants to hear. Hassein asks the right questions, showing a real desire to know, without which Beelzebub would not talk.

Are there beings on the planets of that system with which you were identified? Yes, except on planets too young or too far from the sun, with potentiality of becoming souls. Their external forms vary according to physical constituents (form determined by biology). An element is present on this planet which is not on the others. Try to imagine the same three centers in different physical forms. Creatures on Mars, large trunks, little legs, large shining eyes, which light up the darkness, wings (imagination); eyes (power to see meaning in dark places). On a planet, a little lower, they are coated with fur. Three-centered essences dipped into chemical elements of any given planet and assume a form. This is not incarnation. This is like galvanizing, if one can assume the object was invisible.

There are also beings on a planet of the second order, the moon, which Beelzebub observed. (What is the moon in us?) Frail bodies and strong spirits, figures like ants. Swarm results visible. Hassein should find results visible in him. The climate is variable from extreme cold to extreme heat.

Behind the moon, earth beings have a form like that of Beelzebub except their skins are a little slimier and they have no tail—consciousness; no horns—will; no hoofs—individuality. They have invented boots or personality, pretence that we have true individuality but not real defenses as shown by the fact that we are touchy, open to wounds of vanity, self-pride, etc. The psyche also is imperfect due to abnormal conditions, established after physical birth, leading us to develop abortive, monstrous reason, unlike reason on any other planet.

18 JANUARY 1927

Every one of us uses the word "I." If a prize were offered to ascribe to that word "I" some quality that cannot be found in any other, could you win that prize? When we say "I" we mean "it." And we can talk about "it."

All talk about oneself falls into two classes, one about "I" and one about "it." But talk about "I" is nothing for it cannot be checked. But if you say I am ten feet tall, we say, "Oh, well, now you are talking. We can check that."

"I" is a potentiality resident in us, the development of which will entitle us to say I.

Each of us is in an organism with a particular form, speech, thought, way of walking, etc.—and all have both social and biological history. (Definition of an adult is an individual "I" who wishes to become distinguishable from "it.")

This body yields us sensations.

Wim was wrong in saying that we ought never to regret not having observed during a day. If you don't treat yourself roughly you won't get anywhere. If you say at the end of the day in which you have decided to observe your tones of voice: "Orage, dear me, I did not observe today. Hi, ho." No! If you fail in a vow, stay up all night—don't give yourself that treat you had planned. Fine yourself. Set up a box at home and on those days when you fail in your vow, put in a dollar or a nickel or a hundred dollars. At the end of the month give the money to the institute. We shall anticipate receiving some money, but with all our hearts hope that you adopt this suggestion and that we receive no money at all from this.

[*All the boys and girls squirmed.*]

20 JANUARY 1927

[*He carried on an imaginary conversation with an egg.*]

ORAGE: If you will submit to a process of incubation and make an effort, i.e. peck your shell, you can become a chicken.

EGG: Oh, I've heard of chickens but I don't believe in them.

ORAGE: Well, peck at your shell (that is, observe, etc.)

EGG: Show me a chicken first.

ORAGE: I can't until you get out of that egg.

EGG: Well, what proof can you give?

ORAGE: Peck at it!

EGG: How do I know it isn't too thick?

ORAGE: Peck at it. It's very easy.

EGG: Show me someone who has succeeded then.

ORAGE: I can't. Not until you come out of that egg.

EGG: But I've never seen a chicken.

ORAGE: Well, peck at your shell and you can.

EGG: But how do I know I'll not be worse off? Jump into a frying pan or something and become a poached egg?

[*I have written it badly but write your own dialogue. Very amusing.*]

24 JANUARY 1927

Beelzebub is the prototype of a complete individual; Hassein the nucleus of the magnetic center; the companions and kinsmen are other cells. Beelzebub begins a series of stories in reply to definite questions from Hassein. Hassein is interested like every magnetic center in questions as to the nature and purpose of life; what response to such words as immortality other states of consciousness, etc.

Hassein asks, "What are souls?" and "Are there souls on all the planets?" Planets are emotional states or postures. The body passes through movement from posture to posture, emotions as of body. Can we pass from mood to mood?

The use of the term ship will be familiar to those who know the two schools of Buddhism, esoteric and exoteric, greater and lesser vehicles. They refer to two psychological methods.

Transition from one emotional state to another at will; for example from anger to reverence; this is movement from one planet to another. This presupposes an organization—a ship—a vehicle, found within ourselves. The body kesdjan results from the first three stages of the method: self-observation, participation, and Experimentation. Those who have practiced these three can thus pass from planet to planet, by the technique of change of images. The greater passage from sun to sun requires the third body, a change of intellectual states e.g. contemplation to meditation, to ecstasy, to logic. We have astral matter; but no astral body; mental ditto. The method will do what other methods have been developed for, to form astral and mental bodies—souls, self- and cosmic-consciousness i.e. a consciousness of cosmic phenomena.

These ships the captain mentions here include religious institutions which promised to carry their devotees from earth to heaven.

Three types of ships; three psychological stages of religions development:

1. Everything is done physically. Sacrifices, etc; fumes produced which caused pathological results. Introduced to astral phenomena their appeal to physical senses is a clumsy flight from planet to planet. Brief, uncertain. Astral-plane, physically demonstrated.

2. Symbols. Astral plane symbolically represented.

3. Perfect method with all extraneous machinery left off. Cf. three forms of reason; words, forms and objective. Psychological processes require a method.

The captain is responsible for conduct of the method. (Orage, a junior apprentice.) The captain started young and earned his rank. His father had been made governor of a system (not all those capable of being captains are captains there are other jobs beside those of conducting groups). This captain had intended from the beginning of his interest to be a captain.

Earlier ships were cumbersome and employed substances surrounding all planets; not psychic, not psychological. For example, in séance astral phenomena materialized in fumes of freshly spilled blood.

Improvements were made by St. Venoma, who for his good work was allowed to go to Purgatory. It seems odd that Purgatory should be a reward; but certain ideas can be realized only in certain emotional states. Ideas in the book can only be realized in Purgatory, which is that mood resulting from an emotional understanding of what ones objective duty is, and at the same time realizing that we are not yet prepared to carry it out. Mental anguish is the energy supplied for certain realizations. If we continue self-observation through the three steps, we will certainly go to Purgatory.

In purgatory St. Venoma improved the method by the discovery of the law of falling. This is difficult to understand and suggests two lines of thinking—psychological gravity.

1. Consider the illusion of space in a dream, a psychological space in which things fall. What is the origin of space, fall, gravity, in ourselves?

2. What is meant by fall of tone? From one rate of vibration to another. A note struck dies down the scale. Each planet and each solar system is a note in the octave; one rate of vibration. Transition is a change from one rate of vibration to another.

The practice of the method produces a change in the organism. Strike one note and perhaps the falling note will produce effects on low notes. The change is indirect. The method was invented by St. Venoma (associated with the therapeutics). Link this with the three psychological stages of religion:

1. Ancient Hebraic.

2. St. Venoma, therapy. Jesus sprang from organizations, included by the therapists and was at first hailed as a healer, which was only a minor part of his work.

3. Method of Jesus. No machinery. Abolished all the clumsy

mechanisms of the schools by which he had been trained, with at least machinery used in ordinary living.

Law of falling. Everything falls to the bottom, stable points, convergent lines to the bottom of each mood from the others. No mood is cut off from all others. (At the moment of conception, all planets conspire; according to distance, in rate from rate of germ as hereditarily determined.) There are seven main moods; but also a disorganized cloud of asteroids by which we are ordinarily governed. We very seldom experience purely one of the seven main moods.

Earlier ships were cumbersome, hard to steer from planet to planet, mood to mood. Slow space is an externalization of difference of rate of vibration. How fast can you move from mood to mood by self-observation?

St. Venoma's system had a disadvantage. It felt a pull when trying to navigate past other planets (temptation to fall into by-products). Planets on the left are negative states: depression, despondency, bitterness, despair. On the right are planets where you feel you can do something other than the thing you started out to do (temptation to turn energy into a particular art, science, etc. instead).

QUESTION: Why solar and planetary images?

Major emotional states are related to images in the intellect, dependent planetary images for emotional center. Solar images for intellectual center.

An angel is a fully developed three-centered being. The rumor of this new method soon spread intersolar and interplanetary. Soon after there were experiments open to all. Apply this to Gurdjieff's "last degree of occultism is common sense!"

Jesus exemplified publicly the psychological stages of the rise of the soul from the death of the body. He voluntarily abandoned his body. This ended closed instruction, for the whole world is the occult school of Jesus.

This ship is psychological effort which replaces the older method of faith, hope and love. The captain describes this ship (the method) they are now on. The cylinder is the torso. Juxtaposition. Generator is effort. (At first of self-observation.) The method aims to produce a consciousness of self and the cosmic plan, here, now, in this body. The cylinder in the barrel is hermetically sealed, and its energy ceases to escape by waste (with the seal of Hermes, who taught the method). Gas, fog, planetary emissions (negative states) are automatically dispersed and the ship passes from planet to planet or from sun to sun, very rapidly because there are no conflicting states. The denser the substances to be dispersed, the more efficient the generator works. The passage is more rapid (transition from low to high), more rapid where there is resistance in external circumstances.

These new ships control their own courses. Earlier religions required devotees to stay. There were certain early conceptions of the church as an ark, stay in it and be safe, be carried mechanically to paradise. Contrast this with self-direction. The difficulty a heretic had in getting himself out of the ark. These ships were not only cumbersome but had within themselves no possibility of self-initiation.

CHAPTER VI

This parable is in mechanical (psychological) terms. Perpetual motion; the notion that somehow or other we achieve immortality. An immortal body is a machine capable of perpetual motion, power, etc. This is a satire, on these notions many went insane. Everyone tried to set up a religion, whether he was qualified for the job or not. Some trusted to knowledge, some to luck; and some because they were crazy.

All the systems or cults, all the pathological states produced by rituals, monasteries, systems of breathing and diets were such. But even at their best their values and morals—physiological and emotional—are based on superstition. Amateur religions are a source of degeneration. All religions without method are superstitions.

How would all this have ended if someone had not proved by means known only to himself that perpetual motion was impossible, i.e. that an era of rationalism is negative. They had thought of everything but *air* (air octave), e.g., weight; asceticism. Machine made of astral body, poorly organized may continue as an animal—hence the Birth Stories of Buddha. The length of life of the physical body is cramped by a waste of energy. Under ideal conditions, that of living from birth in a society, not merely a small community, where everyone was engaged in working for development of consciousness with the effects of this on institutions, the body might survive for four or five hundred years; the astral body several thousand times as long; and the mental body as long as the universe. Due to the wretchedly short existence of the body, there is not enough time to organize the astral body, unless one works professionally with the intensity of a fanatic.

Value of reviewing pictorially.
An initiate is one who initiates.

24 JANUARY 1927

Beelzebub's service to Christ was negative but really necessary—i.e. a method. His life having been spent in a search of knowledge, understanding, etc. he was re-admitted to consciousness, to objective reason. An actuality is a potentiality with a "coating." An individual is a microcosm but the only difference between it and the Megalocosmos is that the Megalocosmos is very much more actualized than we (small fry) are. The idea of this book is that Beelzebub is speaking as one of us with potentialities, completely identified with the highest part of the intellectual center; actualized Beelzebub is meant to be here, the prototype of our complete selves.

Beelzebub and Hassein were on the ship Karnak under the glass dome (uppermost brain). Beelzebub identifies himself with all he is and Hassein is relatively his magnetic center. Beelzebub is *I* on the Sun Absolute. He was exiled and permitted to return because of his conascent and modest life spent in the pursuit of the "conascent pursuit of knowledge and understanding" which is what "conascent" means.

Individuals who are ready to learn are all his kinsmen on the ship with him. And Hassein is one even more eager and ready than the others. Also Hassein is interested in the same questions that we are, e.g. immortality, the soul and the future life, sin, super-consciousness etc. You can test people by their degree of interest that they have in regard to these words. So Hassein (i.e. magnetic center) asks: "What are souls?"

(Planets are permanent moods, and correspond, in a cosmic sense, to emotional states—i.e. correspond to postures from which we pass through movement to other postures.)

So Hassein asks: "Can souls pass from planet to planet?"

To be able to pass at will from anger to, say, reverence is to be able to pass from one planet to another. This ability presupposes the organization of the body kesdjan, or astral body in oneself—this is a result from the carrying of the method through the three stages of self-observation, participation, experiment.

So those of you who have been able to do this should be able to travel from one emotional state to another—not at will perhaps, but certainly on some occasions. The mental body is a ship of the solar system on which we travel from contemplation, to meditation, to ecstasy, to logic etc.

Now what have been the methods in other times to attain an astral body? We know that there have existed in history certain institutions for the development of the soul—what are they called? Religions. They differ from sciences or philosophy simply in that they propose to give the ability to travel from planet to planet and sun to sun, i.e. as they say from earth to heaven.

The stages of the development of the ship correspond to the three definite stages of the development of religions. So in the first stages religious ceremonies were conducted in actual pools of blood. Thus people were introduced to astral body in a very curious way, via the physical senses. So, though for a few it may have been good, most people found it very awkward.

Reason forms:	Religious forms:
1st Words.	1st Actual figures.
2nd Forms.	2nd Symbolic figures.
3rd Objective reason.	3rd Method with all extraneous things eliminated.

So the three types of ships correspond to the three forms of religion.

A captain of a ship is one who is responsible for the conduct of a method. For instance I (i.e. Orage) am a humble captain etc., etc.

The Captain spoke: "I have been in this service since a child—I began at the lowest rung. I have been Captain for eight years. I took office of Captain after my father who had become a Master (you will perhaps learn that here are many other forms of behavior open to a conscientious being than public instruction equally to service). Shortly after my apprenticeship I became registered as a ship master. (An agency for the transporting of souls.) (What would you do if you became a self-conscious being?)

At the time your Reverence departed I was only a boy on a ship. (Body and by the way this book can be regarded as a ship.) You were good enough to say that in your day the ships were very cumbersome (so religions). In your day the ships were run on familiar etheric substances in the atmosphere in those planets.

I have been present at séances held in the presence of fresh blood—no medium is necessary. But to obtain this (etheric) substance much material was necessary. This type of ship was afterwards displaced by the invention of an individuum (a technical term describing a being who has, by his own efforts, reached a certain degree of true individuality). And this being was afterward taken to the planet Purgatory. (So everyone of you will go to Purgatory. And remember that certain ideas can only be understood in certain emotional states, i.e. on certain planets say Purgatory.)

St. Venoma invented a new method—from a certain cosmic law—the "law of falling."

Here I am in a certain difficulty. How can I describe psychological gravity? Say you dream—there is in your dream a great space—though you are only in a small room. What is the origin of space and falling and weight in ourselves? Since we can dream them perhaps their potentialities may exist in ourselves. Now we say: "A fall in tone" how far is it actually from si to the next lower do? What actual distance?

So we may say that the planets are each octaves (that is to say likewise notes), i.e. differences shall we say in the rate of vibration. Different notes in the scale so in the practice of self-observation, self-participation, and self-experiment these processes will effect each of us differently.

(So this method of St. Venoma brought about changes in the personalities of beings.)

Three stages to Christianity.

First—Physical demonstration. Therapy was the main object, so Jesus was first hailed as a healer. But he became a teacher second. So his first vehicle was therapeutics. Second—Gnostic (teacher).

Then third the method from which all cumbersome machinery was eliminated. So St. Venoma discovered the law of falling (think of the food scale). Everything in the universe falls to the bottom. So wherever the line of forces converges there is the bottom. So at conception the germ receives a certain essence, dependent upon the distance from, and size of the various states, i.e. planets at this instant. But asteroids are definitely not planets, they are unorganized planetary matter. Our moods are not clear states of emotion but are like these asteroids in this method. We can navigate safely through to the planets, i.e. on the ship "Occasion."

The ship Karnak passes from one solar system to another—but to travel to the nearest solar system of ours—Vega, would take 250 light years. And if the ship Occasion came to the earth from Mars in twenty-four hours it would be as fast as light. (It takes time and effort to change moods or modes of reason.) All that we call space in the world is just changes of vibrational rates in ourselves. The degree of speed of transition from one state of emotion (mood, planet) to another is a test of your ship. How long does it take you to pass from one state (say negative) to another by self-observation?

Although this system was good it had its drawbacks—when nearing a sun or a planet, their navigation became a torture.

So, on approaching a mood or planet, which we intend to pass, the tendency is to fall into that mood—planet. So when we commence to attempt to observe without approval or disapproval or other feelings—we almost irresistibly fall into the influences of certain feelings—or planets. Everything in our sense perceptions is ourselves projected. There is, of course, the difficulty of steering past "by-products." Negative bitterness—wormwood; despondency; depression or despair. All these are negative planets (or moods)—but it is possible to go to the positive planets by means of self-observation.

What is the origin of the evocation of emotional states? Ship "Occasion"—images. There are seven major emotional states; these are related to seven major mental states. What image is to emotion, the sun is to a planet.

(An angel is a fully developed three-centered being)

It is rumored that an improved type of ship had been invented.

So in London we met the objection of a famous Christian gentleman that we were conducting these meetings only in small groups by the truth that there was shown by Jesus many things but that the mysteries were explained to only a few.

And so here the meetings are, so to speak, open to anyone, but no pledge is exacted and no secrecy. Yet with possibility of experiment open to all. The implicit action is in the practice of all groups to permit practically anyone to come to them or to the institute and see an experiment being carried on. So except for medical reasons anyone can come, and see what he can see.

Tricks = first phenomena

Half-tricks = second phenomena and necessitated a great deal of preparation, say, the remembering of a hundred strange words. During the hearing of the words, two centers were actually occupied and so the words were recorded clearly and remembered.

The third phenomena—the real Phenomena—is a form of phenomena which cannot be produced by anyone not especially trained. So in the Neighborhood Playhouse performances what was unique? This question will interest Dorothy?

ORAGE: In me there is no mystery. If there is, it is due to my own inability to express myself—or in you to go from state to state.

The new system was acknowledged to be superior to St. Venoma and was very soon adopted on all the main lines between the planets and suns.

So I would say that if there should be another angel like Christ or Buddha—he will proceed on the design of the method—this new machine.

It is not very complicated. Its principal part consists of cylinder shaped, rather like a barrel (or trunk) and a generator which is placed somewhere within it, i.e to make conscious effort here in this body.

The cylinder or barrel; is hermetically sealed—i.e. the energy is no longer lost—leakage is stopped by observation. (Seal of Hermes.)

When this type of ship is stopped by any substance such as fog, it is immediately displaced and disbursed by the continuance of the generator, i.e. emotional states. (Fog—nebula.) Moreover it is interesting to remark that the denser the substances the better the generator works—i.e. in the presence of resistance observation works much better and more rapidly. If no resistance—there is a tendency to go slowly.

Contemporary ships possess in themselves power, the full ability to control their own destiny.

Formerly religions required that their members remain within its arms and you would be carried to heaven. But an individual might want to go somewhere else—and could. He would become not a cell but an individual. Old ships contained no possibility of self-initiation.

"PERPETUAL MOTION"

"Perpetual motion," Beelzebub interrupts the captain, "surely what you have just described must be that which an unfortunate being of a certain planet called earth used to call perpetual motion. Many beings perished in this pursuit. This idea so took the beings of this planet that they began to think and dream about (i.e. the attainment of perpetual life—an immortal body capable of resisting time).

What heaps went insane over it! (Retired to monasteries—diet, breath control—all for the purpose of creating a soul.)

Many put into this experiment all the values they had had before. If circumstances permitted, many beings occupied themselves, even though they were not natively qualified—with attempting to invent a machine. (Many peopled here in NY now set up such ideas. One here I heard of today teaches contemplation of a flame in an actual brazier—and the leader repeats for them what he calls mantras.)

All these pantaloons expect their friends to be interested in their machines and so had to be shut up in lunatic asylums, monasteries, etc. (This is an indictment of religion or superstition for the degradation of man. For many of the good habits we have had are thus corrupted, making it impossible for us to lead a healthy life.)

But I do not know what would have happened if some crazy old fellow had not proved to himself and others that the idea was impracticable and it occurred to no one to use the simple addition of air in one of their cities. I saw hundreds of such appliances (religions).

Namely, in particular a machine for use by weights (i.e. ascetics.).

We are now trying to review the psychological history of the world. So we see that the introduction of a religion takes an effort on the part of Adam Kadmon—just as it takes an effort on our part.

Beelzebub asks of what material were they built. The captain answered there are parts—wings, etc. which will last a long time and there are parts which will last forever. So we have material now in us of all three states—but though we have astral matter present in us, it is not organized into an astral body. So we have mental substances but we have only mental functions, no mental body. The physical body will last four or five hundred of our years—astral body will last about 30,000 times that—and the mental body because of its power of self-initiation may pass from matter to matter and last forever.

For instance people have dreams of past lives—but they are not of their past lives. Our physical lives are, literally speaking, so brief and short that the possibility of developing an astral body is remote. But the use of one's life consists in living it so fully that in one moment you live as much as a monk in mediation does in a month.

Try to remember this book by reviewing visually. Try to put yourself in the place of the characters on the ship and to overhear from the various angles what was said by Beelzebub, Hassein, Ahoon, and the Captain. Regard the book as a masque on the stage to give a key to students.

Beelzebub with Ahoon and Hassein on a ship in space. The Captain comes in, and goes out. Hassein asks first a question—Beelzebub recalls his experiences—he had freedom of the planets, then earned through a conascent life and modesty how to return to the Sun Absolute, and to stay. Then the Captain returns and describes three ships:

1. ?

2. Operated with air.

3. Operated with a generator—i.e. effort at being aware of the body.

Beelzebub recalls perpetual motion.

This method is liable to fall into the same errors—fall into an illusion of the method.

Our object is to develop a vehicle enabling us to travel from planet to planet and eventually from sun to sun.

It is necessary not only to come here—but to mull over, to ponder over, until next time you see these above ideas in relation to yourself.

[*11:45*]

Try to resist normal reaction, i.e. turn the other cheek. Normal reacting is to return the blow or get out of the way of the next blow. Not even the habit of non-resistance is permitted. It is most difficult to return an unexpected expression. Whereas in our present state anyone can, if he pulls the right lever, make us do anything he wants us to do. Generally speaking our first difficulty is that we react in a mechanical way. If it is a miserable day, say "What a beautiful day" or vice versa. So long as a man reacts in a mechanical way, so long he will remain a slave of circumstances. There is no fundamental difference in our mechanicality only a different gearshift.

First heresy of Buddhism and of Pythagoreans is "How can I observe my moods?" Second heresy is—criticism and an attempt at interference with moods even after observing physical manifestations. But all these extraneous heretical forms of behavior can be cut off. How? By turning your attention with redoubled effort to other physical forms of behavior.

JOHN RIORDAN: But you are attempting to observe memory—i.e. tabulating your various gestures, movements, etc.

ORAGE: No. Because we don't care what your particular gestures may be. The tabulation is so that you can determine afterward if you have been purely observing.

SOMEONE ELSE: But if I observe my walk, it slows down.

ORAGE: No. But it seems to do so. And you at that point are ready for the second step. Not that this means all others present are ready, however it will do you no harm to learn the second step in this method.

1st—self-awareness.
2nd—participation.

I can hold this piece of chalk. I can observe myself holding this piece of chalk. But I can also psychologically "hold the chalk with myself"—as if I were in possession of the organism—though I am not. And the third step is "experiment for the sake of observation." In walking I will vary my usual gait—not with a view of improving my manner of walking, but only vary my usual procedure in order to observe it more carefully. Try this in all six forms of observable behavior. Try looking, for example, fierce—if that is not habitual with you.

STEINBERG: I'm sorry, but I don't see why the second step is not implied or actually implicit in the first step.

ORAGE: The second step has an entirely different psychological sense or touch or taste—when you react as if you were acting—purposive reaction.

SOMEONE ELSE: On a pleasant day I feel as if I were entirely consciously participating in all my physical movements.

ORAGE: Well, but before that you were aware. It is not that you observe from a point outside, but as if you were outside yourself. Thank God I've never been, or felt that I've been outside myself. That would be simply pathological.

At one time we discussed if it would not be better to use another word than "awareness"—so a hunter in a wood hears a rustle, he tries by an effort to "ascertain" what it is. So this effort of awareness for the purpose of ascertaining what you have observed. "Come to grips with it." Not, "Ah! this is a comfortable posture!" But, "Just what is this posture with regard to muscles"—long or short breath, heart is beating, foot is being moved—everything—sensations, weight, touch, taut or relaxed muscles.

I cannot emphasize too much the necessity for making every effort to make every form of observation *vivid!*

A man who had a habit of getting himself into violent rages—afterward he was so exhausted, out of sorts whatnot, that he had to go home and go to sleep. I suggested that he observe the symptoms. So he tried to catch himself, but it was elusive. Finally, however, it occurred and he found himself in a taxi on the way home. He immediately set about putting down symptoms. He became so interested and detached that his rage disappeared and he had the taxi man turn around and take him back to his office. You will discover eventually that everybody's "I" is different, so in observing voice some find it easier than others. There are not two individuals the same.

Becoming aware of genuine duty. This has nothing to do with usual morality. Duty is in the sense of obvious function. We are accustomed to think of the body as a machine, and every machine has its proper use as determined by its structure. This is so with the body. Morality would consist of its use in accord with its structure. Conceive of the arch-engineer of the universe judging us by this standard. But the body has not only an immediate use, it has other potentialities. By analogy, consider a group of savages who find an auto and use it only as a hut. Speaking technically this is immoral. Our psyche is treating our body in this way. This is the morality of which Hassein becomes aware. "Duty" is not to another organism but the duty of utilizing the body in full scope of its functions. This becomes a concept outside of the usual morality e.g., if we assume for the moment that we have three brains and are in the habit of using only one, we are two thirds short of duty that is genuine. Hassein was pondering: "What is the matter?" asked Beelzebub.

Hassein admits having new thoughts; he now understands that everything he has and uses came to its present state through the labor and suffering of many beings, and much unnecessary (gratuitous) suffering. We do not thank those beings, we take everything for granted. Hassein says: "From your talk with the Captain, I have become aware with all my being; and think with remorse as to what and why all these blessings. What are the duties laid upon me by my existence? What must I do in return for all this?" This question is the basis of any morality. The body is not a machine with a function, this has no meaning if it has a function, it is an obligation. Hassein's question is the question of every three-centered being at a certain stage: What is the meaning of my life? And what do I owe? I must make a distinction between, I am a body and I have a body. "I" is potential. Duty applies to "I." Must have had a realization of "I" as distinguished from "it."

I, Hassein, realize I have a body. Presumably it has a designed use; but I do not yet know what its potentialities are. How can I use it?

The final chapter of the book summarizes the answer as developed through the book: good and evil. We are machines with potentialities but the discovery of these potentialities is not in our personal power.

Beelzebub answers: "You must not think or worry about all this just now. When the time comes you will understand and know what you must do. You are still young."

All we can expect from the magnetic center now is a moment of realization. We are still young. No duty now, but will understand and know what you must do, at present can have only the morality of the pupil, the morality of effort. Our only duty is to try to learn our duty, and prepare ourselves. Later, when we become aware of what our job is, we will do it. Let the energies in you move among the energies in it.

He who is too lazy every day to learn everything he can will be unable later, when he realizes his duty, to practice it.

Purgatory: when one realizes what one should do and has not the necessary technique. No need for undue haste. Prepare. Perhaps we knew before we came. Cf. certain myths: Prodigal Son, originated with the Gnostics, Hymn of the Robe of Glory. The son went off, not in a huff but in search of a robe which had been stolen. Fell into adventure and forgot his mission. When eating with swine—i.e. mechanical life, he remembered his mission and returned to his father.

Beelzebub: "I am glad for your future that you have asked this question." This word "glad" Beelzebub might never have used if he had stayed at home, but has lived in foreign surroundings and side by side with his proper nature, a second body was formed also real. Hassein could not have been otherwise and his father could see occasion to rejoice. But Beelzebub, thanks to his misfortunes, is "glad." Differentiate between a being whose completion is mechanically arrived at and a being that develops by effort. Angel—man.

On some planes perhaps beings develop without gaps of scale, without effort, hence without sin, hence without realization, hence without gladness (as distinguished from happiness). If everything which happened could not be otherwise, we could not be glad.

There are planets where everything is natural, evolution without effort; no religion; no gaps in octave.

Beelzebub points out the advantage of our disadvantages. Fully developed man is superior in realization to the angels; man becomes the mind of God. Angels and archangels are His higher emotional centers. God thinks with human entities. It is possible to be unhappy and glad.

Not "good and evil"; but henceforth good and bad—Nietzsche. "Bad" is amateur, failure to carry out.

There is no positive evil force, merely the difficulty of the problem!

BEELZEBUB: Ask me a question!

HASSEIN: Tell me anything you like. I shall be interested because you tell it. (Flattery; he tries to avoid the effort of formulating a question.)

HASSEIN: Tell me about those—eh—those slugs!

BEELZEBUB: What? (He knew damn well.)

HASSEIN: Those beings like us, but with slimier skin. (Smoother, hypocrite.)

BEELZEBUB: I know them well; they are very peculiar. This planet is in certain respects unique and hence interesting, if only pathological. It offers psychological behavior not found on normal planets. (Legend has it that this planet is called "the ridiculous planet" or "the lunatic asylum" of the universe. G. B. Shaw sometimes uses it in this attitude. Shaw inherited this from Lucian, who got it from the Greeks, who got it from the Egyptians and they got it from the ancient Babylonians and Sumerians.)

BEELZEBUB: I saw their rise and watched their development. I almost saw the creation of the planet itself. It had not yet cooled when I arrived on Mars.

First, he will tell about cosmic troubles, genesis of the moon. Beelzebub and his companions were busy adjusting themselves to life on Mars. Suddenly the whole planet was shaken. A stench arose. When it cleared off it was found that the earth had split with two fragments thrown off. The cause was a comet of long path on its first trip. It bumped into the earth and the planet Konda or Kunda. A violent shock. The earth so recently formed that the atmosphere which acts as a buffer had not had a chance to form (effect of the atmosphere on meteorites). His Endlessness was hastily informed. System of nerve communication informs the brain that a stone has fallen on the foot. This takes a time interval; from the Sun Absolute (executive brain) a commission of specialists in world existence was sent. In certain cases definite cells dispatched human cells at a certain stage. Emergencies, when normal methods and instinctive reflexes are not fast enough. (See later chapter on time.) The commission landed on Mars because it was near and Beelzebub met them. Beelzebub was on a planet slightly higher than ours, and therefore knew ahead of time. The commission allayed their fears. There was no danger of catastrophe.

The archangel Algematant, a personified state of intelligence. (Alge=algebra, math, mathematics.) A being whose components are of a nature to understand algebra and mathematics. (Called in the Bible principalities.) Algematant was an engineer and explained: "The split off fragments lost their momentum, before leaving the spatial sphere of the earth and did not pass the edge. According to the law of falling, they began to fall back. But the earth was moving and they came under the law of catching up. Falling and moving, moving is the ellipse, they describe. Both movements have psychological parallels in us. It is desirable that the center of gravity should be moving faster, so that one part should be always catching up but not fall in. "I" must not fall on "it." Perhaps the method striking on it like a comet may break off "I." The falling and catching up may operate. Glory be that harmony is established. This split off of a moon, happened by accident. Archangel Sakaki thought that these fragments might sometime get out of their orbits and cause trouble unless some measures were taken. Danger of hearing the method and understanding it. Measures must be taken about the fragment split off. He decided the earth must supply the fragment with special sacred vibrations, which could be formed only by certain psychic organic forms of life. "Askokin" (the vibration), conscious labor and voluntary (intentional) suffering. Life developing on the moon depends on radiations from this earth, as the earth depends on emanations from the sun. Keep the moon from falling. The effort that subvened the moon is a solar and cosmic purpose.

They ask permission of His Endlessness to create the necessary organic life. His Endlessness gives permission. He does not actively bring about any change in the three centers but oversees them.

The large fragment, "Loonderperzo," became the moon and the smaller fragment is Anulios. The esoteric name of the moon is still Loonderperzo. The contemporary beings on the earth do not even know of the existence of Anulios; but the inhabitants of Atlantis knew of it and called Anulios also by a name which meant: "He that never allows one to sleep in peace." Cf. "The Shaving of Shagpat," by Meredith and "The Discourager of Hesitancy," who carried a scimitar.

Later we will learn what these fragments are in us. Contemporary beings do not know because it is beyond their sight—insight.

Prometheus was the Foreseer—beyond psychological vision.

Their grandmothers never told them, fairy tales feed the magnetic center. But none of our fairy tales tell us that there is a little moon. If anyone saw it through a telescope he would pay no attention. If anyone who was a psychologist or philosopher found in himself an ache for perfection (remorse, duty) he would pay no attention and think it an aerolite, not real.

But we are not likely to see it for we are in the days of mechanical interpretation. Such words as remorse, sin, unfulfilled duty have no meaning. In us is a potential center technically called Anulios; also a partly potential center called the moon. Cosmic analogies—moon, food, conscious labor and voluntary suffering. The labors of Hercules, the Golden Fleece, Ulysses. To supply the moon with a lot of askokin. To relieve men till they are able to do so—Perseus.

The archangel Sakaki saw to it that the laws of seven and three operate independently and concurrently on the surface of the earth, vegetation and other beings and among the bipeds, the slugs.

Heptaparaparshinokh = eftaparabarshinoch, seven making one.

Triamazikamno = triamonia, three making one.

Law of seven is the law of evolution.

Law of three is the law of psychology.

On this planet the two can proceed concurrently and independently. On other planets, they are interdependent.

Sakaki had to produce an organism capable of conscious labor and voluntary suffering. Hence the gaps; and hence the psychic life here is unique.

Perhaps I can recall one or two of the cartoons from the screen to your imagination. Epic parable is that Beelzebub and Hassein and their kinsmen are on the interstellar ship Karnak. Beelzebub possessing full consciousness, will and individuality. Beelzebub and Hassein are engaged in a discussion of the mechanics of the universe (ships)—and all he says is applicable on a smaller scale to ourselves. Try to discover the relation of macrocosmos to microcosmos . . . begins by a description of the manner in which beings on various planets coat themselves. Try to accustom yourselves to a psyche in a different form from that on this planet. If you succeed you will find yourself with a genuine psychology.

Beelzebub is discussing also the difference in psyche on planets—says here on earth in their very psyche the beings are odd. Not only different from other planets in their solar system but different from all other planets in universe. So Hassein being piqued by this assertion will inevitably ask about earth beings.

Then the Captain comes in and an interruption occurs during which ships—say religions are discussed. This discussion is above Hassein's head but it gives him a new idea. It is as if a child awoke to hear his parents talking of means to procure toys and food and so forth—assuming that the child had a spark of something, he would have some things to think about before going back to sleep. Something of the adult world into which he had been for a moment admitted—though not an adult.

Title of the chapter—Becoming Aware of Genuine Duty, i.e. the morality of obvious function. We are accustomed to the idea of the organism being mechanical—i.e. chemicals biologically assembled. Its use should be determined by its construction (as an auto, boat or plow). Their morality consists in their being used for the functions for which they are obviously constructed and intended.

In contrast to animals, vegetables, minerals and metals, it appears that our machine has a use that is not only of immediate value but is also for potential future use. So a savage might use a limousine for a hut but it would be immoral by neglecting is obvious function for which it was constructed. So the man in each machine calling himself "I" has a further duty not to be paid to himself nor due to another person.

The use of such a machine will become the criteria for judging the objective morality of a man. So the word "genuine" was selected to indicate objective.

Suppose we have three brains but use only one—all three must be used and all three must be fed or supplied with fuel.

When the captain had gone, Beelzebub asked Hassein what he was thinking of so seriously. Looking sadly at Beelzebub, he said—Your talk with the captain has given me some very serious thoughts for I had never imagined that things in the universe of His Endlessness have not always existed as they now do—i.e. as I find them. It seems now to me that beings must have suffered and labored and some even suffered more than they need have (voluntary suffering)—that they might give us the conveniences and possessions that we now have. I, for example have existed for a long time—yet until now; I have never realized the truth that these things available to me are not gratuitously provided. And now with the whole of my being I desire to understand why I have deserved all these lessons and I wish much to know what it is that I must do in return for all this in my existence.

In the absence of this attitude there can be no meaning to one's life or morality. But assuming that we are machines created for a specific object and that we owe some duty or obligation to repay, then we can proceed.

[*M. Frank talks a lot about fuel, Orage says why don't we burn all the fuel?—because we need a greater draft or ashes should be raked out.*]

So every being has this question at least once occur to him. Solon says either we are a machine or we have a machine. But, Israel (Solon) I have asked that you make an effort to determine that—for a long time past. Everyone who has made this effort and failed either has passed the possibility of realizing this or has not yet reached the possibility.

[*Someone else actually asks: "Is the duty of the machine or of "I"?*]

The book is presumably written for those who have reached the point of saying: "I have a machine—what shall I do with it? I am prepared to put my machine to its designed use, but in the absence of knowing the later, what can I do?"

Why are we alive? What is the job I would impose upon my machine if I had made it myself? (Hugh—this will please you.) The beings on this earth had the hardest deal in all the universe in that they cannot by themselves follow the natural course of development.

Beelzebub—you must not think or worry about this just at present. You are still young. (Though the magnetic center is at moments stimulated, we cannot as yet do anything about it.) And the time is not yet come for you to pay for your existence—there is only the morality for us of the pupil. That is the morality of trying, of effort, of learning. So a good pupil might be a bad master. We have only the duty of learning the duty. You must not think of doing, for as Beelzebub says: "There's plenty of time later for that." In the meantime, preparation only. Let the energy in you move among the energy in it. Impress upon yourself every morning that he who is too lazy to learn everything will not be able to pay for his existence as he will wish to. Imagine your state if you needed a technique and could recall a time when you could have acquired it, though then it is too late. That is the end of that phase of Beelzebub's reply and it should reassure you of the truth that you need not hasten too greatly. It may be that each of us will sometime realize that there exists in some part of our being, not now realized, remains of the memory of the mission upon which we consciously embarked. So, the Prodigal Son—it was only when he found himself eating husks—that is mechanically—that he then remembered his inherited mission.

Beelzebub says: "I am glad for your future from the fact that you have said these things—that you take it this way."

This word "glad" might perhaps never have been able to use had it existed only on the planet Karatas at home—but I have by chance existed on very foreign and strange planets—and so a second nature began to be formed and because of this I am able to be glad.

For because if one of us were to be regarded by his father, the father would have no reason to be proud, for we are not different from others on this planet, but only mechanical. It may be that on certain planets evolution proceeds without the gap that occurs here on earth and without any effort so that such a being could only be happy, not glad. For if a state were mechanical one could not be glad.

But on this planet hundreds of beings (Rousseau) have had the idea of a world in which the evolution of beings would proceed mechanically. But Beelzebub says here that the beings on the planet earth have a better possible existence than all others. Man is God's mind. Man comprises the thoughts of God. God only commenced to think upon the creation of man.

(Man can be both unhappy and glad at the same time.)

Cherubim, seraphim, angels and archangels constitute his higher emotional center. Man (or Mannas) is the mind of God.

Hassein is only to ponder these things but not yet to assume the duties of an adult. In fact the whole of this planet is in an octave where effort is required at mi-fa and at si-do. But, (here I am passing on a bit of cosmic gossip) there are planets where cruelty does not exist—where in the ordinary course of life the growth of the being proceeds evenly by nature. But here for one thing the life of beings is too short. If an old man, with illusions gone, could then begin this work, he could go far, but he has not the strength.

Try in the meantime not to think of things that it is too early to consider. In the meantime before the captain comes back I will, if you like, tell you some other things.

There is no religion. There is only one God. There is no evil; there is only failure to achieve the good. God without man would be powerless. One of the purposes of the book is to destroy the idea of evil. Good is the use of means and there is only failure of use of means.

Nietzsche said, "No any longer good and evil—but only good and bad."

Beelzebub later explains the problem of creation. The use of certain numbers is the mathematical problem which God set himself in creation—three and seven. There is only the difficulty of the problem.

So Beelzebub invites Hassein to formulate a question. First question: Hassein asks what am I to do? Beelzebub says—good, but wait. Then Hassein's second questions: Tell me anything for I will listen with delight to everything that you will be so kind as to say.

But Beelzebub was not to be taken in by such flattery—he had conducted too many group meetings, so he says something to the effect that Hassein must formulate a definite question.

So Hassein asks "about those slugs"—Beelzebub—What slugs? Of course Beelzebub is not surprised, but has known that this question must be asked by Hassein.

HASSEIN: Those beings on a planet who are rather like us but slimier.

BEELZEBUB: Ah—the beings on planet earth called men?

HASSEIN: Yes, very interested.

BEELZEBUB: I could tell you a great deal about them. They are very very peculiar. Many of the things about them are unique in the universe and only to be found there.

ORAGE: This planet then, it appears, is a little different from all the other planets in the universe. This planet is called the ridiculous planet on the ground that the beings here cut such ridiculous capers. Shaw inherited a flavor of such an idea from —— to Aristophanes.

The whole section of the Book of Job in the Bible wherein occurs a conversation between creator and Job is a "mystery." Read it!

I saw their rise—I saw almost the formation of the planet. I will first tell you of the event which caused the trouble there. For when I arrived on Mars there was not even any vegetation on earth.

Beelzebub's kinsmen on Mars were developed in objective reason but defective in emotion.

Beelzebub—Soon after we arrived on the planet Mars and began to settle down (i.e. accommodate themselves to a new mood), on one of our busiest days a great shaking occurred and a terrible odor. And it was only possible after this odor had disappeared that we could discover what had happened. It seemed that a comet had collided with this same planet earth and had split off a part. So because the solar system Ors was new, this tended to disrupt the rhythm and mutual attractions. (This is obvious even in our ordinary ideas of astronomy. And a planet should be regarded also as a being—a man.)

The earth came into collision with the planet Condor (or Kunda) and two pieces split off. This happened before it was possible for our atmosphere to arrange its formation as a buffer. His Endlessness soon received reports of it.

SOLON: Orage, does this mean that the time element enters into God's cognizance of happenings?

ORAGE: Yes.

A commission composed of specialists was immediately dispatched to inquire into the nature of the happening.

So in the body, nerves convey messages to the executive brain—blood cells are immediately dispatched, so the element of time enters here. When we come to "time spheres"—but put it aside for the moment and let us consider this commission.

This commission arrived on the planet Mars as the nearest planet to earth and conducted their investigations from there.

(Those of you who have attempted to read the future will get a hint here that an event can be apprehended on a superior planet (plane) before it descends to the next plane.)

(Algi = algebra, matant = mathematics.)

Archangel Algimatant is the engineer of the corporeal structure of the megalocosmos. Archangel Algimatant told us that the split off parts lost their momentum before they crossed the line of limit to attraction. (You will remember that the center of each planet is the focus or intersection of certain forces.) With the result that they began to fall toward earth. But the planet was moving and so they fell into the "law of caching up." (Now both these laws "of falling and catching up" are present in us. And it is necessary that our center of gravity should always move fast enough to prevent "I" from falling entirely upon it. By pondering you can perhaps find this relativity.)

Glory be that it has fallen out so. For it will always be so that the moon will always be both falling and caching up, but it will never catch up and fall upon it. ("I" is separated from "it" by accidental contact with this method.)

The archangel concluded that though these fragments could for the present keep their places, there might later eventually occur a catastrophe.

(One of the dangers of hearing this method and understanding it is precisely this danger.)

And it proved upon investigation that the fundamental piece should supply to the smaller fragments a certain sacred vibration and the commission decided to petition his Endlessness for permission to make certain arrangements. (Voluntary suffering and conscious labor.)

So the moon receives not only direct from the sun but also from the earth through is organic kingdom certain necessary substances or vibrations. In other words a special kind of organic kingdom is needed on this planet only. In order to keep the "I" from falling back once it is split off from "it," certain conscious labor and voluntary suffering is necessary.

The Archangel Psycharchy decided in view of this foreseen necessity to set off to secure permission from His Endlessness. He blessed it, the project, and gave His permission. (So "I" does not create but His oversight, consent and blessings are necessary.)

Of the two fragments wrenched from this planet, one originally was called Lunderperzo and now is called moon and the second is called Anulios. The beings of Atlantis knew of the second fragment and called it Anulios though occasionally they called it Kimespai, meaning one who does not allow one to sleep in peace.

(I wish you were familiar with a certain writing of Meredith's in which a court attendant was called the Discourager of Hesitancy. His duty was when he saw someone not performing his duty, to cut off his head. I invite you to remember moments just before you have gone to sleep during which for an instant you were troubled by the thought of how little you had done that day.)

But the principal reason why the second moonlet is never seen is that their grandmother never told them of such a little moon. If one of them should see it through the telescope, they would pay no attention to it, they would say it was just an asteroid. (If anyone should find in himself remorse—ache for perfection—he would reduce it to something speculative.)

None of the beings are ever likely even to see it. For we are fallen upon a time when remorse, aspiration, etc.—because of psychoanalysis, behaviorism, etc.—no longer granted meaning. There is a second satellite of the earth, invisible but nevertheless exercising a real effect upon us and upon the earth. So when the eclipse recently was a few seconds later, it was suggested that the other side of the moon which we never see may bulge and throw out in this way the calculations of the astronomers. But labor and suffer we must. That is our fate. But this necessary labor and suffering can be compensated for by rendering a being here a "mannas"—which is a being greater than an angel.

WHY "MEN" ARE NOT MEN.

Moon in us is not personality. But we are slaves of or food for the moon. Yet it is possible to predigest that food and extract for ourselves certain advantages. In London, Ouspensky was asked: "What, in fact, is man for?" He calmly replied: "To feed the moon." This sounded so crazy to them that it halted their imagination for some time. So someone of us may undertake a conscious labor and voluntary suffering that will relieve the beings here of an enormous amount of otherwise necessary labor and suffering. So the search for the Golden Fleece, Perseus, etc.

HERBERT WOLMER: You said last year that if a great many people practiced this method fully it might be disastrous.

ORAGE: Yes, if a great many people commenced to feed the sun it might cause a cosmic disaster—but this is not possible practically. Another function of man is to cease feeding the moon and only feed the sun—but then again that is conditioned on the quantity of the necessary substance available—and it is limited. It is not possible for very many people to even begin to practice the first three steps of this method—self-observation, participation and Experimentation—to say nothing of conscious labor and voluntary suffering. So the possibility of this work is always limited—say as the quantity of radium is limited. (This certainly relieves my emotions of worry over my fellow beings.) But, practically no one need fear that there will not be enough of the necessary chemicals available for his own use.

Well, my boy, so the Archangel Psycharchy presented the plan to His Endlessness who blessed it and said Be it So. Then the work of the organic kingdom began. So the archangels arranged the laws of three and seven so that they could work independently on that planet. Among the biped beings there was a being called man.

Eptaparabarshinok means only seven making one. Triamasikanok means three making one. On this planet only the law of seven, i.e. the law of evolution, proceeded independently of, as well as concurrently with the law of three (law of psychology) though on other planets these only proceed interdependently, while here independently but concurrently. But psychically speaking, due to this, we have a different existence here. Do you remember a diagram called the enneagram? If you take each point of that triangle as "do" and as place for a shock, you will find fa is okay but si shock is not just right. This indicates that whenever the si shock is necessary we must hurry in order to make it come in at the right place.

2 FEBRUARY 1927

12:30 ON THE TRAIN HOME

Dear Hugh (Ferries),

I have spent this evening around the big table at twenty-seven West Sixty-seventh Street with Ilonka, Wim and Gertrude, going over together our notes of the twenty-fourth meeting (shown above). It is, of all things, the most stimulating. To find three active minds working with great seriousness and purpose on these ideas. Several times we were "stopped" by a sentence one of us had read. You know what I mean? A mingled emotion of joy, reverence, delight, awe, etc.? And shared!?! That's what increases the emotion in a mathematical progression. You are, of course, missing all this—and must be to some extent regretting it. I am not just trying to "rub it in"—but by this to (God willing) perhaps enable you to redouble your efforts to accomplish the first three stages of the method.

There are three or four drunks in at the end of this car—God bless us, how terrible they look. One is obviously pugnacious as I am when drunk—though of course he seems cruel and different from my concept of myself. One is very amiable and friendly.

Hugh, what do the seven major planets denote in moods?

Venus—love?

Saturn—?

Neptune—?

Mercury—will for service?

Earth—lust?

Jupiter—will to search?

Mars—will to overcome.

(Sagittarius—The Hunter.)

This effort makes me remember that I must study Roget's Thesaurus.

I must go find Ilse on the train to get her notes of the Orage group I did not attend to night.

Sherm.

7 FEBRUARY 1927

I tried an experiment last week in order to see how long it is possible for some of you to retain your attention on a subject which has no material counterpart. Those who lasted through one hour—? two hours—good, three hours—good pupil, further—good. In understanding, as I have been able with the help of Gurdjieff, an occasional sentence in the book, I later found it difficult and often impossible to get any meaning from it. For it needed exact context and continuity of the ideas in the book for full comprehension.

The book is an epic dialogue, the characters are of a certain elevation, perhaps a little above humans, i.e. they are like ourselves as we may be for an instance or longer but these beings are able to maintain themselves in such a state. Beelzebub is a fully actualized human being. Beelzebub begins in a position of complete isolation not merely from his physical body—but he attempts to observe the whole material universe, i.e. God's body. So Beelzebub discriminates between "I" and "it" as well as between Beelzebub and the universe. So as he is able to pass at will through the cosmos, we should be able to pass from planet to planet, etc. And in his replies there is always implied a certain attitude in the fact that he speaks of the whole universe having a purpose and he more or less understands it. And beings are an "agency." In fact, the whole material universe has a logical design for the purpose of fulfilling a perfectly reasonable objective. This purpose is intelligible and not irrational. And in so far as this universe fulfills this purpose, it is thereby good or bad, not evil.

And we have a material body. The first thing that one can truly say is, "I have a body," then afterward, "for what purpose do I have it?"

But we differ from Beelzebub in that he can look over the cosmos and say, "these things have a use for me"—but you (we) do not know why the creature bearing your name exists.

What value has your body for you? What each of us has of value to extract from our universe will become clear to us. It has a potential value of the extraction of a particular value which is objective reason—divine reason from the experience of this (your) body. So Beelzebub makes this survey of the body for Hassein for the purpose of aiding him to establish a school for the education of souls to understand what the game is, what the obligation of God is to keep the universe in existence. Only those who reach an understanding of what the game is can be called souls.

There are other planets and solar systems—God is not staking everything on the results on this planet. But Hassein discovers that perhaps this planet is in some ways unique.

So the planet earth was prematurely delivered of its satellite, moon, and an unusual method of feeding and caring for the earth child had to be arranged. So suns "have" planets and planets "have" moons.

So the "Book of Genesis" was not written by dumb fools, but it was written by some people confronted by the same facts that we are confronted with. We know that every time we survey our behavior for one day, we must admit that we have acted like poltroons, cowards, stupid fools—but somehow we do not apply to ourselves such an impartial estimate or judgment. So we go quite comfortably to sleep every night.

We know that for thousands of years men have been on earth, in Egypt—art and science, in Greece—philosophy, in China—personal intercourse, i.e. society. But why has none of this come down to us? Why are we not the heirs of all ages? Instead of as we are, a people who have climbed up from practically a blank. After each civilization a barbarous sponge wipes clean the slate on which that solution appeared. Or taking it that we are human beings of at least 6,000 years of existence, we should be, so to speak, on the shoulders of our forbearers—but cannot ourselves succeed—that someone can?

If I am a politician, why do I think, knowing that I cannot in the smallest respect reform myself, that I can by a League of Nations reform the world?

I have begged you to make a survey of men on this planet as they really are, for example, here are five main races, five main continents, 150 nations, 2,000 different languages on the earth. Now take these sorts of things—make a survey—call them beings, not men, but camels or kangaroos or anything. Note that all of them are mechanical and perhaps becoming more so. (More so, if possible.) If you do this and do it successfully you will begin to understand the point of view of Beelzebub. It is necessary to understand this—why men are not men. In only one respect do we differ from animals—that we possess reason including the use of words. But a man should be one who understands why he is alive.

So sheep do not understand that they live for mutton and wool. Suppose I say to a sheep: "You exist to provide mutton and wool." But the sheep says: "I don't understand." So Beelzebub says: "You are food for the sun and the moon." But you reply, "I don't understand."

One has to play the game of life intelligibly. What would you think of a man who sat down to play chess and played according to the rules of bridge or ping-pong? So at birth we receive a set of cards and we say "play." But no one of us knows how to play them. We don't know the game. Sheep, a least, see the shepherd but we do not see even any superior beings—never have seen an archangel or —— at least I never have. We have no superiors but we are not ourselves superior.

So in the Book of Genesis they tried to explain the fall of man. But we don't even try to explain it for now it never occurs to us that any explanation is necessary. But in the Book of Genesis it says that men succumbed to their instinctive bodies—that they decided they could gain knowledge and understanding without effort. So they ceased effort and soon found themselves outside paradise. We are not discharging human functions.

But how to make self-observation important? Only by making the necessity for effort to get out of a most undesirable and poignant situation, most obvious and apparent. So the book was written.

The myth says that but for the accident of the comet Kondoor colliding with this planet we should not be different. And in breaking it into three pieces, two were split off—so extra effort is necessary now of this planet. Why did such a catastrophe occur? Because this planet is of such a nature that this catastrophe will always recur and every being on this planet will always be affected by it and in just this way. They will repeat the same catastrophe that occurred to this earliest progenitor—earth.

So two parts were struck off from us—self-consciousness and cosmic-consciousness—i.e. consciousness of our bodies and of the world we live in. So a sort of feeding is necessary of the moon (self-consciousness) and Anulios (cosmic-conscious).

Whether the myth is true of Earth—Moon—Anulios, it is apparently and obviously true of I—body—self-consciousness and cosmic-consciousness.

So Beelzebub has by effort attained a consciousness that even angels who have never had to go through such an experience never can possess—a dual being. So we can become not just angel-beings but very sophisticated beings. Beelzebub knows the feeling of gladness—not only happiness.

Those of you who know anything of psychoanalysis will here see an analogy in regard to heredity—i.e. in psychoanalysis you start with the premise that there is a conscious and a subconscious.

Why men are not men . . . we are the planet earth with two satellites unactualized. (Why men are beings with two potentialities—which have names but no actuality.)

The fact is that among those biped beings whom you call slugs (why slugs?—because only instinctive center is developed) and since they had three brains and due to favorable circumstances there began to be formed in them mechanical reason. (For instance it is possible to understand that we are automatic. Behaviorism is a very ancient knowledge.)

When the commission under Archangel Psycharchy descended to earth again to make certain measurements, they noticed the formation of this mechanical reason and decided to take steps. So if men will not by voluntary labor and voluntary suffering try to gain for themselves objective reason and genuine will, then they must be made to suffer involuntarily.

So these beings might by mechanical reason discover their state and also the possibility of higher states of consciousness and they would then revolt and cause us (the archangels), a great deal of trouble. So if we could really feel what we now know that we are in every possible way the result of inheritance and environment—we should at once commit suicide or go mad or become ——.

So behaviorism will undoubtedly soon affect the young men of this country so that they will in increasing numbers commit suicide and murder and engage in ruthless warfare.

So if these beings realized (i.e. emotionally) their state. But the commission attached an organ which reversed everything in their estimation and also made them engage in certain forms of illusory pursuit of pleasure. It sounds ridiculous to say that there was put at one time into the atmosphere of this planet a certain chemical that would so affect the beings on this planet. Well, it is just that which happened. Suppose we created on this earth more radium, what would be the effect?

Electricity is matter and just as the air might be denuded of its valuable nitrogen by a certain action of plant-life, it is possible to denude the earth of electricity, and every one of our movements requires electricity, among other energies.

[*Carl Zigrosser says that Gurdjieff said the ancient Greeks knew of electricity but chose not to use it.*]

We pay for all of our mechanical contrivances (so-called improvements.) So if there be used too much electricity on the surface of the earth, it will effect us, for every one of our present movements of body is electric.

So the Archangel Psycharchy used his chemical knowledge to accomplish something that we are now unconsciously accomplishing by the ridiculous misuse of electricity.

You have heard of the separation of centers by ether, being knocked insensible, etc. and you can in an extreme state of intoxication be doing something of which you are utterly unaware. Why then does this state seem incomprehensible to us? All our centers are at present separated, very, very carefully separated, hence two centers don't fulfill their function—the emotional center's realization of things we know and the second is the understanding of why we are alive.

We all know we are going to die. Why do we not emotionally realize it? Suppose you were in charge of the animal kingdom and had to decide whether or not they were to have the knowledge that they must die. What would you do about it? No one could possibly decide to give it to them.

So Looisos decided to put our realization, i.e. emotionally, into an airtight compartment and consequently we can never "realize" our state.

So too we engage in illusory pleasures, because we do not understand why we live. We know our bodies must perish—but we live for them at least 99 percent of the time. But we have a hope that the reasonable part of our being may perhaps continue to exist, therefore common sense should tell us to live for this part of ourselves. But we don't live that way, do we? Never!!

When we overhear men talking, imagine animals meeting and conversing: "Jolly good hunting over there, the deer here are excellent, such taste I never before encountered. And as for my bed, you should see it—oh, it's great. Always dry and warm. Have you tried this new food that's come out? Rabbits, I believe they call it. By the way, have you ever seen my whelps? Sweet—and my old lady? She's as young looking as the day etc."

So Looisos corresponds to the planet Saturn which is the mystery planet that is both good and bad. So Looisos is also both good and bad. So with the help of the Archangel Looisos there was made to grow in the human species the organ kundabuffer (we are perfectly sane beings but doped) at the base of the spine which inverted their sense of values.

That is, we take for our higher values only instinctive values, etc.

And then Archangel Looisos took his departure satisfied that the organ would do its work well. (Remember that Hassein has not been yet invited to make a survey of man, and so Beelzebub tells him of these things.)

So on Mars he set up an observatory. We are often asked if this is true, how is it that you can bear to let the world go on as it is? And the reply must be: "What, considering the state of the beings here, can we do? Much better to retire to an emotional attitude outside earth since we can do nothing, i.e. to an observatory—observation—participation—experiment, etc.

(Those of us who are on Saturn are the rare ones who understand the first law of life—"Love all that breathes"—i.e. all who share God's emotions—and so Beelzebub says on Saturn. The beings understood this.)

Tolstoy—Beelzebub was on this planet until 1921. And he was struck with this, that Tolstoy, with no more knowledge than you and I, nevertheless got himself passed off as one of the writers of contemporary religion. He was, so Gurdjieff says, who knew him, a perfectly silly man. Why do we give our credence to such or any people when we have nothing by which to judge them?

Though on this planet they have criteria, they never think of applying them to anything of any importance. (Why do we send our children to school conducted as we know by fools?) Why, since war has always been, do we expect it to vanish? We are reasonable beings under insane suggestions. Those of us who have met a number of literary geniuses know what a lot of utter dumb fools they are. For example, I heard an intelligent Chinaman within the past twenty-four hours say: "You know that book of H. G. Wells on China is something to be considered!" Why, even Wells knows better than that. Why have I written books—not because I can delude myself that I can affect more than a small entourage. How? Because beings themselves, though they know a certain degree of actual reality, never apply their actual knowledge to circumstances in which they may find themselves. Well, these beings called men now breed almost everywhere on that planet, differ in color and form of body, race and type—races are not superior and inferior.

(There are seven main conditions by which the seven features of one's face are determined.)

At the same time their psyche is the same everywhere—and in particular, namely, they are all possessed in a high degree of suggestibility, everywhere illustrated by a universal phenomena called war.

So, every civilization has suffered death at the hands of man. And that is why we do not inherit the benefits of preceding civilizations. Because of this suggestibility. And you can do what you like mechanically, form as many Leagues of Nations as you like—or anything else—but it is not certain that the very hardest workers for such a thing as the League of Nations, will not be affected by the war fever and tear down all they have attempted to build up.

As you know, amongst us a hero is one who voluntarily undertakes some labor for the advantage of all creation. (So Gurdjieff went to the East and suffered every form of yogi-training and discipline and diet, etc., and he is in a way a hero.)

But on that planet the word hero exists and those are called hero who during one of those stages called war, quickest and most vigorously engage in this war. How can this be? Why from childhood have they been told that he who kills an enemy (i.e. one who has been due to their suggestibility denoted as an enemy) is a hero.

So by catching beings young, they are so filled up by way of suggestibility that this apparently becomes their customary state.

Next chapter—Beelzebub's First Descent.

It is in Atlantis—whether it ever existed or not is to me a matter of absolutely no consequence. To those who are interested in such subjects, ethnology, etc., and to such others as may be interested—we will read this chapter next week.

14 FEBRUARY 1927

We tried last week to establish a point of view about the human race. Did this state of mind last? A little on Tuesday, less on Wednesday, gone on Thursday or only an intellectual memory without emotion. Great difficulty in maintaining an elevated intellectual-emotional state. It is a great deal to have experienced it for a moment. Parallel the effort to non-identify with this creature who is yourself and the effort to observe and non-identify with the species. Same qualities and phenomena.

In the book is a history of the origin of man and an objective description of him. These facts are not new; but are chaotic and disorganized within us; they are not in our consciousness. Survey your own knowledge of the species, using only information, already obtained with a view to formulating and generalizing. Consider the five main races. Try to imagine in one generalization your actual knowledge of these five main races as they at present inhabit the globe, each has had a history. Can you state the general characteristics, common to all the members of the human species?

Specify in detail the defects under which they labor not limited to certain races or colors, but common to all human beings. The results of the introduction of kundabuffer. A catastrophe split the planet; consequently every being on the planet repeats its history. There remains in us a certain objective standard by which we find these characteristics deplorable:

1. Self-love: from thinking oneself entitled to things one has not earned by conscious effort—in extreme form narcissism.

2. Vanity: a belief that there are elements in our organism of which we may be proud. No matter what theory we may have about the accidental character of our qualities, we cannot help being proud.

3. Touchiness, sensitiveness. Whether a fact is true or not.

4. Hatred, toward those whose radiations affect us unpleasantly though we recognize it as a weakness.

5. Egoism, in the form of believing that an organization to which I happen to be attached is superior to others. Often especially displayed in impudence in which we think that we, without the qualifications are better fitted to render service than others.

These are universal faults. How does it happen we have these traits? The myth answers: because we are biological products of an abnormal planet. We are normally abnormal. We start as abnormal because these traits are abnormal to real essence.

There are two kinds of reform:

- Local
- Universal

Any reform which might be brought about in conditions of civilization, say in the USA at present would be local and the effect on the species microscopic. The great religious reformers have not tried to change any given culture; but to change the chemistry of the human psyche, for the whole species. The level si-do between mechanical and self-conscious is the level of this type of reform. The establishment of self-consciousness as an individual aim is the beginning of the technique of every religious reformer. All reforms take their place in the octave.

In the following chapters will be a critique of the technique of religious reforms. The rest of the book will attempt to evaluate methods of all religious reformers, including Jesus Christ from the point of view of the transformation of human effort.

Why do all reforms die out? Why are all results temporary? The psychology must change. Given this method and the method of each religious reformer, we can institute a criterion of criticism.

The first descent was in help of a Caritasian who had come to this planet, seeing the bad conditions and had undertaken a reform. A Caritasian is such being as we would be if we were normal. Many of us may become Caritasians.

This Caritasian finds people suffering injustice, sweating to pay taxes and carry out purposes which have nothing to do with their own needs. He undertakes reforms and fails. He undertook from a sense of pity to reform the world by instituting what he considered would be a humane form of government. Notice Beelzebub's indulgently contemptuous attitude towards the futility of this type of reformer. Beelzebub puts Hassein on guard against certain sentimental notions about the human race. Those slugs have double natures. They talk as if butter wouldn't melt in their mouths; but when they act they are abnormal and monstrous. Hassein is destined some day to affect a change in the human psyche. The "descent" is a series of lessons in ways not to approach human beings.

[*Orage reads the story.*]

Beelzebub is appealed to for the Caritasian's failure which is troublesome to himself and might became so to all. A failure of a religious reformer has a very bad effect. The failure of Christianity had done much to discredit the principle of love as a basis of religion. It should have succeeded. The principle of love in pursuit of knowledge is indispensable, yet consider how repellent it is to many intelligent people of culture because of its association.

Beelzebub descends to earth, a parallel with Hindu literature (cf. Mahabharata), Krishna, the "I," occasionally intervenes. Also there is a parallel with the steps we must take in observing, participating and experiment.

Beelzebub flew to earth on the ship "Occasion," the appropriate moment, when the maximum of means is present. We are seized by occasions; a self-conscious being seizes one. The home port of this ship was Mars, which is the mood of overcoming, of becoming self-conscious. He landed on the continent Atlantis, which afterward disappeared.

If we reproduce psychologically the history of the planet, what is Atlantis in us and what compares in us to its engulfing? (Maeterlinck.)

The buried continent in us. Essence is what we know to be truly us. We have only a few moments in our life when we act from essence, mostly we are artificial. Self-observation and participation begins to disinter, to bring to the surface that buried psychology in us.

Historical accuracy *not guaranteed*.

The capital of Atlantis was Samnios. This was dominant just as today the intellectual sub-center of the instinctive center. This characterizes our civilization at present. We can chart a civilization according to its center of gravity. "Capital" in the book refers to the center of gravity of the dominant classes.

Beelzebub's "young and inexperienced kinsman" (one who had begun to observe his organism), became friendly with King Appolis ("I" had become friendly with "it.") The human species in their chief center at Samnios, had taken offense and got himself bound (identified) with King Appolis. The king needed lots of taxes. Think of a well endowed personality committed to the necessity of maintaining for its organization the status to which it is accustomed.

PERSONAL APPLICATION?

Suppose self-observation should threaten your ability to do your chosen work and keep up other mechanical status, as intellectuals, philosophers, artists, etc. To maintain this one has to put out a great effort, read books, go places, see people etc. This is comparable to the labor King Appolis has to exact from his subjects.

In general human beings do nothing in regard to obligations, voluntarily undertaken unless some fear is induced of incurring dislike, disfavor etc. of others. In the absence of the possibility of disagreeable consequences, we are tempted to abandon any voluntary resolution, when it becomes irksome.

We are without muscle of our own. We artificially create these disagreeable consequences and attribute them to external agencies.

King Appolis spared nothing, not even himself, nor his subjects' component cells, like a man with a passion for fame in art, literature, or anything else. He had a passion for his objective. He used threats and measures. What threats do you use to yourself? You must do this or that, a passion for self-discipline. We may call ourselves the arch-dodger. Has anyone with this passion ever admitted in moments of candor the tricks he has employed for keeping his organism at work when it wanted to stop? How Orage persuaded his organism for fifteen years to keep on editing the New Age.

This seemed unjust to the Caritasian, who grew indignant at the king and told him so. They talked it over and made a wager. By this the king was to employ only such methods as were approved by the Caritasian. Then, if the citizens failed to pay, the Caritasian undertook to make this good.

(By-products will come; but "I" cannot guarantee any immediate advancement of values of personality. There may even be a temporary decline.)

QUESTION: Will the method improve my efficiency in writing, etc?

ANSWER: Yes.

QUESTION: At once?

ANSWER: Cannot tell; maybe at once, certainly eventually.

QUESTION: But suppose I cannot afford any temporary diminution?

ANSWER: Then do not start the method.

The Caritasian promised immediate improvement. King Appolis accepted; his subjects stopped paying and began to sneak back. (Organism gives up effort.) But the Caritasian's vow was voluntary. If one finds in an involuntary vow, a mechanical reaction, and if in a voluntary vow a conscious reaction, the latter is thirty thousand times stronger.

The Caritasian paid in all he had (effort at self-observation etc.)

Then his kinsmen sought stimulation (attended groups). He appealed to Mars. (His kinsmen are cells in the magnetic center.) He was anxious and appealed to reason. A conference was held. This cannot help "I." The machinery being wound up cannot return to its original state. The literal application of this seems to be the effect on the organism of any premature reform, an attempt to change for experimental reason any one thing, for a moral reason may have incalculable effects. Any local change may bring serious consequences which are not recognized as consequences.

King Appolis is the common sense of the world; and must not submit to an embryological, undeveloped "I." We must not make experiments contrary to common sense although "I" is a being of a higher reason. Such an experiment is against the health of the organism.

Help me return!!!!!

King Appolis retired. There was a conference of "I's," discussing the escapade of one of their number. They advised King Appolis to restore an inferior form of government. The Caritasian thought the subjects would make an effort out of love. (Sentimentality of modern liberalism, idealistic anarchism, Kropotkin.) They labored under the illusion that human beings are naturally just. They are so by theory in our minds but are not so in action. The "I's" advise a return from an idealistic form of government to one tyrannical and realistic, people being what they are.

Why does the prospect, the positive hope, of increasing our conscious powers act less powerfully as a lever of effort than the fear produced by description of our diseased and abnormal state? Logic alone would make the small effort needed very desirable. But not from a mere hope can we get the energy; but from an emotionally understood realization of decadence, of approaching death, etc. A system of rewards alone is not enough it is necessary to have punishments also, e.g. a threat of staying awake till the film of the day is finished, or get up and read or go without breakfast!

A greater effort is needed now to restore; after a lapse of self-observation a much greater effort is needed. Every organization has its own clock. The development of self-observation is like the growth of a seed; it cannot be static and must pass through phases in its allotted time or it will die. Water need not be given every hour; but, say, once a day a liberal amount of time but not indefinite. I must receive food appropriate to each phase or it will be impossible to go on to the next, without going back to the original state.

When beginning self-observation development takes place in a pattern and with a time-schedule; and within this time phase, the food of effort must be given; else the next time will respond anew or not at all. No one knows how many seeds there are in the magnetic center two, three, and four? Limited and in general not more than two. This is why it is dangerous to propound the method to someone who may hear it and not be able to keep in the seed-plot, to keep actively in touch or may commit the sin against the Holy Ghost which is the only sin which may be committed involuntarily, that is destroying in any being the last seed of potentiality.

This time is determined by each organism.

We go back to the story.

There was an attempt to repair, just in time, the trouble which had been caused. The government was restored to tyranny. Does any other method work? Inquire in yourself. King Appolis got results which the Caritasian could not. The Caritasian found this spectacle so distasteful that he returned to Mars, and later on became a good bailiff, i.e. he retired to a school to learn more of himself. Apply this to sociological and personal reform.

Those are entitled to be social reformers who have experience of human beings in all states of existence, action, emotion, etc. Only such are entitled to legislate on behalf of human kind. Otherwise their opinion is based on insufficient knowledge or on insufficient time.

You have to know a person in a state of starvation, terror, panic, wealth, drunkenness etc. His present state is only a temporary criterion. Naivety of style represents naivety of "I's" question. Complexity will give complexity of style.

The next chapter is "The Relative Understanding of Time." Gurdjieff says: "I have buried in this book certain bones, so that certain dogs with great curiosity and strong scent may dig down to them and strange thing, when they have done so, are men."

Effort is useful to understanding.

14 FEBRUARY 1927

I find it a little difficult until I find what your experiences have been during the week. I tried last week to inculcate in you an emotional intellectual attitude that would admit the acceptance of these ideas. I am trying to compare a similar act in observing and non-identifying with the organism and a being which non-identifies from the whole human race—but can maintain that attitude. All the phenomena that occur in the universe on a smaller scale but do occur in this organism—oneself. The difficulty is that the knowledge we really all have is not organized. We cannot generalize on the human species.

Generalize—make a survey of the five races, give the characteristics of each without further reading; each has had a history, represents an anthology of certain characteristics. What in your opinion are the general characteristics of the nature of the human species?

The book goes further—not only supposing that we can do this, but that we can specify the defects under which we all labor. The breed of man has certain defects and can be specified by any ordinary man.

Beelzebub says in order to explain why we are and are not this and that—that a comet named Kondoor collided with and split the earth and at the same time brought about a split in being of the breed of man.

I ask everyone to examine himself for these qualities:

1. Self-love—thinking oneself entitled to certain things—certain discriminatory treatment from some superior being.

2. Vanity—we entertain the belief that we have in us certain elements of which we are rightly proud Even in the face of behaviorism we think this.

3. Touchiness or sensitiveness—we take offense if a statement touches us, whether true or false.

4. Hatred—we hate those whose vibrations are out of harmony with those we happen to have.

5. Egoism—we believe that the I we happen to identity ourselves with is a better one than others. So each thinks he can be of peculiar service in certain circumstances which no one else could perform.

We claim these things; though they are universal among men. We see our faults but can do nothing to remedy them. Why? Because we are the human species, product of an abnormal planet, i.e. abnormal now even in normal circumstances. In actual fact the whole human species begins its existence in an abnormal state.

Now let us suppose that it is possible to hear a messenger from God or a reformer. There are two kinds of reform—local and universal. If a reform occurred in America it would be local. A religious teacher sets out to establish a change in the psyche of man. Such a change could be a lasting change. So Beelzebub is not intent on changing any number less than the full number. All lesser reforms run down the scale again. The interval at which a religious teacher attempts to bring about such a change is si-do.

In the first descent he comes on account of a certain kinsman who has prematurely undertaken a religious mission—critique of religious values. Why are people as they are? Why are they so hard to move, so inaccessible to ideas, why do reforms so soon disappear? The practical mission of any religious teacher is to bring about a change in the whole human psyche. Can we judge from the results what has been the result of each religion and without blasphemy what were the mistakes of each?

A being from Karatas will see, as you should all eventually see, the pitiable state into which the men on this earth have fallen. Taxation without representation. So the kinsman of Beelzebub undertakes upon seeing this state of things but fails and has to call upon Beelzebub, who has remained upon Mars, for help.

Beelzebub is still speaking to Hassein perhaps because he expects one of these days of incarnate upon this planet. He would wish to know something of the planet before coming here. So Beelzebub tries to put Hassein on guard against the influences of these men—they have two natures—one external which looks okay—but inside they are abnormal monstrosities.

I descended several times to the planet earth, and I had to descend there to aid a kinsman who, by associating with one of the beings on the planet earth, had gotten himself in a very serious state.

Beelzebub—objective reason. When they had told me all, I saw that it might be disagreeable to all our kinsmen and to the whole of our tribe.

When we come to the chapter on Christ you will see that since it was founded on love it should have succeeded, but did not for lack of a certain subtlety. At any rate it has become discredited, and one of the reasons for casting these principles in a rather repellent form is that a negative reaction is almost always introduced by the attempt to relate knowledge and love. Why? Since to understand truth, love is absolutely necessary.

So you will find that sooner or later you will find that you too must take these same steps.

So Beelzebub descends after appropriate preparations to the planet earth on the ship Occasion, after finding that observation would not do. (He intervenes at an opportune moment, but we are seized by an occasion—Mars—permanent moods of emotional self-consciousness.)

So we landed on Atlantis, a continent which later sank and disappeared.

Atlantis is essence or that part of us which knows what we are. An essential act is one which we would say was exactly what we should always do, and say it wholeheartedly. The whole of the subsequent parable applies to us from the moment we begin to practice this method. I.e. the essence begins to reappear as does Atlantis in this history. Today the dominant characteristics or center of gravity is in the intellectual sub-center of the instinctive center. (When you hear the word "capital" it always refers to the center of gravity of the time or locality.)

The young kinsman had gotten himself into trouble through the king of that country, Appolis. I learned that this young kinsman had become friendly with the king and was frequently in his house.

That is, he became friendly and identified with his organism. So if by this method I had thought it might be that I could no longer write or maintain a certain pseudo intellectual grandeur, would I have taken it up? So it says that the king Appolis needed a great deal of money and a great deal of labor was necessary. So now we need to do all sorts of things and be with all sorts of things that essentially we don't want by any means really to do.

Is it true that beings do nothing in general with undertakings voluntarily assumed? Certainly it is true in my own case. I need to have a spur in the shape of some disagreeable consequences or I find my voluntary resolution extremely difficult to carry out.

I make a resolve to view the happenings of each day. Unless I tell someone who will snub me in case I fail, I can hardly manage, if at all, to carry out my resolve. So it is recommended that you make your vows public for the present.

So Appolis was very conscientious about his ideas for the public. We are quite capable of a similar state, say an ambition to become a great artist. Appolis had to employ all sorts of means to induce his subjects to do the necessary things, even to menaces.

The subjects added to Appolis the title of king—that of "the arch-dodger." So everyone uses little tricks to keep himself at a task. I, for example, edited a paper for fifteen years every week by promising "it" vacations, trips around the world, riches, position, etc. I was then the "arch-dodger."

Well, my boy, the measures used by the King Appolis, the young kinsman felt were very unjust, about the limit. And he expressed his views one day very frankly. But Appolis did not become angry as it is the custom on earth, but they talked it over and agreed on paper signed by their blood (essential assent) and therein my kinsman agreed to furnish all the money that the subjects failed to provide if the present methods were abandoned.

I undertook that there would be no immediate reduction in personal efficiency. But this cannot be guaranteed—though it could be guaranteed that there will be not any permanent diminution of efficiency—but on the contrary. The organism will benefit eventually but not necessarily in each case immediately.

If you fail in regard to an oath consciously taken the consequences will be 30,000 times as great as in respect to a mechanical oath.

So when the kinsman failed and could not carry out his vows, even exhausting the treasury on Mars; I could not help from Mars, but descended to earth. Appolis says: Impartial friends, I personally am very sorry for what has been brought about—but I am personally helpless to do anything about it. The fact is that the machinery of my government has been changed and now cannot be reassured without great dissension and perhaps revolt upon . . . (So any interference with regard to habits will bring about serious psychological consequences. But it cannot be, once done, easily changed back.)

I bitterly repent in the presence of you all that these things have occurred. For I ought not to have made such a pact with a being who, although higher than I in reason, is nevertheless much less experienced than I am personally.

So I advise each one of you here to retain common sense as the king until "I" has really grown up. There are people here who have done such absurd things on the theory that the young "I" was capable. Never undertake experiments against common sense. Those of us who do undertake some mad experiments will have to admit later that they were mad.

Once more I beg you all and your reverence in particular to forgive me and to help me to return to that form of government which formerly, though mechanical, functioned in my kingdom. We decided that the kinsmen should decide. And we decided to recommend that King Appolis resume the earlier form of government.

So think of the liberal forms of government wherein love is to be subsided for fear. They won't work. Though human beings are essentially just. But essence does not prevail in us. So Beelzebub and his kinsmen advised reverting from democracy to tyranny. (Think here of selling life insurance. The fools won't buy it. They don't know and don't realize that they may die tomorrow.)

Not from ourselves can we extract the energy to increase our rates of self-observation on the conviction that this will improve our state, but if we have a conviction of punishment in case of failure we may do so. Try to impose penalties—no breakfast or tobacco or —— for failure. Every time you cease to exert effort toward self-observation, etc., you will have to make a tremendous effort to resume.

Every organ has its own clock or time program. So when self-observation is begun it is exactly comparable to the beginning of the development of a seed. This does not mean that water must be given to the seed exactly at a certain moment—but that within so many hours it must have water. So with self-observation, a new psychological function begins and goes through a series of phases, each with a time limit. So nobody knows what the consequences may be of introducing self-observation.

21 FEBRUARY 1927

There is an effort in the book to see the human species as one would any other species of animal. As if one read a book on the dog, its nature and diseases; historical, physiological etc.—the beginning of objective reason. Later will speak of divine reason, i.e. a reason contemplating the human species and observing to what extent it fulfills or fails to fulfill its functions, a function of the being in terms of use. It is needful to understand the purpose before we can say whether the being is or is not fulfilling its function, the function of the being in terms of use.

Survey the species to make certain statements applicable to all human beings at all times, either positive or negative. Such a survey has always shown traits regrettable, even to human reason.

These would be interpreted by:

1. A religious observer as sin.
2. A philosopher as stupidity.
3. A sociologist as due to an unfavorable environment.

We do not know what conditions accompanied the end of extinct species e.g., mastodon. Perhaps the planet no longer offered favorable conditions. Perhaps this is true of the human species.

We add a personal survey: each individual finds he has behaved foolish, stupid, and even mad. The philosopher merely notes this and says: Man is uncivilized and uncivilizable. The religious teacher is impelled to deal with this and try to effect a change. The great religious teacher is convinced that the world is as it is but is not yet convinced that it cannot be changed. Can you understand sympathetically his attitude to this problem; his efforts to find proper methods, etc.?

QUESTION: For what does man exist?

ANSWER: To attain within himself objective reason. Half one's time should be spent in pondering how to live in the light of the reason attained.

The preceding chapter dealt with the dangers of a premature attempt at improvement. Until a long process of self-ascertainment has been gone through, an attempt to improve may produce a corresponding defect while removing the defect in question. An animal is what it can be. It has no obligation; but man is under an obligation to develop his potentialities, which have not yet been realized.

• Self-improvement is a re-arrangement between the three centers, an arrangement of what already exists.

• Self-perfecting is a realization of potentialities not yet developed.

Beelzebub's young kinsman was not the only one of his tribe in Atlantis. The others were not interfering by direct means; (perhaps they were teaching the method). They might have been trying to raise the rate of vibration; for the maintenance of a higher rate is the most effective way of causing change.

Our civilization is not built on preceding civilizations. Science is really a repetition although it thinks it is finding things for the first time.

You will find it stated several times in the book (true or not) that in at least two civilizations preceding historic times, electrical inventions were carried to as high a point as in our own times. Gurdjieff claims to have taken part in an expedition exploring the Gobi. Here twenty yards below the surface they came upon the remains of a city; below that another, then another still, present tribes have no traditions or names for these; and this makes Egypt seem of yesterday.

Atlantis is taken as the starting point of man; not because it was the starting point in form; but as a three-centered being. Previous beings had form but the air octave had not yet developed.

We can assume the same quantity of intelligence in the Greeks and Romans as in ourselves; but they applied it to art, philosophy, mathematics, whereas we have applied it to mechanics. It is improbable that the Pythagorean school of mathematics was inferior to modern. Euclid was a beginner's manual.

Our two handicaps: we are not on the shoulders of the past; and life is too short to attain consciousness, even to attain the kind of which we can conceive. We start comparatively late; we can estimate that the job would take several centuries. Considered in cold blood it really does not seem worthwhile starting; but that it may be "worthwhile" is a different matter.

Why is our life so short? Why have we not a normal life of three or four centuries. The answer depends on two issues.

1. Question of time.
2. Question of three centers.

Under the last we are like a clock wound up with three springs, which vary according to heredity and early environment but all three are wound up to run for two or three centuries at least. What prevents them from doing so? The "regulator" is not operating properly. What is this regulator? The effort to become self-conscious. This effort begun from the age of responsibility (seventeen or eighteen) automatically guarantees that the organism would run that long. Gurdjieff has described several people whom he had met, who had found this idea as children and profited by it.

QUESTION: What do we call time?

ANSWER: The duration of the unwinding of the spring.

We are familiar with the differences of time in dreams and when awake. And the experience of the man whose head was dipped in a bowl of water. What is the nature of time in a dream? What is the relation between intense experience and an absence of awareness of the passage of time? Or of the opposite when time seems to go slow? Intense experience makes time short, absence of experience, long. Einstein said: "The more that happens, the less time."

Suppose that under your eyes a tree should be presented in successive stages of its growth, as on the movie screen. How would we feel about time?

Our period up to responsibility ordinarily passes normally, with growth which winds the springs, one by one. Infancy, childhood, adolescence; then man- or woman-hood. A premature adolescence is considered abnormal because we have this series in mind; but manhood now presents disordered phases, with no ordered succession. Gurdjieff says that time is normal up to age of responsibility; and after that it "plays tricks"; as above. This is because the three centers act, not under supervision; but accidentally in response to accidents from without. The natural regulator is removed at the age of responsibility, when this stage is passed a new regulator should be applied by the individual.

The difference between the waking and sleeping state is that in the waking state the three centers are magnetically connected. There is a tendency for each center to imitate the other two, a mutual hypnotism, e.g. an unnecessary knitting of brows etc. during thought. This activity of motor centers is not needed; and there is much waste of energy through this mutual hypnotism. The lack of this hypnotism is a partial explanation of the swift passage of time during a dream.

Up to and including youth there is a winding up; then comes the running down. In early childhood the magnetic tie is not formed. It approximates our sleeping state. The child begins slowly to "wake up," as this magnetic tie is formed. Then it is impossible to "act with childish impulsiveness," that is from one center alone. It draws in the other centers.

It is possible to break these ties by drugs etc; but effort in the instinctive center is so deleterious that it is often impossible to restore the tie or the instinctive center may perhaps be destroyed. It is preferable to use the psychological drug—*effort*.

Illustration: Should this room and we in it shrink to a pin point, no change would be noticed. Gurdjieff takes as an example, life in a drop of water. The heading of this chapter is "The Relative Understanding of time."

Time is the potentiality of experience. The duration of time is in each center wound up; and objective time is the number of experiences potentially contained in the center in question. How many capacities of experience does each center contain? These experiences can be successive or with intervals, sequentially or simultaneously. The time of our lives will depend on the rate by which these potentialities are exhausted by experience, that is, subjectively.

By accident certain difficult experiences with people cause us to unwind in a few minutes, days, or months, years of potential unwinding. We cannot say "our" experiences, when they happen to us and happen too fast for us to be simultaneously aware of and hence profit from them; too fast for us to use.

Time is in this sense, personal. This does not mean that if all beings had the regulator at work that unwinding would take the same time; but each would get the full benefit from it.

Example of two men, one spending one hundred and the other one thousand dollars, each spends purposively. The measure of time is not the quantity but the manner of spending, a difference in the mode of experiencing. The flow may be experienced equally and identically by all beings or cosmoses—human being, planet, sun, milky way, the universe of universes.

Motion is in terms of space.

Time is positive—father.

Space is negative—mother.

Motion is life.

Our visualization of these three; objects; hence three dimensional

At present we experience abnormally because chance can at any moment exhaust our potentialities, either through movement, feeling or thinking. If we in control could choose, this would mean a proper use of time. In saying we "have very little time," we mean we have very few potentialities left unrealized.

[*Orage read a chapter from Beelzebub's Tales.*]

Men use the unit of a year, the revolution of the planet about the sun. The ancients took a longer period than this. We have taken it because of the seasons. The instinctive center attaches itself to the seasons. But there are also emotional and intellectual seasons. A certain emotional season, e.g., which lasts ninety-nine years. A period of an intellectual year extends over an age of civilization. In what intellectual season, am I born? In what emotional season am I? The instinctive year is for children; the emotional year for artists; the intellectual year for real scientists. Certain ancients took their seasons of more importance to them than the external ones.

It is possible to know time only relatively; it cannot be understood by reason, nor can it be sensed.

In different cosmoses, there are all octaves, the only difference being in scale, the element of time is the same, and the order of the unfolding of experience. The way in which they act is the same but the duration is different. There is no end to the octaves (in number).

Only time stands alone—the unique subjective. The subjective is the potentiality of experience. Where there is process, no matter on what scale, time will blend itself with it. For a creature in a drop of water time "makes itself microscopic" and gives those beings the same sequence, the process of experience, the flow of time, as we or beings of other cosmoses. For beings in the drop of water there is the same harmonious relation. They are born, grow, marry, get sick, die, and are destroyed. They have winter, spring, summer. Time never comes objectively into existence and can never be an object. It is the infinite potential, subjective, the potential objective, the realization. Time is the absolute potential of all experience.

None of us live our natural period, nor experience time normally. This is because our three centers are not unwound normally, because they are not under a regulator. Hence we have no normal understanding of time of those who are fully developed and who do not experience faster than they can use it.

21 FEBRUARY 1927

You will remember the idea that the book provides at the same time a description and an exercise—the mind in which you approach this is called objective reason—that attitude of reasonable consciousness with which it is possible to survey mankind, including oneself, as one may lower species—dogs, etc. To this is added divine reason—so that one may in addition survey the human species with discrimination as to each entity's use—duty. And so with every standard, assuming that we know the purpose for which a man was created—we can judge as to a man's being right or wrong.

Making such a survey, as every founder of a religion and every philosophic thinker we shall decide man is:

Religious—sin.

Thinker—stupid.

Biological—defects in environment.

It may be that our planet has ceased to provide those maximum conditions that made us flourish as a race in ages past.

By self-observation and objectively making a review of one's own past—every one of us is bound to condemn himself for a series of foolish and from this point of view semi-criminal acts. But if we, then can we certainly say the entire race as well? But then reason condemns man. And the philosopher comes to the conclusion—"Man is uncivilized and uncivilizable."

Last week we reviewed the various ways that have been employed by various religions in the past for regenerating. So if you can see how each founder of a religion has surveyed, diagnosed and prescribed, you have reached a certain degree of objective reason! Man's first purpose is to attain objective reason. So every human must spend much time in pondering on how he shall live in greatest accord with reason. And it will be decided from these criteria—how much will it contribute to my realization, appreciation and understanding of why I and the world, etc., are created.

Last week I pointed out that we might begin too early to try to correct our defects—and any effort, before ascertaining sufficient [knowledge] about oneself is just as likely to affect one adversely as not. So every effort at self-perfecting should be postponed until the proper time.

QUESTION: Define self-perfecting!

ORAGE: Man straddles the gap between do, re, mi—and sol, la, si.

Self-improvement is to improve the status already evolutionarily obtained. Self-perfection would be to actualize the three higher centers potential in man but not now actualized.

Beelzebub's kinsmen were not engaged in self-improvement but, perhaps by objective art or something similar, in aiming to raise the rate of vibration.

Scientists are now engaged in repeating the discovery of such things as electricity. These things have not come down to us as knowledge but only as fairy tales, myths, legends, etc.

Gurdjieff is quite explicit that there have been at least two civilizations that formerly existed on this earth wherein the development of such things as electricity have been carried much further than we have done. Below the ancient city of Troy there were found, by archeological investigations, several city-layers beneath layers. Thirty years ago an archeologist who thought that history might extend back of Egypt would have been thought crazy.

Madam Blavatsky told of beings—Lemurians—who, though in human form, were not three-centered beings. The emotional had not even gone do—re—mi.

It is improbable that the Pythagorean school of mathematics was inferior to our present mathematics, but it did not take the mechanical turn. So we have no birthright from higher civilizations and yet our lives are much shorter than tradition says the average lifetime of man was in earlier ages.

So if you have measured your progress and determined that it will take about a thousand years to attain the degree of objective reason that we can even now apprehend. Well then, we have only a few years. We have fallen on days when the life of man is very contracted. Why is it that we—the people in this room—have not a life of four or five hundred years? We are a kind of clock wound on three springs—instinctive—emotional—intellectual—and each of our three springs are wound up differently. But each—even the least of these windings—is sufficient for a life of at least 200 years. Wound up by nature.

Now what is it that will determine how long a clock will go on a winding? A regulator. And in exactly the same way our springs, wound up to go 400–500 years, would do so only that the regulator in us is loosened. And the new regulator is called "The effort to become self-conscious."

If at birth we commenced this effort—we should live several centuries. So, self-consciousness is the "regulator." Time is the duration of the running down of any one of our three springs.

Try to recall an actual occurrence in your own life such as it will suggest in order to achieve a state wherein you can absorb the very difficult ideas of objective time in this chapter.

Think of a dream—you may have "lived" in your dream hours in minutes. Try to ponder the nature of time in a dream.

Another day you are working very intensely and you look up to find that the days have flown. Try to ponder the relation between intense experience and time. Also recall the five minutes you have perhaps waited for some doctor—fullness of time is short, emptiness of time is long. You go down the street and the clocks are all different—you are confused. Suppose under your eyes an acorn becomes an oak tree fully grown.

The period up to maturity passes normally.

In these periods or seasons:

1. Infancy.
2. Childhood.
3. Adolescence.
4. Youth.

All these are relatively normal states. So we think of a child reaching adolescence a little early as a bit monstrous.

Beyond these stages, in manhood or womanhood, we can quickly pass down from back through youth to adolescence to childhood to infantilism. There is no normal stage of growth beyond youth. The sequence of our experiences at this point becomes disorderly—because the growth of our three centers begins to proceed not regularly—i.e. by and according to a regulator but haphazardly. We have a regulator that acts only up to seventeen or eighteen.

THE RELATIVE UNDERSTANDING OF TIME

Much of our waste energy is brought about by the unnecessary conjunction of effort in two centers when only one is being used. For example, one contracts his brows and other muscles, etc., when thinking. The period of growth is the period of winding up. Then comes the period of running down . . .

In children the magnetic tie between the three centers is developing with the centers. So we can no longer after youth be free as we have been. The tie between centers is no longer detachable. But it is possible to regain this power, i.e. of detaching at will the centers one from the other.

We have not at present the use of a certain organ or muscle with which we can control the use of glands. The back of the head contains an organ which is in control of the glandular system. But since we are not in control of this organ we are not in control of anything. And it is the exercise of this particular organ that is necessarily our object.

If this room in which we are sitting would get smaller and smaller and we would in exact proportions shrink with it, we would not be aware of any change.

HUGH: I don't believe that.

Time is the potentiality of experience . . . duration of time is the period or sequence of that particular experience.

Objective time is the number of experiences potentially contained within the center in question. These experiences can be made successive and with intervals the centers can be run down sequentially or simultaneously and rapidly or slowly.

At eighteen we have a capacity of say 300-400 years if we live under a regulator. But we are cast into unfortunate circumstances and they are run off. Objective time is a purely individual thing.

If I have $100 to spend and you have $1,000, if I spend my $100 and you your $1,000 purposively and reasonably—I will have had as much as you. So though the "years" of a being may be quite different, every being has the potential equal to that to every other if conscious. Motion is life, space, time.

There is a normal way of experiencing but there is for us now only an abnormal way. If we were in control of our three springs we should experience only when we choose. And this is that which is called the proper use of time.

So in octaves each note is an octave and vice versa and so here is no end either to macrocosmos or microcosmos, so no limit to numbers but we can talk about particular numbers. Time is the unique subjective (subjective is the potentiality of experience).

Time whose works are wonderful manifested this world and may manifest many more.

Time is God of Gods. Instinctive center has potentiality of movement. But not an infinite number of movements. Still, even this is not "determined" for something may happen. But it will not go beyond the unwinding of it.

We are crammed with food eating as we do, but the same quantity of food . . .

The next chapter deals with light and heat. And we, who are entitled to know what this game of life is, are as ignorant as animals. All alone.

27 FEBRUARY 1927

Last week was an experiment in sustained attention of imaginative understanding. Fragmentary attention fails to make up a whole, to bind isolated thoughts into a whole, attention must be sustained. How soon did I give out?

Consider the epic quality of this setting and the beings. It is a sort of dialogue between a fully realized being and one not fully realized. Beelzebub begins in a detached position from which he observes the body of the cosmos, as we when beginning self-observation should be detached and impartial. In all that Beelzebub says to Hassein it is implied always that the whole physical universe has a purpose and that he understands it. Matter is an agency. Part of it is at certain notes of the octave, such as planets, solar systems, beings, etc., have practical not mystical, not theoretical function and each part either fulfills or does not fulfill this function.

Similarly we have a material cosmos; the first truthful thing we can say is "I have a body." From which position are we to observe its use? What can it do? What use can "I" make of it?

Beelzebub can look at the planets and say "I understand their use." The implication is that the universe is logical and rational. For what purpose am I (the listener)? Beelzebub speaks as "I" or mind and refers to the physical universe as a means of attaining something for himself. I can extract from practical experiences with this body an active understanding of its use; an objective reason. The universe is to be used for the education of souls; for beings who have attained objective reason. For those who have understood, the obligation is on God to maintain the universe. Only those who have understood this and taken their part are entitled to be called "souls," partners or sons of God and not slaves.

Hassein takes interest in this planet; but it is one among millions, and not the center of life.

The singular life on this planet is the result of an accident. Our moon was not given off naturally but was the result of an accident. All planets naturally give off moons; but the earth was prematurely delivered of its moon and hence a special kind of life had to be developed to supply special radiations. (See recent scientific experiments on radiations from planets.)

How do we explain the fact that we, who consider ourselves intelligent, if we review our life at the end of each day, find we have behaved like idiots, cowards, poltroons, idle creatures. We would condemn such lives if we judged another impartially; yet we preserve our equanimity. Why such indulgence?

Why after the end of each civilization do we fail to preserve or make use of its excellences? Egypt's art and science; India's philosophy and religion; China's personal relations (Confucius). Why do not succeeding generations build on these? Why are we not in reality the "heirs of all the ages"? There has been only a broken and discontinuous movement. There seems to be a need in us for destruction. Instead of standing on the shoulders of the preceding civilizations, we have climbed up from almost nothing to a place still inferior in many sciences and arts to those of the ancient civilizations.

Why do we believe and hope in "progress" when we have proof before our eyes that the race has not progressed?

Or personally, when I cannot do this (observe) now, how can I expect others to do so? Or if I am, say, a reformer and observe my own failings how can I expect my effort to be carried out?

Make an impartial survey of the world, its continents, its islands, its races, its history, its languages. What impartial judgment can we make? We are growing more mechanical every day, if possible. Devote a few minutes each day to such a survey. Such effort must precede any understanding of the following chapter:

WHY MAN IS NOT MAN

What claim do we make to be superior to the animals? In reason, we think. What is man? One who understands why he is alive. (Does a sheep understand mutton, and wool? Do we understand moon-food and sun-food?)

What is the body for? What is life for? What to do with the body? How to live and what values to attain? Not one of us, in spite of all philosophy knows why he is alive. We receive body at birth to play with, and not one of us knows which or what game he is playing. The sheep can see their shepherd; but we can see no biological species superior to us. Who are they? No one employs physical force over us. We are so complacent and uncritical that we take it for granted that we are fulfilling human functions. The problem of why not, never presents itself to us as a real problem (emotionally, intellectually) as it did to the writers of Genesis, for example. They said mythologically but intelligently, that degradation came through succumbing to the temptations of the instinctive center. We were put in a garden where we were expected to care for the garden; but we ceased to make effort and soon were out of paradise. This is the psychology of Genesis.

Gurdjieff gives a myth which is related to the method, and is designed to produce a poignant realization of our state—premature delivery of the moon—catastrophe of the comet (unusual state of emotion). Two pieces struck off, leaving the earth deprived of two functions for normal development. Take this personally: Why have we not the advantage of normal methods of education and development?

The nature of this planet is such that the catastrophe will always be repeated in the organic life on it. Individuals will pass through the same stage that the planet passed through. The individual repeats the history of the species, back to the original parent, the planet which had two parts struck off.

1. Consciousness of my body.
2. Consciousness of the world in which I live.

(Both are normally accompaniments of life, but since no longer organic parts, they must be re-conquered by feeding, i.e. each of us must make special effort, must feed these potentialities, to make them actualities.) Such words as God, service of God, religion, etc. have no meaning for us. On some planets there is perhaps a natural development of education, science, etc. On our planet, the sponge of oblivion is always passed over every great system. There must be always effort. Thanks to this effort Beelzebub can say "I am glad," "I understand disease as well as health."

Beelzebub talks to Hassein; these slugs had three brain systems; but due to external conditions began to develop unexpectedly mechanical reason. With mechanical reason we can for instance understand the idea that we are organic mechanisms.

When Sakaki and his commission returned a little later to see how life was coming on, he found here mechanical reason and had to decide what measures to take. If creatures will not make voluntary effort, labor or suffer perhaps by virtue of their mechanical effort will avoid involuntary effort (to attain self-consciousness and cosmic-consciousness) realizing by their mechanical reason that they were mechanical slaves, used for a purpose, they do not understand. It was possible they might prefer not to live.

If we realized emotionally our mechanical nature, that is without the possibility of self- or cosmic-consciousness as in behaviorism, suicide would follow. Sakaki saw that our mechanical reason would one day discover this and arranged to prevent these effects, i.e. we would refuse to be such slaves with a resultant upset to the cosmic equilibrium. With the arch-chemist Looisos, an organ was designed to turn values upside down and provide imaginary pleasures.

The physical analogy is with the use, especially in the East at certain periods, of opium—or consider the limited amount of electricity in the atmosphere. Its greater mechanical use has allowed less biological use. If will requires electricity, then as the use of electricity increases, will will diminish. Looisos must have done one of two things; either released certain elements in the atmosphere or denuded it of some.

Our Lucifer was a chemist. Superstitious notion of a special organ, all rot. Atmosphere was treated to prevent realization. We have heard of the separation of the centers, e.g., when taking ether, by drugs, or by such fatigue as induces autointoxication. But all our centers are separated from two other centers, with which they would be connected if we were normal.

- Emotional realization of things as they are (true emotional).
- Understanding of why we live (true intellectual).

We know we will die; unlike animals we are aware of our mortality, yet we behave like animals. We know we are all to be butchered but we do not know when. How is it possible to love? Our emotional center is separate from our mechanical knowledge. This was the work of Looisos—imaginary pleasures. We have three groups of our activities; intellectual, emotional, physical. We know the body is mortal; perhaps the intellect is not. Obviously we should in theory live for understanding, reason, etc. Yet 99 percent of our effort, time, emotion, is spent on pleasures of the body. Paraphrase ordinary talk in terms of animals.

The forces of heredity are not mechanical (?) Saturn, Looisos, both good and evil, responsible for doping and for the possibility of living kundabuffer . . . Sane beings but doped and therefore behaving as if not sane. The organ kundabuffer turns values upside-down, men take instinctive values as the highest in the face of proof to the contrary. Looisos returns satisfied that the organ will work. Men will not suspect they are doped and will live in illusory satisfactions. Beelzebub will later point out to Hassein the results of this dislocation of centers.

Beelzebub and his kinsmen return to Mars and set up an observatory. (Mars is an emotional attitude outside the range of faith, now doped.) They visited Saturn, found beings more highly developed. Saturnians are rare among us. They have understanding of the first law of life: "Love all that breathes," which is the first obligation on all responsible beings. These people were congenial to Beelzebub.

Later on he gives an example of Tolstoy, though not naming him, who without any real knowledge of life or self became regarded as the author of a modern gospel. Gurdjieff knew Tolstoy, who was naive and self-ignorant. Why do we give credence to his statements, when we have no way of checking them up? Suggestibility. Do not apply reason to ideas presented to us in certain ways. Not susceptible to ideas but to forms in which they are presented. Why will we, knowing certain authors to be fools, read their books with respect? We, knowing certain education to be bad, will send children there; knowing certain bad ideas will act on them. Flying in the face of our knowledge. This is fundamental in man. Analyze this. Why are books written? Why do people believe Tolstoy's gospel? Because we never verify by applying personal knowledge and effort. Why not? It involves effort of self-knowledge and consequent estrangement.

Beings on this planet differ in color according to climate, and race distinctions are purely a matter of prejudice. Personal distinctions vary according to main causes, among which are heredity and conditions at conception; but the psyche is always the same, especially in suggestibility. Mass suggestion especially in relation to war. Why are we not the heirs of old civilizations? Every civilization has been destroyed by man in the madness of war fever. So long as we are susceptible to war fever, so long can there be no general program. Later Gurdjieff gives examples of Leagues of Nations going back to Babylon.

Take as an example the conception of the word "hero." Beelzebub says to Hassein: "A hero is among us one who voluntarily undertakes some labor for the benefit of creation, the whole, not some part of it." Cf. the discovery and promulgation of the method, involving effort of which we are utterly incapable. Gurdjieff spent thirty years in the satisfaction of a rational curiosity. Gurdjieff is a juvenile hero. On the planet earth the word hero exists and is usually applied to those who most easily fall under the war fever and slay many others. Admire those who do not fear death, who do not fear those whom under suggestion, they regard as enemies. In this state of trance, we are ready to destroy or be destroyed. No gods or devils are to blame; beings induce it in themselves and in each other.

The first descent is the period of Atlantis.

Whether Atlantis ever existed is here a matter of no interest; but that Atlantis exists in us is of great psychological interest.

BIBLIOGRAPHICAL NOTES

Iamblichus' Life of Pythagoras, translated by Thomas Taylor.
The Golden Verses of Pythagoras.
Pythagoras, by Edouard Schure, translated by Fred Rothwell.
Mahabharata.

28 FEBRUARY 1927

The previous chapters are on abnormality. In this there is a certain suggestive statement of the nature of normal man. What should a normal human being do, be, know? From our abnormal understanding of time, experiences are too fast to be received into our consciousness. In this room, different colors, sounds, etc., affect my chemistry; but I am unaware of most of them.

Beelzebub says our lives are growing shorter; by this he means we make conscious use of fewer and fewer experiences. The title of this chapter: "The Arch-Absurd."

Gurdjieff is aware that what he is about to say is almost incredible. Its subtitle is: Discovery. According to the tales of Beelzebub our sun gives neither heat nor light. Beelzebub is indignant; he is capable of pity. He makes a survey of the planet he has left, with sympathy but in a detached way. They live in conditions created by themselves, which are not becoming to three-centered beings, "becoming" means both fitting and that which will enable them to become. Any normal cognizance of the cosmos in which they live has disappeared from their psyche. This is the first indication of what a normal, three-centered being would be. Just as we are aware of the flora and fauna of nature and the characteristics of civilization, so three-centered beings would be aware of the functions of the cosmos, those of the moon related to the sun—all the cosmic phenomena, in the midst of which we dwell.

This means a direct personal knowledge, a "being knowledge" or a personal knowledge, not just hearsay (have we any personal knowledge of the structure of the atom?) I have a personal knowledge of the difference between the city and the country. Gurdjieff says that every three-centered being should normally know the cosmic phenomena which affect us without our now being aware of them. This is caused, according to the myth, by kundabuffer. (Some Hindus used a metaphor of mirrors.) Kundabuffer was introduced to prevent the acquisition of such knowledge for fear of destruction. But kundabuffer was removed later, that is organic conditions were removed. The responsibility is now on human beings.

Plato said his republic could be set up only if he could have newly born children to start with; but since he would have to employ adults for their education, he regarded the problem as practically insoluble.

Fumes being no longer generated, by fumes, education being continued. There are thousands whose intelligence is superior to their conduct; they are freed from superstition in regard to religion or morals, but teach their irrational conduct to their children. How many subscribe for others to that which they would not consider proper for themselves.

What do we know about heat, dark, light, cold? We know by personal knowledge. We assume that light and heat come directly from the sun. What would human beings do if they knew (sensed), that nothing so material as light comes from the sun and that the sun is itself cold and icy. Would it send heat to their misshapen planet, which is the shame of the solar system but which eventually may redeem the whole solar system. (The Ugly Duckling?) This is in many fairy tales, the doctrine is often enshrined there, where they would not be suspected of propaganda. The troubadours were emissaries of an occult society.

Light and heat are not universal. They are particular to certain localities and to certain conditions (certain planets). The vegetable and animal kingdom have different perceptions than we of light and heat. We are contributing to these phenomena.

The whole of our universe (all observable phenomena) exists owing to one system: trogo (I ate) auto (ego) ego (I) crat (government) by "I, myself eat"—I eat myself, and this is the nature of my life. The food I eat is changed into the cells of my body, I am what I have eaten and digested. The universe is a comparable being which eats to live and lives to eat. Every part of the physical universe is the product of eating of the "I" (God). This idea ties up and throws light on many myths: certain early rites of cannibalism; the Holy Communion; the tradition of the early Christians that Christ cut off parts of his flesh and that the disciples literally drank his blood.

My body eats—and is substantiated; where is "I"?

This system was created by His Endlessness, when only the Sun Absolute existed and where His All Gracious Endlessness still exists. It is impossible to explain clearly at this point. We have a body whose every cell is accounted for. Where is "I"?

We can offer no evidence of the existence of "I," yet we can be sure of it. Similarly we say "God is." Gurdjieff never says "lives" but "exists"; ex = out, of; ists = manifests, to be; that state of being which is capable of manifesting itself. The primary fact of being is "istence," but the "ex" is necessary for proof, communication. This does not affect its essence.

Essence—existence.

"I"—"it."

It is always passing up or down the scale; all elements are undergoing change, a conflux of chemical elements, some moving up the scale of their own octave, others down, in evolution and involution. These are proceeding in accordance with two cosmic laws (one system, two laws):

1. Holy triamazikamno (later triamonia), three making one
2. Efta para barshinoch (later hepta etc.), seven making one.

The first is the law by which cosmic substances can interblend and form the cosmos according to law two. Every note is threefold; and the succession of notes is sevenfold. The eighth note is a repetition of the first (see modern physics). All elements yet discovered tend to fall into groups of seven or eight. Why is seven so common in natural phenomena? In completing a circle, by what impulse does it return to its starting point? Number is not subject to kundabuffer.

An attempt to objectify what we have hitherto called "I"; to empty "I" of all objects which can be objectified. "I" can never observe "I." "It" is under the law of seven; "I" is under the law of three.

"I" is composed of consciousness, individuality and will. Can these ever be seen? The subjective world is seven; the objective three. The phenomenal is seven; the noumenal three. "I" is a vacuum from which is excreted phenomena. See later experiment which might be reproduced of generating forms in a vacuum.

To understand this chapter, one should have a metaphysical background and be familiar with failure, any previous answers which have failed. One should be capable of understanding the difference between the potential and the actual.

The potential exists. Read Saurat on this problem.

Before the universe was actualized, God existed on the Sun Absolute. He planned and constructed the universe on laws of architecture, so to speak. Everything objective was threefold, everything subjective was sevenfold.

Sitting is the result of seven reciprocal thrusts. Why do certain buildings stand and others fall? Those that stand are sevenfold. Why do certain sentences fail to stand alone? They are not aphorisms and must have the buttress of introduction and subscription. They are not under the law of seven. Certain works of art of the ancients were built on the law of seven, so as to stand, to be a thing. Ruskin's Seven Lamps was on the trail but became confused. Make a work of art on the same laws as the universe. Only those were creators who could create things which exemplified the sevenfold laws of the universe. Hokusai said that when he died, he hoped to join that body of artists who drew in light and created flowers. Blakes "Tiger, Tiger etc." The contemporary use of the word "creator" is ridiculous.

This body will wear out; we take the wrong food or the right in insufficient amount or excess. Suppose one took only the food needful to repair worn tissue. We don't know how to do this and consequently are always taking into the body substances whose decay leads to death. We live under ignorance, hence time.

When God saw his own demise approaching, he made a survey of the law of existence and saw that if he could establish self-feeding, absorbing only the food needful to restore wear, he could become endless. That is he could defy time. Having assured his existence, he then could say I have time for self-perfecting. We, as component cells have a chance to share this endlessness.

Beelzebub has great gratitude, greater than we are capable of, that he exists in this endless body; but refers with slight disrespect to His Endlessness for being willing to remain in this state. Beelzebub is not convinced that it is worth it for an intelligent being; if that is to be all. This criticism is really directed at human beings who, when they achieve a certain state of content, cease to strive to realize their still undeveloped potentialities. Our weaknesses are the source of our striving. Energies which should be turned into developing of new powers are diverted into producing gratifications, for the planetary body. If happiness is taken as an end, the fundamental illusion of kundabuffer, truth, development, etc. become by-products. If our aim is truth and self-perfecting, then happiness may be a by-product from the actualizing potentialities. Certain stages may sometimes be accompanied by happiness; sometimes by unhappiness. Happiness is not a criterion.

28 FEBRUARY 1927

"THE ARCH-ABSURD"

During the reading of this chapter, I shall make comparatively little explanation because the reading itself is the most important yet to read in my estimation until we reach the chapter Purgatory. Unless you can, from the point of mankind, establish some gulf of objectivity, nothing can have more than literary value in this book. This chapter defines the nature of normal man. Therefore here have been described diseased animals who have failed to strike the note intended—or a least to maintain it.

In contrast to this we ask what is the type of human being which none of us has ever been able to define outside the terms of our usual environment. What should we do and what should we know?

Even time for us flows abnormally—the springs are released in an abnormal way so that we liberally realize only an uncertain small percentage of our experiences. Our time is defined as a series of experiences which can be felt and utilized at the rate at which they pass.

We are becoming more mechanical—and Beelzebub here deplores this fact. Hitherto Beelzebub has been a very cold critic but here shows pity.

"The Arch-Absurd." Our sun gives neither light nor heat.

Later when I relate the facts regarding the existence of three-centered beings you will understand that, for the causes of that Babel that exists on earth are not becoming to three-centered beings.

(We can make a survey of conditions as if we were dead and perhaps intending to reincarnate.)

There has tended to disappear any sensation of cosmic phenomena proper to a three-centered being. (We ought to know the function of the moon, planets, sun. We have not inherited the knowledge of our whole environment as we should have, being what we are.)

None of them, i.e. beings on the planet earth, have any being sensation of the cosmos. ("Being" as an adjective always means "personal" as opposed to "hearsay.")

I personally would not bet a penny on any of the atomic theories extant—even when they work. Do you know the difference between the city and the country? Of course you do—no one could convince you that you don't. So you should have just as accurately, knowledge of the difference between moon, planets and sun. Something has been interposed in our psyche which prevents us from having a "being sense" of our true environment.

Indians—mirrors.

The method of Gurdjieff introduces the possibility of a self-reeducation. Return to essence.

Many situations become less intolerable when we know that the cause of the difficulties present have ceased. So now, it is well to bear always in mind that the causes of our condition have disappeared. But we "inherit" the results and we in turn pass them on to our children.

Daylight and dark, heat and cold—we understand how heat in this room is produced—or light. But what do we know about it?

These beings are persuaded that heat and light all come from the sun. The genuine causes of these phenomena never even occur to them.

Fairy legends—troubadours were the messengers of a certain occult group and undertook to purvey the knowledge they possessed in spite of laws of church and government. So many of the fairy stories still contain certain tones and vibrations of a higher quality.

Light and heat as we know them are peculiarities of certain planets—so the vegetable and animal kingdom probably do not feel light and heat as we feel them. Laws of world creation and maintenance are chief cosmic laws.

The whole of our great universe depends on one law called "trogoaftoegocrat."

Trogo—eat—observe.

Afto—myself—it.

Ego—I—I.

Crat—government by.

"I eat myself." This is true, isn't it? Every particle of oneself has been eaten. So this universe is a comparable being which eats to live and lives to eat.

Note that Gurdjieff never uses the word "live"—always "existence"—that state of being that is capable of being manifested. The primary fact of existence is "istence." "I" do not depend on existence but Orage does. That does not mean that I cannot continue in being.

So in the book we are speaking of the creation of "its." Processes of involution and evolution. Every particle of your body (including the food you have recently taken) is in a state of conflux—moving up or down their octaves. These processes proceed in accordance with two fundamental laws—the chief laws of the universe—triamazikamno, meaning three making one and Eptaparabarshinok, meaning seven making one. These interblend and gradually form ——.

The whole of "it" falls under the law of seven but "I" falls under the law of three—but never can the manifestations of "I" be observed—yet always we have the three (individuality, consciousness and will) observing the seven ("It" and the universe.)

Law of three maintains world of noumena.

Law of seven maintains world of phenomena.

This table can only stand because of seven reciprocal thrusts. I can only sit or stand, but not both simultaneously, on account of the law of seven.

Every being has it within his power to remain alive for ever—by gaining the power to renew one's body.

A conscious being could use the law of seven as it now exists in our universe to create bodies, flowers, anything—real works of art. Thus we have the resurrection—and the legend of the great resurrection—opening of graves and walking, etc.

A boat is sinking—a storm is coming up—a man is leaning over the edge with a microscope.

"What are you doing?'"

"I'm engaged in scientific investigation," he replies.

"For what purpose are you doing this?" the other yelled.

"I am a devotee of pure science," he loftily replied.

God understands the laws of seven and three so well that he can guarantee himself immortality against time.

Beelzebub always has a little contempt for His Endlessness for he wonders religiously if one can exist eternally contented without change. But remember, however blasphemous any statements about God may appear, there is always God behind a God behind a God.

[*After the meeting I asked Orage if Beelzebub's criticism of God was that he had stopped after perfecting himself in consciousness, will and individuality.*]

ORAGE: No, it is that he has stopped far short of that. He has not perfected himself. He has established himself securely against time and rests there contented.

MANCHESTER: Is it as it would be with a man who has amassed enough money to make himself secure financially and thereafter relapses into complacency—i.e. in his instinctive world consciousness he is immortal beyond the reach of instinctive want?

ORAGE: Yes, exactly. (Dear me!!!)

7 MARCH 1927

It seems presumptuous for anyone to pretend to write on this subject—the ultimate meaning of the universe. It seems presumptuous on our part to attempt to understand and yet it is often reiterated throughout the book, that the normal state of a human being is to attempt to understand this. Renan said that no men should be ashamed to be unable to answer ultimate questions, but should be ashamed not to be interested in them. Cf. the first Book of Genesis where God brooded over chaos. This detached reason should be our attitude.

Suppose we are asked at death Nietzsche's question: "Well, what has been your experience of being a human being?" The question assumes that you have experimented with life and that you have brought home a report. This is the attitude of a scientific observer, who is also an experimenter.

Consider the species; one can make a series of objective statements on the race; a critique of human beings. In the preceding chapters the conclusion is reached that human beings are degenerates; that is through thousands of years they have become steadily less and less actual, with less desire to realize their potentialities. The race is still at the head of biological evolution but is deteriorating. The result is that we accept as normal things which are abnormal. Let us suppose a race that in isolation loses interest in educating its children, developing its intellectual life, etc. If none were exempt, no one would be aware of the deterioration. If confronted with the works of his ancestors, he would be faced with a problem. Without any objective standard we have no way of telling whether we are degenerating—and if so, how much?

This book attempts to set up a standard for a normal being, perhaps not even in historical time. But there are certain records, e.g. it was said last week that one of the normal senses of a human being was an awareness of the cosmos in which it is living. Our common birthright is to understand this cosmos. Just as a man, who is born on one continent, is aware of the existence of another. Astrology and ancient religions were often based on personal sensations. These now become superstitions because these sensations are no longer ours. Others (below) which include certain powers for which at present we have only names.

Before coming to the personal, we must have a certain analogy with the universe. We cannot understand the universe unless there is a certain correspondence with us, whether we are its product or it is our projection. Otherwise, there is no contact. If we are, e.g. three-centered, it must be for us to understand. This does not mean that our knowledge exhausts it; but our knowledge is conditioned by our means of coming into contact with it. One of the frequent exercises of imagination in the book is the frequent shift from the personal to the universal.

Trogo-auto-ego-crat. Have you during the week thought of the significance of this? Man is the result of his eating; the universe is the body of His Endlessness. Was there a Sun Absolute before the universe came into existence? What does this mean? This is unintelligible to one who has not tried to make a distinction between "I" and "it." If I have experienced this immediacy, I can understand the statement that God was before the world. The Sun Absolute in us is the highest of reason, the brain. If our first being was threefold, everything subsequently in creation tends to become threefold. This is called Trinity, or three-in-one, or God, or triamazikamno (triamonia). It means simply that the nature of man is inherent in creation. There is a tendency for it to manifest itself progressively in a threefold manner, hence we have three brains. Each brain corresponds to one of the three original forces (We repeat that our knowledge may never exhaust it). The degree of our realization is the measure of our development.

What are the three brains? What are found in each? Why do two alone produce the animal, and not human? It takes three to produce reflection.

Two produce sensation and emotion.

Sensation, emotion, image.

The animal lacks the third brain which combines sensation and emotion into the image, hence it is incapable of reflection and imagination. We see things in three. In absence of the fourth center, we have no ground for discussing what we see.

Indications in preceding as steps of evolution. Fully revealed only in a perfect product. There are no sharp lines. It shades off as in the octave; but there are notes—although this does not destroy continuity and the "restorials." Continuity and discontinuity. It is impossible to say where one leaves off and the next begins: universal matter, vegetable, invertebrate, vertebrate and man.

Return to daylight. Following these explanations to be neither accepted nor rejected; but first will clearly formulate and understand.

This phenomenon of daylight manifests itself to human beings by the presence in the atmosphere surrounding the planets of a chemical substance—okidanokh, electricity. The three forces of the world are assembled as three in only one element—okidanokh.

Hence, when it enters any planetary body, the three forces are then distributed to their respective centers and proceed to build up. It is often said in modern physics that we are the product of electricity. The three forces are in themselves:

- Affirming—positive—image making.
- Denying—negative—sensation.
- Neutralizing—reconciling—emotion.

We will later discuss the misuse of electricity.

In entering into any being there takes place a process called Aa-ee-o-u-a. Remorse, or wish to evolve. In practical terms the wish of an inferior to be like a superior when in his presence. Any rate of vibration when in the presence of a higher rate, strives to become the higher. Remorse in the elements. One of the means by which evolution is brought about, i.e., not merely by inner impulse.

Mechanical progress is aided by shock, which is merely the presence of a higher rate. Threefold electricity; cf. atom of hydrogen: one electron, one proton; the third force is that which holds these two in relation; cf. man and woman become father and mother only in relation to the child, proton and electron are related so as to produce an atom.

What is the atom in itself? It is invisible. We are third force blind. We cannot see the group; we see only the individuals making it up. Have you ever seen a crowd? Only the individuals.

- Proton positive.
- Electron negative.
- The relation between them is the atom itself.

One atom of electricity consists of three forces, yet is one.

When Aristotle began his section of his book on metaphysics, he meant to discuss space, time, thought, force, in light of the doctrine he had received from Pythagoras; but he never got on with it. Refer back to what happens when in the presence of a higher rate of vibration. Just as a given note will go sharp when a higher note is struck—Aa-ee-o-u-a.

Electricity is the active or growing element in a being. It is this which responds to the higher rate of vibration.

QUESTION: Has the rate of vibration of thought been measured?

ORAGE: Yes, we are constantly making this measurement but roughly. Why do we say, a weighty thought, a light remark?

[*He is interrupted by someone who says: "What about a sweet girl?"*]

When we say this in any particular case, it gives an indication of a certain physical criterion of taste. Electricity is not the only source of vibrations; the whole universe is their source. Our bodies are materialized sets of vibrations. We compare with the outer world as a piano with a series of players who play as passing. We can only respond to the extent of our abilities.

Electricity produces the possibility of being aware. The external world does not consist of objects; nor is our own body an object, merely temporary conglomerations of ability to respond in the presence of vibrations. The process of physical evolution is owed to one growing element of electricity. Both Dewey and Whitehead have this idea that there are no objects; that there is nothing in the universe but forces. But how can we catch a force? Only in a temporary conglomeration.

But every constituent element is always changing. The real thing is what Whitehead and Dewey call process, change. Fixity is only relative and rough. Change of what? We say "matter"; but matter is only a prejudice. The universe is really the actualization of forces.

MARY JOHNSTON: Is this remorse of the elements connected with Anulios?

ORAGE: Yes, a higher rate than the earth.

Anulios, Earth, Moon, three centers. The Earth is between Anulios and the Moon; between higher and lower rates. The tendency of the higher to go toward the lower, the abnormal to the normal.

Our education leaves off where very ancient education began. Between the ages of eighteen and twenty-one, "the idealistic period," when waiting for something to give more meaning to life than they see demonstrated in the lives of those about them. Life is especially full of electricity at this period. There is no institution to give training. Then the most idealistic become the most disappointed and turn cynical, become cranks or commit suicide. It is the aspiring period, aspiring to a realization of potentialities, full of okidanokh. When in a civilization which tends to become more and more instinctive, that is food at one end and sex at the other, disillusionment is most sharp. Then most idealists become mostly instinctive, indulge in sex etc.

Extreme use of electricity for mechanics means less for psychological use. Gurdjieff says two previous civilizations have gone down because of too much such mechanical use. We become very clever in the instinctive center and unable to grow after, say, eighteen, that is to grow psychologically. Electricity broken down, degraded to a lower rate of vibration. Daylight is the first response that okidanokh makes to the higher rate of vibration reaching this planet from the sun and moon.

Emanations from the sun are not in themselves part of the nature of light, when received directly in the atmosphere surrounding this planet; they produce in okidanokh a certain aspiration or remorse which we call light because we then can see objects. The use of ritual, music etc., to produce an emotional state in which certain ideas may be understood or "seen" and not merely translated in street-terms, is an analogy to light. When the elements are in this state we can "see" objects.

Self-observation is a higher rate of vibration. When we observe, the elements of the body will themselves aspire, suffer remorse, i.e. adapt themselves to "I." This must be direct. If one merely thinks about self-observation, it is not direct but is refracted through the mind, hence this excludes a wish to change any phenomenon observed, which would be the process of self-observation refracted through one of the other centers. Direct observation causes sunlight.

Digression:

In any being, the three systems tend to become coated making three centers. From each tends to develop a body:

1. Planetary.
2. Spiritual (kesdjan—astral).
3. Body of mind or objective reason or soul.

Corresponding to each is a form of reason:

1. Planetary—instinctive.
2. Spiritual—being or essential, capable of understanding forms and ideas.
3. Mind—divine, capable of understanding reason or why things are.

1. Things we are accustomed to.
2. The what of the world—perhaps modern physicists at their best.
3. The why. God created an intelligible world and also a corresponding sight.

1. Ordinary sight.
2. Spiritual sight, not psychic but insight.
3. Gives foresight and behind sight, i.e. simultaneity of sight.

Three bodies; three forms of reason; three forms of sight—a complete human being.

But we have at present one body only (within it two other centers without corresponding bodies).

Planetary sight and spiritual and intellectual, dreams and words not facts.

The three brains are developed to the extent the bodies are e.g. a good body-brain, partial spiritual, very slight mental. The cerebral is the least developed, visceral next; the instinctive, the best.

96 percent of our experience is instinctive; 3 percent emotional; 1 percent intellect. 96 percent of our civilization is concerned with the body, 3 percent with art and 1 percent devoted to why.

The quantity of pure research that can be carried on is limited to about 1 percent. Great inertia is not only in individuals but in civilizations. Humanity stands on its head. The instinctive is now the positive, the cerebral the negative.

Emotional is neutralizing but leans toward the instinctive. All this is abnormal. We should change by opposing the instinctive with something in the name of reason.

The characteristic of the instinctive center is *inertia*, which is to continue doing what it has started; habit, in the largest sense. Intelligence is against habit; because no two situations are really the same. Intelligence would make a new activity each time; the instinctive merely offers habit.

Breaking of habits experimentally is for positive intelligence, the beginning of reason. If it is broken for utilitarian reasons, then it is merely the instinctive center, but if experimentally then it is merely subserving reason.

7 MARCH 1927

ORIGINALITY AND INITIATIVE VERSUS REPETITION

Although circumstances and our minds change, this is the instinctive. We can continue to subserve our natural functions and also develop our own consciousness. In any being are brains—the place in the total organism in which the origins and collected results of impulses and reactions are located; the springs and milieu for collection of responses. Simultaneously sources and registers, these three brains are his life and experience; his precious possession, hence the second commandment: "During ordinary existence it is commanded beings should avoid those perceptions that may injure the purity of their brains, i.e. the maintenance of reason; cf. our fear of going mad. Only beings who have lost their reason can ever admit that reason has not the highest value.

Only three-centered beings can be conscious of the possibility of becoming fully developed, i.e. reach divine reason. But in us these three possibilities exist in vain. Beings of the earth, because of their conditions of existence have made this planet a festering wound in the cosmos. We have almost a sane equipment.

- Affirming in the head brain.
- Denying in the spine brain.
- Reconciling we have in us, but it does not act as a mass as in other three-centered beings. Instead of the heart we have the solar plexus, a congeries of nodes, not harmonized into single systems capable of emotions. They are on varying things at the same time and hence are not capable of will.

With the process of self-observation, there begins a consolidation, a gathering of the limbs of Osiris by Isis. This reunion cannot be brought about through the instinctive center, only by the affirming brain with relation to the whole. "I" is these potentialities, as yet unactualized.

7 MARCH 1927

Perhaps you remember the title of the chapter.

Let me say that when we've gone over this chapter we shall have passed over the most difficult part of the book for us to comprehend. Later on, with Hassein also, bits will be remembered and will take their places. It is certainly presumptuous on the part of anyone, including the writer of this book to make comments on the nature of the universe and meaning of life.

Renan said: "It is not disgraceful not to know the nature of man and the meaning of life but it is disgraceful not to be interested in these questions."

And the writer of this book, you will recall, constantly reiterated that it is the duty of a human being to understand himself and the universe. Can you cast your eye over nature and make some real observations on the nature of this biological being called man?

What does it "feel like" to be a human being? One should be a scientific spectator who is also an experimenter. Men have certain characteristics. We are in a position to make some real objective statements about men. Make a critical survey.

Men are degenerate—have become less and less actual and have less and less desire to actualize their potentialities. This is abnormal, but so gradually has it come about, that this abnormal state is regarded as normal.

Men have no proper regard for their children, no proper regard for their intellectual development and so on.

Without an objective standard of what a human being really should be, we can not determine whether we (that is, men) are declining or progressing.

There are some records of ancient times that show men were once very different. It is the birthright of normal beings to understand that the solar system is our natural realm. In early times it was "felt" that planets were neighbors but now we have for that only superstition.

We will proceed to find here further qualities which ought to be the normal qualities of beings on this planet, but for which we have only names now.

Gurdjieff in this chapter passes from the universal to the particular and vice versa.

Three centers in the universe—and three in man.

We are what we have eaten—and so the whole physical universe is just the same, "God was on the Sun Absolute." Can you make the distinction between "I" and "it"? God existed before and apart from the physical world. In the same way "I" must have existed before and apart from "it." If I am by nature a threefold being then what I make will be threefold. So three in one the trinity—three making one—triamazikamno. The word of God.

The nature of man was inherent in things before creation. An original threefold force that inspired creation was bound to manifest itself in three characteristics forms. What the meaning of the universe is we cannot yet know and we must apprehend it as threefold. Animals would apprehend it as twofold.

Time is the potential of all potentials—the source of all actualities. We come here to the question of why three-brained beings produce a particular sort of being. Man has imagining—sensation—emotion. Animals have sensations and emotions, but not third force enabling them to possess images. It can be speculated as to whether animals may sometimes possess reason and vegetables emotions—but this is because threefoldness is inherent in them. So as in the scales, tones flow into each other, yet there are specific restorial notes and it is hardly possible in certain cases to distinguish between metal and mineral or animal and vegetable, etc.

Now I must try to correctly represent to you what the ideas of the school at Fontainebleau are—not what I know or believe—but faithfully transmitting.

Light manifests itself owing to the invariable presence of a certain chemical substance in the atmosphere of all planets. This element is called okidanokh—or electricity. The three forces of the world are assembled in only one element—okidanokh—or electricity. We are mainly products of electricity. These forces in us are called:

1. Positive—image making—affirming.
2. Negative—sensation—denying.
3. Neutralizing—emotion—reconciling.

These three systems in ourselves are the origin, cause and conditions of our being as we are.

There takes place on the entry of these three forces a process called ache for evolvement—envy—remorse (of the elements)—ache for perfection. Any rate of vibration in the presence of a higher rate strains to achieve the higher rate itself. I.e. a shock being present, elements will strive in addition to the mechanical desire to raise their rate of vibration.

Proton and electron are held in relation by a third force. Man, woman, child—but father and mother are not altered by the child. What makes the relation of father—mother—child?

Third force blind. We cannot see a group—we cannot see other than a large number of individual people—never a crowd.

1. Proton.
2. Electron.
3. Relation between them.
4. The atom.

Aristotle commenced a chapter called metaphysics in which he intended to deal with space, time, form and force.

Lower notes aspire to higher notes—what is there in the nature of things to produce such an aspiration?

The one active element in which are contained the three forces.

Take "I" and "it." You owe it to the one fact—that you have a body, "I," that you have any experience whatever. If light affects it, it is thanks to the fact that it is impressionable in that way.

Circumstances pass us and as they pass they play upon us as a series of players may play upon a piano. Of course they are limited to the number of notes. The whole external world consists of no objects—only of a conglomerate of manifested vibrations. The universe is a constant flux of three forces.

Moon is lower vibration—Anulios is higher.

Positive—Anulios—intellectual.

Negative—Moon—instinctive.

Neutralizing—Earth—emotions.

Youth—idealists—will adopt all sorts of forms of sex indulgences, become cynical, become pathological in some way, commit suicide.

It may be that the increasing use of electricity will bring about a very serious, possibly disastrous, situation for human beings. Until it will become impossible to grow even to the age of eighteen as now.

The emanations from the sun when it encounters this substance electricity in our atmosphere, it sets up among other substances "remorse," which exhibits itself to us as light.

So in a certain state of emotion you can understand certain ideas. Under self-observation certain tendencies in the elements of our bodies will become active—"remorse."

In any being the free functions tend to become coated or they tend to have a corresponding system built up around them—but from the continuation of this there are built up three bodies:

- Planetary—instinctive reason.
- Spirit—essential reason.
- Mind or soul—objective reason.

Objective reason is capable of understanding why things are as they are. Being reason can understand the formulations and enunciation of scientists, i.e. the "what" of the world. Objective reason is capable of understanding the "why" of the world.

- Planetary body—see external objects.
- Second body—insight.
- Third body—foresight and "hindsight."

These three forms of bodies will give us, when completely developed, a complete understanding of ourselves and the universe.

According to Gurdjieff, these are represented in us by three brains:

1. Instinctive brain highly developed.
2. Visual or emotional brain only partially developed.
3. Intellectual brain hardly developed at all.

96 percent of our experiences are instinctive. 3 percent of our experiences are emotional and 1 percent are of the intellectual.

As should be:
Intellectual—positive.
Emotional—neutralizing.
Instinctive—negative.

But we are:
Instinctive—positive.
Emotional—neutralizing.
Intellectual—negative.

So we are standing on our heads.

There is nothing evil in the "instinctive" center—except habit in the largest sense of the word. Instinctive offers its only rule—its tendency to repeat "its" experiences. But as soon as habits are commenced to be broken, reason will commence to exercise itself. Put in contrast initiative, originality and repeated habit. This tendency is instinctive.

The brain is in general merely one of the means for the transposition of material, but it is possible for an individual to also at the same time utilize the experiences, i.e. to use the trogoaftoegocrat machine for the development of consciousness. The brain as collection of results of impulses, reactions and responses as the three springs are unwound. We live by their impulses and grow by their records. So brains are sources of experience and at the same time records.

The development of an individual is always possible and depends upon the development of these three brains.

First commandment: Love all that breathes.

Second commandment: During ordinary existence to avoid all those experiences that will tend to impair the maintenance of these three brains.

What do we fear more than death? Insanity—to become insane. Why? Because of his second command which is laid upon us even though we do not know it. Even the cynic prides himself on reason.

It is only possible for three-centered beings to be conscious of the possibility of achieving divine or objective reason.

But on earth owing to the conditions—abnormal, monstrous as they are—that place has become a nasty sore on the cosmos. We have in us a variety of contrary wishes instead of will. "I" is a potential yet unactualized.

14 MARCH 1927

BEELZEBUB'S SECOND DESCENT TO THE PLANET

The Timaeus of Plato contains the cosmogony of Pythagoras.

Before taking up this chapter, let us remind ourselves of the beginning of the book, its place, time and personnel. Beelzebub represents ourselves with our potentialities realized, the normal or ideal man. His function on this planet is finished; and he has all of human experience behind him, including a critique of human nature. He is objective, without prejudice, in fact benevolent. He had been existing on this planet for some fault. This suggests that the "I" is already in exile and that we have made the error of identifying ourselves with a part of our potentialities instead of the whole. He has made use of his exile to lead a conscious life sparing no effort to develop all the technique possible. He begins with accounts of life on other planets. Whether such life exists or not we need not say; but at any rate such life, if there, depends on emanations or radiations from solar sources. Beelzebub and the captain discuss trans-solar ships. Under this parable are discussed various techniques for developing super-consciousness. There are four forms of consciousness: sleeping, waking, self and cosmic.

The peculiarity of beings on this planet is due to special conditions; they are unique, especially in the nature of their reason. Why do I think that the majority of people I meet are fools? Why do the majority of people whom I meet think I am a fool? And why are we both right? Why do we all recognize the essential senselessness of people? This is taken for granted and used in all dealings with crowds. Why do we have such difficulty in behaving reasonably even in a crowd with our own standards?

In discussing ships we encountered the "law of falling," giving a psychological meaning to the law of gravitation. The tendency of a high note of vibration to fall to a lower note. In this sense, space becomes merely a difference between rates of vibration.

What is the distance between two notes? If you're interested in space and time, read S. Alexander, a physicist. You will meet such sentences as "Space is the mother of time."

Then discussion of ships led to perpetual motion; and under this . . .

[*Parable, a discussion of the old question of the immortality of the soul.*]

We, here, to night, are bodies, not souls; and shall probably not survive death.

In certain periods, whole civilizations have made this the touchstone of values. Is it possible to conceive a machine which would last and work in any substance? The answer is yes.

This discussion arouses in Hassein reflections on "becoming conscious of genuine duty." On becoming adult, we enter into certain responsibilities. Hassein thinks: I am here on this planet, among two hundred thousand million others, surrounded by nature who supplies enjoyment etc. How much does it cost to maintain this? What do I owe for all I am getting? Is life of value? Possibility for experience belongs to life. Hassein realizes: nothing just sprang into existence; and everything is maintained and developed by effort. Not only nature but people labor to maintain this civilization. Hassein is overcome by this realization. We come into the world "entitled" to nothing. What entitles us even to mother-love?

Nature prompts it; and ultimately we must repay in conscious effort. But it is now entirely premature says Beelzebub to Hassein, to consider, or even to think of repaying. It cannot be that until you understand how much you owe etc. Any attempt to repay now would be premature and even lead to greater debts. Hassein's only duty now is to an increased understanding. Our morality is that of pupils.

In return for Hassein's display of genuine emotion, Beelzebub will tell him what he wants to know. Hassein asks about slugs. A slug is a one-centered being which has no further potentialities; but we as three-centered beings have the possibility of developing three bodies. As long as we are satisfied with one body, we are slugs in regard to our potentialities.

In order to explain what we are, we must go back. The myth of the genesis of the moon. The earth was going along peacefully, when it collided with a comet and had two pieces struck off. If the planet was a whole it was left deprived. We are organically the product of the planet and may be expected to reproduce the organic deficiencies of the planet.

All that we call nature, including ourselves, is a sort of skin on the planet. This split personality is native to all life on the planet. All of us at any given moment are "I" and "it." Discriminate between what I do and what "it" would do, cf. St. Paul. In the myth a commissioner is sent from the Sun Absolute, to see what must be done to preserve the equilibrium of the system, for altering one planet affects the others, i.e. if earth's weight was reduced by one-half, other planets would find themselves nearer the sun; and their year shortened, with catastrophic events produced. No pebble can be thrown into a stream without affecting the balance of the earth on its axis.

Sakaki comes to investigate and finds the two fragments had not gone beyond the solar system. They had gone part way and then began to fall back; but meantime the earth had gone on in its orbit so that it was always falling and never catching up (i.e., our higher emotional and intellectual centers).

These must be supplied a certain sort of radiation from this planet supplied only by labor and effort. Why this curse of labor, this necessity of effort? Why the apparent malevolence of God. According to the myth, this is not malevolence; but a result of necessity. No one can escape the necessity of effort. Even when idleness seems possible, men engage in various unnecessary enterprises, leaving peaceful circumstances to put themselves into action.

The substance derived from effort is called askokin. What is it? A sort of sweat, physical, emotional and mental. This is perhaps the only service we render at present to the universe. This may be paid, either consciously or unconsciously (as at present). If voluntary or conscious, the same substance is yielded but the individual himself profits from it. In this way, the curse itself becomes a blessing Plato said: "God's curses are opportunities."

Sakaki undertook to farm on this planet, in order to produce this sweat. He arranged that on this planet the law of seven and the law of three should operate not interdependently but independently. Sakaki is responsible for the split personality between "I" and "it." "I" is under the law of three (only three functions of consciousness). "It" is under the law of seven—color, sound, even processes of the body, digestion. Bodies do not help in consciousness. Why is the body not reflective of the mind? Why this unfitness between the body and consciousness? Why are we like strangers in it? Distinguish between the three functions of consciousness within or during any one of the four states of consciousness.

Sakaki made it practically impossible for men to be men. We suffer but we are not to blame; the fact that 99 percent of the time we are without sense, hysterical, vain, egoistic, stupid etc., is the truth. It was arranged to insure effort or suffering. A suspicion that we were used for this purpose might arise (see later) so another device was introduced. Accident merely means, not within our possible calculation; but an accident of collision between the earth and a comet is within some cosmic calculation and for some purpose.

Abnormality includes not only human nature but all fixture, cf. St. Paul in "Romans": The whole of creation groaneth and travaileth, etc.

Earth suffers for something which happened far away. But misfortunes are also opportunities, if met and handled experimentally. If met by complaining and asking why one is picked on, one will suffer just as much, if not more. If met experimentally as an opportunity to solve a problem, there is a muscle developed, of the highest use.

There is a relation between Beelzebub's revolt and this catastrophe. Beelzebub represents mind. The form of intelligence which he represents is only possible through meeting and overcoming certain difficulties. Effort is needed to convert knowledge into understanding. Beelzebub had to sweat to understand what he knew.

The organ producing this split was called kundabuffer; it was the effect of certain conditions in the atmosphere, just as certain conditions produce, say, baldness. Sakaki and Looisos, the arch-chemist (physio) arranged that human beings should develop a certain disease, producing certain psychological manifestations, native to the disease, as intestinal disorders produce irritability. This spinal disease produces the same effect as if one had taken opium. We walk down the avenue in a state of somnambulism or we undertake some job which we do not know how to undertake or carry it through with an extravagant expenditure of energy. We have the facts but we are unable to assemble them.

Kundabuffer has been removed. Its function is no longer necessary; the organ is vestigial. It once had the function of keeping us crazy. Now, we are born sane but become insane through the influence of our elders, education, convention, desire to be like our neighbor. Education is the enemy of the human race.

Sakaki returned and Beelzebub set up an observatory. Self-observation thus gave him additional lenses, so that he was able to observe distant planets etc. It is impossible to make an objective survey of the human race as a whole which is what is required to understand the book, without adding the lens of self-observation. We may not be able at present to see the relation between listening to the tones of one's own voice and carrying on certain imaginative acts.

War is one of the peculiarities of the beings on this planet. It is due to our conventional education. We discuss it and carry it on without realization of its horror. An inhabitant of another planet where the idea of carrying it on and killing was repugnant as some loathsome crime among us would shrink from coming here. Then why did Sakaki and Looisos arrange this lunacy? Perhaps there had to be more blood. Cf. Séances of early religions; evocations in fumes of blood, a crude and obvious means to strike the limited imaginations of primitive peoples. It gave them real horrors to convince them of the supernatural and create respect for the priests.

Perhaps the normal death rate was not enough; the moon cried for more. So it was given wars. (See later chapter on war.)

This peculiarity was not unique to certain moments of madness; but was prepared for from birth by certain trance conditions. Call a man a "hero" who is prepared to throw away his own life, i.e. to commit suicide in order to murder. We have only to consider what would be a reasonable line of conduct to realize that this is the acme of unreasonableness. The "hero" has been specially conditioned.

Then came the first descent to Atlantis, whether geographically correct or not is not our concern. Beelzebub was on a mission: a Caritasian reformer had come to a hasty conclusion that the way to reform was to let people do as they wished, believing they would do the "right thing." They had not first taken the trouble, which Beelzebub had taken, to understand human nature. How much will we do merely through love of the good the true, the beautiful? There is disillusionment of the premature reformer who does not realize that he is attacking not local, but universal problems, and must have a universal understanding. So with us, attempts to make reform without first preparing ourselves.

Time is the unique subjective, the essence of what we call "I."

Experience is due to three factors: external stimulus; organ receivings; medium of communication. What is it that experiences? "I."

Alexander says that time is subjectivity and space is the field in which time actualizes itself. The subjectivity of time. Our time limit, the degree of our possible experience, in the three centers. Time passes fastest for those whose centers are run out without our being aware of it and them. Noting our experiences as they pass is called "making use of time."

14 MARCH 1927

NEXT CHAPTER — "THE ARCH-ABSURD"

Light and heat are local on this planet. Cf. self-observation produces no direct effect only consequential effect. The sun does not light nor heat. Emanation is the influence exerted by any object or person, which does not involve any passage of matter. It is comparable to a magnetic field surrounding a magnet. Every being exerts an emanation by its presence; even a table does this and its being is not negligible and its presence has an influence, the planets and sun of our system exert two influences on us: radiation, emanation. Has this some bearing on the modern doctrine of catalysis?

The sun though cold and dark by its presence within our system produces by its presence an effect, a sort of shiver. As for example one goes into a room and says: "I don't like the feel of it." It is the effect of its emanations and radiations. Electricity shivers. Remorse wishing to be more than it is. Perhaps this is the origin of the growth of plants—stimulation of awareness, in the presence of a higher rate of vibration. The mystery of growth is perhaps dual: within and external stimulus.

If we fail to attain light, we only attain heat. (Heat is "the light that failed.") If we make an effort to understand certain ideas and succeed, we have a sense of light; if we fail, the sense of the impossibility produces an emotion, which is heat. Then we can understand why the image of remorse is used; this image is a snake trying to bite off its own tail, in anger and disgust with itself. One fumes "Why can't I?"

A human being is the product of his own digestion. "I" watches this cannibalistic process under the law of seven. Psychology functions under the law of three. God is the same. We are the seeds of the tree Yggdrasil; acorns around an oak. What is the resemblance between an acorn and the oak? What is the resemblance between us and the cosmos? We can only understand the world as we can come in contact with it. We are acorns and we can see the law in us. Can we see the laws in the universe? Gurdjieff says "Yes."

The primordial substance is of three types or kinds. Electricity has positive, negative and neutralizing. Matter, energy, electricity, is there any difference in these terms? Modern physicists speak of these three. Can you differentiate, e.g. in a hydrogen atom the proton is the nucleus and the electron the orbiter and the movement of the electron around the proton gives the exhibition of energy. This is a highly metaphysical concept. Close the book.

Of these three it is electricity which contains all three. Substance here is named ethernokrilno. Cf. doctrine of Maya in Hindu philosophy. Maya is the potentiality of matter. This ethernokrilno becomes differentiated into matter, energy and electricity being the first emanation from the Sun Absolute. The Sun Absolute is "I" who dreams. Of what substance are dreams made? Of this primordial substance. These form in our sleeping state and take shape according to our thoughts. In our waking state they move slowly but still are the results of consciousness.

Our waking state is an objective dream. Thought alone will not shape them. We must use hands, tools, etc. Even in dreams the three elements are present. In consequence of this primordial threefoldness, the most developed show a threefoldness most clearly. Hence we have three brains, each manifesting one of the three forms of electricity: positive, negative, neutralizing. A normal being is one in which these correspond. Cerebral is positive, instinctive negative and emotional is neutralizing. "Yes" is of the reason, "no" of habit and the body, while the emotions reconcile these. In this sense the emotions are spoken of as "The Holy Ghost."

Negative emotions are the result of the failure of reason to overcome the inertia of habit. When this is inverted, like Peter who was thus crucified, the inertia is greater than reason, there is the negative. The only evil is the substitution of negative for positive. Beelzebub's attempt was to invert; to restore the positive to the part positive by electrification.

Corresponding to the three bodies are the three forms of sight:

1. Sight.
2. Insight.
3. Through sight, or seeing the reason of things.

One understands the how of things.
Two, the what of things.
Three, the why of things.

This presupposes three bodies. We have a good understanding of how, a slight understanding of what; and no understanding of why. Nature will not help us to develop the second or third. We are unconsciously supplying the emanations and radiations needed. We can develop the others; for while nature has supplied the substances we squander these substances in aimless pleasures. We should use them for conscious labor and voluntary suffering.

Original meaning of the word ecstasy—standing outside of, a non-identification. Today it has an opposite meaning. We must continue building the second body. We cannot have objective reason without the third body. Is the book an objective survey of humanity? If so, Gurdjieff must have the third body. Did Pythagoras practice the method? Plato?

How does money give roots? The objective attitude; the positive attitude; is it possible to take a positive attitude mechanically? Gurdjieff when he went to the East. Whenever you have a purpose, is not that purpose itself of the first body? My case, Napoleon's?

Attempt to imagine a normal being.

Electricity and element?

Bertrand Russell says: "The way in which things behave."

Matter, energy, electricity, but if all—matter is an actualization of force.

THE SECOND DESCENT

This is the second descent from Mars. Atlantis had been engulfed in the earth, not drowned. After the genesis of the moon, the earth was revolving a little unsteadily; but soon settled into permanent equilibrium which it has since maintained. It was in this settling that Atlantis was engulfed. Consider the psychological parable. However, spreading of the human race took place. There were three main centers of civilization on the continent of Asia. The aboriginal continent was replaced by three centers. We are born with essence, which begins at once to be engulfed by personality, by society, by suggestion. Essence—our biological potentialities, what is biologically native to us. Personality is what we have become. Personality may or may not be harmonious with what we are biologically.

By the time of Beelzebub's second descent, the race had begun to grow up, to develop personality.

The three centers located geographically were:

1. Tiklandia (Karakum) desert in Eastern Turkestan. The sand with which it now is covered was due to a planetary catastrophe.

2. Goblandia or Maralpleicie, where is now the Gobi Desert was once a highly developed civilization. (See Churchward, one city below another.)

3. Gemchania India.

THE REASON FOR THE DESCENTS

One day on Mars an etherogram was received, by hearing. The commission was sent from the Sun Absolute to the earth to investigate the effects of the engulfing of Atlantis and to see if any adjustments were needed in organic life. The commission arrived. Looisos was accompanied by his retinue of angels and seraphim (incarnate powers of reason and emotion). He concluded from Mars that the catastrophe was not so terrible and an immediate visit not necessary. Looisos invited Beelzebub to undertake a commission to visit the earth and attempt to limit the custom of blood sacrifice, which was then a prominent feature of all religions. In each of these three centers blood sacrifice was on such a huge scale that the atmosphere was charged with the fumes and organic life on the moon began to take on monstrous shapes.

[*Orage speculates that perhaps the monsters of old tales were a sort of spiritualistic materialization caused by emanations of blood fumes on other planets causing abnormal experiences here.*]

Looisos asked Beelzebub to limit or end this custom on the earth, not only because of its effects on the earth but also on the moon. Like a good political agent, Beelzebub descends; takes the ship Occasion and reaches the Caspian Sea. He travels by river (Amu Darya, near the Aral Sea now dried up) and arrives at the city of Kunkali, the center of Tiklandia.

He visited local cafés. He attaches importance to a strategic point of observation from which civilization is to be viewed. He talked with the natives. After a month or so he decided to employ a local and prevalent superstition and build on it a doctrine.

We must be on guard even against divine messengers, who may use prevalent superstitions for their own purposes, as Beelzebub did for benefit of the moon. We assume that the doctrine is for the avowed purpose e.g., we assume that if Jesus taught love it was for our good; but he might have foreseen deleterious effects on us which were good for the cosmos.

Beelzebub found that the natives thought that the sacrifice of something dear to them was pleasing to God, and since their flocks were dear these were sacrificed. Beelzebub had merely to suggest that they sacrifice themselves instead of animals (might not be so good for human beings but if animal sacrifices diminished, Beelzebub had accomplished his mission). This idea spread rapidly and soon animals became almost sacrosanct. How do we explain the attitude in India toward animals? They are regarded as holy; Beelzebub's propaganda. The same people, who once had sacrificed, now revered them.

Beelzebub's method: Beelzebub talked at great length to a prominent pulpiteer, and did not divulge the real purpose of his arguments; but they sounded plausible. He suggested that God wanted the development of reasoning and that all creation up to man presupposes man and a fulfillment by man of his organic functions. He exists to produce individuals capable of objective reason. Supply of objective by reasonable beings expected from this; planet and all nature is for this use. He continued: "If you use nature for this purpose, you are using it ethically i.e. objectively, because for a purpose designed."

Another argument he used—there exists a certain force called (in India) "prana"—life-force. Beelzebub said this was a substance (will scientists be able to take it and animate a table?) or essence. It exhibits itself in a series of biological evolution and as it develops, it reveals more of its potentialities, capable of will, consciousness and individuality. Life-force in us does not differ in any respect except maturity (quantity of experience) from the animal and vegetable kingdom. There is only one life and we are the highest biological development. Man is more actualized, and more conscious but in essence the same.

The purpose of man is to develop from this essence a certain type of reason, which will constitute him one of the permanent brain cells of all life.

God is both the creator and an evolving being. He aims at developing by developing his brain cells. As we develop will, consciousness and individuality we become more ready to take our place as one of the brain cells of the universe. It is a necessity for the universe taken as a whole to develop individuals having these three functions. At about the age of twenty-five George Bernard Shaw had a realization that nature aims at brains. All his paradoxes and plays flow from this mechanically. But let us define "brains" more clearly. Ponder for a moment the thought that nature aims at individuals having will, consciousness and individuality. A realization of this will draw together all other knowledge and ideas, as opposed to modern attempts to find a unity of thought. It is like lifting a tent-pole with the canvas which had before lain shapeless on the ground.

The third argument Beelzebub used was:

We have senses, so that we can attain the objective which God wants us to attain. They are prepared to make possible the development of that reason which God wants. What do I hear? What do I see? What use should I get from my tactile sense? These are tools for the production of consciousness. If so used then they are ethically used; if not so used then either childishly or monstrously. This hits art. If sensations are used for aesthetic purposes there is degeneration; they are enjoyed for themselves instead of being used to attain an objective. Self-indulgence masquerades under the name of art. This priest took Beelzebub seriously and spread the doctrine that animals should be used instead of being sacrificed. Since Beelzebub had not given him his objective aim, they went to ridiculous lengths; sentimentalized animals, which is another self-indulgence masquerading as humanitarianism. But other priests attacked him as a heretic and put him to death. Beelzebub buried his body and arranged for the education of his soul. "He who loseth his life etc."

Beelzebub was recalled to Mars by another etherogram, more exiles were coming from Caritas including the woman intended by the local astrologer to be his wife. He had two sons; Tooloof (father of Hassein) and Tulan.

THIRD DESCENT

Soon after the honeymoon, which lasted perhaps a Caritasian fortnight but an earthly half-century, Beelzebub goes back to earth to Goblandia. He landed on a sea now covered by sand, the sea of Gobi; in the midst of the Gobi desert. He proceeded upstream, that is he did not follow his inclination. Our psychological experiences follow an inclined plane and run downwards. Gurdjieff has excavated and investigated in the Gobi desert, he used a special raft—that is an artificial device for opposing our inclinations. (Self-observation.) This with participation and experimentation are going upstream on a raft.

He reaches the capital; the citizens there took opium, chewed poppy seeds. The custom had spread widely and the population had degenerated. The king was a great-great-grandson of a being who had been conscious and he had inherited certain traditions, like the modern intelligentsia. He tried to stop them by legislation; forbade it and issued fines. This aroused curiosity and increased the habit. Cf. prohibition. What is the poppy seed? What are its effects?

- It made it impossible to see reality.
- It made people invert values.

It made it impossible for people to take their own experience as a guide, e.g. tried one way of life which had not aimed at wealth or happiness and yet would despise it and seek other things because recommended by others. Compare in our day the role of advertising and the number of things we do and obtain which yield us no satisfaction. Publicity. We are dupable, open to that kind of suggestion. We chew a poppy seed.

This begins in our infancy when we take our parents and nurses seriously. The obedient child is the foreordained victim of the big salesman. Effects, continued: people mistook insults for words of love and words of love for insults. If a person tells me a useful tonic truth, which helps my growth and I resent it; but if he tells me something flattering though perhaps deleterious to me, I am his friend for life.

[*Orage's story: "You are a weak minded liar; you are planning a public career. Look out for yourself."*]

This made people mistake a crow for a peacock. How many people who pass as celebrities, as peacocks, great names; and in private we find them to be crows. H. G. Wells when rather young fell in with Hinton's books. These were filled with extraordinary ideas. He was a good mathematician. He put these ideas in story form but was a very bad storyteller and remained obscure. But Wells developed Hinton's ideas in his "time-machine." Hinton died obscure. The value was in Hinton, the salesmanship in Wells. We require good advertising such as Wells' wrapping of Hinton's ideas. We want what others are using.

Swift answered a question as to what natural intelligence was as "Seeing things in the bud."

The original phrase which Gurdjieff used was "Time is the unique subjective." That is the bud. Now, think about it. From this a whole chapter unfolds.

Ouspensky asked why different beings had different time-perceptions and Gurdjieff said: "Think about it; time is breath." This is developed in Ouspensky's forthcoming book. How many of us could take Gurdjieff's doctrine neat?

In Goblandia, Beelzebub preached the same mission as to sacrifices. He went to India. The party set off from Goblandia to India by caravan. Comparable to forming a group for the study of Hindu philosophy. (An essay by Bertrand Russell on the Freudian method of dream interpretation could be applied to waking dreams.) Hypnopompic, the only distinction between waking and sleeping dreams. Sometimes dream figures are visible for a moment after waking, In relation to self-consciousness, our present waking state would appear to be what our sleeping state now appears to us to be. With this in view we could interpret the day at its end like a dream; but must take all motives into account, not merely sexual. It would reveal the physical nature of the being. Russell's essay: accidents which occur—accidents in dream. Also true to what we encounter in "real life," equally subjective. We are deceived into thinking them objective but are the product of hypnopompic imagination. During a dream we think it real for we have no other criterion.

Beelzebub passes with a motivated caravan from Goblandia, which was doped to India in search of pearls. Suppose this was a dream, how would we interpret it? Gurdjieff is describing an objective dream. Beelzebub joined a party which was going to study Indian philosophy. They made a conscious effort to reach a state where they could find reality.

They passed over places of enormous elevation, Himalayas, and places devoid of even the possibility of vegetation; suffered cold and hunger. Mountains are an attempt to pass from one form of idealism to reality. Can only describe great altitudes with great aridity of expression. (Orage's attempt to get content into two Eastern terms used by Max Mueller. Died en route, i.e. gave up). Hard to make the passage but this party made it. Arrived at Indian philosophy and Gurdjieff now gives his critique of it, a critique by a man who actually arrived and understood. We have had no one to give a Western report on Indian philosophy. Gurdjieff in his youth read Mme. Blavatsky's "From the Caves," "Jungles of Hindustan" and "Secret Doctrine." Gurdjieff went and reported that nine out of ten of her references are not based on firsthand knowledge. This cost him nine years.

This party got to India and dissolved the myth that this was the land of wisdom. Gurdjieff was the Dalai Lama's collector of dues for the monastery and was entitled to enter every monastery in Tibet. He discovered extraordinary elevations, abnormal developments, so called magical powers; but did not find one universal intelligence. Occult powers were developed but they differed only from Western geniuses in type (scientific, literary etc.) They were diversions from normal type.

He arrived in India, the third center (like the three centers of civilization in us).

- Tiklandia, blood sacrifice, instinctive.
- Goblandia, poppy seed, publicity, emotional.

- India, Buddhism, intellectual.

Cf. Put Buddhism back earlier. Sinking of Atlantis 8,000 to 4,000 BC. Local tradition in India says that Gautama was the seventh of a series. Perhaps Gurdjieff means the first Buddhism had already degenerated. Buddha had realized that all humanity suffers from a planetary disease and called it kundabuffer. (Buffer means "reflection," see life as it is in water, upside down.)

Buddha told certain truths, planetary disturbance, genesis of the moon etc. and our planet being left lopsided. But with the sinking of Atlantis the need for kundabuffer was gone. Beings were now born naturally but education is based on kundabuffer and keeps repeating an education based on a state of things which no longer exists.

The Buddha said: "I will show you a personal method by which you can return to a natural state and begin your own education," on self-observation, participation and experience in two forms.

1. Conscious effort.
2. Voluntary suffering.

He divided these:

1. Conscious effort.
    a. Self-observation, the "only way."
    b. Participation.
    c. Voluntary suffering. (This is not pain.)

This mistake bred the dervishes etc. It is suffering in resisting a mechanical response caused by another person who is distasteful. It is self-restraint in resisting inclination and forcing a contrary action. This is summed up in Jesus's remark "Love your enemies." Not actual pain; but psychological. If for instance you do not return a blow, be on guard that you have not merely suppressed resentment, humiliation, etc, which would take hypocritical forms. One must take an action to express this love, thus converting a negative emotion into an active one.

If you overcome these consequences by these two means, your own growth will take place, inevitably, like taking a couple of bricks off a plot where a seed is trying to sprout. If you try directly to develop understanding and consciousness, you will fail.

Within one generation of Buddha's death his disciples had decided it would be easier to be either alone, or with those who were also trying. They would found a monastery or institute. After the group instructed by Buddha himself had passed away, the successor groups picked out very inaccessible places, great heights and they attempted to develop abnormally, yogi powers. This was based on a misunderstanding. Those who go to yoga are on the way to Tibet.

Beelzebub finds that all that Buddha had taught has been so corrupted that his most sincere followers were most sincerely mistaken. This doctrine, originally concrete, objective, normal, had become monstrous.

When you do something wholly intellectual, wholly emotional, wholly instinctive, you are sacrificing the two-centered being (the other two centers). Every great intellectual genius had become so by a blood sacrifice of two centers. Blood sacrifice is the abnormal development of one center, at the expense of the other two, since animals are two-centered beings. The doctrines of Buddha are still extant in a form intelligible to those who knew the norm.

- Prana. (Beelzebub seized on this.)
- Kundabuffer.

Beelzebub tried to recall to some of these degraded Buddhists, the doctrine of prana. This is the life-force and in human beings is objective reason; in animals instinctive reason. Beelzebub tricked them into thinking that every time they killed an animal they killed a cell which might be necessary to their own development and understanding. This is true in terms of centers but is silly as they took it.

The idea took root. Beelzebub returned by way of Tibet, passed some monasteries, the self-tamers. They had realized that our mechanical reactions were like beasts and undertook to tame themselves, thinking they were following Buddha's teaching.

But Beelzebub says they had to keep nightly watch in front of a ring of fire to keep off wild beasts (only at night). When we are conscious, these wild beasts of negative emotions do not appear; but when we are off guard, they can destroy. On the way to Tibet he met voluntary self-immurers in sentry boxes. Beelzebub felt pity. No one who has not been human can feel pity at the sight of something so admirable and so imbecilic; tried to make up for lack of neighbors by ferocious treatment of self. On the heights of this effort no life is possible. A distortion of Buddha's doctrine of enduring manifestations of others; for he had required them to stay where they were.

Another etherogram—Looisos was on Mars and getting ready to

come to earth, making a survey of earth. If he were spending a year, 389 of ours, Looisos is not yet come but may be expected any time. The earth has been giving trouble. The Himalayas have been rising (making a corresponding depression elsewhere) and the rotundity of the planet was getting uneven; this affects other planets. The height must be reduced. Maybe use the magnetic currents of the sun with possible quakes. Beelzebub went back to Mars to tell Looisos about the earth. He got interested in the canals on Mars, one-half arid, the other water. Our brain, front-half in bloom; back-half empty. To get the back into communication with the front, maybe has something to do with Looisos plans.

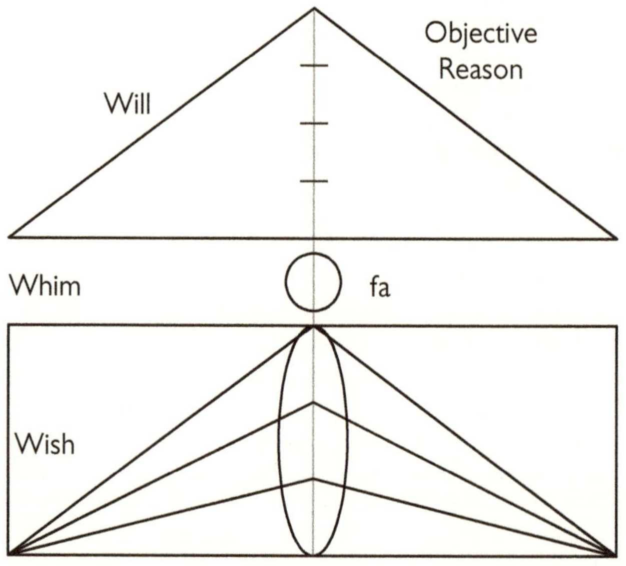

In the lower triangle objects presented, in the upper triangle objects chosen. Three successive magnets; the three wishes of fairy tales, toward which one becomes positive. They must be sequential, i.e. if the first is money, the second must involve the use of money made, and the third involve both the preceding. The development of a positive attitude toward the first, not as an end but as a means for carrying out the second. Perhaps it will be necessary to go around this series several times. E.g. Gurdjieff wanted to find out certain knowledge in possession of someone 4,000 miles away. He took up a trade and earned money in order to make the journey, in order to get the knowledge.

This perhaps repeated, do, re, mi. When a positive attitude is established on this section of the scale it is impossible for anyone else to present a magnet which will attract. Pass through the emptiness of fa, then choose objectives, exercising will, to attain objective reason.

In do, re, mi, the aim should be to develop the professional attitude of attaining each objective with a minimum of time, effort, waste of strength etc., eliminating non-essentials and keeping the body in proper health. The lower triangle then becomes a training to undertake the much more difficult, strenuous and prolonged pull in the upper triangle. Work in the upper triangle will thus be based on work in the lower triangle.

Distinction between a practical mystic and a theoretical mystic.

[*The above was the result of asking Orage:*]

"You have put the suggestion in my head that I should make money. In adopting this suggestion, am I not just succumbing to one more magnet, or mechanicality as if I had fallen under the influence of a banker who had stimulated me to go into banking to make money?"

ORAGE: It is a magnet; but the difference between making money for a purpose and making it for a career lies in the attitude; and is revealed in the use made of the money, after it is obtained. For the young banking apprentice, the career is an end in itself and the attitude is negative. If your ultimate aim lies far beyond that however, the money making becomes merely a tool and the attitude is positive.

We have always diagrammed as follows; but strictly speaking is:

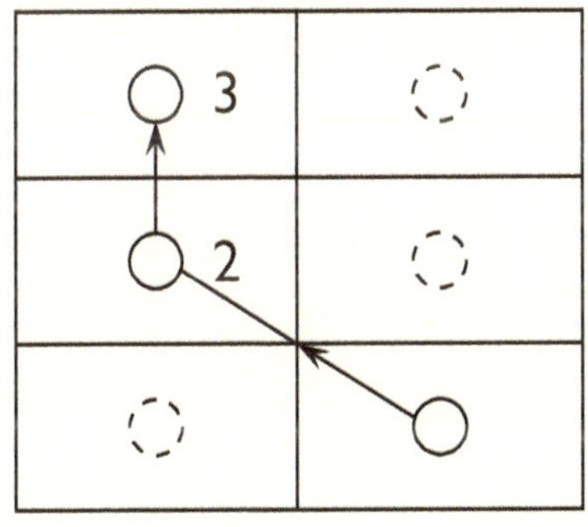

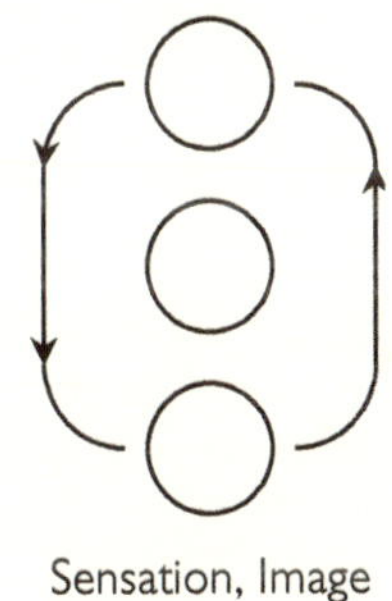

Sensation, Image
Emotion, Action

At present drop back from intellect and emotion into sex (emotional center re-stimulates sex; intellectual re-stimulates emotional, and thus emotional, sex.)

Artists and philosophers are either suspended on top of the third center without roots, yearning for the bridge, without being able to find it; consequently they become pathological, sentimental, idealists of one form or another, anemic, cynical; or drop into emotional and become altruistic; or into sex.

Food. Normal return to sex is indicated by the dotted line. The general current of society today makes the circle up and back to sex and food. Line will be drawn A–B and all activity in this civilization goes on in sex and food and unless artists and philosophers have sent down roots they will be cut off.

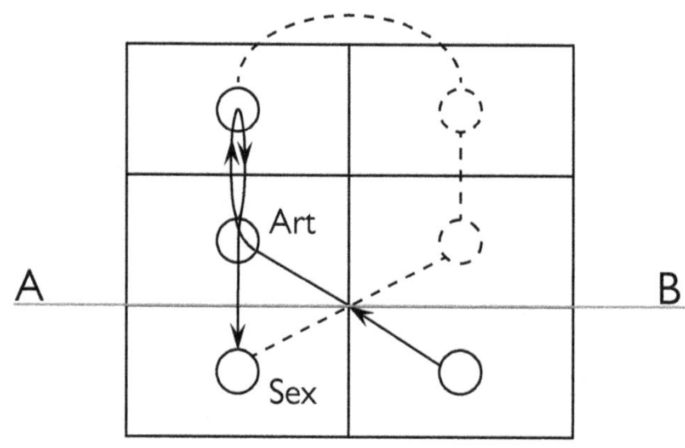

Beelzebub's second descent to the planet—but before embarking I remind you of a number of the stages through which he has passed.

Place, time and personnel—the protagonist is Beelzebub—to be conceived as a being like ourselves but with all our potentiality actualized.

His function on this planet has ceased—he having had all possible human experiences. And his critique of man is one that any impartial being might, or rather surely, would arrive at. This is to help Hassein so that he will not have to go through all the difficult phases of experiences Beelzebub has been forced to undergo.

Exiled for some defect in reason—but he uses his exile.

Life on the planet is conditioned on their access to certain radiations from the Sun Absolute.

The captain enters to discuss certain difficulties of navigation. Talk of ships—i.e. techniques of religion for developing self- or superconsciousness.

The peculiarities of the earth are of a special kind due to the peculiar conditions encountered here.

Especially in reason—why do I think that the majority of people I meet are fools—and why do the majority of people I meet think I am a fool? And why are all of us correct in this? Senseless or mechanical we are.

In the light of plain logic I should act in a certain way—but do I? Never. Why not?

We encounter the "law of falling," i.e. psychological gravity—the tendency of a vibration to fall to the next lower one. The space between two notes in music is not measurable but is nevertheless space.

Certain recent works by Alexander are worth reading. "Space is the mother of time," he says.

Then perpetual motion was discussed, i.e. immorality of the soul. Then the possibility of developing such a body as will live forever.

The discussion of ships, etc., awakes in Hassein "the becoming aware of genuine being duty." Suppose we were to be born in a labor colony—upon coming of age or before, we might become aware of a certain duty laid upon the community as a whole.

I am here on this planet amongst two billion other people with many pleasures, etc.—what does it cost to keep it going? Are you glad that you are alive? Do you appreciate that nature, etc., has provided for your circumstances of existence and being? Hassein becomes aware that nothing springs into existence or being without effort. And that he reasonably may expect to find it is his duty to repay for his life. Who inspires a mother for that love that protects her children? Nature. And sooner or later we must repay nature.

Beelzebub says to Hassein, for the time being it is impossible to begin. You must understand first how much you owe and how to repay. Only one obligation—that of a pupil, i.e. to understand.

Now in return for this real feeling of Hassein—Beelzebub offers to explain anything. Hassein asks Beelzebub about those "slugs." But slugs have only one center and in that way are innocent. We are obligated to develop three bodies from three centers, Beelzebub goes on to explain, but must go back some time in order to explain why we are what we are. History—at least in the form of myth. But the myth herein described is of a much more modern character.

The planet while peacefully developing, encounters a comet and two pieces were struck off, and a similar catastrophe would then occur to every biological being on this planet. For we are just the outcome of the influence of the sun on this planet. We and all of nature are about the same as the skin on our bodies. Nature is like a sensitive skin on this planet and we the microbes on that skin.

A commission was sent to inquire into the procedure to be set up to restore equilibrium in this solar system and other solar systems as well.

The Archangel Psycharchy was dispatched with a commission to see what should be done. They discovered that these two fragments have not gone entirely out of the influence of the earth—but, though always falling and caching up can never fall upon the earth. But these fragments must be supplied with a certain radiation from the earth due to effort and labor on the part of beings on this planet. So even when leisure is possible, men promptly engage in wars.

So, a substance is derived, askokin—or sweat (so "slimy"). Can be done either mechanically or consciously—but if done consciously and voluntarily the same substance is yielded but the individual himself benefits tremendously. So Plato said: God's curses are opportunities. Psycharchy undertook to "farm" beings that would provide this substance.

And so he arranged that the laws of three and seven operate independently and not interdependently or reciprocally. So the body is under the law of seven as also is food, color, sound. But my consciousness is under the law of three with the result that our bodies do not help us. Why is not our body immediately responsive and reflective of our thoughts? Thanks to this arrangement of Psycharchy.

In the various states of consciousness, sleep, waking, self-consciousness and cosmic-consciousness, there are three phases of consciousness.

Why men are not men. So many difficulties are put into our way that we are not to blame for our state. All these were the result of an arrangement that would guarantee this necessary suffering and the resultant substance.

When we refer to an accident we refer to an event not within our possible calculation. But it is not outside the possible calculation of all beings. Since this accident occurred to the earth before the evolution of man, it was an accident from our point of view. But a curse or mischance is also an advantage. If you encounter misfortune in life personally, you can either say I will accept this experimentally, or you can say: "I'm the Jonah man—I am picked on, etc." But if accepted in the first way you will eventually thank your fate for having met such circumstances.

Beelzebub represents mind, and perhaps a certain form of understanding is only possible to beings that have had certain experiences.

A certain state of being implies certain effort to understand what one knows. Then kundabuffer was attached. So if one has intestinal disorder, one will be irascible, moody and irresponsible. We are afflicted according to this book, with a spinal disorder—and—are as we are.

99 percent of our mistakes are made with all the necessary knowledge to have acted correctly. At the base of the spine there is an inactive organ that used to keep us insane. And now we could be sane except for the contact with our elders through education.

[*Education is the enemy. (Sherm's interpretation.)*]

Beelzebub, by inventing an observatory and telescope—i.e. self-observation, was able to see beings straight. Through this he observed beings on this planet and they behaved as other beings except for certain peculiarities.

So if one saw someone disemboweling himself, he would be horrified. But in war we cannot feel this because we are doped. No being of any other planet would consent to come to this planet of lunatic shambles.

And it is not to be wondered at that we have not yet had on this planet the pick of divine messengers.

[*Orage suggested, "If you are interested, as I am emphatically not, in séances in the presence of fresh human blood to be obtained from a hospital . . ."—and the room became suddenly intensely quiet.*]

These phenomena do not occur occasionally but men are especially trained from childhood—and put into a trance state—for war. Fakirs who hang by the sinews of their calves all their lives are so crazy because they are conditioned to it.

Beelzebub made his first descent to the planet Atlantis on a certain mission. Once there he felt that people would, if permitted to, act as they would, act righteously. That they would follow the good, the true and the beautiful. But we know from self-observation how true or false this is. So came the disillusionment of the premature reformer. Unrestrained benevolence.

We are up against a universal problem and only a universal understanding will permit us to do anything about it.

Time is the essence of all that we call "I." The potentiality of all experience—the unique subjective.

Experience—transmitting medium of the mechanism which receives it. This is all we have.

Alexander says time is the subjective which actualizes itself in space.

Write an article on space in dreams.

Our time limit is contained in the experiences which we are capable of in our three centers. So those who live longest who note, register their experiences. Hence it is desirable to note every possible experience possible.

THE ARCH-ABSURD

Self-observation produces no direct effect but only a consequential effect. The sun is cold, yet it produces our heat, light and life . . . by emanations. An emanation is the effect produced (not by radiation or any substance) by any object, form or being upon another object, form or being. The mere presence of a table will exert an influence upon us. So the planets exert an influence, in two ways—by radiation and by emanation. The sun though cold and dark induces in certain elements in our atmosphere a certain shiver. So in our atmosphere a substance called archidonis (electricity in three forms) is effected by the emanations of the sun producing "remorse," or an ache to grow, or an aspiration toward a higher rate of vibration.

So if you succeed in thinking a thing out you "see the light"—but if you fail you are in an emotional state—i.e. heat. Heat is the "the light that failed."

(The image of the word remorse is derived from the image of a serpent so enraged that it is biting its own tale.)

Then we were introduced into . . .

Every hair on my head was once food on my plate. But who am I that does it? "I" stand apart from this spectacle of trogoautoegocratic process—i.e. I eat myself—watching. Acorn—oak tree. I—the universe—microcosm—macrocosm.

We can only understand the world in proportion to the amount we have contact with it. The laws in us we can see—three and seven. Can we see these in the universe? Everything that breathes tends to become three-centered, but exists under the law of seven.

What is the difference between matter, electricity and energy? Say in an atom—proton (matter), electron (electricity) and movement (energy) of the electron around the proton. These are the three aspects of the original emanation—positive, negative and neutralizing. Substance is named here "ethernocronone"—primordial prime source substance.

Self-observation—is what you call "I." Who dreams? Who makes the form in dreams? Of what substance?

We are such stuff as dreams are made of—i.e. "ethernocronone." In dreams, substances take shape directly from thought. The substances of this life are of a lower vibration than those used by us in dreams. Nevertheless, in dreams there are these three forms of electricity—the same primordial threefoldness thus we develop three brains, positive, negative and neutralizing.

1. Cerebral—positive—yes.
2. Spinal—negative—no.
3. Visceral (emotional)—neutralizing—reconciliation.

1. Reason—plan	}	*Failure* of reason
2. Habit—cannot	}	to exert sufficient
3. Emotion—despair	}	positive energy

So man inverted—King Solomon's seal represents both man upright and inverted. Substitution of one for the other is only sin.

14 MARCH 1927

Corresponding to the three brains are possibilities of development of three bodies—we have one and the beginning of the other two.

The how—sight—practical understanding.

The what—insight—scientist, understanding of principles.

The why—through sight—seeing the reason of things.

These three forms of reason imply the development of these three bodies.

1. We (and even animals) understand "the how."
2. We understand a little of the what.
3. We don't understand at all the why.

Nature does not help human development and the reason is that we are quite unconsciously performing the functions of nature. But from this we do not benefit. Aimless pleasures squander forces that could be used in conscious suffering and voluntary labor.

21 MARCH 1927

Last week we spent the whole of the time on a review leaving this week for the reading of the book.

Herein he describes the first group that used this method.

SECOND DESCENT

First descent—Atlantis. Five centuries have passed. Not sure whether Karatas or Ors. 389 times longer is one year on Karatas than here. The narrative continues in the form of stories to Hassein.

"We return from Dimickfargo"—a special form of food taken on the ship with them—a special form of impressions.

In the interval, Atlantis has disappeared. Not submerged, but engulfed in the earth. Due to special causes—after the collision which left the earth busy—i.e. until a new center of gravity was firmly established.

Thanks to the fact that the circumstances on earth resulting were particularly favorable, three new centers of culture were by that time established. We were born with a potentiality for a certain amount of experiences in the three centers, but we have become, thanks to the circumstances of our environment, either what we might have been, or, conditioned by these circumstances, not what our essence biologically would have indicated.

These three centers of culture were:

1. Tiklandia—Sahara.
2. Goblandia and Karakum—Gobi desert (Maralpleicie). Not only one city below a city in Goblandia but a city below cities.
3. Gemchania (India).

The reason for my going to the planet earth was a commission given me through an etherogram received on the planet Mars. (So the message was received not by reading but by hearing.) That a certain commission was being sent from the Sun Absolute to earth to investigate the consequences of the sinking of Atlantis. It consisted of that sinister Archangel Psycharchy (Looisos) and other angels (or incarnate powers) and the commission decided that the consequences were not so catastrophic. At the same time, the Angel Looisos invited me to undertake a mission to earth regarding blood sacrifices. For these so affected the biological character of beings on the planet that on the moon they commenced to take monstrous forms.

It may be that certain monstrous forms that have come down to us in myths may have resulted from conditions on other planets. It is amusing to think that biological forms are derived from a series of stations through which the forces must travel.

So Beelzebub alit on the Caspian Sea and traveled up a river to Tiklandia. There he visited the cafés. (As he also did on subsequent visits. So later you will see that he indicates the importance he attaches to commencing observation from a certain center of the community.)

So after a month of observations he decided to employ certain superstitions to aid his work. (His work was to preserve the fate of the moon. So Jesus may have had a much larger end in view than the benefit of the men here—say the stability of the universe.)

So all that Beelzebub had to suggest was, that the beings sacrifice themselves. He found very soon that the idea he proposed rapidly spread. (The use of veils when insects were in the air lest they should swallow and kill one. Their refusal to walk abroad during certain hours of the day, lest they step on and kill certain insects. But why? Since there was no sense to them.)

One of the influential pulpiteers said: "In view of the fact that God wishes on this earth the self-creation of a certain number of rational souls, the whole of the rest of creation has been created." (All creation up to man presupposes the evolution of man, and man presupposes the development of objective reason.)

And the rest of the material is for this purpose, and if you use it so, for this object, you are acting ethically, and vice versa.

And there exists a certain life force, prana, or essence, that is substantial (and that this substance may be discovered soon) and which exhibits itself in a number of forms—so you will see that the life force that manifests itself in vegetable and animal does not differ from that which is in us except in maturity, age and quantity of experience. Its essence is less developed —— to less experience. The purpose for which man exists is to develop a certain form or power or degree of reason. God is at the same time the creator and the evolving being and is engaged just as we are—in developing brain cells in the totality of His or our being. G. B. Shaw: "The darling necessity of evolution is the development of objective reason by an individual." So those of you who would be three times more brilliant than Shaw spend one month on pondering that the darling necessity of man's evolution is the development of three brains—not one. The true search of science is to discover a principle around which all our knowledge will arrange itself.

So Beelzebub said why has God endowed you with these faculties? They were politically designed to produce this faculty of objective reason.

For what do I hear? For what do I feel, taste etc.—experience? What!!? So the French regiment who were so overcome by the aesthetic effect of the bugle sounding the charge that they all sat down and called for an encore. So Beelzebub could scarcely refrain from laughing at the extremes to which these beings sentimentalized their reverence for animals.

So the priest started a counter propaganda, denouncing this priest, and secured his death. So Beelzebub took pity on this priest and took his body back to Mars and there saw to the education of his soul. He was recalled a little early by an etherogram saying that a party would shortly arrive on Mars among which would be that woman who was to be his wife—one who was assigned to him as his wife—the lady whom the stars had sent him.

Tooloof and Tulan were the two sons born to him—and Hassein was the son of Tooloof, his favorite son.

Whenever we follow our inclinations we are travelling downstream (not evolving). When we go against our inclinations—i.e. upstream—we are using real will.

THIRD DESCENT

He landed on the Gobi desert and followed a river upstream as usual. (So we follow vice versa "an incline"—downstream) by an arrangement of rafts (temporary structure—equivalent of self-observation, participation and experiment—always opposed to "natural" methods—artificial). Finally he reaches the capital where inhabitants have an opium habit—or chewing poppy seeds.

Now the King of Goblandia was a grandson of a conscious being—and he tried to install a legal prohibition with fines, etc.—with the result that the curiosity of many was to taste it. (So in the USA we have prohibition. What is poppy seed here now?) It distorted values—made it impossible for people to take their personal experience as guide and made it necessary for them to take another's experiences as their guide.

Say advertisement—suggestibility—the whole art of modern publicity salesmanship—our parents catch us young and so we fall victims of these black arts later in life.

The result was that they mistook kindly men and serviceable words as deadly insults—"et au contraire." "And a crow was regarded as a peacock." So many people adore H. G. Wells—but Wells took ideas, etc. from Hinton. Hinton's books are now reprinted and greatly influenced Wells. Hinton was a bad writer but an original thinker.

Swift said original intelligence is "seeing things in the bud."

Gurdjieff said—only—"time is the unique subjective."

Ouspensky was interrogating Gurdjieff on the different apprehensions of time. Gurdjieff finally said: "Well think about it—time is breath."

Every civilization has its own particular form of poppy seed.

From here Beelzebub passed to Hindustan. (Buddhism and monasteries.)

Dream figures remaining in the room after actually waking—our life is a dream in relation to a self-conscious life—so as Freud has taught the world to interpret dreams, but not only on sex. There is where Freud failed—mixed motives. The Freudian method is correct. Bertrand Russell showed that a day's events could reveal exactly as a dream an objective interpretation of our psychic conditions. So whatever we encounter is equally subjective—hypnopompic imagination. In a dream we don't doubt that the dream is valid. We have no criterion but in our waking state we have another criterion and can say in relation to the dream this is real—but in relation to another state this is not real.

Beelzebub joined an expedition in search of pearls (real philosophy—a conscious effort to reach this) they passed over places of enormous elevation, very unusual, devoid even of the possibility of vegetation.

An attempt from one form of idealism to inform of realism. I (Orage) spent many years in attempting to get some life or meaning into Eastern terms—but could not. And the vast majority of those who attempt this die en route—as I did. (But this expedition succeeded.)

Gurdjieff's personal history happens to conform to this—at age twenty-one he encountered Madam Blavatsky's works and he took it seriously and he went to every place she mentioned in the Secret Doctrine—and he reports that nine out of ten of her references were entirely false. This cost him years of terrible effort and suffering—with only negative results. He was at one time engaged as a collector of monastic dues for the Dalai Lama and it gave him access to every monastery in Tibet and he says: "I will truthfully say that it is true, I discovered extraordinary developments.

I did not discover one single being with universal development—only monsters. A particular variety of monstrosity—but no attainment of objective reason, no more than in the West, only different."

The expedition arrived at India—at its center of development.

- Tiklandia—instinctive—blood sacrifice.
- Goblandia—emotional—poppy seed.
- India—intellectual—Buddhism.

The tradition of the Buddha in India is that the Gautama Buddha was the seventh of a series of occurrences of the Buddha.

There are two schools of Buddhism—the exoteric and the esoteric.

What had been Buddha's aim? He realized that the whole of mankind suffered from a disease—kundabuffer—meaning a reflection, or seeing things upside down.

Buddha told them exactly these things—planet, collision, lopsided, recovered its balance, i.e. that kundabuffer was removed, that there was no longer a natural reason for continuing as before, for beings are now born quite naturally normally, but socially the consequences still persist. So he said I will show you a method for returning to your normal state. And his method was self-observation, self-participation and self-experiment.

Conscious effort—three sections:

1. To observe yourself (the only way).
2. Participation.
3. Changing reactions.
4. Conscious suffering—but it is really the suffering that we all undergo if we resist the inclination to react mechanically, and further to force ourselves to react contrary to the inclination. It involves a conscious refraining from the mechanical reaction and the conscious actualizing of a different reaction.

Refrain from hating your enemy and love your enemy. Turn the other cheek. Converting a poison—a negative reaction to a positive one.

By these two means your own development will naturally ensue.

Take the brick off a plant, no further effort is necessary. All we have to do is take the bricks off. Not by trying to improve yourself—for thus you will fail.

Conscious suffering:

1. Resisting mechanical reactions.
2. Reacting consciously differently.

"So they set up an institute of the first groups after those under Buddha himself, and immediately set out to scale heights—Tibet."

There are in America a number of quite competent yoga instructors who will undertake to instruct one in extraordinary occult powers—but their followers are going to Tibet. They will be lost en route or still more hopelessly when they arrive in Tibet. The more sincere the modern followers of Buddha, the more hopelessly wrong—the more monstrous.

Every time you do something wholly instinctive or emotional or intellectual you are performing the blood sacrifice of the other two centers. Every "man of action," artist or intellectual. So when Beelzebub speaks of the reduction of the sacrifice of two-centered beings—animals—he means just this.

SECOND KUNDABUFFER

He tried to recall to them the original doctrine of prana or life principle. Its natural fruition would be in animals, natural reason, and in men objective reason. So he persuaded them that every time they killed an animal, they killed a certain center in themselves and that they would inevitably suffer. So their attitude changed and they became absurdly changed. And he left them to stew in their own juice.

Then Beelzebub went back by way of Tibet. He came across the sect "the self-tamers"—they came to the conclusion that they had in themselves a jungle of wild beasts, (i.e. mechanical reactions). Their passage was greatly hindered by the necessity of guarding against the attacks of wild beasts (negative emotions) that never appeared in the day due to the presence of the sacred substance a-o-r-o-u or aspirations. But at night it was necessary to set up around the camp a ring of fire.

[*A significant dead silence while Orage tells of priests who voluntarily immured themselves in a kind of sentry box, etc.*]

No angel of normal development can ever experience the kind of pity that Beelzebub felt on seeing these marvelously admirable but incredibly stupid performances. For on these peaks which they thus reached, there is no possibility of growth. So no residential institute or monastery or such is ——.

This work must be practical without change of scene and among normal people.

Now Looisos sent an etherogram, saying that Looisos was again about to appear (and it is interesting to hear Gurdjieff say that Looisos is even now preparing to come here again). The peaks of the Himalayas are growing, rising and the rotundity of the planet is becoming a little uneven and is beginning to affect the planets surrounding it, so something might become necessary, say by the use of electric currents from the sun resulting in earth tremors.

So Beelzebub returned to Mars where certain canals were being constructed, for on one side of Mars there is only dry land and on the other only water. So canals and drainage.

28 MARCH 1927

FOURTH DESCENT

The second and third had been to stop the sacrifice of two centers to a third. We now discuss the sacrifice of one center to two. Keep in mind the proper relationship of the centers:

Positive, passive, neutralizing.

Male, female, child.

Beelzebub enjoyed completing his observatory on Mars; i.e. the method by which the unknown part of our psychology may be "observed," including "heavenly bodies" which are the higher emotional and intellectual centers.

There was a person on Saturn whose knowledge of the method and observations were superior. As if to present these ideas to the Western world he went to Tibet to find a person who was permanently in a different world (on different planet). The method is so improved that the heavenly bodies are a million times nearer; that is, the method is so improved that an ordinary being can understand it, though still far from a realization. We can now ourselves form a notion of objective reason, playing roles, etc., without being able to actualize these ideas. Cf. Addition of book.

Gornahoor Harharkh and Beelzebub were observing the earth. Beelzebub came to the earth to collect a number of apes to take them to Mars for experiment. While telling Hassein this, a sailor hands Beelzebub a tablet, which when placed at his ear, enabled him to hear a message which had been received by the ether. Beelzebub says: "What a strange coincidence, this message from Mars tells me there is a great to do about this problem on earth, in America." (He's referring to the Dayton trial. Dates do not agree in this conversation since it is supposed to be in 1921 and the Dayton trial was in 1926.)

Earth men have long been interested in apes, usually in one of two theories: either men are descended from apes or apes from men. In Tiklandia, 8,000 BC. it was that apes were descended from men. Now, thanks to Darwin, it is said that men descended from apes.*

But we should apply the saying, "Cherchez la femme" from Mul-

* Note by M. E. B. This is an entire misstatement. Darwin held that apes and men were both descended from a small mammal.

lah Nasruddin: If there are any anomalies in nature, examine the feminine principle.

After the sinking of Atlantis the races were scattered and often the sexes were segregated. In this condition, men satisfied themselves with homosexuality; but a woman entered into relations with male animals and the results were apes. The psychology of all apes is that of females in a hysterical mood. Physically they resemble their quadruped male ancestor. They have the psyche of the female and the body of a quadruped. Gurdjieff is here referring to philosophers and priests. Take a critical attitude towards the race and ask how these two classes of beings came into being, continue to maintain themselves and obtain respect.

The philosopher is a speculator who deals in words.

The priest does not even deal in words but in symbols, but their meaning he no longer knows.

When essence has disappeared (Atlantis sunk), there remains personality in which the three centers are separated. Not one of us is one being. That unification is burled; and at the surface is only separated centers. It is possible to be highly developed in one, rudimentary in another, and atrophied in the third.

In the history of the planet is our psychological history. Development of the theory—the embryo before birth repeats physiologically the history of the species. Gurdjieff says that after birth, we continue to repeat.

From the point of view of breeding the positive and negative are the two important ones because the neutralizing force is a child of the first two.

Positive, male, intellect.

Negative, female, instinctive.

The emotional center is the child.

Now, the intellectual center does not seek out the instinctive and does not demand a body for the intellect. The penalty is homosexuality, titillation—the attempt to make words take the place of breeding.

Consider the volumes of metaphysics, where the intellectual center is of itself trying to produce, the positive alone produces no child. Intellectualism is words and produces no effect on the emotional center. The yogi type is self-abstracted. The instinctive center is left to find some positive element, and because of not finding it within itself, it looked for it in external stimuli. (Priests and all activity into which no true intellectual element entered.) The outcome is something, since there is a positive and a negative. A certain kind of emotion, but not human. Apes are those active beings amongst us whose activity is directed not according to objective reason. Beelzebub takes some of these to Mars to see if it is possible to make human beings of them. (Can we, who are active apes, when this method is promulgated, become human?)

He alights in the same ship on the Red Sea because it is near to Africa. This was the first continent to be peopled by three-centered beings after the sinking of Atlantis.

Three centers:

- First—center of Africa.
- Second—Egypt.
- Third—South Africa.

He decided to spend some time in Egypt, where his observatory (later a corrupted form known as a pyramid) was being built. He proceeded by the Red Sea, via Sinai (of the moon) to Thebes and Cairo, within easy reach of Cairo was a campus with buildings devoted to the observing of the heavenly bodies.

But before describing this we must tell something of what had happened in Atlantis. For the first time, a public society had been formed to discover the nature of man. While in Egypt, he put himself into a certain state of meditation in which it was possible to read certain thought forms left there by previous beings that had attained a certain degree of objective reason. (This may throw some light on certain phenomena; of automatic writing, visions, etc., e.g. "Light on the Path" which was automatically written. Mabel Collins showed this book to Mme. Blavatsky who said it was a translation of a book of which only one copy was known.)

In Atlantis, there was a certain being that had attained a power of making records in "thought matter," as I might mould clay or write on paper. These would last practically as long as the atmosphere. These were visible to Beelzebub. He could put himself into a certain state of vision and become fully aware of the contents of this particularized substance, in certain forms which can be tapped and read in certain states. Thus in Egypt, Beelzebub learned of the foundation of this society of Atlantis.

Belcultassi one day realized he had made some bad blunders and was so disgusted that he reviewed his past life, impartially; he found this incident no more stupid than all the others, though this time the consequences were worse than usual. How many times have I done things so foolish or stupid, that if found out would have ruined something dear. When one brings consequences it seems more stupid because it's more vivid.

There was no correspondence between what he had done and what he had wished and thought. A contradiction between his ability to do and his wishes and theories of what he was doing. We apply this reasoning to others and can point out their folly. Belcultassi applied this reason to himself and said: "I must be an especial fool. Others cannot be as foolish as I for they all look so well balanced." He decided to question his friends, confessing his folly, and ask them to condemn him. But so disarming was his sincerity that the others confessed they were leading equally senseless lives. He found a few serious ones and formed a society—Akhaldan—those who seek for an aim and sense to existence. A research society looking for the cure for a radical insanity of our being, in possession of three centers, speaking different languages—"the meaning and aim of existence"—a society which takes the discovery of this as its aim. Begin as a small private group, begin to meet and confess and observe. Kept diaries between meetings of observation:

- Undertook review of past life.
- Observation of current behavior.
- Formulation of results put before group for criticism.

After some time they decided they could do nothing about it unless they had access to some special knowledge. They divided into five groups for special research. Each individual must take all five to be complete:

FIRST GROUP

Observation outside their planet, i.e., outside the physical body—behavior of other people with the idea of classifying them according to type. Each of us knows hundreds of people and has enough information to set down. If we had done this seriously we would not ask: "What are the types?" We would have a working knowledge.

28 MARCH 1927

SECOND GROUP

The second group was concerned with mathematics in its broadest sense. It has been suggested that thoughts vary in weight and in rapidity; feelings in intensity; muscular movements in stresses. Can you distinguish these weights, intensities, stresses? This will be introducing measure into psychology. Modern psychology is physiology, investigating physiological changes, applying vibrometers. But this is not psychological measurement, changes in psychological state.

Who can discriminate in himself between the weights of two thoughts, e.g., in one chapter Gurdjieff says, "Time is the unique subjective." Contrast this with two volumes of Alexander on time, space etc. Alexander says, "Time is the father of space." In the latter, so much is being implied as being understood before the sentence is understood, fanciful and yet has nothing to do with me. But Gurdjieff's phrase has at once greater personal impact. In Indian philosophy it is often said "Time is I." This is similar to Gurdjieff's phrase; but is slightly different because it is of different weight.

Take emotions; there is a familiar saying in America: "I am crazy about it," where there is really but a moderate degree of interest. Those who have had genuine emotions do not thus use superlative expressions for mediocre feelings. When genuine emotions come, they drop this use of superlatives. Even when speaking of the most intense experiences yet had, if they can imagine more intense experience, they will continue to use the comparative. Distinction between stresses: can you tell the difference between seven, seven and a quarter and seven and a half pounds?

THIRD GROUP

Observation of the perceptions and manifestations of beings. Observe in our own manifestations and if possible in our perceptions. We receive perceptions and yield manifestations. We receive at the rate of ten thousand per second. These undergo changes of vibration and issue as behavior. Like a threefold mill. A reduction of behavior to mechanical transformations of perceptions; drastic and radical. Perceptions are always rates of vibration and depend on the vibrations present in us, whether perceptions will change up or down. If your vibrations happen to be low and in this state encounter low vibrations, behavior will become still lower. Your organism lowers the rate of vibration in atmosphere at large. (See last week on voluntary suffering, an attempt to react non-mechanically, assuming a certain ability to control this mill.) Perceptions if run down, emerge as behavior, i.e. potential perception for others of lower rates of vibrations. It is possible in the long run by this means to determine the tone of each center. This gives collection of material for the next group.

FOURTH GROUP

Physics and chemistry, i.e. observed changes produced in them by the passage of perceptions. Every perception effects a change; it may only disturb one or two neurons but to that extent we are changed. I didn't say that manifestations had changed anything "no guilty act." Act is merely a product. It can be stopped only by something done within the organism, i.e., by change of rates of vibration of the organism. This can only be done if the organism is insulated, that is, it can only be done through self-observation. Act is merely reaction to perceptions as affected by the state of the organism. This includes opinion (thought), feelings and physical movements. It may be considered physically or chemically. We speak of the "struggle" within us, one force of vibration encountering another force. We call it embarrassment, etc.

FIFTH GROUP

Engaged in a study of those phenomena which occurred within themselves, owing merely to the fact that they had three centers, e.g. while reading the newspaper, my lips move. When the intellectual center works, the instinctive tends to work too. Or, I observe a person in a certain state of feeling and though the perceptions which caused the feeling are outside of my field of perception, I tend to have analogous emotions. This group studied exclusively human phenomena, human psychology.

The Akhaldans discovered however that there was still further work necessary, they had done their best . . . They decided to send delegates to see if any more advanced students of this problem of their senseless conduct were elsewhere to be found.

The first they sent to the center of Africa. (Africa is the substitute for Atlantis—emotional.)

Then to Egypt (intellect) and then to South Africa (instinctive).

Return to Beelzebub in Egypt. He studies their observatory to see if they have any good technique he had not thought of. These ancient Egyptians, descendants of Akhaldans were seriously at work. They had a huge structure, five tubes pointing out and converging in one chamber with an underground mirror, forming one image. Consider the five types of behavior, cast into one composite image. But the center of focusing was underground. Then Beelzebub returned to Mars, he put the center of focusing above ground, i.e. objective. Makes focus as it were, outside oneself. The Egyptian focus was in the mind. In Egyptian mysteries the focus was inside. The Egyptian method was only possible with the intelligentsia and developed a special hierarchy of intelligence. But anyone can employ Beelzebub's method. In Egypt, it was never taught publicly. Other buildings in this campus; one had as its purpose the charting of winds and changing of climates. They knew how to affect weather, i.e. psychologically, also externally; currents, winds, observation of emotional states; changing of moods, weather. You are in a low damp state. Can you change negative to positive?

While the Egyptians were doing something psychologically, they were also affecting external changes. Called by the Greeks: "Masters of Dreams."

They had a deliberately imperfect copy of a figure seen at Atlantis (when they discussed with King Appolis in the center of the Akhaldian hall). This figure had the head and bust of a virgin, connected with the main body by a piece of amber; it had the legs of a lion, the body of a bull and the wings of an eagle. Thus there were four parts, of which three were connected; for amber insulates. Okidanokh of an organic kind, which makes it impossible to transmit the energy from three centers to the fourth.

Meaning: In order to recover our normal state, which had been rendered abnormal, four things are necessary:

- The laboriousness of the bull: ability to continue working indefinitely even blindly.
- The legs of a lion: this labor must be executed, with self-confidence knowing every other being is unable to destroy it.
- Wings: bullish labor is not enough; work must be carried on with aspiration.
- Head and breast: stand for love; insulated to indicate that this love must not be associated with the functions of the three centers.

None of the intellectual, emotional or instinctive experiences of the body as such.

- Breasts of the virgin: indicate as yet no result, only potential.
- Virginity: is potentiality.

The same symbol, though changed, was at the entrance to Thebes. The name in Atlantis was conscience; in Egypt, the sphinx, meaning a question, an interrogation. In Egypt there were no wings; for the essence which had stimulated aspiration was now missing.

Beelzebub returns to Mars with some apes. He has to go to Saturn to be godfather to a child born of Hermaphrodite. On planets with satellites there are two sexes; the penultimate plan must differentiate energy into two sexes for satellites. On planets without satellites there is either one sex or three: one, hermaphrodite—three, three beings required. This is to say the hermaphrodite contains two centers, positive and negative produce emotional. The three beings are the three centers which produce the fourth.

How angels are produced: At birth they already have three bodies, each subject to development but not as with us, successive. On their planet, three sexes, each specialized one of the three forces (of electricity) but each was truly a sexual being. These three take part in a mystery called immaculate conception. Then each goes his own way and during the period of conception each thinks only of the Messiah and of its particular conception. When the miraculous birth draws near, the three draw together and become one being. Eventually from them emerges an infant angel. On earth there are only two sexes; the neutralizing force is rare and hard to come by. These two on earth produce beings who develop physically but only partially emotionally and but potentially intellectually. They are born incomplete and must work to obtain this neutralizing force. Hence voluntary suffering is local to this planet.

28 MARCH 1927

[*9:20*]

May I make one announcement? Numbers of people have expressed a desire to hear the book read again. On Thursday there will be a reading on that evening at $1.

You will remember that last week we considered the second and third descent and this week the fourth descent. You remember the reason of the second and third descents to put at an end the sacrifice of animals or two-centered beings.

FOURTH DESCENT — "DESCENT OF APES"

Discussion turns on one center of two—need a parallel thinking—three—positive, passive, neutralizing.

He was engaged in completing his observatory on Mars (a method by which unperceived aspects of bodies within ourselves—heavenly bodies—may become perceived.)

It occurs to him that on planet Saturn there was a being who was an expert on observatories (say a being in Tibet who is familiar with self-observation, etc.), Gornahoor Harharkh. It is now easy to define objective thought—simultaneity of thought—casting and displaying roles can share in a degree the attitude of a being like Beelzebub. Can describe actualizable ideals not yet attainable.

Beelzebub undertook to return to earth and capture a certain number of apes and carry them back to Saturn for examination and experiment.

Came an interruption—sailor brings in message—Beelzebub turns to Hassein and says at just this moment: "There is a great 'to do' on earth regarding the origin of man, particularly in America, for many generations. There are two classes of speculation:

1. Man from ape.
2. Ape from man.

Neither is true.

Tiklandia, 8,000 years ago, had the theory that man was descended from apes—but now conversely. But both wrong. Cherchez la femme, i.e. inquire of feminine principle. I.e. after the sinking of Atlantis, beings found themselves segregated so that in many sections there were only females and in another only males. Males contented themselves with homosexuality. But females took male animals and therefore the apes. (Apes are describable as female in their hysterical moods.) He is referring to philosophers and priests. There are two classes of beings—philosopher—speculator who deals in words. Priest—not even in words but in symbols to which he had entirely lost the meaning.

Sinking of Atlantis = disappearance of essence and sex. Instinctive education is one—emotional education is another—intellectual education is still another. Each is left above the water. Each of these is so separate that it is possible for a person to be highly developed in one, rudimentarily in a second, and not at all or dead in a third.

So Gurdjieff says even after birth we continue to repeat embryologically. Immediately after birth, the history of this planet: intellectual—positive, male; instinctive—negative, passive, female; neutral—emotional, child.

Philosopher—yogi type—one perfectly willing to remain separate from the instinctive, therefore what occurs in him is an attempt to put words into the function of breeding. So metaphysics is self-indulgence in which the cerebral center merely engages with itself in the hope of producing offspring. Mere intellectualism produces nothing but words.

But the instinctive center by itself can produce nothing and since positive has become concerned with itself only, the instinctive must mate with a lower center. The outcome is something—something in the emotional center. But it is only pseudo human or apish or bestial—so all those activities we customarily call great but which lack the positive element of reason—are apish. Apes are those active beings among us who are active but whose activity is not directed by intelligence. An attempt to see whether, when the method is promulgated, active apes like ourselves can become human.

He alights in Africa on the Red Sea. Africa was occupied in three centers (parts). Egypt—the scene of the building of the extraordinary observatory. South Africa. . . .

So Beelzebub stayed in Egypt to study the observatory and came to the city of Thebes and not far was Cairo—and within that a campus devoted to buildings holding observatories. But before that, Beelzebub says: I will tell you of certain experiments there (i.e. the first promulgation of this method). First—put myself into a certain trance form under which certain thought forms were apparent.

"Light on the Path" (Mabel Collins wrote this down who afterwards became maniac.)

There were in Atlantis, beings who had attained the power of making thought molds, which would exist practically as long as the atmosphere. So Beelzebub put himself into a certain state of intellectual contemplation wherein these thoughts could be read.

A man, Belcultassi, in a negative state began to seriously review his life and came to the conclusion that the particular event had been not only unusually stupid but that herein the result had been particularly disastrous. (The fact that an event doesn't have to result in disaster doesn't change it from folly.)

What he did was not in accord with his feelings or thoughts (We can be relatively objective with regard to people to whom we are indifferent.)

Belcultassi said to himself: "I must be a singular fool. Other beings surely are not thus. So he invited other beings to consult with him over his own deficiencies but they, attracted by his own sincerity and candor soon admitted that they were in the same fix. So they formed the society of Kaldeans—to determine the aim and sense of existence—the meaning of existence. There is not one society on earth today that knows this.

They began to meet and discuss and to compare notes—and kept a diary of all observations.

1. Detailed review.

2. Current self-observation.

3. To formulate conclusions in order to put them before the group for criticism.

But they decided to divide into five groups with special work for each group.

1. Group examined those phenomena that occurred outside their planet. External observation of oneself and others posture, facial expression, etc., to determine type, etc. Each one of us knows a least 500 people and without going beyond these, one could find ample material for dividing humans into the types to which they belong. Physiological and physionomical.

2. Group concerned with mathematics and algebra—psychological exercise—thoughts vary in weight and rapidity, feelings in intensity, muscular actions in stresses. Can you turn your attention to the qualities as above, i.e. to employ a measure to weigh thought, to determine intensity of feeling, to determine degree of energy, stress in actions?

3. Group to observe the perceptions and manifestations of beings.

We are mechanical beings operated by perceptions and thereupon manifesting behavior. Try to think of yourself as a threefold will, always receiving and manifesting perceptions: 1—verbal—opinion; 2—emotional—negative feeling; 3—physical—turning away.

4. Group of physics and chemistry—proceeded to examine what changes take place in us by (or resulting from) the impressions (perceptions) we receive, at the rate of ten per second. Therefore no guilt in actions or manifestations. For they can only be stopped by one means—by changing the rates of vibrations of the perceptions we receive. Behavior is a reflex—including opinions, emotional states, and all behavior in action.

5. Group to study those phenomena that occur owing to the fact we only have three centers, for example—reading the newspaper, lips move. Why? Because so closely related. Or we see another in an emotional state. The cause does not interest me, but I receive from them certain images which arouse, due to an analogue, emotions in me. I.e. study human psychology.

But they then discovered that further knowledge was necessary. So the Akhaldan society sent certain of their members to various parts of the world. South Africa, amongst other places, and they came into the center of Africa, i.e. the personality began. Asia is fully developed personality. Five tubes by mirrors concentrated observations in the pyramids of Egypt into a single complete image (i.e. one's own organism, observe five forms of behavior and resolve them simultaneously into a complete and accurate image). But Egyptians had focus underground. Beelzebub adopted the method of the Egyptians but produced a result of focused awareness above ground and outside (i.e. objective, not subjective), this was possible only to a few—the intelligentsia—the hierarchy. It was not taught popularly in Egypt.

Another accomplishment went toward charting winds and controlling climate. Climates—moods. Winds—currents of emotions.

By observation can change negative into positive emotions.

At the entrance of the campus there was a certain symbolic figure—a deliberately faulty copy of a figure seen by Beelzebub before on Atlantis.

The Atlantean figure was:

1. Head was that of the bust of a virgin, connected with the main body by a piece of amber.

2. Legs of a lion.

3. Body of a bull.
4. Wings of an eagle.

Amber insulates okidanokh—makes impossible transference from third center to fourth. The meaning of the figure is that in order to recover to a normal state there is a necessity to obviate the consequences of the organ kundabuffer.

1. Body of bull—laboriousness, self-indefatigability.
2. Lion—self-confidence arises from knowledge that nothing can destroy him.
3. Wings—aspiration—labor and fearlessness alone are useless.
4. Head—love—not to be associated with any of the functions of the trunk or the three centers.

So the Egyptian figure had no wings—called the sphinx—i.e. question. The original figure was called conscience.

Beelzebub returns to Mars with a number of apes. Finds he must attend the ceremony of a child born of a hermaphrodite, as godfather. Three sorts of planets having one sex, two sexes and three sexes. This refers to two centers producing a third, one a second—or three producing a fourth.

Angels have at first already three bodies and although they have all three potentialities of development it is not in sequence. On planets where angels are born there are three sexes—positive, negative and neutralizing, but each is truly a sexual being. When there comes the necessity of the creation of a new body for a being there takes place a process called immaculate conception, during which each thinks only of the Messiah or Christ. During this time the three beings become one.

The method of conscious labor and voluntary suffering are peculiar to this planet. Protagoras (Belcultassi) was in Babylon, Egypt, etc., before setting up his school or institute in Sicily. So Napoleon and his critics and the futility of critics by us.

4 APRIL 1927

The rate of time of the rational center, is one-seventh of one-seventh shorter than the rate of time of sense perception. Make an experiment of restating in your own terms and pondering many of the frequent statements in the book. Reason will then serve one of its functions, i.e. shortening the time necessary for personal development that is shorter than arriving by trial and error through the senses.

FIFTH DESCENT

Babylon was the fifth cosmopolitan center in the world. It was between 3,000 and 2,000 BC. Tiklandia, Goblandia, etc. had all been of one nationality, provincial. Babylon was metropolitan. It was the acknowledged metropolis of the whole planet; and to indicate its position in the East people wrote from right to left, i.e. towards the West, towards Babylon. In the West they wrote from left to right, if North of Babylon, from top to bottom, if South from bottom to top. Present indication of historical position of ancestors.

Cause of the fifth descent. Beelzebub had noticed from Mars that the length of men's lives was declining. It had been from seven to ten centuries. He could not tell the cause of this from Mars, so came to earth to study. He makes effort to survey the whole species. He traces history and degeneration of the species. It was the first opportunity to observe that certain centers were no longer three but one, i.e. Babylon was the first "modern" center. Ideas were current there of science, art, and religion that are still current. Until then the conception of science was based on the development of normal potentialities of normal beings. It had been assumed that to develop the second and third bodies was one of the obligations of life. This was taken for granted just as education, marriage, etc. are taken for granted now. All conditions were adapted to this. A scientist from Babylonia took advantage of conditions to develop normally—art, literature, occupations, etc. were subordinate.

With Babylonian times, intuitions of potentialities were waning—substituted by techniques and the accumulation of knowledge and facts, cf. certain animals and primitive individuals. As intuitions waned, mechanical means were substituted; until we arrive at a "highly developed modern scientist," who had no intuitions but an amazing command of mechanical technique.

Science is based on sense perceptions, a property of the human being as such. Compared with science based on accumulation of knowledge, and not through first hand sense perceptions, but by substituting technique . . .

In Babylon, there was a congress of the new type of scientist, who had lost the sense of potentialities and thrown back on effort to discover . . .

We should be able to see examples in elders; this example is gone, intuitions were so lost that we are even in doubt when we hear them stated. Let us assume them to include the development of two other bodies. Which of us can imagine that we will in this life develop emotional and intellectual potentialities, that we will become Platos or Hypatias, which in pre-Babylonian times was normal. When we look at trees, e.g. we see them as material for our use. The pre-Babylonian scientist recognized their utilitarian use but also saw intuition as the latent potentialities in each individual and intuition as a function of each living being.

In dealing with animals, e.g. the first intuition that they fulfill their functions in the cosmic scheme, as we fulfill ours. Man is only entitled to make use of animals insofar as he is fulfilling his own function, i.e. development of reason. If he is using them only for his appetites or comforts, he is missing one of the natural values.

In this decline from intuition to rationalism came the idea of the decline of religions; and we owe Babylon for the origin of the idea of "good" and "evil." The world is an enormous apparatus for the transforming of energy up and down, with a balance maintained by reciprocal feeding of rates of vibration. "Absolute good" would be the maintenance of this equilibrium. The idea of "evil" was introduced when the individual identified himself with the whole process.

Now what appears a digression: distribution of races; after the sinking of Atlantis.

- Tiklandia.
- Goblandia.
- India.

About 5,000 BC, due to the third cosmic misfortune that befell this planet and continued for several years, there were winds of such intensity that the mountain peaks were abraded and sand storms followed. Tiklandia and Goblandia were obliterated. There is currently no plausible explanation of how so large a part of the earth's surface should be covered with sand. It lies in the Gobi for a depth of thirty or forty feet. Gurdjieff says these sand storms were caused by the moon, because the atmosphere of the moon surcharged with electrical elements received by the earth and fell into a sort of friction with the earth.

Of the people of Goblandia one part went East and settled in China (old histories of China say it was settled from the West), one part went West and settled in Europe; one part South to Persia.

Babylonia became the center under the influence of the Akhaldans who made a world capital out of the city; a university center.

The subjects of especial interest to these Akhaldans:

1. Physical sciences as we know them.

Gurdjieff says that all we know about electricity was known then. They aimed at the accumulation of facts under the illusion that the complexity of the existing civilization produced a change in psychology, but on the contrary, to the extent one is forced to depend on external, force, technique, help, etc. we measure only weakness. Knowing and doing were developed at the expense of being. The inauguration of the modern period.

2. Morality.

In absence of intuition of world purpose, they were forced to collect data and give the subjective interpretation.

What world view do I have? Is everything pure chance? Is the universe governed by an all wise and benevolent being? Do I depend on a kindly providence? Or do I view the cosmos as a school where I am set to acquire a certain understanding, or as a penal institution? Or as a gymnasium (as some Hindus) to acquire certain powers? Set down your conception of life, accidentally arrived at, one of a few. Interrogate yourself. Find your conception, however subjective and particular, heard in one of the stories heard in childhood. It is not an original but a derived conception. Originality and generation of the truth is disclaimed; yet all our thinking and lives are colored by this broad concept. The Greeks, the Romans and we in our modern time also are continuing to think the thoughts which were formulated in Babylon.

One of the Babylonian Scientists, Hamalinadian read a paper on the "Instability of Human Reason"—"Skepticism of the Instrument." Assuming the mind has been developed in evolution, in response to needs, just as the hand has. Hence the brain has been developed only for the purpose of survival and cannot be of value for the discovery of truth as such.

Second line of argument: We know the origin of our dialectics. Each of us has seen only a small part of natural phenomena, so small that we have no ground for passing judgment on the whole.

Third line of attack: Kant. A species of logical introspection; our structure presupposes certain (characteristics) concepts of time and space over which we have no control and which limit our perception. Yet each one attaches some importance to personal judgment. Hamalinadian was a crack scientist; had gone to all the schools including Egypt, "making thought material."

In ancient Egypt as in modern India, the highest yoga classes materialized thought. This merely makes clearer the subjective nature of thought. Hamalinadian could see thought; but this was no help in solving the problem: does man survive death? Hamalinadian admitted that in spite of the abundance of learning, he knew nothing by personal experience about the soul, though he had written books on the subject which his colleagues had admired. This is our state. Does anyone *know* that man has a soul or about its fate? Hamalinadian invites anyone who has a method he has not tried to tell him and he will try it. No offers. Hamalinadian retired and became a farmer (related to first food).

[*Orage reads*]

Pan-scientific congress to settle the question, is there a soul? The Tower of Babel. This is the hope that by putting together all theories, he might combine them and build a structure which would reach heaven. Hamalinadian began by the analysis of the brain, the origin of our opinions and our impressions—analysis of current behaviorism.

As Hamalinadian spoke his voice began to grow, moved with realization of what he was saying. He admits that in one mood he could prove that men were just bodies and in another that they were just minds. Yet he was not a mediocre scientist but had completed the highest studies. During this congress he had followed all the conflicting theories and had agreed inwardly with all. A tower built of theories, all plausible, yet of various consistencies and so must collapse. Hamalinadian left them. He is the type of the disillusioned modern scientist whose reason is being based on sensations, which is insufficient for any essential conclusions.

Pause and distinguish these:

- Being.

- Knowing.
- Doing.

The three broadest types.

The "being" type is the rarest; and the degeneration of the species is measured by the decrease in this type. Everyone here is in the first instance a being. We are distinguished from the animal. This does not mean that we are superior but differentiates between animal and human being. Can you distinguish, not instinctively, not emotionally, and not behavioristically? Then what is the difference? We can only say it is self-consciousness, awareness of the state of being. It is possible for us to classify ourselves in the order of beings.

Comparison of orders. I can distinguish between a state of well-being and a state of ill-being. I can measure the degree in which certain faculties are sharper in well-being than in ill-being. Suppose for the moment there was no external world. Close your eyes and try to be merely conscious of yourself. Can you distinguish changes taking place in your state (psychic), can you distinguish three main forms of states: thinking, feeling, moving (motor activity)? Each of these is susceptible to many sub-states. Collect names of emotional and intellectual states:

Intellectual: concentration, attention.

Instinct: pain, lightness.

Interrogate yourself; the beginning of a technique for the science and art of being. Be aware of psychic states as they occur. Take an illustration: anger, how many varieties, as many as shades of red?—Indignation, rage, spleen, vexation, etc.

Someone in pursuit of knowledge would proceed by reason, based on reading would be able to define. He might say "indignation is anger and surprise" without any personal knowledge. Someone pursuing being might be able to distinguish shades in himself without perhaps being able to define them in current terms. There is a difference between knowledge and analysis of words and understanding of self.

Babylon instituted word reasoning and put an end to the pursuit of being. Substitution of verbal thought for trained intuition. We come into the world educable and are corrupted by words. Knowledge is not the outcome of experience but of crystallized concepts. Possibility of the self-discovery of a means, with a series of exercises and arriving at a greater self-understanding.

Each of us is a Hamalinadian. Suppose science succeeds; the disillusion of Hamalinadian is awaiting us. How shall we start?

Method:

First Step—physical behavior

Second Step—observation of psychic states as such, attention on changes. Until now nothing on this has been said, because external behavior is a language with three meanings. Three centers simultaneously express themselves in our behavior.

Consecutive and increasingly subtle readings bring to light. (Later on in connection with our drama we will see part of training in "acting.") At present all this is premature but now giving to distinct states. Interrogation based on words, a useful experiment.

Morality in Babylon—two schools: dualist or idealist, materialist or atheist. The first assumed the existence in the world of two principles: good and bad. We find in ourselves tendency to classify things thus, not only in relation to ourselves but absolutely. That each species should so classify things relatively, i.e. in relation to its own purposes, is natural. "Good for me," conducive to my purpose. This judgment is purely relative and implies no judgment of the object itself. If I say "good in itself" I am applying my personal judgment which has nothing ethical in it (instrumental), with cosmic meaning. This double meaning of the word "good" is the cause of most of our confusion. This false attribution of personal to absolute values, we call morality; a universalization of which is strictly speaking personal. There is nothing in the world which is universally good or bad. In spite of the fact that this is clear, none of us can refrain from using "good and evil" and feeling that we have some claim to pass judgment, thanks to an educational system which originated in Babylonian days. Morality was instituted following the decadence of the intuition of God.

The non-moral view was held in Babylonian days by a group who were mechanicians. Everything in the world is a series of causes which produce effects which in turn become causes and produce effects. It is a circular change without meaning. Speculation as to origins and ends is impossible. The first school had turned organic good and bad into ethical good and evil. The second school came to the conclusion that there was no psychology and no being. The price that will be paid by modern technical psychology (see Watson)—no psyche, if the whole preoccupation is with external behavior. It is a subtler physiology. It loses sense of experience other than senses. If psychic activity is directed outward continually, the ultimate conclusion will be that nothing real exists.

Logic is based on impressions; if we collect no impressions for the psyche, logic will compel us to predicate the non-existence of the psyche. We cannot reason about the psyche with a being all of whose impressions are all physiological. Watson said: Your theory cannot interest me because it is based on facts which are not of my experience. I understand you to say: collect the facts.

We cannot talk yet, can only go, do. Collection of facts begins to give ground for new judgment. A half-century after Hamalinadian came St. Ashiata Shiemash. Hamalinadian was the most highly intellectual scientist of his day.

Before considering Ashiata, we must go through the steps of viewing the human species objectively. Each of us is the product of a long biological history; and also from the moment of conception, this biological heredity becomes subject to variations due to the particular time in the civilization in which we find ourselves. If the environment is discouraging to normal biological purpose, we find hostility to normal development. If favorable, sociological materials will aid biological development.

In this critique, there are certain implications; one of these is the conception of a normal human being. It is impossible to arrive at this by taking merely the average of individuals. The species in process of degeneration may offer an average but ceases often to be normal. This distinction between average and normal is very important. This book defines the normal; and needs to be long pondered before being grasped.

(Gurdjieff often said to Orage: "What I am saying now, you will understand perhaps in a year or two years." Although the statement was clear.)

A being, irrespective of sex, who at the age of about twenty-one begins to find quite naturally in himself the development of that state of consciousness which we call self-consciousness. He becomes aware of his body in the sense of being psychologically in possession of it. This happens normally and is accompanied by devotion to certain interests and employment of means.

At the age of about thirty, another crisis in which he begins to become conscious of the world in which he lives; not merely this planet but other planets and his relation to them. This varies in individuals but the character of the stage is the same. Aware of total life purpose, function, etc. At first he just senses them.

On other planets there are normal three-centered beings. On this planet are no phases, turning points after the age of planetary majority. After this a normal development is dependent on external impressions received up to this time. More or less chaotic, unfolding in the possibilities of experience laid up.

Beelzebub's first effort was to understand why this state is. He reviewed the history of the planet, as it is useful for us to review the history of our individual lives. He found a catastrophe and split; each individual repeats this planetary accident. The results are serious but not fatal. The Moon and Anulios remained within the gravitational field of the planet. This split is not ineradicable. It is possible to develop normally if only our sociological inertia which we call tradition had adapted itself.

Kundabuffer is vestigial but tradition continues it. This sociological tradition must eventually be overcome and seen through as a condition of normal development. It is impossible to develop through sociological ideas; it is not a question of eclecticism among the knowledge we have acquired. All this knowledge is useless in the absence of the development of essence, the biological germ. This is the origin of the insistence on "being born again," not spiritually or occult but by returning to the biological state before we were subject to sociology, hence the value of reviewing life by pictures. It develops the center of observation; and "I" becomes something, as the panorama of the metamorphosis of its own body passes before it. It also leads to seeing the layers or coatings and the transparence of the layers. The sociological attainments do not drop off. One sees the essential reactions due to period, place etc.

Comparing ourselves with a conscious being, aware of function, ask the question which Ashiata asked himself. He appeared in Babylon, shortly after Hamalinadian. Hamalinadian, an intellectual, had analyzed mind. Impressions are accidentally received. Are they sufficient for any objective judgment? He decided there was no salvation in cultivating the mind; and went out to grow food i.e., to collect impressions, which no one could give him. He had abandoned reason and self-analysis, the ordinary sense of words and he was thrown back on the simple pastoral task of taking impressions of his own physical behavior.

Ashiata was perhaps taking advantage of the wave of intellectual skepticism and disillusionment—no solution of essential questions by gathering data. He decided that an emotional awakening was needed but for the intelligentsia, an emotional appeal on the instinctive center is not sufficient; it must come over an idea, from beyond reason. Hence Gurdjieff speaks of objective reason.

Ashiata spoke of objective conscience. He began by questioning his own competence to undertake a reform, realizing that he also had been subjectively determined. He set out to make the coating of education transparent. In a state of objectivity he began to formulate the means to carry out his mission; and left a document for a line of initiates, of whom today in Central Asia (psychological as well as geographical essence) a few members remain. (Asia—essence; Europe—personality.)

The steps he took: Legomonism transmitted, occult doctrine, original fully formulated and transmitted by human means. Title of the Document: "The Terror of the Situation." Suppose it is true that all of us are abnormal, that we have never seen and never shall see a normal human being on this planet. Suppose this species is degenerating and that we can be but dimly aware of this; that we as species and as individuals are being carried inevitably downs the scale of evolution. Consider efforts by Ashiata, Buddha, Egyptian civilization, etc. Many attempts and all have failed. Our stakes on Ashiata's efforts. The situation inspired him as we know. This may give us an understanding of the intensity with which Ashiata went at it.

[*Orage wishes he had the music which accompanies this section; this has the same ideas emotionally realized as intellectually realized in the book.*]

Ashiata's meditation, he began with the following prayer, i.e., he put himself in a definite emotional attitude, as precise as the physical posture, an arrangement of emotions.

"In the name of the cause of my arising," is used instead of being born, i.e., we exist sensibly as a result of coating ourselves, cf. electrolysis. "I" am always; periodically comes to a manifestation. Thank whatever powers that "I" has it; that we live as well as are. My aim shall always be to be just toward everything already coated and toward all originations of those existences still to be. To me, a trifling particle of the all-great essence, it was commanded to be coated with a planetary body of the planet earth. (And help men free themselves from the effects of kundabuffer.)

Previous messengers had taken one of the three functions (faith, hope and love) of three-centered beings. Ashiata says that these three functions are natural to three-centered beings, resident in the essence of man as such. At first he thought to use one of these. At seventeen he began to prepare his planetary body in order to be during the rest of his life impartial. Gurdjieff attaches importance to striving for impartiality.

In Babylon he observed the effect of sociological conditions on beings and began to doubt the possibility of using any one of these three functions. He had anticipated the failure of Christianity, which assumes in us enough essential faith, hope and love, on which to base a religion. He observed his intellectual contemporaries. They had not enough faith, hope and love. The properties of kundabuffer were so crystallized that their education became a substitute for their being.

He decided to bring this planetary body to a state of emptiness of impressions received in this life. Attempt to think of a consciousness blank of content but vivid. Only in this state would he begin to choose a method. He ascended the mountain of concentration, forty days and nights and another forty days, and neither ate nor drank. Then he reviewed and analyzed all the phases of experience through which he had passed. He became merely an active experiencer. He spent the next forty days and nights on his knees and to maintain his relation with his planetary body, every half-hour plucked out two hairs, to remind himself that he is incarnated in a physical body. Usually exercises of concentration cause a separation of a certain body, which leads one to think one leaves the planetary body. After these three periods he was free from physical and emotional associations.

Then he considered how to *be* more in order to carry out his mission; development of being as such. To know more is not to be more; to do more is not to be more. It became clear to him it was already too late to use faith, hope and love; these functions were degenerate. Probably due to the fact that when kundabuffer was removed the taste for —— was so strong. They have faith, hope and love, but how do they love and hope and what is the nature of their faith?

Faith: They have faith but not independently arising from their own nature; it flows from other functions formed in them from infancy, with the result that they believe in what happens to have been presented by impressions received. No essence centers. It is possible to induce in them faith, caused by things of which they have no experience. Beliefs are superimposed, chiefly on tickling of their weaknesses.

Love: The differences in descriptions of ten different persons; none would describe genuine love. Three suggestions:

- It functions to serve as mainspring for desire for perfection and a rest from labors for perfection.
- For sensations of bliss in the intervals which follow rest and effort.
- For mutual possible aid in striving to overcome the effects or kundabuffer.

Now one loves because others give encouragement or stimulus

or praise; or because features resemble oneself for whom one has a physical polarity.

Hope: Worse than the others, in a mangled state adapted to the weakness of the psyche, consequently more and more crystallized and cannot get real faith, hope, love. The artificial hope is always hoping of something unreal, a paralysis of those functions by which they might overcome the properties of kundabuffer. The result is a nervous illness called "tomorrow." This afflicts those who by chance learn of the presence of undesirable features and the efforts necessary. They always imagine they will be better able tomorrow.

He returns to the mountain and looks for other means. Is there anything in us worth appealing to? Reason is ineffective because we flow into subjective moulds. No use preaching sanity to madmen; a mere presentation of a new truth in reasonable form is not enough. In this chapter is also a critique of the emotions. Not only our ideas, our sincerity, our faith, hope and love, our emotions, which we think are more profound, are here questioned.

Then what is there still in essence which is not acquired nor corrupted? A product of a few real impressions of our subconscious. He discovers a fourth sacred function: objective conscience. It is still in its primordial state because it's never used in ordinary life and hence not corrupted. He devoted himself to the development of conditions for a few who would aid him to rediscover and develop this function.

Attempt to discover an analogy in us with what he means by objective conscience (by function he means psychological activity); e.g. an occasional sense that there must be some meaning to life and that happiness is not a sufficient explanation. A "sense of sin" but not in the conventional sense, a curiosity with a sense of guilt, a dim sense of having a purpose. Ecstasy, delight, etc. tinged with sadness. But no conscious external appeal can be made since the conscience and even the subconsciousness listens through threefold corrupted channels. Hence the individual must do something in strange conditions. Self-observation with self-review. Draw out from the subconsciousness and put into the conscious, the voice of objective conscience. Beelzebub adds that during his sixth descent (1900–17) he looks for traces of Ashiata's brotherhood. He found only one tablet with sentences erected in the city of Babylon; texts and reminders. One of these is the treasure of a brotherhood in Central Asia. (Asia is our substitute for essence) These sentences of faith, hope and love are:

1. Faith with reason (consciousness) is freedom; faith based on understanding—that reasons why.

2. Emotional faith is weakness.

3. Instinctive faith is stupidity.

4. Love with reason (consciousness) evokes the same in response.

5. Emotional love invariably evokes its opposite.

6. Physical love depends merely on the accidents of type and polarity.

7. Hope, a reasonable aspiration, with reason (consciousness) is strength.

8. Emotional hope is slavery.

9. Instinctive hope is disease.

Ashiata's effort from Gurdjieff's point of view is the most intelligent effort made by a human being at world reform. He began by preparing himself; and concluded that all his ideas opinions etc. were conditioned.

He made a review of his past life and emptied himself of all accidental impressions. Until then he could have no objective view of different methods, he came to native essential judgment which had not been conditioned towards faith, hope and love. He found a native human quality not dependent on the chances of environment. It was not necessary to use a special vocabulary for people. He looked for something as fixed in the species as the nature of a lion or a wolf. He named this objective conscience and set about finding a number of people in whom this objective conscience was nearer the surface than in most. He chose thirty-six, mostly from monasteries in the neighborhood. He does not mean buildings but independent thinkers, capable of thinking against current sociological trends. Every independent thinker "lives in a monastery." He taught cosmic truths, not yet truths to the thirty-six.

a. Ideal pattern of the potentialities of man; the relation between man and the cosmos. Octave and semitone as difficulty, presented as theories.

b. Then he directed their psychological effort so as to increase their awareness (taught the method of self-observation).

c. Taught them so as to persuade and convince one hundred others.

Two requirements:
1. Self-understanding.
2. Ability to persuade and convince others.

He called these thirty-six—priests. These persuaded and convinced one hundred so that each of these could persuade and convince a hundred others, "sons" and "grandsons" who could persuade others, initiates. 5,000 to 6,000 BC was the beginning of priests and initiates—self-perpetuation. Since Babylon was the metropolis of the world, all intellectuals were soon within range and in a decade all were familiar with the concept of objective conscience; and it became a universally accepted standard of value among intellectuals.

For about three hundred years the civilization built on this prospered. The political state, racial prejudice etc. disappeared; art, science etc. underwent change and were related to the standard of objective conscience. During this period of three hundred years was something approximating the Golden Age, with works of an international character with universal values. This was ended by a counter-revolution whose leader was Lentrohamox. (Lenin-Trotsky. Hamox, being Egyptian, served to give a mystical connotation with political significance.)

Look at the form of government that eventuated from this propaganda of Ashiata and how this government was destroyed by Lentrohamox. You can draw a parallel between a sociological story and individual application. In each of us there is an Ashiata and a Lentrohamox comparable to these "epic motives" in the sociological story. Appeals to faith, hope and love made to us today, have already a tone of sentimentality. An appeal made with these for a base would bring out a little revulsion. We would say this is not logical, i.e. we are intellectually on guard against it as a result of education. Same as the Babylonians. We are equally civilized and equally corrupt, demanding intellectual proof.

Yet Ashiata had before him the example of the world's greatest dialectician, subtle reasoner and logician in Buddha. He's acknowledged among the Hindus as the greatest. Yet Buddha made himself so misunderstood that within a generation of his death his own disciples misinterpreted him. Why? Because our reason is as conditioned as our emotions. What is rational is determined by our education. Hence a fair skepticism includes reason.

Ashiata realized the way reformers before him had failed and that so would everyone after him who appealed to faith, hope and love. He proposed to appeal to something we have not yet rationalized; and which few of us unless in desperate circumstances has ever had personal knowledge of.

Why is a dog always a dog? Why does it always behave like a dog? Why in certain circumstances does it go to its own death? Why not behave, as we would say, reasonably? It behaves as it does because it is obliged to be what it is, be the outcome what it may. A dog is indifferent to whether it's rising or dropping in the scale, whether multiplying or becoming extinct. It is innocent; has objective conscience. Mineral, vegetable, animal, instinctively obey the law of their species. No need of psychological effort. A fixed species, no evil. Man is fixed externally, but psychologically has in him every species. He can on occasion be a dog, mouse, lion etc. Examine yourself and others. Elasticity produces doubt as to ones real fixed nature. Man is note "si" in the octave in which all other notes are fixed but with the potentiality of other notes. Man is an elastic species with possibilities of dropping or rising psychologically. This introduces the problem of objective conscience as a matter of choice and responsibility. Consciousness that no other animal possesses as a possibility.

Animals are incarnate actualities. The note "si" is precarious, a responsibility. Now it's possible ascent or descent, the realization of possibilities—The Terror of the Situation, Ashiata. Objective conscience is the awareness of possibilities, latent in us. What is right and wrong? Among our possibilities are those of growth or of degeneration. At one time our choice of possibilities has a degenerative character; we are becoming "apes," not animals. Our criterion of values is between up and down; this implies that man is a free agent.

Nature as such is indifferent as to the direction of which possibility is actualized. We have bodies, in a biological sense, for either movement. The criterion is within. This "right or wrong" is nothing natural, it cannot be sought in biological values and biological welfare, it is not a criterion. There is not only a standard of right and wrong in biology but to what ought to be. This introduces the idea of values for outsiders. This introduces the idea which Ashiata calls "God," i.e. a determinant that each develops his potentialities in a higher direction. The species below man does not need this. In man who is the first of a biological species to occupy this critical point in the scale and to cooperate with the plan imposed on the universe by its founder—the evolution of the universe.

Ashiata said that part of the scheme required that at a certain point should appear a number of self-conscious agents, not servants who would cooperate in carrying out this arbitrary plan, i.e., no universal right and wrong. We have the choice between cooperation and frustration. In every human being this is the ultimate criterion of value; exemplified in experiences in which one has felt that there is something one will not do, come what may. Will not and cannot—essence of essence.

Ashiata proposes to bring this into consciousness and build upon it. The measure of the distance that our ordinary lives are from this consciousness is the un-seriousness with which we regard the things that happen to us. We should carry a vivid sense of values into everything we do. Hence Ashiata instituted the method.

Objective conscience means "consciousness of our cosmic duty." Trees subserve certain cosmic functions as they change certain solar energies (emanations) into terrestrial energies, the vegetable kingdom acts as a transforming agent, deposits energies chemically into the planet. Human beings were not possible until this had preceded us. Human bodies are made from vegetable and animal substances. We are also chemical transforming agents. We enrich the chemical composition of the planet with our bodies, energies not otherwise collectible. There are three transforming centers; each transforms in a special field of energies—solar into terrestrial.

But it is also according to the theory of possibility. That unlike mineral, vegetable and animal, this can be done and at the same time potentialities and powers are developed which will result in individuality, consciousness and will. This is not biological but normal for human development—normal man and normal objective development by which this norm can be attained. What is this norm? (See last week, the difference between normal and average; between standard and statistical.)

What is the aim of existence?

Ashiata defines it in five items or commandments; and objective morality for pupils:

1. Maintenance of a state of readiness of the planetary body which we happen to have inherited; this is to be interpreted in a larger sense than merely health. "Readiness" excludes crystallized habits and special skills. Elasticity kept so that the body is ready for the use of intelligence. Special skill which is obtained by the loss of elasticity is a violation of instinctive morality.

Gurdjieff mentioned forty or fifty crafts he had been interested in. In none was he a specialist. He had two purposes: to give the instinctive center the feel; to be ready for potential needs.

Ancient drama, destined to develop and maintain elasticity of function. A variety of roles, each role necessarily employed the body in different techniques. This had to be played physiologically.

We find in ourselves a feeling of criticism in regard to a specialist in any physiological field, e.g. gymnastics. Consideration is only partial but is based on a sense that the ideal development would be in the direction of wholeness. Maintain an elastic and ever-ready state.

2. The aim always to have an undiminishing curiosity and hunger and thirst for improving oneself in the way of being.

There are three main possibilities of human development: being more, knowing more, doing more.

It is yet impossible to formulate methods for increasing being: "Oh yes, he knows everything but he himself is nothing," or, "Oh yes, he has done all sorts of spectacular things but himself is nothing."

3. Our criticism implies a "conscious aim to know more and more concerning the meaning and purpose of world creation and world maintenance."

The characteristic preoccupation of moments of seriousness: what does life mean? We are only reduced to this question in moments of despair or danger; i.e., reduced to essence. Most of life is spent in socialization and when one is indifferent to sociology, one asks this. This is of the essence. (Story of the cathode ray.)

The Akhaldans in Atlantis took as their scientific objective, the discovery of the meaning and purpose of life. This question recurs to all of us in our essential moments.

The Akhaldans were the first and last scientific society to openly make its objective to answer this question. Modern science does not begin to touch the questions that arise in every man in essential moments, "Why are we alive?" If an answer to this is necessary in order to cooperate and cooperation is a conscious obligation, the interest in this becomes a practical need and not a parlor curiosity.

4. To pay off as quickly as possible the debt we have incurred in the process of becoming conscious beings.

This introduces a sort of terror. That we are here as biological beings is a fact. At the same time, we are conscious, an individual. For individuality, plus biological existence, we are indebted to something. This does not say whether we are glad. At any rate we are psychologically and biologically experiencing through a physical body and psychical mechanism of coordination.

Can I say that I owe my biological body and nature, and that I owe my entity? But this already puts me in debt. I start my conscious existence in debt for the fact that I exist. Pay off? How? In order to leave myself free, in order voluntarily to undertake real service for the cosmos.

This is where voluntary effort begins, not to discharge debts but to carry forward a movement, which depends on individual initiative. Only when this voluntary (conscious) effort begins are we in this fourth: "To aim to pay off, quickly, the debt for ones arising and individuality in order to lighten the burden of His Endlessness, a burden carried by a comparatively few shoulders."

5. In the aim always to help the speedy improvement of all beings including those like oneself and others, to self-realization, in the ability to say "I am," with a content not dependent on external phenomena; or at least not put hindrances in their way.

These five objectives dictated by essences. Everyone in whom objective consciousness was active would find himself formulating. Our ordinary lives are far from this; we may have thought of these—as ideals but not as practical obligations. What sort of morality do we have in place of it?

A lion is what it is; we are without a sense of good and bad; have right and wrong but are corrupted into a sense of good and evil by sociological forces yet our individual sense of right and wrong is so vague, that only in occasional moments can we formulate with assurance. "How do we come to be without this clear sense of what is proper to man?"

Let us assume for the moment that these five are correct aims. Then why have we not been trained to pursue them?

The answer is mythologized in the book as a split in the planet, into essential and artificial. Sociological values are produced at the expense of essence. A restoration of the species man to his original potentialities is necessary. Atonement—at-one-ment, a reintegration of the psyche of man. This implies that at one point of history there is a possibility of reintegrating man, who previously had been doomed to be fragmentary. The habits man acquired when he was necessarily fragmentary and when it was impossible to develop self- and cosmic-consciousness, persisted in civilized forms. All civilizations have become impediments because they are based on conditions which no longer exists and in which self-consciousness is impossible.

National distinctions, racial and caste; science and art, these began during the fragmentary period. Not one based on essence. If essence demands the development of self- and cosmic-consciousness, it follows that race; caste, etc. are not based on essence.

From a consciousness viewpoint an individual might be entitled to rank as superior, a high being; but from the point of view of race as inferior. Sociological values are not cosmic and vice versa, superior and inferior. There are men and women honored sociologically who from the point of view of the cosmos are empty of value.

How does it come that we, unprejudiced as we think we are, are subtly under one or another of these prejudices, and cannot think essentially without coloring our impressions?

A candid, rigid, self-review of life will lead to the answer to this question. We will discover the degree to which all essential values are colored by prejudices of race, education, profession etc.

Ashiata undertakes to rouse this essential standard and leaves his disciples to their own devices. He aids by formulating a norm. It is very important to make this review. You will observe that you find yourself in making this review predisposed to make judgments of good and bad based on the conception of self-interest. A radical critique of our existing conscious psychology, which all presupposes one value: egoism. Ashiata's critique is that our greatest implicit value is egoism and not voluntary cosmic service. Our individual conscience is the voice of self-interest.

Take the simplest example—castes. Usually in three main groups:

1. Ruling—possessing.
2. Fighting—professional.
3. Laboring—industrial and agrarian.

What is the difference found to be in the character of their egoism and selfishness, the character of their cunning, the presence or absence of domineering; a federation of individuals in whom selfishness is supplemented by certain vices, such as cunning, hatred and inhumanity? How did the different castes come? Not by self-interest since all are equally egoistic but by cunning. The ruling class has selfishness plus cunning; the professional as such selfishness but with less cunning; and the manual has still less cunning. There is a contest between varying degrees of cunning. When the three combine we have a nation; when nations combine we have a race. None of them any guide to cosmic values.

[*Orage spoke of his connection with the radical labor movement.*]

Egoism and cunning are sociological values while cosmic values are essence and voluntary service. Cosmic service is versus interplay of egoisms. A crowd of individuals is equally selfish; neither proposes a greater value to which they are willing to submit. A larger number whether nation, mob or race has merely a numerical advantage.

Ashiata points to a criterion higher than both, by the degree to which objective conscience is individually realized. Ethical conflict between individuals and races reconciled. Not for human functions but for developing functions.

Special technique: self-observation, self-perfecting; self-expression. This is the first step toward self-realization and bringing into consciousness objective conscience. As this is pursued awareness of purpose begins to dawn, and the five commands begin to take on a personal meaning. They cease to be merely intellectually interesting. The individual then begins to lose his sociological coloring and sheds his sociological moralities. He grows more free and more responsible, he takes on a severer morality. (Ordinary anti-moralism is quite mechanically moral.)

Lentrohamox fell under the temptation to substitute for the aim of cosmic-consciousness the aim of happiness. Happiness resulting from the discharge of a cosmic purpose is divine happiness; but happiness pursued for its own sake is the opposite.

18 APRIL 1927

I should be extremely interested to know how many have been able to retain the thread of the discussion in mind from last week.

The efforts of a reformer—first to prepare himself.

Ashiata Shiemash decided that all his impressions from infancy were subjectively formed, i.e. conditioned. So having gained an attitude of impartiality he did permit himself to consider his conclusions as of any value. He then concluded that here was in the essence of all human beings an untainted, native quality—named objective conscience. He thereafter set about his task by first of all selecting a number of beings (three A's) chosen chiefly from the monasteries of his neighborhood—not buildings but lone thinkers—whose essence was a little nearer the surface than usual. First he instructed them in certain cosmic truths:

1. True pattern of man—his relation to the cosmos—the law of the octave, including introduction, influence, necessity of the introduction of the semitone.

2. Self-observation—increasing awareness.

3. He taught them to formulate these truths so that they could each persuade a hundred other beings in such a way that each of the hundred could and would be able to persuade and convince a hundred additional by their emotions and their reason. Then each was called "priest," these when able to persuade 100 others were called "initiates." So in ten years all the intellectual, instinctive, and emotional outlook of all the intellectuals in and about Babylon was changed.

For three hundred years this civilization prospered—racial differences, caste differences, national differences disappeared. This was the Golden Age lasting five hundred years. It was put to an end by a sort of counter revolution lead by Lentrohamsanin (Lenin-Trotsky).

The form of government that eventuated from the propaganda disseminated by Ashiata Shiemash.

We must make a parallel between physiological and psychological development.

The first thing to realize by self-examination is that which appeals to our hope, love, faith. It will be regarded by us as a little sentimental, as a little under suspicion—due to our education. We say—prove this!

Buddha appealed to logic, subtlety, and reason, but though he was a master of dialectic in one generation his teachings were perverted.

Our reason is just as unreliable in its usual state as our emotions.

Ashiata Shiemash knew that every reformer had and would fail if the subjectivity of mankind were not taken into account. He proposed to appeal to something in us that we have not yet rationalized.

I propose to speak of this now, though we have not—most of us—experienced it. I will speak of the objective conscience of the whole of the animal kingdom.

Why does a dog always obey the obligation laid upon him, to be what he should be? It is a matter of indifference to dogs whether their kind disappears from the earth or not—whether they are going up or down the evolutionary scale. They cannot do what is wrong, for they obey the law of their being.

But man, psychologically, is "capable" of being any animal which produces in him a state of doubt which makes a choice possible. Because he is the note si in the biological scale. Man is not a fixed note but may proceed up or down the scale. Animals being a fixed note do fill all their requirements.

But man is capable of first, a simple awareness of possibilities. It is possible that man is a free agent, i.e. he has the possibility in him of either proceeding up or down the scale, actualizing either the lower or higher series of possibilities. It is a matter of difference to nature which man actualizes.

Not right or wrong—but "something that ought to be." This introduces God as the final determinant which decrees that a being with choice must actualize the higher series. So man has an objective conscience which may make him consciously determine to cooperate with the design of God.

So Ashiata Shiemash created thirty-six beings as his sons, not slaves but conscious beings.

In every human being there is this criteria of values—you may have felt that there is something that you will not do, come what may. The alternative of death by torture or giving the life to one you love. In such a case you may find you are pushed against a wall beyond which you cannot go—God, Devil, or man notwithstanding. This would be objective conscience. But the truth is that in all circumstances this consciousness would operate. A vivid sense of right and wrong would operate.

Consciousness of our cosmic duty is objective conscience. Trees act in accord with their own objective conscience—certain emanations of the sun are conveyed into the atmosphere and contribute to the chemical constitution of this planet. Humans were preceded by vegetable and animal kingdoms necessarily for the substances to form a human body, were by them transmuted into earth material.

So we in turn have three transforming instruments which transform solar energies into terrestrial substances. But in addition we have the possibility of simultaneously attaining by conscious effort: individuality, consciousness and understanding or will.

What is the difference between normal and average? It is the difference between standard and statistic—what ought to be and what is.

What is the aim of existence?

1. Maintenance in a state of readiness the planetary body which we happen to have inherited—the idea of health plus readiness, excluding the idea of habits or specialized skills. One should be potentially capable of any accomplishment that might be required. Gurdjieff had familiarized himself with fifty or sixty crafts in order to keep him in a state of readiness, elasticity for any effort directed by intelligence—this is the first aim dictated by objective conscience. (So we feel a little contemptuous of a highly specialized development in a man—a gymnast for example.)

2. The aim always to have an undiminished curiosity and hunger and thirst for improving oneself in being. Always to have the wish to be more and always to know more. Usually the more knowledge a man has the less we find him to be when we meet him. The same with one who has done much. Although there are no institutions to help us, we all feel that unless we become something more we shall have failed in our lives.

3. A conscious aim to know more and more is not at all in the nature of an answer. Not merely a parlor question, but a state in which everything including our own behavior will present itself as a possible clue to the solution of this one problem. But I am tonight for the first time—not second time—in a state or attitude where the statements seem not quite defensible. I am in a horrible state due to subjective lack of confidence. I came to you in the hope that this may be the result of chief feature, i.e. chief defect rather. Certainly I shall—so help me—continue to attend these groups. For I cannot reasonably do otherwise.

4. To pay as quickly as possible the debt we have incurred in the process of becoming conscious responsible beings. This introduces a

sort of terror. We are here as biological beings and at the same time we are conscious, i.e. individuals, in order thereafter to be able to lighten as much as possible the burden of our common father.

5. To aim always to help the speediest development of all other beings up to the scale of reason—to the sacred degree of self- individuality.

These are the conscious objectives. You will understand as a usual being on earth today, how far from realizing these normal obligations of a being of man we are.

There occurred a split by virtue of which our total planet became separated into something essential and something artificial—so that we human beings owe to this the fact that we have both an essential conscience and an artificial one. So we are producing sociological values at the expense of essential values.

This is an effect of kundabuffer and during the time of its presence—it was not possible to attain consciousness, self-individuality or will and certainly not cosmic-consciousness. And on account of traditions imposed during this period we now find it almost impossible in the absence of that organ to do so. Due to our civilization which is a product of that period, we still fail to develop, or perceive the possibility of developing.

The criticism of Gurdjieff of indicting man for egoism—putting self above cosmic good is, cockeyed.

It is exactly to say that one cannot fight his own kind but that he can engage in a cosmic war. And the noble thing, he infers, may well be to sacrifice himself to that cause. What difference between that and international war—nobly undertaken, as we say?

Selfishness plus cunning:

1. Rulers.
2. Professionals.
3. Laborers.

Gurdjieff criticizes God and man—negatively.

What is cosmic service?

He never says:

Why?

Where do we go from here?

What is beauty or love?

Certainly he has suggested a valuable method, i.e. to include, first of all oneself in all observation of phenomena.

It looks to me as though I were to find myself down among the swine feeding on husks soon. Well, so be it, if it must be so.

Split personality in the case of Mrs. Piper, see account of Dr. Brinc. Mrs. Piper was subject to attacks of amnesia and perhaps a year after would turn up pursuing a different occupation. She has about nine variations of her personality. This is an extreme case of a split or multiple personality.

The diagnosis of the psychic condition of man is that he is suffering as a race from split personality. Do some of us under the influence of a strong emotion, drug or drink ever suffer temporary fracture, so to speak without memory? Try to imagine one of our friends attacked by amnesia. It is impossible to remind them in this state of their normal state. What means would you use to remind him of what he is? This is the problem of the religious reformer, dealing with the race to remind it of its normal condition.

It is familiar to history that people under certain emotional stress ask: "Why am I alive?" The vagaries of such are very much alike in all times and races. This is responsible for religions, folklore superstitions, etc. as well as poetry. There are occasional flashes as when Mrs. Piper says to herself: "Who am I?" There are moments of partial recollection of states of consciousness which once were. There is a Hindu-story of the child who sang in the womb "Let me remember who I am." And his first cry after birth is: "I have forgotten!" We have drunken from the River Lethe.

At one time doctrines were concealed in fairy tales—lost doctrine and lost memory, the sleeping princess, which is each of us. If we were awake to this we would be aware, the prodigal son (see The Hymn of the Robe of Glory.) Voluntarily or on mission we leave for a foreign country with knowledge of our mission—objective reason and objective conscience. En route we begin to forget. We are absorbed in our associations. After a long period of feeding swine, there is a flash of recollection.

The problem of Ashiata was that of anyone of us who was dealing with a friend suffering from amnesia. We begin by talking about things they used to be familiar with and real, memorable incidents, hoping the chance word will reawaken the memory. Or we take him back to familiar scenes; or begin to talk in terms of present reason, e.g. Mrs. Piper in a shop. How do you like it? Where were you before? Or if the present condition is below normal one might try reproach. The prodigal son realized it because he was lying on husks the swine ate. The method of Ashiata is the same. There is nothing occult about it or supernatural. It is just common sense.

Ashiata began with thirty-six three-centered beings with the possibility of development to six centers. (Three higher centers.) Enough to start with. He began by trying to remind them of their early associations, e.g. by instructing them in cosmic truths, with which they were once familiar. This implies that this should be childhood possession; for it is not abnormal to be aware of our place and function in the cosmos. Our abnormality is that it was a matter of guessing. Ashiata hoped that as he talked, some chance word would awaken their own knowledge of these truths. Not trying to substantiate logically, but to reawaken ideas buried in the subconscious. He supplemented talk with directions as to personal method—self-observation. Ouspensky uses the phrase self-remembering—by attention to the organism to reawaken original identity, so that they should cease to be identified with the planetary body. (The far country to which the prodigal son had gone.)

By attempting to review the past life and by doing it daily it was hoped that a detached and objective attitude would be made easier to take an objective attitude. Try reviewing your past life pictorially. Help in the daily review to take this attitude; *these things happened to my planetary body.* Wake each morning with a little more detachment. Arouse a personal sense of shame as a fulcrum for objective conscience.

Two kinds of shame: by discovering failure in some conventional duty or a sense of contrast between what you had been and what you have become. Recognition—first think of objective conscience. Not necessarily associated with an understanding of objective reason. We realize that we know nothing; we have no sense of purpose, driftwood etc. but these moments may merely leave us a little more desolate.

The first difficulty encountered by Ashiata and later the cause of his failure. Nevertheless this state is the only sufficiently intense state to provoke the necessary energy or impetus for attaining objective reason. Not one of us will ever understand the cosmos until it becomes a personal problem; that is, that we feel the need to end this ignorance. But how long may this Purgatory (emotion without power) last? Ashiata formulated simple rules of objective morality. If entertained they will induce intensification of understanding of objective reason and objective conscience.

Be more—more conscious, more will, more individuality.

These five even if taken only mechanically will aid other measures for awakening objective consciousness (emotional center) and attain objective reason (intellectual center). Our present consciousness is in the instinctive center. Ashiata—trying to develop the two higher centers. Awakens the emotional center which gives a push to develop the intellectual.

Ashiata prepared a propagandist body. Consider the remarkable organization of the Knights Templars or Order of Chivalry, where some of the noblemen began apprenticeship in the kitchen. Compare the energy with the effect of any propaganda now to make people forego certain comforts.

[*Orage was familiar with Ely Cathedral; before the site was a swamp, occupied by wild fowl, there was no stone. A small group of people came using the name of the Christian religion. Stone was brought by the river. It was apparently a hopeless project. Those who began it must have had a high degree of will, consciousness and individuality.*]

Ashiata proposed:

1. Unlearning.
2. Re-education.
3. With a small number of re-educated people he would re-educate the whole race.

A religion reformed by purely psychological means. 300–400 years, inscriptions, doctrines, sculptures, religions, traces of world-culture about 5,000 to 4,000 BC, with a ruling class in agreement as to the ends, aims and means of culture. A universal language of ideas and ideals. Speech in terms of value with local variations.

Reaction was incarnated by Lentro-hamox, embodying certain resistance (Lenin-Trotsky and results). Propaganda simply based; with awakening of objective conscience it unfortunately happens that objective reason does not come to life and hence for a time one suffers a sense of guilt without having the means of coming to a rational understanding, e.g. to go somewhere with a purpose. By leaving, the remembrance becomes fragmentary and the situation changes and cannot be carried out. The degree of suffering is the degree of importance once attached to the plan. Thus we have the same pang when we try to formulate whence we came, for we cannot remember. This state is almost unendurable. Most people in this state will take some narcotic, such as religion, service to others in desperation. Lentro-hamox is the personification of the unwillingness in us to tolerate any larger objective conscience without objective reason. Lentro-hamox chooses to work on those who have not yet developed any objective reason. He started methodically. There were a small number of the dissatisfied who were beginning to think there was no hope of attaining reason in proportion to the suffering. He said there was only one thing for us in life and that was the pursuit of happiness and happiness means not being obliged to do anything. Freedom is the definition of man; and freedom means choice, freedom from obligation.

Ashiata had said that man had a sense of obligation to discharge the service for which he was created and would find himself evolving only to the degree he carried out this obligation. We did not choose this. Lentro-hamox critique is that of a good philosopher but a pure rationalist. He said that if man was created for service he was therefore created a slave. He will repudiate this service and attain to absolute freedom. Very crafty and plausible plea. It finds us in certain moods, ready to consider it very convincing. Why should we after just escaping from the role of mutton and wool find ourselves morally obligated to take on another service? He presented this under the terms of freedom and happiness and countered the propaganda of Ashiata. Lentro-hamox was neither a monster nor a traitor; there was nothing diabolic in the defeat of Ashiata. There is already enough in our reason to defeat Ashiata, Jesus Christ or Buddha.

The weakness of the Lentro-hamox position. Only from a state of urgency can one realize understanding; then without this urge such understanding is impossible. Credit God with some subtlety, when Jesus said "Love your enemies" he knew the impossibility and therefore taught a method by means of which these commandments could be practiced. When undertaking the incarnation of a world, God made certain emotional and moral experiences as a prerequisite for development of reason. Lentro-hamox figured it was possible to attain understanding without paying the price of emotional experience, etc. Rationally he was right; but wrong in fact. There can be no cosmic-consciousness without a sense of cosmic obligation (objective conscience). Lentro-hamox left out of account the emotional element both in himself and in the world. In this sense he becomes the forerunner of our spiritual ancestors—the Greeks and Romans, the beginnings of civilization for us. Anything before them we consider "ancient," "Barbaric." Gurdjieff says the Babylonian civilization was superior to the Greek. We date from the Greeks. Gurdjieff says the Greeks descend, not from Ashiata, but from Lentro-hamox, the rationalist without any higher emotional urge. Two possible streams but we inherited this one.

A period of world culture, then revolt. We are the inheritors of the revolt. The tradition was that the followers of Ashiata withdrew into small groups. Small communities found down even to the time of Alexander the Great; but the main line of tradition was rationalism. Geographically limited, individually limited. These little caves and occult schools are in our subconsciousness. Lentro-hamox inaugurated the modern, negative and subjective. Transfer from cosmopolitanism to egotism.

All explanations of life are now based on personal prejudice, for our preservation. We cannot formulate a philosophy except from the point of view of personal interest. Nietzsche said, "I no longer ask of a philosopher, is it true? But what was the interest for the philosopher?"

Even reform movements, industrial, radical movements in England must, if there is no sense of cosmic obligation, become personal. Without higher emotion all philosophy becomes a matter of the head with a view to personal welfare. Subjectively colored and egotistically determined. Our reason, being subjective, is already degenerated, that is egotistically determined. Our world view is subjective, i.e. the notion that the world is not an instrument formed by God for use and that he has no use for us; that God did not create the universe for any practical purpose, like a sensible being but out of sheer benevolence and only wants us to be happy, he accordingly likes chiefly those who are themselves happy or who make others happy. The implication is that it is our chief purpose to be happy and the path to happiness is to make others happy. This is a childish attitude; yet it is Schopenhauer's. Another variation is that only individual happiness counts; this is the philosophy of the ruling class, the subjective error into which Nietzsche fell, that mankind exists for the development of a few supermen. This assumption is common to certain types, the Napoleonic. The opposite is another variation that the individual does not count. "What matters my happiness if there is a little progress?" Sociological progress may be at the expense of the individuals who make up society, resulting in a collective organization of individuals devoid of essence. Still another variant is modern science, which proceeds by accumulated facts in the hope that some later generation will receive understanding. Will not the habit of collecting more facts continue?

Always postponing the struggle to understand till tomorrow—a habit of putting off. Tomorrow and a later generation—the utilization of means which in themselves are of no use. Typical scientist.

The notion of God as a father varies with subjective experience. Or the notion that the universe is a sort of school, where there is teaching. Maybe it is a school where there is learning but not teaching.

Objective reason is not to be attained by any subjective or egoistic emotion, personal anguish. Objective conscience is necessary. Gurdjieff's cosmology may sound ridiculous, but in competition with the infantile concepts which are implicit in our point of view they are manly and intelligent. We think we escape the cosmology by being frightened of specific words. It is a fact that the world has a meaning and also that we have a relation to it.

Ashiata says: there is a method by which we can arrive at an objective understanding of what is. Lentro-hamox says: there is a means of accommodating ourselves to what is, without understanding what it is.

The success of Lentro-hamox was established by Greek tradition. The Greeks were responsible for the corruption of human reason. As a result it is almost impossible for an objective conscience to be developed since then. The Romans are responsible for the corruption of the organic conscience.

We had been considering the purpose of the fifth descent.

Now the sixth descent to discover why the existence of three-centered beings is diminishing. Recent statistics in Europe and America show an increase. Why does Beelzebub assume a decrease? Consider the parable. (Exercise of the faculty which later becomes intuition, guessing in reading the parable, perhaps this indirect method of formulation is used to stimulate this faculty. Exercise patience and remain alert, reading between the lines.)

What is Beelzebub talking about when he says existence is contracting? Not directly of the body. Our existence as three-centered beings demands the exercising of all functions, remaining elastic in all three centers. At about twenty-five or thirty, the majority of men cease thinking, not mechanically but originally. At forty they cease to have originality of feeling. They continue to vegetate due to sociological hygiene but are one- or two-thirds dead. Perhaps it is in the light of this that Beelzebub's statement is to be read; as "vital statistics" of three-centered existence. What is the cause of this premature death? The failure to develop in children an objective conscience; the absence of this crystallization of emotional-moral realization.

This stresses the importance of two questions in reading this book. By what can we recognize objective conscience? Have we got it? Knowing why we were born, what is proper to me and what is not proper or becoming for me, apart from sociological right and wrong. An innate sense of what is proper to a three-centered being. This would give us a compass as a guide to what for us would be right and wrong. Also give a stimulus, what is proper is desirable, emotion leading to motion; steer to a recognized goal. This would have been a natural growth, beings normally brought up would have had this compass and consequently would steer toward development of will, consciousness and individuality.

Normal human society with normal education would have found all its members consciously arriving at development of astral and mental bodies with the objective of finally arriving at objective reason. To understand at first hand the reason of world origin and world maintenance.

But we have a split personality (stealing our birthright, Esau, similar allegory of a split personality).

We find substitutes for objective conscience, objective reason, will, consciousness and individuality, etc. We have these things by name only: philosophy, science, art, religion, sport, health and well-being. These are merely names, shadows like ourselves.

Amundsen's airship passing over polar regions, so near that his compass pointed nowhere in particular but merely moved; he had no criterion of direction. Suppose a conference on board; it would be forced to rely on guesses. Conceive this state of mind. Any direction might be wrong. Even if we agree, this is no criterion, merely a practical unanimity (fallacy of the pragmatic school). This is our situation, our compass being gone. None of us has any clear interior sense of the direction of life. We are in space and compelled to move. The only direction in which we can move is that agreed upon by those around us. Hence the confidence in sociological conventions, morals and ideals. It is a pragmatic agreement. The subjective criterion is either individual, idiosyncratic, rebellious, etc. or conventional. From an objective point of view there is not a pin to choose between them. Both are subjective.

In these circumstances we fall into various sophistries, e.g. the criterion of value is adaptation (evolution). Much of psychoanalytic ethics is based on this. The whole of Jung's school is based on this: "Are we adapted?" Then we must be right. This might be called "hanging on or running down." It is the posture of maximum comfort—the substitution of means for ends. If one has no end one will tend to overvalue the means (and in proportion the end ceases to be realized), e.g. the end of philosophy is truth; our means is reason. But in absence of truth we tend to admire ingenuity of reasoning, in any given school. We succumb to brilliance of process, epigram, reasoning, etc. This is worshipping the means. The end of arriving at justice is the end of law. The means of arriving at justice is impartiality. The method of impartiality is formulated by rules applying to all. We have become legalists. We pursue legal forms and legality instead of psychological forms and justice.

Also, what is the end of sex? From an objective point of view, it is twofold, procreation and self-creation, the creation in us of an astral and mental body. The procreation of planetary bodies; the creation of emotional and intellectual bodies. Thanks to the Romans we find ourselves using it objectivelessly. We have substituted the pursuit of pleasure derived from the process, for the satisfactions derived from the realization of the end. Playing with reason; playing with sex. Playing with forces, titillation, masturbation. Doomed to sociological standards and approval. "Beware, when all men speak well of thee." "Do this to the Lord and not to men." A warning against taking sociological criteria. We are bound to do this in the absence of objective criteria; the interior spring of action being gone.

We run on three springs of a mechanical kind, which are wound up by external circumstances. Like a clock with three springs, depending on external circumstances and which cannot move, with self-determining. In this chapter are some details of the winding, degree, intensity and kind of winding:

1. Heredity and general biological ancestry.

2. Conditions and environment at the moment of conception (conditions means planetary; environment means local circumstances).

3. Life in the complete sense of parents and the part of the mother during period of gestation.

4. The being manifestations of parents during the period of growing up of the child, the behavior which arises naturally from the being of the parents.

5. Corresponding being or essential behavior of others than the parents who come into contact with the child.

6. Good wishes of beings of the same blood, whether absent or near. Old wives wisdom. What is the reason for this? Celebration of birthdays etc.

7. Character of effort made by a growing child to understand why he is alive. This is hard for westerners to understand. The form this wonder takes is often embarrassing to parents. When we are asked "how was I born?" meaning "why am I alive?" we give only direct sexual significance. If a true answer were given to a true question we would probably find ourselves telling a series of fairy tales with implicit and not explicit answers to these questions. This would satisfy the emotional craving.

These determine the potentialities of experience, which we later "live out." Having been wound up the child goes out of this enlarged sociological womb into the world. His potentialities are fixed.

Not all thoughts may be thought by it, though later there may be an intense desire to understand certain things. Not all emotions may be felt by it but certain emotional experiences later, at thirty or forty may be made possible by certain contacts with strangers or associates for ten minutes. Also physical.

Experience, what is it? Dewey's problem. The release of springs in ourselves by external agencies, that gives what we call consciousness of thought or emotion or action, assuming that we can experience a thought or emotion or action. Will an external agency tick it off? Accident? Chance? As a rule our emotional potentiality is ticked off slowly, so that we still have reserves. In cases of shell-shock large reserves are ticked off in a short time. It also is possible for the intellectual center to be so stimulated by thought that the potentialities run out. Not through shock but through titillation, reading to excess, thinking without an objective, following our interests, playing with reason. In reading we respond with intellect to the thought presented and in responding, the potentialities of being are checked off. He is passive and after a few years of reading is incapable of an original thought.

Art: Those who pursue it have as aim an object of beauty. But when the object is presented they must make an emotional response automatically; if this continues response ceases, e.g. curators of museums. Those who make pursuit, sooner reach the point of having no more responses. They are then forced to repeat the formulation of what were once real responses, a psychopathological state. In this state they think they are now ready to enter a creative stage; that having exhausted the meaning and significance of the past they can produce—cubism, futurism etc. These are offspring of the aged, imaginary children. Socrates begs a contemporary artist not to give birth to wind-eggs.

Greece is responsible for the deterioration of the intelligence, and Rome is responsible for the degradation of organic shame. Germany is responsible for the further subjectivity of the intellect in subordination to the emotional center. England has spread the propaganda for sport. How many times we hypnotize somebody into doing something against his own good by saying: "oh, be a sport." Why has this such an influence? A phrase of black magic: "play the game," "cricket," that is effort without an object. The quantity of effort is always the same. Again we are considering the means. Intellect—titillation.

Art and the aesthetic impulse exist for the discipline and stating of beauty, which is the harmony of a being with its cause. The aesthetic sense gives a criterion of proper function. If used apart from its purpose, merely for pleasure it has psychological results, psychopathic.

Similarly, ability to make effort for the development of will. Effort apart from will corresponds to titillation of reason, pleasure of aesthetic etc. It is a substitution of the pleasure of the process for the satisfaction of achieving a goal.

We are wound up with potentialities to develop will, consciousness and individuality. But power is mechanically ticked off and the age of each center depends upon existing circumstances. If we are merely passively responding, we remain untouched in essence.

Is there any means of arousing our still unwound reserves? Of ceasing to be an agent? Gurdjieff takes the example of a clock, which is wound for a certain period. But by changing its regulator we can change its period of unwinding. Loosened it runs faster; tightened it increases longevity. The regulator is in us, but we cannot change the winding.

But if we can control the regulator we can determine the period. We have to refuse to respond to external stimulus in a mechanical way. How?

1. The method. Self-observation automatically tightens the regulator on all three springs. Or if we can wind up we can control intellectual, emotional and physical longevity, the regulator is in us. We cannot change the winding. But why is a short life undesirable? Because it is hostile to the development of objective reason. No chance.

Life is too short. Anything that promotes the lengthening of the intellectual, emotional and physical life has this reason.

2. There is a subordinate method. "Iransamkeep." At present we have three centers wound up by the means described above; they have been ticked off to a certain degree; are partly unwound and exposed to the chance that one may be unwound at any moment and certainly passively. "Iransamkeep"—"I keep myself." Not giving oneself up to the associations arising from the functions of one center only. Giving oneself up and being absorbed. "I was absorbed in my reading" or in watching a game. Often regarded as a highly desirable state. "One center only." One should never become wholly absorbed: in processes of reason; in love, beauty, art, religion. Each of these is a necessary means toward an end but a total absorption has bad results

3. Associations of physical activity; craze for adventure, travel, sport. "Iransamkeep," avoiding absorption. If you are aware of your physical behavior you cannot become absorbed. Always try to be doing two different things at the same time. If pursuing art, also reason; if reasoning, use your hands. One of the Pythagorean schools, arranged for the artist to be talked to and argued with and made to answer questions, while engaged in his work. It might have prevented him from doing good work; but in his purpose he did better. We can now see the traces of those ideas in his work.

If an American is travelling, he should think. If thinking, you should also do.

Now I would like to go on with the narrative with the sequence unbroken. First thing to realize is the possibility of contact with a case of split (or multiple) personality.

Mrs. Piper had been subject from time to time to attacks of amnesia—loss of identity. She became a seamstress, shopkeeper, domestic servant etc.—under the influence of drink, drugs, etc. We may act in a way that will be both forgotten and, to us, also inexplicable. Diagnosis of man is that he is suffering from split personality. Say a friend of yours is suffering from an attack of this sort of amnesia—he has forgotten his identity. What should you do?

What is the meaning of existence? What is my mission, if any?

The problem of how to revive your friend's memory of himself is exactly that of the religious reformer who desires to perform his service for man.

The cry of an Indian child in the womb is: "Let me remember who and what I am after birth." After birth: "I have forgotten the meaning and aim of my being." So it is for all men.

Fairy stories are the first food for the magnetic center of children. Sleeping Princess (or royalty or divinity)—The Prodigal Son. Refer to more elaborate myths than in the Bible—Mead's, "Hymn of the Robe of Glory." Have you ever undertaken a commission and become as involved with, and absorbed in some personalities that you suddenly exclaim: Jove, I forgot my . . .

How would you try to arouse your friend? You would commence to talk of familiar things—also to take him to familiar places—to talk to him with the reason which he has acquired since the attack of amnesia—or again if the role he had fallen into was lower than formerly you would perhaps violently reproach him in the hope that you could arouse him.

So Ashiata Shiemash when proposing to treat mankind for the affliction of split personality employed exactly the same means—by talking to thirty-six, i.e. three-centered beings with the potentiality of six centers—i.e. specimens of split psyche. He began to instruct them about cosmic truths—their place in the cosmos, their responsibilities and duties laid upon men. (Nothing abnormal in being perfectly familiar with the meaning and aim of our existence, on the contrary.)

Continued association with these ideas will reawaken in themselves ideas now lost in their buried subconscious—plus an additional method for reawakening. (Ouspensky uses the phrase "self-remembering" to recall to oneself one's self-observation, self-participation, and self-experiment. All so that one can non-identify with the planetary body and recover a real knowledge of ones being, aim etc. By reviewing one's past life one can non-identify so as to review even the current days happenings to one's planetary body.

So to awaken a feeling of shame, the fulcrum of objective conscience, not conventional shame due to being discovered in social dereliction—but the shame of the prodigal son to find himself competing with the swine for the husks in the light of what he should have become. But a thrill of objective conscience does not carry with it the development of objective reason. Not one of us will ever understand the cosmos until we feel the shame of not understanding the aim of our existence, nor can we ever commence the achievement of objective reason.

1. To maintain the planetary body in a state of readiness for the attainment of reason, readiness to understand.

2. To be always striving to have more and more consciousness, individuality and will.

3. Always having at the back of your mind that every act, circumstance, happening, may throw light on the meaning of existence.

4. To treat all those beings with whom we come into contact justly with complete tolerance.

5. To aid all other beings in these four ways.

At present all our consciousness is in our instinctive center, the other two centers are to be brought up to the same degree of consciousness. Ashiata Shiemash tried to do this.

There have been great things done in the world—the establishment of chivalry—of Knights Templar—of Masonry.

Is here enough material among us—the fifty or sixty of us here to establish anything comparable? Could we undertake to build Gothic cathedrals, so to speak? Take the cathedral of Ely which I am very familiar with. It is located in a swamp—no stones there. Here came a small certain group under the name of Christians. The swamp was drained, tons of stone dumped in it, masons trained, got money from barons. These beings must have attained an extraordinary degree of consciousness.

But Ashiata Shiemash did more, he proposed an un-educational system, then an educational system, then through these, a religion reformation by purely psychological means was undertaken. So at one time for say, one hundred and fifty or two hundred and fifty years there was a world culture.

Then it began to come to an end by means of a certain kind of Lentrohamsanin—a species of psychology that is comparatively simply based. For with objective conscience, objective reason does not spring alive and so suffering results.

You remember, with a pang, that you have a mission which had been forgotten. Then when we begin looking about for the means to even formulate, not to say understand, we find ourselves helpless.

Narcotics are religion, service to others, etc.

Lentrohamsanin—the state of being unwilling to entertain a state of being aware of objective conscience without possession of objective reason. So Lentrohamsanin selected these beings and began to work on them just as Ashiata Shiemash had done.

He said the only thing for us in life is the pursuit of happiness, which is freedom—absence of the obligation to do anything one does not like. (But one did not make his essence and if our essence demands the service of God his creator then we must follow this.) But Lentrohamsanin said the state of being under moral obligations was undignified and proposed that man repudiate such an ideality if we escape from the use of mutton and wool, again surrender to a further demand. (I hope you will see that here was nothing diabolical in the attack of Lentrohamsanin on the work of Ashiata Shiemash. If it is the fact that only from an urge of a realized obligation is the attainment of objective reason possible then this means that it is barred for some of us forever. But we must not fail to accord to God a sort of subtlety—God is no fool. God himself would be the first to admit this—that God has the highest reason in our universe today. Certain emotional states are necessary for the understanding of certain truths. The attainment of cosmic-consciousness is impossible in advance of the sense of an objective conscience. So Lentrohamsanin was rationally right but in fact wrong.

So he started a movement which resulted in our spiritual forefathers, the Greeks and the Romans. We date from ancient Greece which dates from Lentrohamsanin. To our misfortune and perhaps to our ruin so far as this life is concerned. Rationalism without any higher urge. We are the inheritors of Lentrohamsanin, rational successful revolt on the spiritual plane.

Monasteries in little Tibets in our subconscious.

Cosmopolitanism to egoism. Instinctive titillating. We cannot formulate a true theory of life if it is not favorable to us. Nietzsche said: "I look always for the motive my philosopher had in formulating it."

Schopenhauer's idea was compassion.

Nietzsche—superman. Ninety-nine exist for the happiness of one—Napoleonic complex. The individual (or the opposite) exists only for the good of society. What does it matter if I perish if society benefits. (Socialism and sociology.)

The pursuit of science through successive generations keeps on accumulating facts for the use of future generations. I believe that each generation will continue to suffer from the disease of tomorrow—and will continue to accumulate facts of no use to them but for some future realization.

Here is the supposition that God is our father—the "father complex." (Heine said that God is a witty fellow—why? Because Heine's father was a witty fellow.)

(The world is a school in which there is no teaching—only learning.) But some will tell you that he is a teacher and that every event of his life was carefully designed by God—the teacher to instruct him.

ANNETTE HERTER: Why couldn't the activity of a scientist be the result of objective conscience and a resulting search for objective understanding?

ORAGE: Because the emotional urge from such a motive would be so strong that he could not be content with an activity which may have a result a hundred years hence.

We are prepared to make any sacrifice for instinctive good but what are we prepared to do for the development of reason? The price of objective reason and objective conscience is not to be attained through any instinctive emotion.

I say to you who are saying to yourselves—how fanciful. I say that these ideas are manly and intelligent. And all the time we are speculating that facts are facts. God is what he is. Human obligation is what it is. The objective fact that the world has a meaning and that we have a relation to it remains, whatever our subjective interpretation of it is.

Ashiata Shiemash says there is a method for understanding and Lentrohamsanin says he has a method for adjusting oneself to it.

2 MAY 1927

I'll read first of all a particular chapter on Greeks and Romans. How the Greek and Roman civilization arose. In terms of individual psychology:

Greek—reason.

Roman—instinct or body.

In Europe long ago there were only two-brained (quadruped) and one-brained (reptiles) beings. A few three-brained beings engaged in destroying the quadrupeds and reptiles.

One group—maritime, sea fishing. Hellenic—fisherman.

Other group raising cattle, land. Latin—shepherds.

In Latin more and more prolific because earth needed vibrations—especially quantity vibrations arising from the death of three-brained beings. This is always true when three-brained beings fail in conscious suffering and voluntary labor. The other group migrated wither to the Western shores of Asia or to the Dardanelles, dividing Asia from Europe, called Hellenic—Greeks—fishermen, etc.

One of the chief features why the reason of European beings has become mechanical is because of Greeks and being-shame has become atrophied due to the maleficent Latins. ("Being" = native or specific; "shame" = prohibiting them from doing that which is not becoming to that species.)

So the fishermen during bad weather retreated into caves, etc., and invented games—chiefly "the game of pouring from the empty into the void." In all ventures, at the beginning, there will be bad weather—do not retreat or the consequences will be serious. Little by little these plausible answers to nonsensical questions became what they now call science.

Romans—guilty from the fact that "being shame" became atrophied. From bad weather, the shepherds retreated with flocks for shelter—and having talked out everything, one of their number proposed to the others a game called "cinque contra uno." They invented devices for their own depravity.

The Greeks borrowed the finesse of the Romans and composed "Athenian Nights." Romans borrowed from the Greeks their form of depraved mechanical reason and composed the "Roman Law."

When the Greeks and Romans made a conquest of Asia, there remained in the Asiatic essence non-resistance, due to the command of Ashiata Shiemash: "Never kill, even when your own life is in danger."

So war swept away all the results of the labor of that conscious-essence, living-sacred and well-wishing being Ashiata Shiemash and can never occur again. For the reappearance of such a messenger of His Endlessness on earth again is almost impossible.

There is a sort of shame common among the earth beings now, but not at all like that of beings on other planets—here they are ashamed only when their unconventional behavior is observed or may be observed by some stranger.

The diagnosis of the human species is, that it is a species of split or multiple personalities. Take the war—public opinion approved, but ninety-nine out of every hundred privately had exactly the opposite opinion. This is characteristic of the race everywhere.

It occurred by a collision which split the planet and psyche on the planet. But it became possible for this split to be cemented, yet customs continued even in the presence of a fundamental essence which is sane, whole and sound and normal.

There is in us the possibility of objective reason and of objective morality. Emotional center is objective conscience. Instinctive center is objective morality.

Right and wrong for the organism is to be determined biologically. Criteria of behavior is native behavior determined by objective conscience native of essence. We have instead an acquired conventional morality and a conventional conscience which make us ashamed of unconventional behavior.

We have no innate criteria of values in the absence of objective conscience so our reason depends on what we have learned from education, etc., and behavior also. Philosophical speculations are pouring—nothing from nothing into nothing.

But we could use the word "law" instead. Law or justice. Our conception of justice is always colored by law or what we call law. But in fact there is no more relation between legal law and justice than there is between truth and our present reason.

Roman law depends upon the maintenance of the welfare of a community of physical bodies and has no basis upon objective conscience—(i.e. the mutual aid of souls) based upon physical values and physical welfare. So shame in regard to our neighbor. But shame in regard to God would result in justice. Our law should be creature to justice creator (God), but is creature to creature.

"I am a body but I have a soul." This is the sin of identifying with one of our centers. Truth is "I am a soul and I have a body." It would pay to repeat these two statements a few thousand times and then examine law and philosophy. But half an hour after I will find myself thinking: "perhaps there may be something in some of these philosophic theories or possibly justice in a law court."

Sex:

1. Purpose for the continuation of the race.

2. Creation of a being self-conscious and objectively developed in point of reason.

This power (sex) has these two natural objects. Amoral use of this power would be already dictated by is confinement to these two functions. The Latins used this force in "cinque contra uno"—i.e. either single or double (mutual) masturbation. But degeneracy occurs in the rational intellectual center or instinctive center. (Words or physical comforts—altruism.)

Lentrohamsanin is idealized consciousness that imagines the truth can be arrived at by rational process without feeling or emotion. A hasnamuss lives according to reason without any emotional obligation:

Intellectual development = degree of 3.

Emotional development = degree of 1.

Instinctive development = degree of 3.

Germany has carried on this 3-1-3 development. Craze for imaginary sciences. Experts in inventing every possible imaginary science. Heirs of Greeks. Also spoil bodies of men as well as their reason.

The human being is a mechanical laboratory for transmutation of chemicals. They undergo in us, by a process of metabolism, either a raising or a lowering of rates of vibrations of materials taken into the body.

Germans invented various chemicals—satkaine, aniline, cocaine, atropine and alizarin. Satkaine—something that makes you "croak." What German philosopher really makes you croak? (Keyserling is one—recent book.) Steiner, Freud—psychoanalysis is voodooism with obscene rites and human sacrifices. Dr. Peterson, associate of Freud and Jung.

Thinking is a chemical of high vibrations and can destroy mind, psyche and body. Satkaine is a highly rarified gas and when concentrated can be released into the atmosphere thereafter at will.

Aniline is a chemical color for dyeing. But substances so colored exist for only a short period. Previously vegetable dyes were used and articles lasted centuries.

Quick means of education, schools, universities, dyes human psyche, so for a period it appears to be brightly colored but at the age of thirty years the colors fade.

Even genuine pieces of ancient art are destroyed by this aniline. So we find it dangerous to look on old ideas, when true, for the colors we have acquired destroy them.

Cocaine is equivalent of kundabuffer—idealism. It makes us believe that things are as they are not. The theory that without effort on our part further real development will occur is "cocaine." It induces fantastic potentialities—i.e. prosperous imaginary potentialities—not real.

Atropine put into the eyes makes them dark—i.e. you appear to earth beings kindly and agreeable. Getting ourselves liked. But as judgments in others is all mechanical, we try mechanically to make ourselves mechanically agreeable. Affectation of universal amiability after the age of forty-five goes.

Alizarin is chiefly employed by confectioners who prepare the essential food for the beings of that planet.

Propagandist puts forward this theory or whatnot as attractively as possible. The human chemical laboratory is aided by these chemicals to degrade chemicals to a horrid degree.

9 MAY 1927

We were engaged in considering the purpose of the fifth descent. For the purpose of objective reason generally—but specifically to determine why the duration of man's life is decreasing. But if we study statistics, we find it increasing. It may be that the effort required to inquire into—to guess—is one of the necessary efforts of the development of intuition and reason. Say—divination, reading between the lines.

It is obvious from my view that he is not referring to physical life—birth to death, but of existence as three-centered beings. Not the life period of men but of humans. Men cease "thinking originally" at thirty-five years, women at forty years. The majority of people over forty are one-third to two-thirds dead and merely survive thanks to circumstances over which they have no control.

Beelzebub's object in this sixth descent is to observe the totality of three-centered functions. What is this prematurity of old age in regard to one or two centers? He attributes it to the absence of a certain emotional crystallization that can be called objective conscience.

We were born to know why we were born. To know what is "becoming to three-centered beings." In this sense what is proper and what is improper for us as three-centered beings. If that should have developed in us we should have had an infallible individual compass. We should have an emotion of propriety and have been impelled to an appropriate behavior. These were the natural circumstances in which we should have been brought up. But this catastrophe occurred. What if it had not?

We should have this innate sense of objective conscience. We should have aimed at the development of will, individuality and consciousness—i.e. objective reason—divine reason—an understanding of the mechanics of the universe.

Every one of us should have been consciously aiming at the development of the second and third bodies and to understand the meaning and purpose of world creation and world maintenance. We have lost our birthright of wholeness.

What is the absence of these things? Do we do or can we do? We must find substitutes for all these things. So we have all things by name only. We seek substitutes because we have to. As being shadows we pursue shadows.

We have a compass but the needle points at any and all points. How shall we direct the ship? One way is as good as another. Think of Columbus on the open sea—lost—compass in this state. In the absence of this instrument we have no sense of what direction is life. Yet we are compelled to move—to act—we must decide. So we agree to take that course which is agreed upon by those people with whom we are associated. This is pragmatism. Since we have only subjective criteria and no objective criteria—we are dependent upon suggestion. So we fall into every variety of sophistry.

Criteria of value is adaptation to environment. The whole modern concept of solution rests on this, despite the known fact that many species have disappeared while pursuing just this course. Jung's whole system is based on so silly a basis that it won't bear one moment's objective consideration. Mechanical adaptation of an accidental set of circumstances for comfort.

Substitution of means for end. Means tend to be overvalued just to the degree to which the end is lost sight of.

Philosophy is certainly search for truth. But we read Spengler and we admire his processes—his style—his whatnot. We admire the means and pay no attention to the end. What is the end of law? Justice. But now we are all legalists—we regard the substitute—end of law and the substitute end of legality, instead of justice.

Take our spiritual forefathers—the Romans—what is the natural function of sex for three-centered beings? One is for procreation and one for self-creation. That is for creation of bodies. Procreation of bodies and self-creation of emotional and intellectual bodies.

We have substituted the pleasure of the pursuit of sex for the satisfaction of its proper end. Masturbation or playing with forces—all the result of split personality.

If we have the approval of those we associate with, we cannot easily form an impartial estimate of ourselves. We depend upon social-psychological criteria.

So in the absence of this spring (individuality) we exist mechanically. We are dependent upon three springs wound from without and which run down independently. We have a fourth which is self-winding but it is not usable in us at present.

Here are the elements that wind our springs!

- Intellectual, by the intellectual circumstances we encounter.
- Emotional—same—emotional experiences.
- Instinctive—health, etc.

1. Heredity in general—our biologically ancestry.

2. Conditions and environment at the moment of conception—planetary conditions and local circumstances, the local terrestrial conditions as well as the astrological planetary conditions affect us.

3. Life of our parents and particularly of our mother during the period of gestation.

4. Being manifestations of parents of the child coming of age—during the period of majority. Essential behavior as a totality during this period.

5. Correspondent being manifestation or essential behavior of other beings with which the child comes in contact during the period of minority.

6. The good wishes of beings of the same blood or tribe—an old wives tale. Yet it is real and important—birthdays, etc. and sending good wishes.

7. Character of effort made by the growing child to understand why he is alive. Wonder. Sometimes these questions take embarrassing forms—"How did I come into this world?" Not that they want sexual account, but really want to know. A true answer would be telling a sort of fairy story with an implicit attempt to explain life. Not explicit. We now "live out" our lives—but we should "live up."

So children were introduced in ancient times into the presence of sages and certain vivid persons so that after majority they should have the potentiality of certain intellectual and emotional experiences.

Let us consider what experience is. It is the release by an external agency of a spring in us that gives consciousness of thought or of feeling or of action. Every one of us has capacity for a certain quantity of emotional experience. Thanks to an accident it has been kicked off slowly—but an accident might kick it off in almost no time at all. Shell-shock is an example of this. The spring has been run down. Such a one has the capacity still to act as if emotion were present but it is like a watch in which the main spring is broken—it will stop. More examples are: Reading to excess, phantasm fancy—curiosity without end—following our interest—flirting with one's reason—thinking without end.

Art is another way to run down one's emotional spring. To pursue art. A curator is the most cynical of beings—yet no one can go into a gallery and encounter works of art without response. It is equally true that no one can incessantly encounter them without inevitably losing all capacity to respond. This is true of all mechanical responses.

Modern art is an offspring of "the aged." Socrates warned someone that though there were all the signs of pregnancy, it might be merely a "wind-egg."

Greeks substituted the pleasure of reason for the pursuit of truth. Romans were responsible for sexual depravity and for sinking of objective conscience.

England is responsible for the introduction of sports and games. We say to seduce a person into doing something we wish, "Oh, be a sport." Why is this phrase charged with black magic? Why would a sensible person run away faster from this phrase than he would from an inverted cross?

The phrase "play the game" or "play cricket" in England. One says of a politician—thus and so—yet "he plays cricket."

Effort without object. Effort will be made, but effort not voluntarily made runs down the spring. The indictment against sports or games is that it involves effort with no object.

Reason is for the discovery of truth if not so used ——. Art is for the discovery of beauty—i.e. the discovery of and performance of objective functioning. The ability to make effort is given us as a means for the development of will. Effort for its own sake is titillation—so in sport, effort is directed toward the pleasure of effort.

Every one of us started with the power to achieve will, individuality, and consciousness, but this power is being kicked off mechanically. Recurrence for the vast majority of us is a mere repetition because we have ourselves used none of this potential power.

The possibility for us is to cease to be victimized by external stimuli. The analogy of a clock. If there is no regulator or if it is loosened it will not go twenty-four hours—but one hour—six—or a very short time. In us there is a regulator and it can be tightened so as to extend almost indefinitely the running down of our three springs. We have to resist the mechanical running down.

1. The introduction of the function of self-observation into physical functions during this activity—it will wind another spring. This

is the secret of the maintenance of your age. Not merely therapeutic. Why live longer? Because a short life is absolutely hostile to the end of developing objective reason. This is the terror of our situation. Ninety years would be necessary for development of the second and third body.

2. Iransamkeep—We have three centers wound up to majority and ticked off since to a certain degree—leaving certain parts of them unwound. "I keep myself." Not giving oneself up to the associations arising from the associations of any one center only. Not to be "absorbed" in the associations of any one center at a time.

- Intellectual—In the associations of an intellectual reaction alone—yogi.
- Emotional—Not to be wholly absorbed in any of these: art, love, beauty, religion.
- Physical—Not to be wholly absorbed in: health, sport, adventure, holidays, travel.

Absorption in one center is to be avoided by:

1. Being aware of your physical behavior, and you cannot be wholly absorbed in any one center. It prevents it.

2. Always to be doing two different things at the same time. Ignore the advice of society which says to become proficient you must concentrate. It is true you will become proficient—but you will arrive also at a sad state of being absorbed within yourself.

If you are engaged in art—reason. If in reason—do something with your hands.

16 MAY 1927

Our objective inheritance is that we should know why we are born, know it early in life and be trained to carry out our functions. Animals and vegetables in their natural state do this. Plants produce seeds and, although there may be frustrations which delay, they do not divert the function. The vegetable world has great powers of adaptability for overcoming obstacles. Three-centered beings have three brains for the development of the germ of objective conscience, but education and environment from birth press down and bury this germ. Like Esau, we gave up our birthright for the mess of pottage of ordinary life; this is the meaning of the story. We have no natural criterion. The difficulty is increased by the fact that we have no accurate knowledge as to the origin or history of the planet, its geology or its races. We have speculations by scientists and geologists and ethnologists. Can anyone recall the preceding civilizations, their sequence, etc. and call himself their heir? There is only a rumor that civilizations have preceded ours. We do not even know their culture, art or philosophy; much less inherit these. There is no continuity of knowledge. As species also, we have no direct contact with our origins. There are always rumors of the existence of beings who have charged themselves with continuity of knowledge, cosmic and planetary, a secret knowledge. These have regarded themselves as custodians of a race. According to Gurdjieff there has been since Atlantean times a chain of initiates or Masters who have claimed to have such knowledge.

[*Orage says that for himself he has never met any such and so has no knowledge as to whether there is any such continuity or as to whether such rumors are or are not true.*]

The book:

We hear of the decline of Babylonian culture and a pan-scientific congress. There was a club of the friends of the legomonism or the friends of traditional culture (knowledge). Moors, Chaldeans and Pythagoras were members. They decided to adopt another means of transmission than by initiates because they had noticed that in the case of war, the best were the first sacrificed and among these were initiates. They devised methods of transmitting knowledge and art. They wished to transmit to remote descendants, across periods of war, changes of civilization or possibly even planetary upheavals. They were planning for thousands of years. What material should they use? Paper was too perishable. But there were certain works of art into which consciousness had partly entered—music and song, religious and social ceremonies, architecture, painting, religious and lay dance-forms and movements, sculpture, drama. It was argued that wherever there was civilization, these occurred.

What we call art is as natural to men as building nests to birds. These forms are indigenous and aboriginal to human beings as such. Pythagoras and the rest did not count these as anything unnatural. Another thing: a marked characteristic is conservatism and tradition. Pythagoras counted that any innovation introduced by them could be counted on to endure, e.g., religious forms. This "committee" proposed to introduce into current art certain innovations to serve later as a reminder and perhaps a language. They rejected literature not only on account of the perishability of paper but because literature is the most subjective of all the arts. It depends on languages which change and die. Do you know any ancient languages now? Also literature is a shape of shadows. Pythagoras wished to depend on things. Babylon at this time was the metropolitan city of the world; had museums etc.

There are two types of work of which we should call art.

1. Subjective.
2. Objective.

Subjective works of art are those which issue for self-expression. Common in modern art, it claims that the artist merely needs to delight himself to find himself thereafter delighting others. This art is related to the subject or person or ego. This is inferior to objective art which is art devoted to an object, the transmission of a state or an idea from the artist to the beholder; a species of calculated influence; not in the sense of self-expression; but in the sense of self-conveying, e.g. primitive form of begging letters, or for money or "third degree" in which it is proposed to exert upon others an influence. This is not confined to advantage for myself but for them, this is major art.

Minor art: soliloquy and money making.

Major art: effort of converging certain ideas for the benefit of the beholder. E.g. the Bible, with its purpose to create a certain state of being in the reader. This is not for the advantage of the writer. This "committee" was in a position to choose the best examples of objective art. They picked up the best examples of natural art. They proposed to prostitute the greatest works of art of their day in order to write upon them their own doctrine. They did not intend to harm them but on the contrary to introduce a new element to make them more capable of expressing along side of the works of art, certain ideas.

Consider the difference between what we would consider a perfect work of art and a perfect work of art, when they got them in it. We say a perfect work completely satisfies our sense of harmony that is every part of our sensory, emotional and intellectual being is satisfied, a harmony of impressions. From Gurdjieff's point of view, this ideal state of harmony is the last thing to be desired; it is not tranquility but merely a state of higher sleep. Because nothing is aroused that caused disharmony, "aesthetic contemplation" is a sublime sleep. Consciousness is in abeyance.

But the object of this "committee" was to make people remember and—not forget. If without injury to a work of art, they could introduce something which would arouse a conscious question, which in turn might provoke a further curiosity in regard to the work of art itself. What is it which fails to satisfy and arouses curiosity? Something strange. Nobody says of Greek art: This is strange; what does it mean? It completely satisfies, the mind fails. It evokes no curiosity.

But one looks at certain Egyptian frescoes with a feeling of something strange and wonderful which it means. We cannot despise the artist of the work; it is clear he had the technique and was not inferior to the Greeks as a craftsman. This strangeness in a work otherwise perfect is a device. It is aimed to disturb and not to please. But for this is required a work which otherwise would have pleased.

Leonardo da Vinci, when examining ancient art had a question: Why with such obvious mastery, did ancient artists make such and such juxtapositions? Gurdjieff says that Leonardo came near to finding the answer. This third form of art is the only kind to which Gurdjieff gives the name of *art*.

Summarize: subjective art aims to gratify the artist. Objective art aims to satisfy the beholder. Conscious art which stimulates the beholder to question consciousness which creates consciousness. The "committee" allotted a day for each variety.

SUNDAY: MUSIC AND SONG

We are three-centered but we are not always thinking, feeling and sensing together. The ordinary work of art happens to stimulate all three centers. We have no sense of any interior disharmony. They introduced a variety of rhythms calculated to induce in any average hearer a variety of disharmonious responses, e.g. intellect, say, sadness; in emotion, joy; in instinctive a funeral march. It simultaneously awakes grief, joy, associations of burial. On hearing such melody, it is impossible to give it a name; strange beauty (as when a dog hears a piano and has its centers disharmoniously aroused). A hearer pulled in two or three directions would find himself uneasy. Instead of a higher state, one of unrest, yet not an unpleasant one because each of its components are beautiful. If these could be heard separately we would be pleased; but there are three separate rates of vibration. Only when there is a conflict within the three centers is there a chance of reconciliation by a fourth. Art was used to induce in hearers the necessity of developing consciousness. We will reduce you by music to such a state that you will be forced to self-observation to free yourselves from this aesthetic misery.

MONDAY: RELIGIOUS AND SOCIAL CEREMONIES

Consider the large number of religious ceremonies extant. What was their original purpose? For example the ringing of a bell at mass. Introduced in ceremony which preceded Babylonian times, to break a ritual which might otherwise be soporific and then to arouse to question, why? Take ceremonies: coronation of kings, inauguration of presidents, masters of masons etc. antedated Babylon but began to have new elements introduced. They are nudges to a sleeper, e.g., postures are often unnatural, i.e. into which we would not naturally fall and which is difficult to maintain. They are intended to make the question, why this, a divergence from the natural. All ceremonies must include this element of the unnatural and not intended.

TUESDAY: ARCHITECTURE

Innovations in structure, in interior, e.g. a cupola would naturally rest on four supports for the distribution of weight. It was arranged to have cupola rest on three dissimilar pillars and that part of the weight of the cupola should be in itself. In St. Michel this is considered merely an oddity. The Taj Mahal is a classic existing example of conscious art. Competent students can read in its construction, the record is made. Form and deviation from form are a language. The interior is a more subtle form of record, with different volumes of space. E.g. we can consider this room as a series of volumes of spaces, one larger, one smaller and a third broken with beams. If these volumes were broken, we could have a series of symbols. But every interior has a different pressure of air (as in the subway when passing under the river). The pressure of air in this room is different from that in a room differently shaped. It has different associations. If we know what associations with pressure of air, we could arrange pressures to produce certain desired associations. The pressure is different at the nave of a cathedral from that at the altar. Pythagoras et al. proposed to use architecture as one would music and song to produce this disturbance and this query. These associations are not merely historic as we are inclined to think.

WEDNESDAY: PAINTING

The latest examples of the introduction of divergences is in Persia in the fourteenth and fifteenth centuries. Again we have an agreeable disharmony, using contiguous colors in an unnatural way. After seeing one color the complementary color is formed on the retina of the eye; and this is a natural sequence for the eye. It gives pleasure for the eye to pass from one color to the complementary one through the spectrum. The Babylonians knowing the "expectation of the eye" put next to one color an unexpected color, which required a conscious adjustment. It was pleasing but also disturbing.

THURSDAY: MOVEMENTS AND RHYTHMS

The rhythms were of two forms, religious and social.

Varieties of dance of modern civilization:

1. Physical center—popular dances of the day.
2. Dances of expression—Isadora Duncan
3. Ceremony—rare in modern time
4. Religious—Hopi Snake Dance—an invocation, but of what? They have forgotten. But there is introduced an invocation of a higher center in the dancer himself.

A movement if accurately done, will produce a certain psychological state. Popular dances were taken and variations introduced. Whoever practiced them would experience. They evoke certain disturbing contrary states. We cannot find a name for the effect. These movements were not designed by Gurdjieff.

FRIDAY: SCULPTURE

Representation of ordinary forms. Modeling of imaginary objects: sphinx and Assyrian bull. They introduced variation in accordance with a theory now lost. According to this theory each body was constructed on the principal of seven, so that each feature is a multiple of seven in some other feature. The same is true of its details. If one feature were missing we could replace it from measurements of others; a mathematical relation. The committee of Babylonians found this canon of seven taken for granted and employed no other. There were no oddities; even a monstrosity was created according to law and not according to an idiosyncrasy of the artist.

Parallel between the foregoing and the method, these works of art are usually devised for the stimulation of harmonious impressions and disharmonious associations, to create an impression which is new and memorable. First, it strikes one with surprise and then is never forgotten—this is characteristic of impressions which reach the essence. Conscious works of art give new and memorable impressions to those who had experience. A designed experience; the object of this is to transform the life of the beholder into a work of art. It would introduce a variation into his natural behavior. This would tend to make him a conscious being and in proportion as he could make this sequential and objective would it exemplify a work of art. The committee faced the fact of the Babylonian decline, a period of dark ages coming. How over this chaos should certain things be transmitted? How to transmit memory?

Parallel: you become to a certain degree conscious of certain ideas and certain values—intuitions of objective consciousness of certain ideas and certain values—intuition of objective conscience, reason. Why do they not remain? Why do we forget? One reason: wars and civil wars. What are wars and civil wars in us? Emotional states of a negative kind as a result of contact with others or of strife between centers. What we knew passes from the mind and it is practically impossible to recall without having recourse to the original stimulus; oblivion of our state. Art is a constant re-stimulus. We need parallel means to these: music, architecture, etc., in our own conduct for the maintenance of certain states, e.g. like a man in training for a race. We have moments of consciousness and need technique to maintain a memory, e.g. I have a body. This parallel will be made clearer in the discussion of drama.

16 MAY 1927

You will remember that last week we were in the throes of attempting to understand the effects of objective conscience in life practically. That we decided that—from a standpoint of objective conscience—man was entitled to understand the cosmos and his relation to it. So it is with the vegetable kingdom. Nothing one can do will divert the vegetable from its natural growth. Nothing will do more than arrest its growth. No potato will become an orange by growing in an orange grove.

We have no history of this planet—no real ethnology or history of evolution. We are cut off from our parents both on earth and in heaven—i.e. "Esau." We have no knowledge of our origins, sequence of evolution, etc.

There are legends of many civilizations that have reached great heights of culture in the past but we have no continuity of history which can be relied upon to tell us about these.

But it is said there have been from Atlantean times downward an unbroken line of initiates or masters who have preserved a genuine knowledge of the history on this planet and before its development. But I, for one, have never known such a one.

At Babylon it was proposed to transmit such knowledge through some other means, because the method of transmission by initiates through an oral or written tradition was too precarious. So they conferred to decide upon some means. They devised a method and gave it the name of "art." They formed a club—"Friends of Legomonism"—Pythagoras, a Moor and a Chaldean were members.

Let us suppose that we here in this room possessed knowledge, valuable knowledge, which we desired to transmit to our remote descendants. What material could we list that might reasonably be expected to endure? Paper won't do—it won't last. Music and song, religious and social ceremonies, architecture.

Painting, religious and lay dances and movement, sculpture in all forms and drama. In all civilizations these activities appear. So they decided to introduce certain innovations into the arts.

Literature is the most restricted and subjective of all the arts. It depends upon languages which soon disappear. Literature—only a shadow of a shade—since it substitutes words for things.

They found two types of art or work—subjective and objective. Subjective—those that issue from self-expression. These "artists" claim that all an artist needs to do is to delight himself and hence others as he thinks. Objective—those that issue because of the object outside himself held by the artist. It is calculated influence.

Beautiful is that which fully satisfies—that which simultaneously and harmoniously satisfies sensuously, emotionally and intellectually. I.e. it induces a higher state of sleep—called aesthetic contemplation of beauty. Memory of consciousness is in abeyance.

But the object of these beings in Babylon was the opposite—to make remember. So they decided to introduce elements into works of art that would cause the observer to question, to ask what is there strange about this. Egyptian frescoes produce or provoke this state. Greek art does not. To evoke the question "why." They proposed not only to evoke the question "why?" but to raise a specific series of definite questions in a definite order. Leonardo da Vinci almost alone among modern artists asked why were certain colors arranged in a certain order and juxtaposition? That is, they introduced into otherwise harmonious works of the above nature, certain provocative disturbing elements.

SUNDAY — MUSIC AND SONG

We are three-centered beings and we are not always thinking, feeling, and sensing harmoniously. (Sometimes so essential that we exclude thinking and feeling.)

Same melody means to:
Intellect = sorrow.
Emotion = joy (holiday).
Physical = funeral dirge.

We are familiar with the fact that a dog may be unable to lie still or keep quiet at the sound of a piano. It is simply because its two centers are being differently stimulated. So it was upon three-centered beings by these melodies. Gurdjieff has written music which induces such effects simultaneously—such a conflicting state in the three centers that only the introduction of a fourth element, i.e. self-observation, etc., would make the hearing satisfactory.

MONDAY—RELIGIOUS AND SOCIAL CEREMONIES AND RITES

The tinkling of a bell in the mass is an example. Oddities were also introduced into social ceremonies, coronations, ceremonies in masonry, etc.

Priests were induced to assume certain postures; say in holding aloft a bowl, he will stand in an unnatural position or posture, one you never would assume. All ceremonies must include an unnatural or "intended" element.

TUESDAY—ARCHITECTURE, STRUCTURE

A cupola if made by anyone would be made to rest upon four equal pillars, but they are arranged that it should be supported by three unequal, against the ordinary tradition of good builders. St. Michel has such oddities. (See public library.) The Taj Mahal is the classic example of conscious art because a competent student can read by an exact alphabet in it the text of the Koran. Composed of divergence of architectural forms.

WEDNESDAY—INTERIORS

Here they used different volumes of space. It gives the eye the greatest pleasure to look at colors as they appear in the spectrum. But they did not follow this—they just put a color in which required a conscious adjustment of the eye.

THURSDAY—MOVEMENTS AND RHYTHMS OF DANCES OF RELIGIOUS AND SOCIAL NATURE

1. Dances of physical center—popular ones of today.
2. Dances of expression. (Isadora Duncan).
3. Religious—Hopi Indian Serpent Dance. Invocation dances. Invocation of one's own higher self.

Conscious art is art for inducing consciousness.

Friday—Sculpture.

Sphinx, Assyrian bull. Everything in nature, including what we call ill shaped—is constructed on the law of seven. Every item is a multiple of seven. There are seven features in every face, each bearing a certain mathematical relation to the totality. So there were introduced elements contrary to the expected natural law of nature, i.e. the law of seven.

Before I conclude I would like to make one parallel with the work we are attempting. A novel impression arriving from otherwise harmonious impressions of an objective work of art will actually have reached essence—a memorable impression. So someone observing these works would become changed—in some proportion a conscious being. Conscious art is a designed experience to awaken the observer to consciousness. To awaken in him the desire to be in possession of consciousness, will and individuality.

Why do we find ourselves forgetting? Failing to remember those values which we accept here? In historic terms—because of wars. That is, negative emotions towards others or our own centers engaged in a civil war.

I may be able in a certain state to formulate certain ideas and an hour or two later you could search me for any vestige of the ideas.

So we must find parallel means in ourselves for the maintenance of these ideas. Training required for physical regime. We must maintain a state of training. We must find a technique for the maintenance of ourselves in a state of memory—self-remembering. I have a body—I am a soul.

Chief feature. What is essence?

Well, I observe you have brought your bodies—that you have no control over their height, behavior, type, history, pre-natal life, circumstance of our embryonic life—not to age three. But at that time the major part of our physical bodies were already determined at age three. You don't need a messiah from Sinai to tell you what you already know.

We are brought into a world at birth containing other people. At that time we begin to receive direct contacts hitherto only indirectly through our mothers.

We are essential up to birth and social afterward. Essence and personality.

We were not born to speak English—we weren't carried by our mothers to speak English—language is not an essential thing. We are sitting in chairs instead of squatting on the floor—by accident. Before birth we were beings—not fully developed of course—but not forced by sociology.

Essentially—that is, in accordance with our heredity and influences at conception. We are nine-tenths social or personality imposed by environment.

Lion or tiger cubs, however highly trained, will become ferocious if pushed beyond a certain point—i.e. they will become biological.

I remember a group of twelve people who flattered themselves that they were naturally polite to each other, Russian aristocrats—all excellent friends. Gurdjieff offered to reduce them to such a state that he would need a revolver to keep order.

So at the first meal there were only eleven plates—they all fought politely to be the one to drop out. Next meal only ten plates, then—nine plates—not quite so polite. Eight plates, seven plates—drew lots, six plates, same. Five plates—then arranged that dinner bell be rung at an unexpected hour. Then all ran and those who could run faster grabbed a plate. Only four plates and there were two people ripped up. Ninth day—only three plates—fight. One person only who never rushed, pushed, fought and Gurdjieff said he was the only one with natural human or humane essence. (Hubbard has it.)

The reason none of us ever know each other; because we never encounter each other in moments of desperation—where perhaps life and death may be at stake. Shipwrecks, for instance, among a party of friends is a horrible affair. Of course you may find that you are the natural superior of all the cultured people you know or the opposite.

The two systems of education in the world today are Eastern and Western. Occidental aims at development of personality. Oriental aims at production of essential values—not at uniformity.

Wall Street man may adhere to conventional business practices but eventually he may be a shark. But education has done nothing for him. In the East you will find all essential types fully developed.

Saints, storytellers, liars, murderers, yogis, bandit—(tiger). There he won't be appearing in a dress suit but will be a member of a bandit-guild.

The East is wrong because it doesn't realize the value of personality—the West is wrong because conversely it does no realize the value of essence.

Where is the school or where are the teachers who can teach us simultaneously both values—essence and personality. Each is by itself a monstrosity. A thing that is neither East nor West, yet it may be both.

The first aim of this method is to undo our Occidental personality training—to become essential. At the moment of birth all of us started on a Western career. We must get back to the point when our Occidental training commenced—i.e. moment of birth, then we must begin a simultaneous development of essence and personality. Occidentals will say: "Nothing is ever true." We have therefore two sets of half-baked idiots. The only way we can ever understand them is to consciously unlearn our Occidental ——. How? I can prescribe the means but I cannot give you the energy to carry on the method prescribed.

Why do we stress this principle of self-observation? Unless you employ yourself to the fullest extent observing your physical behavior—and not at all because of any value in knowing your gestures, and so forth—attendance at these groups for a thousand years won't do more than give you one or two more ideas to rub together. But constant effort at this fundamentally uninteresting task will give you the energy and power to do anything you may want to do. Problem to increase the light in this room . . .

So there are a set of people who say, study, another says go to church or engage in the arts, a third who says exercise, diet, etc.

So a man, who goes out of the door to the main wire and turns more current from the main, is called a mystic . . . And the professors say: "See, we have produced more light by our splendid work." But the artists cry, "No, we did this!" And the ascetics call them both liars and claim for himself the credit.

But the electrician worked out consequences by working on causes. So if you do the work of self-observation you will find that the light in you will increase.

Can you sustain meditation for a half an hour? Can you think of three things at once? Can you look at a picture for three seconds and draw every line? Can you memorize a hundred lines of poetry in half an hour?

Well, observe every day as much as you can quite honestly—for a month, then try anything of this sort again, I will guarantee that you will find you can do perceptively more and better.

Man can lift 150 lbs.—two weeks of observations—he can lift 175 lbs. But the degree to which we observe ourselves usually won't make a very perceptible difference.

If you want to know how awake essence is in you, it can be determined by the number of times you can observe yourself. Divide your day into sixteen hours—if you can observe one-sixteenth of this time you are rather good. If you can observe one quarter the time each day you can depend rather definitely on how you will react in a crisis. Self-observation will develop essence. But it is equally unknown in the East and in the West. People are sometimes reduced to essence by shock—but usually leave them insane and so forth. Shell-shock for example—social/racial/caste/clique/profession = prejudice—will be stripped off by self-observation.

Essence stripped bare of personality by shell-shock, hysteria, pathological conditions, will speak without any regard for the effect. But essence reached by self-observation will not act like that. Essence knows why we are alive, what we wish to be and do.

Wall Street man and Greenwich Village man are both ghosts. The man in Greenwich Village is merely open to too many winds and will be blown about in all directions. The Wall Street man merely happens to have his sails set so that only one wind can perfect him. We are at present sailing vessels. Some are blown into very good harbors—others into Lapland, very bleak, etc. All sailing is called luck, fate, etc.—but it is due to the set of our sails and the prevailing winds in our neighborhood. But we can pass to the age of steam. That is, of the age of will. (The Indians regarded steam vessels as being possessed of the devil.)

By means of the same force generated by self-observation, light, heat and power—not only will you know what you really want to do but you will have the power to do it.

1. Light—thought—self-understanding.
2. Heat—feeling—wish to do something.
3. Power—physical energy—ability to do it.

I understand what I wish to do and can do it—*now*. But our present state = I do not understand what I wish to do—I wish to do what I cannot do—I do not approve of what I wish and can do. A ghost in hell. We are born in three—not in two. Perhaps we are in hell—and lost and damned and served up hot to God.

Nothing will satisfy us but success in all three centers. Specializing in one center activity will not satisfy us. First thing we must do is self-observation and first thing it will do is produce heat—arouse a wish to do something for oneself. Ignore your psychological state, just observe your physical.

Be aware of what you are doing. Not a proposal to assemble data—merely an exercise. When you speak as "I" you speak as owner of your body. But when you speak of what you think you will be, speaking of what your body is thinking. "I" am asleep and if "I" awake "I" will only observe the external behavior of my body. As though you were in a car—and if it jogs over a bump you don't say: "My God I just had an inhibition"—but if you were asleep you would dream something of the sort. If you were awake you would say: "Went over a bump, jogged the car." Will you try to be currently—along the stream of—aware of these five things?

Imagine a room without sunlight but good soil in it. We dig it up, get some manure, drain it or moisten it. It grows a little something. But let in sunlight (self-observation) and it will commence to grow what from our point of view is much more desirable. Call it silly, magic, etc., but it happens like that—neither criticism nor gardening. The room may become an open space.

Movements merely illustrate in bodily posture and movements what ought to be our psychological work. It is an enormous aid to have some sense of physical coordination for psychological exercises; before you can begin to think you must have something to think about. Before you can feel you must be aware of feeling—before you do either you must be aware of stimuli.

So we must first increase our awareness. Mental processes presupposes awareness. Prehension is Whitehead's word for that which occurs before it becomes locomotive, is felt or thought about. Intuition is an accidental working of thought and feeling. We are looking for another kind of intuition.

23 MAY 1927

DRAMA

Drama presupposes knowledge and control of the body. I am a soul; I have a body. This proposes that the soul shall use the body. A three-centered being is divided into parts:

Planetary body—three brains—three centers. A divine mystery is associated with this conception. The soul aspires to be the actor. There is a technique by which the soul can manipulate the body to express knowledge of, and control over, the instrument for living. This also presupposes knowledge of types of people. The number of types of planetary bodies is limited. It is therefore not hopeless to expect to arrive at final conclusions, personal idiosyncrasy maybe subsumed under about twenty-seven types. The actor never acts alone. It is necessary to recognize types. Also it presupposes that he has a conception of the role he is to play in order to function as a soul; that is, he must be aware of his mission, he must know his reason for acting as he proposes to act, in cooperation with the whole cosmic plan.

It is said that the ancient occult schools used drama as exercises for behavior in life. Putting plays onto the stage of life. Today we just put plays on the stage.

The teachers had to know:

The nature of man; that he was three-centered but that these centers almost never acted simultaneously from all three centers, varying in age of centers according to degree of experience. Each new stimulus evokes for each center a parallel response according to distribution of experiences already received. So we say, over-intellectualized, over-emotionalized. Now "over" is impossible. We mean "under" in other centers, "over intellectualized" means "under emotionalized." This makes impossible the perception of real drama; always melodramatic. Odd triangles, a "non-whole view." Teachers are on guard against irregular responses and would train to bring about a harmonious response, he can evoke discordant responses (see music, above).

Types; the knowledge they were after is not occult and can be expressed mathematically relative to the three centers. Or colloquially: suppose you were asked to draw up an appropriate setting, speech, etc. for a miser. This would be inappropriate for Don Juan. Miser, Falstaff, Hamlet, Micawber, etc. Some novels specialize in a few types, e.g. Dickens. Each of us falls into two in greater or lesser degree according to idiosyncrasies, a type. It is true that few of us manifest this clearly. In the Occident especially, the type is concealed. The divination of types beneath the idiosyncrasies is sociology. The method is practical. We often say: You have to do it, to get the feel of it. Pupils are expected to try things out to feel what it is like, become aware of manifestations. A being is one who experiences.

Experiences are physiological processes taking place when we are not aware. They are changes of direction or division of streams in our blood vessels. These have psychic counterparts which we call our consciousness, while in the process of experiencing. Simultaneously there is the behavior of the mechanism of the manifestations. Manifestations are the means of communication. Stage set: a being undergoing experiences; manifestations the only form of communication. My subjective never becomes the spectator's objective. He can see only my manifestations. He will understand just in the proportion in which I manifest sincerely.

Teachers wished to give control so the pupil would not just convey his experiencing but whatever he wanted to convey. A technique of insincerity? Yes. This is a charge against a conscious actor. It is an assumption by the critic that spontaneity, a lack of ability to control a manifestation means greater sincerity. But being unaware of and unable to control manifestations, nine-tenths of his experiences are beyond his perceptions and hence nine-tenths of his manifestations. A fractional sincerity. A conscious actor aspires to be aware of all and to choose and arrange in relation to the type with which he is dealing. In order to do so he must sometimes, but very rarely, act from one center at a time, i.e. presented as a purely intellectual problem. The tendency is for other centers to join and distort the action of the center engaged.

Actors had to learn to act in one center or they would be otherwise excluded from efficient participation in many situations. They must also learn to act simultaneously in all centers. St. Paul said, to be all things to all men. A technique of playing roles. Mimicry is part of the play of children. Adults single out merely a few impulses likely to be sociologically valuable and leave others without development (except in pathological channels). Guessing is the green blade of a power which, if trained, would develop into intuition with certainty. Children are discouraged from guessing or imagining or telling lies. Modern thought is suffering from a lack of scientific imagination. Mimicry is a second neglected faculty. It is preservative of the elasticity of the planetary body. If trained it would give control and make dramatic school and mysteries unnecessary.

Method:

Pupil appeared on the stage and a play was improvised. Gurdjieff says that certain of the earliest plays of the Greeks were thus and there is some testimony in Plato; for he reports on improvised plays. There must be a critical audience.

A pupil on a stage, he is not thinking of plot but self-interrogating as to his inner state. What impulse do I feel? To shout? To go home? To write? To speak to a policeman? "I'd like to tell the cop what I think of him." Catch one of these odd little thoughts as they pass through the mind. In the wings, pupils are nervously waiting wondering what role they will be called on to play. "Hey, policeman, don't you see those two bums fighting?" Another pupil enters the stage, he must play the role of the cop. How will he behave? In order to qualify, every pupil went about observing types and technique, the relation between this school and life. Older pupils had to play rarer roles. Origin of introduction in earlier plays of gods. Not intended to represent gods but men in states of ecstasy (ex-stasis). Echoes of blank verse, poetry, spoken in ecstasy. The Iliad was perhaps dictated and repeated verbally long before it was written down. In these roles the actor had to produce actual manifestations. In this sense, a dramatic school is a training-ground for a universal life. Pythagoras committee introduced variations. What has just been described is natural and could develop anywhere. The troubadours would improvise on demand Pythagorean variations:

The enneagram, a nine sided figure with seven main points and three sides of a triangle. The body under the law of seven; the psyche under the law of three. The "I" experiences in three; the body manifests in seven. But in the octave of seven, there are two semitones, necessity of an external shock. To make the mechanical law of seven correspondent to the conscious law of three requires a psychological jolt at the proper moment. Counterpoint between experiencing and manifestation. The dotted triangle in the enneagram. A miser is not conscious of his experiences or manifestations. The intention of the schools is to control experiences in order to control manifestations. If we could control experience and act through the semitone to give manifestations a different turn, we could indicate conscious action. First; an actor had to pass a test of playing roles. Then he was allowed to take part in the second form: i.e. mysteries.

The difference between these mysteries and a play in general:

Introduction in the mystery of the semitone in the octave. Pythagoreans were scientific mystery creators. E.g. a policeman on some critical occasion, when manifestation was expected, would act differently indicating that he was only a policeman by role but not bound to be a policeman. He could introduce an original act, not determined by the role or nature. In mystery is the extraordinary.

Begin by inducing in the spectators an anticipation; but then the actor became himself and illustrated what the conscious soul would do under these circumstances. The spectator might be challenged at any moment, concentration and self-interrogation. It could not be said that the actor broke down; he had proved he could play the role perfectly. The spectator was provoked to say "Why"? The question led to the anticipation of something concealed of value to the spectator.

Third form: life. Here the pupil was expected to take any situation and play with unconscious actors but so that he could be understood. The Christian Mystery was rehearsed first in occult schools, then rehearsed by the Essenes. Then it was played historically, to affect thought, feeling and conduct through many generations.

It is possible the Christian mystery was the final outcome of these Babylonian schools. It is logical whether there is historical continuity or not. See "Fragments of a Faith Forgotten" and see how Jesus trained his pupils to dance, play roles etc. Judas may be said to have had to play a most difficult role, certain to be misunderstood; and like the villain on the stage to be hissed by a naive audience. Playing roles assumes a knowledge of our manifestations, not critically but instructionally (sociological improvement is a negligible object for the soul). If you try to play up merely to improve for social praise, it is little; but if this is regarded divinely, you learn what you are and how to use it.

First class of dramatic school.

Second class, types. Review pictorially people I have met. I will find they fall into two groups; then study these types in action.

Third stage; begins in pantomime.

Fourth: Intervene in role, either for personal development or to convey something important to the spectator—a significant act. The life of Christ was not the life of Jesus. Before and after Jesus the divine mission was consciously Christ.

(Orage has seen Gurdjieff play roles which few would condescend to, deceiving even his intimates.)

What is left of the Pythagorean concept of the drama?

Contrast ancient drama with the modern theater. The modern has two purposes:

Amusement, propaganda or education. (Ibsen, Shaw, Galsworthy.)

Not as mystery, which is impossible because it requires conscious actors. Our actors imitate not from within but from without. They merely produce an illusion in the spectator, whereas the ancient actors had illusion and also elasticity.

The spectator is never challenged; he is merely stimulated to recall previously recorded experience. Pictorial associations are provoked "sympathizing with himself." The drama today is not an experience but a re-experience—titillation. It is not an influx of new material but a stimulus which sets old material in motion. It is evocative and not representative, procreative but not creative, its effect is the intensification of the mechanicality of both actor and spectator.

The ship was now nearing the planet where Beelzebub was going on a mission. His hoofs moving on the surface of the deck evoked phosphorescence thus indicating they were nearing a planet. Coming within the magnetic center of the planet. They began to make preparations to land.

End of first volume. Later volumes will deal with matter on this and on other planets.

The drama of the life and crucifixion of Christ. It is possible that this event was the final outcome of the Babylon schools. Jesus trained his disciples in dancing, playing of roles and other things, taught by the Babylonians. Judas would have been the most difficult role. Playing roles implies knowledge of our own manifestations—I wish to know my manifestations—not to change them for the better.

We run the risk of substituting sociological approval for objective approval. We must try to see our manifestations "divinely." The first class in such a drama school would be playing roles, the second would be knowledge of types. These types will fall into groups naturally through impartial study. Then you would learn how to act as a type. The third class would be in pantomime. You would be required to convey without words to an audience your interior state. A test would be to try to deceive an intelligent audience. Such a trained audience would acquire a genuine clairvoyance. You would acquire the ability to change your role at will either for the purpose of developing consciousness or for some real purpose.

Gurdjieff gave a dinner—told dirty stories—first his guests had attitude he was kidding them—later the Archbishop became convinced that he really liked such stories so he told one himself. Then another etc.—finally Gurdjieff yawned and stopped them. He said: "See he is not just priest inside." He was adopted by a priest—brought up to go into church—has no any real priestliness in him."

Modern theatre exists for two reasons—pleasure and propaganda (Shaw). None are used as a "mystery" because there are no audiences for it. Gurdjieff says every actor today acts from without not from within. He says the spectator is never challenged by any unexpected manifestation of an actor in character. The drama today is not an experience but a re-experience. Gurdjieff calls it titillation because there are no new influx into one's centers but only associations. It procreates but does not create. It induces but does not produce states.

Phosphorous in the atmosphere noted on the ship Karnak—has approached its own planet. Conversation ceases. Book one ends.

Responsibilities—possibilities.

Soul is actor—body is medium through which it acts.

Planetary body—three brains. Drama of life is the use to which the body can be put by the soul. Every soul can become an actor:

1. Acquiring knowledge and control of its medium, learning to manipulate it in any form of expression.

2. A soul must have knowledge and understanding of types of beings it is likely to encounter—the number of types is limited (twenty-seven) and so experience and understanding of types would enable one to deal with them and to handle them.

3. Necessary to soul as actor is some conception of role it must play in relation to object for which it exists, i.e. must have a degree of objective conscience and of objective reason. In ancient schools of occultism, drama was employed as a series of exercises for playing roles in life. Teachers had to be familiar with nature of man.

Man is a three-centered being, acting un-simultaneously.

We vary in behavior of centers according to degrees of experience we have had in each center. Every stimulus varies according to experience we have had in that center.

Over intellectualizing is impossible—means under emotionalizing and so with other centers. We are irregular triangles. Always one center in us is more developed than the other two. This makes melodrama our sole experience. Thanks to our education, this predecision to take a non-dramatic, non-whole view of life has become a pseudo non-essential. Ancient drama induced threefold harmonization. It is possible to evoke discordant responses from same individuals when the same spectacle is presented.

The number of people you have met if you recall them pictorially will illustrate all types. You can characterize them 3-1-3, 3-1-2, etc. Other method—as miser, Don Juan, Hamlet, Falstaff, Micawber, etc. There are only twenty-seven of these. This is the framework for knowledge of mankind. "There but for the grace of God . . ."

Sociology is the only reason our type is apt to be concealed. By playing roles in drama you become familiar with types.

A being is one who experiences. At any moment something is happening to us psychologically. There are psychic counterparts to our physical states. This is experiencing. Imagine yourself to be seated in a room being unaware that your experiencings are being made manifest in a cartoon. Experiencing = manifestations. Manifestations are the only means by which spectators become aware of one's experiencings.

Art of drama—to be able to produce the effect of manifestations as if they were the result of experiencings.

Inability to control manifestations is real sincerity. One who being unable to control the manner of his manifestations, selects from his experiences one element, then claims he is sincere. Actor is first aware of manifestations, then adapts them to his means.

Never do we act in one center at a time. It should be possible to act in three centers simultaneously. This would make it possible to respond to all types, to adapt to every individual.

Mimicry—a fine game of childhood which we squelch. Guessing of children is simply green blade which would evolve into intuition with certainty if it were not discouraged. We are suffering from the defect of scientific attitude, which discourages guessing, lying or mimicry of children. Mimicry of children if trained would develop into power of controlling manifestations. We have to work to recover what should have been our birthright.

Critical audience in front—pupil on stage—directed to engage in self-interrogation in regard to this first impulse. Can he do this? What does he or you feel impelled to do? Pupil's first idea might be: "I'd like to give that policeman a piece of my mind." He therefore looks into the wings. Would say: "Hey! What you doing? Can't you see these people over there quarreling?" then play is begun. Fellow addressed must behave as a policeman—must carry illusion—next soldier and then cobbler—etc. He had to be able to respond with any technique. This was basis of the old Greek plays. Dramatic school of those days was training for universal life. It's possible that groups here in America might do likewise.

Enneagram. The whole of our body is under the law of seven. Psyche under the law of three. In the octave there are two semitones. Mechanical law of seven will be perfectly fulfilled only when the law of three necessitates intervention at certain critical points.

Every one of us is a channel through which two streams are passing—experiencing—(law of three) and manifesting—(law of seven). Experiencing—think, feel and do. These are not under our control now. If we could control them our manifestations would indicate conscious acts, (and conscious art). Actors had to pass the test of acting according to any type, before being allowed to pass to mystery.

Mystery differed from ordinary play by introduction of semitones into the ordinary octave. This was done so: the policeman aforementioned would occasionally manifest his ability to regulate his conduct on occasion by introducing an act determined by his own soul and not by the role or any imitation.

The design for the spectator was to induce the expectation of normality and then for the actor to change from acting a role to acting as a conscious being. This required a terrific degree of perception by spectator and questioning.

One's soul had already all this knowledge but it is inaccessible. But if we ponder the material already given to us we will gradually begin to see light.

30 MAY 1927

Here is a parallel with the Bible in that it opens with cosmology and cosmogony, an account of the world and why. It proceeds through a series of semi-historical episodes interwoven with myths into which eventually come clear the major and minor prophets. The reader is expected to become aware of duty to God. Compare with Ashiata. After the objective conscience is awakened comes the New Testament, which is the method, taught by individuals. Objective reason after objective conscience. Proceeds by instructions assuming the method. It culminates in the elevation of the personal nature in the most diligent of disciplines.

Thus the Bible may be considered as a drama, an objective work of art. Gurdjieff's book is perhaps a bible for the future. (At any rate Orage thinks Gurdjieff had some such purpose in mind.)

Ships: Methods of communication within the individual, how to go to places and find forgotten things. We are also a megalocosmos with unknown parts spatially distant; time and distance. Cosmology is a concrete psychology.

Old Testament—actualities.

New Testament—potentialities.

Gurdjieff's work has text, music and exercises. It is a complete method.

- First phase: self-observation, participation, experiment.
- Second phase: voluntary suffering.
- Third phase: conscious labor.

The thesis of the book is that we as human beings suffer and labor. This is obligatory although at times so distributed that some seem to escape; but the total tax is the same, two thousand million people annually yield this tax. The purpose of religious reformers is to show how this tax of suffering in addition to being paid can be turned to use. There is no idea that it can be lifted. (Stories at times of task masters who have taken too large a share.) But a personal advantage may be derived:

- From voluntary suffering may come *consciousness*.
- From conscious labor, *will*.
- From self-observation, participation and experiment, *individuality*.

Buddha's disciples within one generation fell into the error of thinking that they could surprise consciousness in other than normal circumstances. This resulted in Tibet.

Chapter on Apes: An ape is a caricature of a three-centered being. An experiment to see whether man can be made to behave normally. Visit to Egypt: A scientific theocracy. Distribution of temples, school etc. according to human patterns, organs with physiologic and psychic functions over the whole country. It is possible to go to a spot and say here was a temple, a school and excavate

Fifth descent: An epic event. Which events on the planet stand out for me personally, real or imaginary? (Effect on Orage when at age of fifteen he read Plato's account of the death of Socrates, was profuse weeping.) We do not know where we are. We may be lying asleep on an island of the Sun Absolute. Space and time are psychological. Experience may be second hand intuition and divine meaning of dreams. This is historically unimportant. What is important is its effect on us. An objective truth becomes a subjective fact.

Hamalinadir—no personal key.

We are speculative in regard to the nature of the world, our function etc. Our reason, objective reason, divine reason. Hamalinadir still thought that two times two was four.

Ashiata's study of human nature finds divine forces of faith, hope and love degenerated through association with purely mechanical meanings. Reasoning had also no use. Appeal to objective conscience and memories of childhood. Platonic doctrine of recollection, anamnesis. Already know but must be reminded. Hence Socrates interrogates and does not state. Dialectic developed in this. The result of the work of Ashiata was a planetary culture. At preset Babel, laboring for a cosmopolitan culture, a belief that by introducing enough different languages and culture and values, we will find a value. Ruling classes not in agreement; not working toward the same aim. If so the effect on institutions would be revolutionary. Under the regime of a world state, the planet would be organized for functions.

Ireland: psychic, lines of force, magnetism.

India: philosophy.

The reaction of Lentro-hamox constantly happening to us. Realization becomes merely verbal, e.g. what realization do you have of chapter on time? Reaction. The Greeks are responsible for technical degeneration. The day after you read the chapter on time, take up Alexander and engage in dialectics. Technical postmortem on a dead realization, Greek dialectics. The Romans are responsible for technical degeneration of objective conscience. The memory of objective conscience in Roman law. Greek dialectics are responsible for the degeneration of human reason, Roman law for the degeneration of objective reason. Later physiological inventions. Greeks and Romans at least corrupted on a higher plane. Later on lower. The German spirit (which has nothing to do with racial or geographical Germany). Prototypes of psychological characteristics of German type that degeneration takes the form of something physiological.

How many people whom you know have understanding. It is of two types: logical understanding based on fact and rational understanding as applied to the problem of ourselves. Why alive? What values? Understanding is neither intellect nor intuition but equally positive.

Positive—father—the intellect.

Passive—mother—the intuition.

Neutral—the child—understanding.

The creation of the neutral quality is the object of this work.

Psychological systems based on: norms and averages.

The usual psychology is the sum of facts provided by current behavior. Contemporary psychology measures by the average of contemporary manifestations at any one period.

Man exists for a purpose not his own; this includes all beings. The norm of man is the discharge of the design for which he was created; like a machine made to do a certain work. He was created normal.

Owing to certain circumstances this planet has developed as an abnormal machine, which no longer fulfills its design. Hence life exists on this planet by sufferance (grace). A by-product of the fulfillment of a normal aim would have been complete happiness for us. We are no longer capable of the happiness which accompanies the fulfillment of a design. We suffer in consequence. Define what is considered to be a normal human being (see Bhagavad Gita—how does he walk?) Ponder the formulation of a norm. We cannot begin to develop non-psychopathically except on the basis of a norm. Abnormality: self-pride, vanity, touchiness, egoism, etc.

Third statement.

There was once on the planet a race of normal men and women. Then what happened? A planetary catastrophe. The nature of this planet is now inimical to the development of a normal man. Renan in 1865 said in his "philosophic dialogues": "Nature is hostile to the development of man and desires mans imperfections." Gurdjieff's theory is that this is true but not totally irremediable, though the chances are a million to one with the handicap of education and the present attitude of society. This chance is strengthened by two things.

1. The wish of the creator that his machines should function normally, hence messengers have been sent to point out the abnormalities.

2. The continued existence in all, except hasnamusses, of conscience as an inward unrest about our abnormality. In a hasnamuss the germ of a conscience is dead; he is beyond shame.

There is a striving for perfection, which is practically impossible to attain. All messengers agree on:

1. The terror of the situation.

2. This to be overcome: degeneracy, dependence on others and absorption in current ideals; social values instead of personal.

We substitute aims instead of making a good job of whatever we are doing. This for ourselves. Man exists for perfection. The method is observation of self in contrast with the norm as defined by union of conscience with intellect (intuition). The norm becomes a framework into which observation is fitted. This reveals the degree to which we are normal or abnormal; what is in contrast to what ought to be.

[*Here begins Orage's review of the book, trying to formulate ideas implied in the allegory.*]

Preface: There is a certain grammar of association in every mind, in two forms: association of words, association of forms. Reasoning, verbally and by ideas. Nine-tenths of what we call thought is mechanical association of words. Say "agony" to a superficial writer and he will say "anguish, sweet, dark night of the soul," etc. as readily as a parrot. The association of form is dependent on personal experiences, still an association but different from mere words.

It is the form in which peasants often think; or those whom we call "understanding." It has strict reference to experience, a grammar with people in whom the experiences exist; avenues to a language not in words (gesture, voice etc.), a strict grammar. Attempt to use language of understanding.

Man is (normal) a being (a machine that feels) designed to encounter, to create and to overcome difficulties. Contrast this with view of man who believes that man exists for happiness, peace, etc.

You may create difficulties in fields of your own choice; but make aims which require effort to attain. Overcoming counts; results are the test. No sentimentality, no attitude of the cricket player "well missed old chap." Read Milton and see he was a fighting machine and spared himself no blame for his failures, no crown for the splendid failure. See essay by J. A. Froude on Reynard the Fox. Practical effectiveness in overcoming.

We have respect for the person who encounters great difficulties even though he did not wish to. If he is crumpled, we pity; if he survives merely, we cannot help according him our respect. Or who voluntarily creates difficulties, i.e. who undertakes jobs which require effort (stretching himself) to achieve.

Never do as others do (advice given by Gurdjieff's grandmother), become responsible for the way chosen and its results. That is: do things in your own way. Man is in essence a passion for attaining a reasonable understanding of the meaning and aim of existence. It is the value of value. You may not suspect this of yourself, saying you are a humble person. Take off the onion a few more skins and all the troubles, criticisms from dissatisfaction are revealed.

31 MAY 1927

The body we have is simply a creation of nature—we have no quarrel whatever with modern psychologists, physiologists, physicists, embryologists, etc. We can hand over the body to them. We wish to see that all this time we have been associated with this body. We might have learned through it, done something in it actually and really have grown through it. Biologically how this body was created by the planet or nature, is no concern of ours.

We have one word only to remind us that we are not just a body—"I." But I have had no experiences. Every hair of my head I have eaten—yet I have not transmuted the food. Nature has done this. But out of this aftoegocratic process which necessarily goes on, it is simultaneously possible for an individual to get something out of the process truly for oneself (for I).

I am an immortal being capable of all experiences—of individuality, consciousness and will. But the body is capable of only a limited short existence. Even thinking takes place as inevitably and automatically in us as it does in a cat. We have no more control over our day dreams than we have over our night dreams.

What can I do then?

One thing. The truth is, we are souls and have bodies—but there is current a lie to the effect that we are bodies and have souls.

Now we can do one thing. Observe this body with non-identification as "I." After several years of effort at listening to the tones of my voice—without wishing to change it—without approval—merely aiming at a purely recording act of "I." Yet after all these years of such effort it is not easier to do. The only difference is that with equal effort I can hear this voice longer at one time and at more frequent intervals. There are only five forms of physical behavior to observe under this method. There are forms of behavior that one must not, in truth, attempt to observe. (We must not observe emotions, though it is dangerous for that to be said, for you will, tomorrow morning, if not sooner, have lost the "not" and say "Oh, I remember. He said to observe my emotions.") The result of observing the five forms of physical behavior—one thing will be accomplished—you can some time realize the meaning of "I have a body."

In the Pythagorean school the pupil was put under a vow of silence regarding this method for a period of seven years. Not because he was jealous of this knowledge being disseminated but because of the effect upon the pupil himself. The first danger is that you transfer merely into words the energy aroused in the emotional center and in the practical center. And second, if you merely talk to someone and do not at the same time guarantee to yourself to do ten times as much work as you can properly expect from the people you talk to.

A white elephant is no more creditable than another one. If we are tall, strong, beautiful—this is an accident. So we guarantee to take the pride out of anyone—not by humiliating him—but by setting him this task and letting him prove to himself that he cannot do it. A human being is an animal in the possession of a soul. We all start with a sleeping soul and a waking body. It is not more difficult for one of us than for another, the quantity of effort is dependent on ourselves. If one of us could put the same energy into this work that you could easily put into arranging your affairs to go to some desirable spot in France or elsewhere—for one month—you would have transmuted the psychological condition from a most squalid state to one of a comparative paradise.

Well then, how shall we begin to prepare for this journey? You know a savage can count to four—one, two, three, four, but more than four is "many." A hen can distinguish between one and two but not between two and three or more. Well—how to observe these five forms of physical behavior?

Well, which is most important to begin with? None, they are exactly of equal importance. Don't spend a second on determining which of them to begin with, just begin at once on the one at hand. Say—posture, facial expression, gesture, movement, tone of voice—it does not matter which. Take one of them and determine that you will finish that job. Know every gesture all day long.

Don't make excuses. I've made them all. But the difference is that I have made them all and can't bear repeating any one of them. Tell me a new excuse and I'll use it, at least for one night—and I won't make that day the nightly review. What is "nightly review"? It consists of going over the behavior of your body in a series of pictures—what would have appeared on a three dimensional screen, not as shadows but as figures. Recall before the mind's eye in a series of three dimensional pictures the panorama of your body's behavior during the day. If you do this you will acquire a real imagination with power.

QUESTION: What can one do to eliminate worry over past events and fear of future ones since we should not observe emotions?

ANSWER: Observe the physical symptoms. My hands are cold, my eyes are welling full of tears, my knees are shaky, etc. Enumerate them all. But perhaps you cannot finish all such symptoms before the grief has—unfortunately quite disappeared.

Suppose the state is a happy one. I observe a good startling manly tone of voice, a disposition to jump or run or whatnot—eyes sparkle, etc. Now what happens? This positive emotional state is surprisingly intensified.

"To work is to pray" was meant in this sense. Of course it was very soon turned to the so-called advantage of slave owners or drivers.

Next, participation. Well that simply means "taking part in." Taking part in these five forms of behavior. When you are speaking—say I will speak a little more clearly than usual. Though the larynx will still be doing the same work you will be running alongside so to speak.

Or in a posture, say to body—"No, don't move from that posture. It may not be comfortable but I put it here and I will participate in that posture." There are two blood circulations—one keeps the body going and the second is your own private property and with it you can participate in the activities of your body.

Then experiment. Experiment for the sake of seeing if you can change. How I see at once all of the thousand and one notions of self-improvement coming down upon us! "I don't like that facial expression—I'll change it. I don't like this or that so I'll change it, etc., etc. So this surely means I put myself to school to improve myself. Don't believe it. Wring the neck of any impulse to improve yourself. Be sure you are as a body utterly beyond hope of improvement. No! Experiment only for the sake of seeing if you can change. Experiment only in matters of complete indifference—let all matters in which you are concerned go without interference.

When you awake in the morning open only one eye at first, get out of bed in an unhabitual way, don't look at the clock for a moment—just for the sake of varying your behavior. In this case you send energy through a smaller pipe and it is thus a means of saving energy. It will surprise you to find how fresh you feel as such a day goes by.

These experiments are part and parcel of this ancient and occult method that is so simple that it confuses most of us very greatly. Five minutes of practice is worth a thousand years of just listening. There is a deadly opinion prevalent to the effect that one can be changed by just listening.

So here, if those of you who listen, are intellectually interested, but who have done little, do not do something, it may become unnecessary to bring one here who will deal with these very differently.

Voluntary suffering is suffering the unpleasant manifestations of other beings. A snake, mouse or spider—will produce a sharp emotional state in many of us. So some people will affect some of us. And voluntary suffering consists in controlling your facial expressions and other forms of behavior or in concealing them or in changing them. A man enrages me—I want to strike him. But voluntary suffering requires that you respond as if he pleased you, etc.

Conscious labor. Make a vow and keep it—dress for a week in a different way from usual. To clear up the indebtedness you may have within a certain period. To write all the letters you owe. To do twice as much as you ever have in one week on some definite work. You are to meet a friend—have a number of topics you will discuss that are interesting to him and to yourself. Be and exist purposively. Man is placed on this planet and put into the occupation of a body to develop individuality, will and consciousness.

Individuality—by separating "I" and "it."

Consciousness—by manifesting differently mechanical negative reactions.

Will—by always living purposely, always with an object, a purpose

You know the object, the means and you know that no one will help you in this world. Conscious effort is continuity in always having a purpose.

17 OCTOBER 1927

Ponder the sentences of last time, drawing on memory, reading association to use as pegs. Whether you accept or not does not matter,

Grammar in mind always operative; two kinds:

1. Verbal.
2. Forms, ideas or mental energies.

Those who have understanding. This can be cultivated by pondering, which is an effort to think of abstract subjects (metaphysics, cosmology). There are many ideas in this book we are incapable of understanding. We assume on the contrary that if the truth is stated clearly we can understand it, but we must develop understanding, not only by direct pondering but by handling present situations practically. Relation of time to needs; money and expenditures.

A normal human being—designed to encounter, create and overcome difficulties. A psychic being consists of its appetites. When we speak of psychology, we speak of the kind of desire which animates it. Essence is the kind of desire. In the case of a human being, the desire to encounter and overcome difficulties. A fighting edge for the universe. We are completely happy only when thus engaged. When diverging from this norm we are abnormal. This explains the accumulated hatred in this book for artists, scientists, poets in general. They substitute for normal aims (encountering and overcoming difficulties) some temporal forms such as pursuit of beauty, acquiring of riches, material conquest of the planet. And as the artist influences other men, the book regards him as an evil influence. He tends to withdraw man's interests and energy from man's normal aim, hence hostile to the great scheme.

In the essence of man in his normal state is a hunger and thirst. A biblical hunger and thirst for objective reason (meaning and aim of existence). Man is executively equipped to meet difficulties, emotionally passionate for knowledge. He is a sword bent into a scythe of interrogation.

Never do as others do. Do things in your own way. If we consider we are forbidden to imitate others, we will concentrate on the situation and ask what we can do uniquely in this situation. Ponder so that the theory may be definitely our own or else be also definitely rejected.

Try and set down in your own words, the idea of life entertained by any one of your friends or by yourself. The man on a desert island has to settle such problems himself. What is your idea of the world?

Materialistic hypothesis: Is the world merely by chance? Is there design? Is there any conscious purpose? Any aim or object? The current view is that there is no aim; that protoplasm formed accidentally etc. If life were accidental were conditions of life also accidental?

Or any other current point of view? Such as, that God is omnipotent and all loving. The world is being designed for us entirely, not us for God, done out of benevolence and gratuitous. At no time does he need help and presides over the universe with no other idea than that his children should be happy. That we have no obligation and no responsibility, no duty except to each other. At the same time man was commissioned with power over the inferior species; and the sacrifice of millions of the lower creatures is authorized etc. All this is a replica of the attitude of the ordinary, selfish, overindulged child towards its parents. Not old enough (not in years) to realize that nothing comes to them which did not cost somebody, or nature, something. This is a wide spread attitude and is the Christian doctrine. Cosmological view. Implicit in each person is the key to his behavior (chief feature); chapter one is the first adumbration of this view. That the world that is knowable, the objective universe is a work of conscious creation; that it is consciously maintained and for a conscious purpose. It is like a machine created for a conscious purpose. Of drawing from the machine something which the creator of it wished. This is not merely for our delight, nor for fun but in pursuit of an aim entertained by himself. The onus of the reason is on God. The point of view may be criticized as anthropomorphic. It is also theomorphic. If it makes God in the image of man it also makes man in the image of God. Animals do not make machines; man has reason to understand the meaning of machines; and is possibly in a position to understand the meaning of a machine, vaster than any he could himself make.

Though designed to have a passion for understanding, and power to develop it, man has departed from the norm. Man is in a state of hypnosis. His normal understanding has been converted into abnormal. He has only glimpses, shadows of his real passion to understand and to overcome.

We cannot, while the fumes of the drug remain, pull ourselves together and reason. We want to be reasonable and cannot. We have a haunting conscience that we are not acting reasonably. The parable of "The Prodigal Son," in a far country (psyche) feeding swine and aware of it, yet cannot remember his father's country—the problem is to bring ourselves to realize what we know and how to awaken ourselves.

There are no magical means which would not destroy the possibility of a normal awakening. The only sure means is a daily attempt to ponder the meaning of life and by an attempt to deal with the situation, not only without complaining but spiritedly. Here we have a taste of normal activity.

The physicist's conception of the nature of energy. Solar energy is not inexhaustible—Bertrand Russell. Dissipation of energy: inhaling and exhaling breath of Brahma in the Indian tale. The solar system runs down. This is not the point of view of this book. A section is devoted to the creation of a perpetual motion machine, brought into existence in time, but once made it, runs. Its characteristic is that it had a beginning but no end. Though each part is subject to decay, it must be replaced. The objective universe is a perpetual motion machine. At one time it was brought into existence and arranged that the parts should be replaced. For this work of watching the machine and replacing the part there is great need of attention; and with an expanding universe there is need for the superintendence of the mechanism.

This quite simply is Gurdjieff's cosmology: A conscious being created a perpetual motion machine, always within his power but needing constant attention (growing family of worlds) and so he prepared three-centered helpers of God. We can be a society of helpers, instead of being slaves, which we are in any case. But to be conscious helpers means co-working and understanding.

Is there any response to that suggestion? It may be one of negative emotion to the sense of our painful realization of our inadequacy, realize our plight—the terror of the situation. And yet we are within easy reach of sanity, only a thin veil of illusion separates us. We are "poverty-stricken millionaires." Starving and no way to food by ordinary reason; and yet we have potentialities. Those who have tried to draw out of themselves with sentences are sometimes surprised at their potentialities. Think highly of this output in comparison with complete ignorance; but little in comparison with potentialities.

Everything and nothing, a double emotion in everything real. Man has a passion to understand aims and meaning. Fitting himself executively to overcome difficulties, and to cooperate voluntarily. His freedom is service; it is a paradox in all reality.

Threefold classification everywhere:

1. Sun Absolute (will talk later about what it means), representing reason.

2. Any sun.

3. Any planet.

Three orders of matter are associated with intelligence, emotion, instinct. God is conceived of as a being whose intellectual body consists of the Sun Absolute; his emotional body of all suns; his planetary body of the planets.

The design for the three-centered beings on the planet is that they should develop; and with the pursuit of understanding etc., the other two bodies will develop. The normal life of the astral body is a passion for understanding; of the intellectual body, the power to understand. By pursuing this normal development we gratify the need and create the body, there is no other way of developing normally. The pursuit of any minor aim will have the result of distorting the growth, understanding etc.

Here occurs a section entitled "Being aware of genuine duty."

Not arbitrarily imposed. We already, so to speak, incarnate this duty, as the structure of a machine carries embodied in it its purpose and functions. Structure is purpose manifested. It is not a question of discovering a duty in us, not congenial to our mechanisms. Organic duty: i.e. duty of acting according to our mechanism, organism. Distinguish the normal organism and present abnormal state. Start by asking: what do you think is wrong with the human race? And try to formulate what you regard as the characteristics of a normal human being. Use imagination on one side and criticism on the other. To discover in ourselves divergences from the normal and so get stimulation for attempting to become normal. Use pencil and paper, and being Western trained, write it out. For increase in articulateness and formulation of what you understand. Pass back and forth between self-observation and thought.

Question your personal problems. Do you feel like risking having your feelings scratched? Reason is a material substance. By living constantly and actively reasoning, making use of every chance, as when inhaled, to enhance insight, imagination, etc. Like an atmosphere where monks have contemplated. Appetite for reason best exemplified in questions. Man's reason is questioning, while his emotion desires.

In understanding people who are unsympathetic is a question of associations. All my words are related to my associations. The same words in the vocabulary are related to different associations. Associations much the same, words are different. Experiment with different words. Interrogative attitude; intelligent trying. (Sympathy is chemically determined and outside of understanding. You can hate and understand.)

We are always engaged in avoiding difficulties, trying to reach a point where effort will cease. "Man is a boat, rowing in one direction and looking in another." Freud's discovery that whatever the explicit aim, we are really heading towards extinction. How much do I desire this cessation? How far do I diverge from the norm?

Is there a third grammar? Association of words, forms, logic.

Forms are manifestations of logic, e.g., a physicist says dissipation of energy (i.e. in time, the unique subjective) and merging. A creating physicist must meet the logical necessity of circumventing this process. He had no wish that it should be one form or another. He had no forms in his mind, merely the abstract logical use and logical possible solution. Thinking in forms: man is a three-brained creature. Not the example of man as he is, but the idea on which he is built or designed. For example in a book on botany, a plant is an ascending spiral but at certain points by line, the tree is a combination of all spirals in the vegetable kingdom. Why the variety of forms? Why a mechanism of spirals thus formed? We are still interrogating that. We find answers in objective reason as to why. Forms—Plato: the idea of a chair, "the quality of a chair," an abstraction in the concrete. This is what is meant. Man is in essence a passion to understand and a will to overcome. Why? Because he is designed to be an active cooperator.

We have a wish. The wish is already an entity; you have harbored a being. It may be of the ephemeridae for if not gratified it soon may die. Or if a little higher, it may live as long as its energy permits. If your nature is rich, you may find desires which will last all your life. Further, you may have desires which will outlive your body. In Saurat's point of view, our immortality depends on our having desires which outlast the body. This might be a passion for understanding which outlives the planetary body.

24 OCTOBER 1927

Accidental association of words: man who got emotional over "vengeance is mine" because his father who was a minister had used it in anger. Association of ideas; when trying to acquire any different technique, at first we fumble; then "I've got the hang of it." I understand, I'm onto it. Similarly get onto the idea that the universe was created and we, for a purpose of producing certain forces.

Curiosity in regard to:

- How—practical.
- What—scientific.
- Why—philosophical.

What are they in their essences, these sentences? What is Gurdjieff saying? There is a verbal and a formal understanding of death. Try to reformulate; the effort of doing this will result in formulations crystallizing almost automatically. The progress from one form of understanding to another is not by extension.

Gurdjieff classifies scientists into real and pseudo. The real seeker wants to know "what" only in order to answer the question "why."

Technique for developing:

Verbal association is developed by words.

Formal association is developed by association with wiser people.

Certain persons who have associations with peasants, Arabians, etc., return with developed understanding. Logical understanding is developed only by conscious preoccupations with questions of what is the meaning and aim of existence.

Every individual has as his genuine duty the development of objective reason. Done by inquiry and preparing himself to inquire. Thus like an oyster, he develops his pearl. Conscious labor is labor for consciousness, effort is psychological effort. Positive self-observation etc. Voluntary suffering in increasing the effort expended. Effort is painful. Conscious labor: questioning as to why.

According to Gurdjieff's psychology there are only two fundamental emotions:

Love of being and fear of non-being.

All negative emotions can be traced to fear of non-being. They threaten to contract our being. All that expands our being etc. expanding our ego-life, with love we expand our being. With hate and fear, we contract it.

The Book of Dzyan, a Sanskrit fragment in its opening stanzas asks these questions. Madam Blavatsky's "Secret Doctrine" is a commentary on these. All beings are classified according to their reason; each is a step on a ladder. The reason of a being is the coordinated sum of his normal functions. Man's is higher only because the elements entering into it are more complex. Since the majority of human functions are abnormal his reason is also abnormal.

Man by definition is superior to the animals but in fact, his reason is abnormal. Abnormality of man is summed up—the absence of fear of non-being. A rabbit threatened with death runs; man does not run. (Man knows that he inevitably will die some day, but this has no consequences for his life.)

What cosmology?

Pondering for example, the phrase "creative imagination." What was intended to be meant by it, by the person who coined it, and to us imagination is imagery. Can I image something which I have not seen? Which is not composed of objects I have seen, in a void? No! How does fancy differ? It is less precise. In greater artists we have imagination; in lesser, fancy. What distinguishes? What gives a difference of value which we naturally assign? Come back to the word "creative." Is it fancy versus creation? Where is creation? Perhaps creative is an exaggerated word; perhaps "directed," recollecting and recombining images. It can be thus used for fancy is undirected. Directed imagination is something more. What did Coleridge mean by it? Perhaps the phrase is related to creator? What effect has the faculty on an artist or thinker? Did it create something in him?

What does imagination create? In the reader an elevation of mood, to a higher plane, a climb. But perhaps this is only a feeling. What is the evidence that I am not fooling myself? What evidence that I have climbed? I see a wider expanse and less detail. Make imaginative exercises. Survey the population of this planet as an exercise in directed imagination. It produces an elevation of spirit with inability to consider details.

Normal versus average. We have never seen the normal; only average and abnormal. We are sub-ordinary. We must progress from abnormal through ordinary to normal ordinary. Byron was lacking in human sensibility, which makes possible the genius of his verse. But we think super ordinary.

Birth. Development of "I."

The birth of the body is natural. In the development of the body we can find only the pattern, but stages are identical.

Self-observation, I. Experimentation. Youth of "I." Voluntary suffering. Conscious labor. The result is a fully grown "I," and therefore its normal life would begin. The soul has reached its responsibility and enters on its functions.

External phase. Classify according to type. Modern psychologists are explorers without a map. This psychology (Gurdjieff's) offers a map to the traveler. There has been given to this planet a particular attention because it is abnormal, a mote in the eye of the universe.

The moon was split off on account of an accident, perhaps to develop a certain kind of soul. Reading is a modern substitute for opinion with the same effects only on the cerebral center instead of emotional. Sakaki kept the passengers on a doomed ship playing poker. Just as the English government keeps the unpaid classes distracted with cinemas, races and gambling.

Kundabuffer is vestigial. The pineal gland is a vestigial eye. The appendix, though still with some functions, is vestigial. Customs and habits are continued by sociological causes.

Consequence: do not people judge by what they have for theory and hear say and not by what they know. Practically anybody can be persuaded that reading about imaginary people is a form of experience. We also are apt to believe that experience is communicable, that we can be taught by it. Or that we wish rest and peace; or that to be rich is a happier state than to be poor; that people are inferior or superior according to their station in life, or for their possessions, or charm, or education, or gifts. Such as a gift for writing, comparable to a wart or a prehensile thumb. That national greatness is a condition of individual happiness. That amusement amuses. That distinguished company is brilliant. That inspiration can take the place of work. That other peoples praise is satisfactory or that their disapproval is debilitating. Praise acts as a sedative and disapproval provokes a sharp practice and a provocative attitude. That books, music and pictures are stimulating, a pathetic assumption that we are receiving passive impressions. That leisure without previous work is agreeable. That it is possible to do nothing. That fame has a real value or the possession of power or success. Continue this list.

These are due to a general property of kundabuffer. We are unable to ponder because pondering might disturb our self-calm which is a peace of mind without understanding the meaning of life. Egoism is the substitution for right and wrong of "I like" and "I don't like."

I like or do not like.

It is good or bad.

It is right or wrong.

Tastes are of the instinctive center.

Emotional center; it is good.

Intellectual center; it is right or wrong for the effect intended.

The words "I like" and "I don't like" should be left to children.

Means by which the influence of the properties of kundabuffer act: suggestibility is sociological, born in our biological structure. Of all the impressions received we note those indicated by suggestion. "Blood-stream" the continuum of biology, suggestibility the mechanism of our psychology. We shall never understand anything without personal effort—conscious labor which is labor to understand. We do not acquire understanding by experience. Most obligations are fulfilled because of punishments and rewards.

Essentially there is no difference between man and woman. Perhaps man meets his problems with an intellectual emphasis and woman with emotional. But differentiation of sex does not arise until embryo has passed this note in the third month of gestation.

Vine and the tendril—tendril sent out by the vine to reconnoiter.

Sociological origin of a split personality for a child says: "Billy did so and so." We teach him to use "I," bringing about his own identification with his planetary body. We must attain the right to use the word "I." We must be able to objectify the body, consider it as a possession.

"The kingdom of heaven is within you and if ye know yourselves ye shall find it." This saying was attributed to Jesus in a parchment discovered about forty years ago. Also: "Know yourselves and ye shall be aware that ye are the sons of the father," date about 350 AD.

Pondering always refers to the question why, ratiocination to what. Why am I alive? Start by eliminating all the familiar answers. Find all useless. No answer is left except the craving for an answer. The body can only dream: "Who shall deliver me from the body of this death"? I can only escape from dreams by dis-identifying. Then "I" can wake up though the body continues to sleep.

All undirected thought wastes the organism, wastes time, wastes energy (the daily ration). In the intervals when not thinking of anything, think of something. If not pondering on these matters, think of practical problems. The material for pondering is the forms of experience. Pondering requires thinking in forms.

All verbal communications are really impossible, or at least relative. We communicate by recognition of a similarity of experience. All experience is ineffable; but we try to formulate certain forms of thought "at which we throw words." But the formulation is not the form. There are many possible formulations for each form.

The wish of wishes in man is the wish to understand, but this wish is broken up into a variety of wishes; a bush instead of a trunk. The variation accomplishes nothing but the fundamental wish remains.

Myths: Osiris was cut in pieces and scattered over the planet. It was the work of Isis (wisdom) to reintegrate, make whole. Then man is man.

SECTION ON TIME

Time is a process that cannot be sensed, felt or understood. Only phenomena can be known but time is the unique subjective, never subject to be known.

I am an ability to experience; but this ability to experience is determined by the organism. The potentials of my personal experience are conditioned by the winding of my three centers or brains. At the present time our three brains act according to chance. The result is that experience teaches us nothing since the order in which such experiences occur depend on chance and not on logic or reason.

Illustration: a motor car that is run properly is subject to wear and tear; but if improperly run the rate of wear and tear is not determined by its original structure. The incidents of life are not graded in the order in which we can derive real understanding. With the development of essence, experiences would begin to flow in the right order. Coincidences begin to occur more frequently as essence develops. As if providence—a coincidence of octaves.

Our planetary body exists for two purposes:

- A transforming of energies between sun, earth and moon. Like tides.
- To provide a soil in which a soul can develop.

At present only the cosmos in a physical sense makes use of the planetary body. In this sense, we are agents for the supply of food to the "moon."

Thought varies in weight and rapidity; emotions in intensity, body in muscular stress. Try and catch a thought and approximate its weight. Compare the intensity of emotions. And muscular motions in tension.

Act as if "I" exists and it will. Say "I have a body" and you will have one. A man is responsible for all his acts except in death pains.

Sleep, food, etc., should be scheduled for organic needs. The body has many needs for which it has no wants. Satisfaction of wants destroys us; satisfaction of needs builds us up; cf. Wagner's prose works. There is a margin between need and want, e.g. sleep.

5 DECEMBER 1927

[*Orage reads from Bertrand Russell's: "A Free man's worship."*]

Bertrand Russell is the Hamalinadir of modern Europe. Another extract—Russell's dream of happiness (cooperation instead of competition). He diagnoses to psychic causes in man which prevent cooperation. He is describing consequences of the properties of the organ kundabuffer. Contrast modern psychology and philosophy's point of view with that of Gurdjieff. Make a list of ten questions which puzzle you.

SECOND DESCENT

Planets are mutually dependent on each other's emanations—and these emanations proceed principally from the organic kingdom. On each, the organic kingdom is like a thin coat of varnish on the surface of a football, a skin. As a ray of light falls on a substance, one color being radiated and the other rays absorbed by the substance. We absorb . . .

On each of the planets, nature provides conditions for souls for the creation of those souls necessary for the creator. The body with all its organs exists for one product which is seed, the ability to reproduce. But at the same time, Gurdjieff says that that is to end ——.

In addition to reproducing, there must be producing. In addition to procreation which is biological there must be creation which is psychological. Instead of prolonging the species through a succession of time, the prolonging of the individual and the abolition of time.

Nature provides conditions for both and is indifferent; but the creator's motive is to produce the souls. "On all the planets beings are graded according to their reason." Reason is the sum of normal functions. And there is a natural relation between beings and different "reasons." Relations as in physics. Standards in reasons are impartial. If beings of different reasons meet, the lower would not dispute the superiority. A man really normal would not be harmed by a normal beast. Abnormal conditions of society result in natural conditions being changed. A respected being demanded by inferior beings. Real respect would be natural and inevitable. Men become famous because of oddities, defects etc. The reasonable or rounded man does not attract attention; the oddity does.

5 DECEMBER 1927

THIRD DESCENT

The whole universe exists as to its physical body for the sake of the Sun Absolute. The Sun Absolute is the universe. The body exists so that "I" may understand. The best use to which the cells of the body and the body could be put, and which would give them the most satisfaction is to increase the understanding of "I" who is their God. Analogy—Sun Absolute is the soul body of God. Suns. What is called essence (G. B. Shaw, life force) on certain planets in certain beings coats itself as a cosmic unit. In which the divine reason may exist individually in time after this. It aspires to become a constituent cell of his brain, a cell in the highest brain of God.

The substance of essence is called "prana." (Sometimes said to be the blood of the nervous system.) Life for the planetary body is blood. Life for the astral body is prana.

If crystallized in anyone, thereafter one must improve it in divine reason or reincarnate perpetually. Current occult groups say we all reincarnate and have already done so in time. According to the theosophist, not in recurrence. According to Gurdjieff this is untrue. Reincarnation is the exception occurring only when individuality has begun, when one's prana has begun to crystallize. Then there is no escape; one must go on while the seed is gestated. Gurdjieff: "Blessed is he who has a soul; blessed is he who has none; but unhappy is he who has the conception of one."

This concerns only a few in relation to the rest; essence is thrown into the melting pot from which new beings emerge but never the same essence—Peer Gynt and The Button Moulder. Many of us have an essence, not yet crystallized and therefore not yet recognizable.

In proper conditions, kundabuffer however developed, from birth, gradually atrophies. What are the proper conditions? Buddha's eightfold path of right thinking etc. When kundabuffer is atrophied normal development begins. The souls may develop rapidly.

Akhaldans—seekers after the meaning and aim of existence, ponderers. Members grade according to their intensity of desire. They affirm nothing, they are only seekers. The bell tent and the central pole, the aim and meaning of existence may be an impossible aim but that aim must be the tent pole. Pursuit of this aim is religion.

Men used to live between twelve and fifteen-hundred years. (Orage has no idea how this is to be taken.) No evidence of any literal truth. Perhaps to be taken in the sense of activity in three centers. The centers run down, the period of learning is over, a creature capable of learning which has ceased to learn. It may be said this creature is no longer man.

The reason that certain parts of the planet become centers of intensive population and other parts become war areas is that nature demands from those parts of the planet vibrations only provided by congested population or by death.

QUESTION: What is it to be ordinary?

ANSWER: A workman-like attitude to any job. If one has an extraordinary gift, this does not mean that one must cease to exercise it, but must not be with an extraordinary psychology attached to it. Must regard this extraordinary gift from an ordinary point of view; not attaching too much value to what is a product of biology.

Ordinary—subordinary—extraordinary.

To become normal we must first become ordinary, in psychology. Subordinary and extraordinary are identified with the lack or presence of some special gift. "Ordinary" does not refer to the organism but to the psychological attitude to it. One must be non-identified.

The method cannot be proven theoretically. The psyche is always active and demonstratively never passive and logical. Potentials are only experienceable but never logically demonstrable. Stretch your mind with exercises, efforts of real imagining in reality. Such as the exercise of imagining the total population on the planet etc., or in place of the planet on the solar system in relation to Hercules in the milky way, to other milky ways.

14 DECEMBER 1927

FIFTH DESCENT

Ashiata reforms can be scaled. Which plane is it on? Speculate as to how you would begin to change the human species. Ashiata began by distrusting all his beliefs due to sociology. He made himself capable of intellection without image content, i.e. capable of impartiality. He concluded that the species was too far gone in subjectivity for any appeal to love, hope and faith. He settled on objective conscience, representative of God in the essence, not dead but dormant. It could be brought into consciousness. Then man would have an infallible guide as to the nature of his duty. Men understand and cooperate in the scheme of things and pass from the category of slaves into that of sons. He taught the method of self-observation, etc.

Five points of objective morality:

1. *Satisfaction of the planetary body*. Satisfaction here has no connection with gratification; but means the satisfaction of needs. There is an obligation to keep the planetary body in trim, in lean health, without excess or deficiency, without its complaining and making it answer to one's needs. The range of life is conditioned by the planetary body; and it must be regarded as an instrument.

2. *To improve ones being*. What is the meaning of being? I cannot be defined in terms of the intelligence, or of ability or of the state of the planetary body. It is not what we know or can do; but what we are. Ponder the meaning of the word. Have you any fear of being alone? The state of being is the only thing which grows or declines. Most things are determined by the planetary body and in this sense the behaviorist is right as to 99 percent of life. Whether I become facile in languages in art or in earning money is due to chance. Individual growth consists in the growth of being, essence, not personality. Personal attempt to say: what sort of being am I? Am I chicken-livered or do I feel some sort of dignity, apart from my external stupidity? There is only one method of improvement of being—"by effort," being effort. This phrase may have many meanings if regarded by the intellect; but personally one knows what effort has been made. By voluntary effort, the being grows; and fails from the reverse. Review the day for voluntary effort. There is a feeling of strength from having performed this exercise. Life is a gymnasium. St. Paul—always running in the great race. Gurdjieff says: "Always in a state of puff, not

excess but always a little ahead of inclination. Will feel more strong. Self-consciousness passes, disappears and gives confidence, attainment of strength." Gurdjieff uses "spiritual" in the sense of "spirited," a spiritual horse or dog.

3. *To aim always to know more and more of the world, and of its laws and of its creation and maintenance.* The aim of philosophy is the understanding of life. This is not a privilege of a few but a normal function of the human being. It does not require that we give the right answer; but the dignity of man consists of his concern with the question. That he ask of the existing conditions and of his life. What is the meaning of it? One should always be curiously questioning experience. In every situation there is material for questioning. With one faculty one is inquiring while with the other faculties one is behaving ordinarily. There is no need to be aloof or idiosyncratic. Understanding is of the intellectual center. An effort to ponder the meaning and aim of existence automatically stretches all the faculties of the mind, memory, attention, imagination, concentration, etc. become enlarged, not by direct but by indirect exercise. While pondering may be seems to have no result, after a half-hour there may be not a word to say. Worse than that there may be merely an increased realization of ignorance. Socrates said wisdom is realization. Gurdjieff says: "The more you realize you don't know, the more you know, as you will find." Exercise by assembling all you know about beings on this planet; with every breath one is born and with every breath one dies, "breathing this planet." (Refer back to number 2.)

Strength—effort usually on two objects:

a. Over body. Work until painful and then do a little more, a little more than you feel you can do. This is the effort. When a little more painful, then stop. Voluntarily create conditions in which you pass to your second wind.

b. Over feeling. When you feel you can't contain yourself any longer then contain yourself a little longer. That is, waiting a little longer before your manifestations become expressed. Look for your occasions within the bounds of common sense, e.g. difficulty in formulating questions, difficulty in asking questions in the group, overcoming silly little fears. How much stronger are you than three years ago when you started attending these groups. Absence of will to make effort because of the failure to realize the necessity for it.

4. *To pay one's debt in order to be free to serve (duty).* Wordsworth, Ode to Duty. Recognition of performance and justice. Generally speaking we are all of us parasites. Not one of us has discharged his debt to nature. To be alive is a unique miracle. The cost to nature, the preparation of planetary conditions and long periods of civilizations, instrumentalities. In return, the majority of us does nothing but childishly enjoy. In the family of nature, we are self-indulgent children. Recognition of services rendered. Emerson says: "Earn your Living." You may earn it by gratuitous effort. If you have a thousand dollars, spend it intelligently. How dare you squander the efforts of others? "What I cannot think is how nature can let you live."

5. *Helping others to self-individuality.* The key is service. Discriminate between gratifying the weaknesses of others in order to obtain their good opinion of ourselves and helping them to become what they really want: independent, self-conscious, healthy, strong, understanding, capable of performing duty. Usually we merely cater to kundabuffer. On the other hand we dare not be hard on others because this involves the obligation to be doubly hard on ourselves. The only service we can render human beings is a service that will help them discharge their functions as human beings.

"Reason" is defined as the sum of normal functions. Which are these functions to you? A normal human being has five activities or functions:

1. Health.
2. Strength, (quality or force of being).
3. Inquiring for the sake of understanding.
4. Paying the cost of one's living.
5. Service to others.

Relatively to these same values, it is not a question of being Christian disposed. Not a virtue. Question of being a man or a woman.

Any one of these can be isolated and made an idol of, becoming offensive. These five compounded make a normal hum an being. Man is a passion, etc., he has these five processes and behind them, a passion which is integral. Ponder the word "passion." It is an intensification of "craze" and is lifelong and enduring. "Holy" is wholly, a holy (wholly) passion. Every person is holy to the decree of his passion.

[*A question was raised of recurrence and reincarnation.*]

The aim of the tree is to produce seed. There is a difference between a seed and the leaf. In the autumn, the leaves fall; but they do not fall until they have returned their sap to the tree trunk. A certain amount of life is confided to a tree. The leaves breathe. When the season for breathing is ended, life is withdrawn from the leaf. The leaf falls, wasted; next year, there is another leaf. Leaves recur. There is no individual persistence. Life coats itself in a new leaf. But the dropping of a seed is very different; the leaf surrenders its life back. But in the case of seed the life passes into it. It can go anywhere and the life of the tree goes with it. To the tree, a seed is a dead loss, and yet it is what the tree exists for. The leaf is not a dead loss. In the Norse mythology, on Yggdrasil—the tree of life, occasionally seeds appear. Gods and men, they incarnate, having crystallized prana in themselves into seeds. We are recurrent leaves with the possibility of becoming recurrent seeds.

27 DECEMBER 1927

I have been reading current psychology in the Atlantic Monthly, the article "The Paradox of Humanism." The first serious statement after considering behaviorism; the first swallow after winter.

The psyche objects to living in a fool's paradise. Our duty is to anticipate the inevitable pessimism, the breakdown of modern science, religion and ethics. Many people still imagine they have some free will. The theories in Gurdjieff's book are at present premature and useless, like recommending a doctor to a man who thinks he is in good health. But it is desirable that there should be a nucleus of people with certain positive ideas. It is inevitable there will be pessimism, which will reach the finest minds. Not all will escape as easily as Bertrand Russell, who is "terribly at ease in hell" and emotionally a child.

PRELUDE TO CHAPTER ON PURGATORY

Last week we discussed objective morality. But there was presupposed the ability to distinguish between "I" and the organism, and to realize that the organism is a mechanical organ of heredity and social history and with behavior corresponding to that history, over which we have no control.

We cannot affect behavior in respect either to emotion, thought or conduct. When one has realized this, the rules of objective morality become obligatory. When you realize that you cannot do, then realize that you must do, thereafter do not act from inclination or wish but from will. Will is "activity without wish."

As "I" awakes for a second and begins to be aware of its organism, it begins to grow. That "I" is the soul. In the present chapter, we will pass from objective morality back to behaviorism again, in a more detailed way than is attempted by contemporary science.

Ashiata lists seven factors which make the organism what it is. Not a simple reason, but a number of contributing factors, divided into seven groups.

1. *Heredity in general.*

This is the determinability of the experience-ability. It is not one's immediate parentage but the whole family, and behind the family the race. Five major races, each with a peculiar psyche, with history and experiences. Behind the race is a biological history; animal, vegetable, mineral. We can distinguish certain characteristics. The body is the result of a complicated biological history back to the appearance of organic life on this planet.

2. *Conditions at the moment of conception.*

At the moment of conception we start as a unicellular being. This moment includes the factors of the physical and psychical state of the parents, including their recent history; also the geographical position, condition of the air, soil, magnetic forces etc. What determines? It is too complex for us to attempt to analyze this. Our life is not determined by secondary causes which we take to be primary, such as health etc., but our experience-ability, which is determined by these factors just given. A machine with a series of windings; if these are favorable the experience-ability is both long and rich. If fewer, nothing can prolong this. It holds the same relation to our life as our dreams. We cannot control either their length or their kind.

3. *Planetary emanations.*

Operative on us, through our mother during period of gestation. This sounds nonsensical. We know of the effect of the moon on the tides. There are subtle tides in us. It is here stated that we are affected by the planets associated with our sun. Again, it is impossible for us to have any knowledge.

4. *Being-manifestations of the parents during the time that the children are arriving at adolescence.*

By "manifestations" is meant whatever the parents do from "essence," genuinely. This is rare. An act of complete sincerity has an enormous effect on a child, upon its character. One reason that children grow up without character is not because the parents do not have it, but because they conceal it in their behavior.

5. *Nature of being existence of people with whom children are brought into contact.*

Modern civilization brings about all kinds of artificial behavior, unnatural food, clothing, sleep, posture. We usually exercise one center at a time, belonging to a sedentary type, unnatural or active type, we breathe unnaturally, artificially. We have spared ourselves fatigue and have not been compelled to take long breaths as a manual laborer does. We find thought almost spared us—by reading newspapers and books. While real teaching is replaced by a mechanical exercise of memory. Food, air, thought; children have not the advantage of copying the behavior of normal beings; but are made artificial. This is why children brought up on a farm sometimes outstrip city children.

6. Thought waves of those of the same blood.

We are not in a position even to discuss this.

7. The exertion to understand, which children up to the age of adolescence have been encouraged to make.

The presumption is that they have curiosity. Our habit is to gratify this at once, thus sparing it its own effort to gratify. An appetite would exert itself but fuel heaped on a fire puts it out. Curiosity is so valuable a manifestation of life that its gratification should be delayed. The teacher, instead of being anxious to teach, should just encourage curiosity. Gurdjieff says in the East there are no teachers, there are only learners. They will carry them throughout. Life is vitally curious.

Life from adolescence has been simply unrolling an objective film corresponding to that which had been wound up in us. Our life was like a cinema until adolescence. This film was wound unconsciously. After adolescence it begins to unwind in the objective form of experiences we meet. E.g. you choose a profession. Your fate is not determined by what you will do in it; but what you will do in it is already determined by these preceding factors. We are not living now; we are watching unfold that of which we are the unconscious victim—our little spool. As it unwinds, we, as we say, live. This is behaviorism with a vengeance! This, says Gurdjieff, is why the behaviorists do not yet begin to realize to what extent they are determined. Not actually living. It is true accidents occur, the wound up spool maybe dropped, may have a premature unwinding. Three spools, one by accident unwound quickly. The result being that the individual cannot again experience in the field of that spool. E.g. terrible experiences which turn the hair white in a few hours or days—shell-shock. This may be by accident or by the unwise initiation of others. The latter is one of the perils of civilization, as opposed to accident. About what is an "accident" it is useless to speculate; but about the other disaster, it is possible to speculate.

What is it aside from "accident" which causes a premature unwinding?

Suggestion. E.g. each of us has a fixed capacity for thought. Suppose we act not from native wish but from invitation of others. We find ourselves reading a great deal, attending learned lectures. This passive titillation exhausts our potentiality without our having actively thought. Similarly, with emotions. By association with pathological artists "devotees"(read "victims") of love, of beauty, find their emotions not genuine. To pursue an aesthetic career not actively but appreciatively is a short cut to a loss of taste and power. Similarly in the physical world. Sport—a premature aging of the heart from exercise, not taken because one felt the need for it but because of pseudo reasons of rivalry, publicity, etc. If one spool is gone, the possibility in this life of a normal development is gone. One specific against a premature running down of our spool is "Iransamkeep," i.e. never to abandon oneself to the activities of one center only, never to become a specialist; never to aim at greatness; intellectual, emotional or physical; but at a balance between the three, cost what it may in sociological values.

Society is always creating monsters; because it is difficult to resist the inducements society offers. Leonardo da Vinci was one of the greatest of Europeans because he refused to become a specialist although promised much money. He would throw up the contract when he felt himself becoming unbalanced. A working rule for everybody; and nothing esoteric about this. Modern schools take this into account but when the pupil leaves school he is expected to specialize.

ANOTHER METHOD

Attempting to become self-conscious. Among the by-products is this, that it is impossible to become specialized. One may excel but cannot become identified with his pursuit. The difference between identification and non-identification is not one of efficiency; but of putting or not putting one's life into it. This is a specific against a specialization which is really pathological, the fate that otherwise lies in wait for victims of society.

This brings us back to the definition of the final goal. We said at the outset that man is a passion for the understanding of life. This is the master, magnetic current. But we are negatively polarized. The positive magnetic pole is the cerebral, the negative is the instinctive. When the current is rightly passing, all functions begin to fall into proper place. But when, as in us, the current is passing from the spinal to the cerebral, then things go wrong. We are abnormal and are crucified like Peter with head downward. What is the positive magnetic current? The psychological being is a passion for understanding. Those who have had it increasingly, find their functions increasingly normal. First psychologically then physiologically.

But the prime requisite is the presence of that active passion for understanding. Why? Because man was created for the purpose of producing a soul. And a soul is defined as a being capable of objective reason, that is, of understanding the meaning and aim of existence. To the degree to which we are suggestible in regard to objective reason, admonitions of ideas in this book may cooperate in developing us. This completes the circle, of the ideas in this book from the preface.

The last effort of Ashiata—to introduce normal standards.

The key to the analysis of modern conditions which follows and which at first blush seems too drastically pessimistic. (Orage has given us the logical order of the book but leaves it for us to formulate it during his absence, bearing on ethics, science what are its values? (Pondering is a species of digestion of ideas. Orage recalls a New Year's vow of two years ago. Something that people wanted to do; something they really wished to do. One man to complete a book that had been rotting on the stocks; another to complete a mural, etc. Orage invites us to make a vow, with the year ending at end of February and to carry it out at whatever cost to inclination and to human values and influences.) A vow is made to the sun. An inclination is to the moon, converting energy. To achieve something nursed and hitherto not weaned. A hair shirt or goad to the ability to make decisions.

A rehearsal of what would happen when the passion for understanding grips you. Vows are exercises. A taste of what being committed to something by a voluntary act really is. It must depend on oneself and not require cooperation from others. A vow must be personally accomplishable. To achieve something nursed but hitherto not weaned. We must not shift responsibility onto others. A vow is our own. If undertaken and we fail, we forfeit any claim to consideration of our "promise." It is an impertinence to promise, then. We believe we are "people of our word" accidentally; but let it be difficult! Because we have no free will and until we realize this, until we have buried our false idea of free will, we cannot have it. Why as a group do we make so little progress? Because as individuals we contribute so little energy. Everyone knows it is easier to think when in certain groups than when in theirs. If all make a vow and all keep it there will be increased understanding. A collective atmosphere. (Sometimes when Orage is reading his notes he is able to formulate things he has not been able to formulate before.) Objective reason is thousands of planets off; but there is only one means. A vow is a being-effort consciously made. Negative emotions cost us years of our life, our real life. They are a drag on intellectual and instinctive energy. Emotional energy is the spendthrift of a three-centered being. A vow gives a psychological model, a working model in psychical experience of the passion of the whole being.

[*End of 1927. Orage goes to Fontainebleau.*]

19 MARCH 1928

Look up Swift's "Tale of a Tub." A straightforward narrative, with plausibilities maintained. It is an allegorical history of schisms in the Christian church. Swift is England's greatest prose writer, the greatest man who wrote English. This is allegorical like Beelzebub's Tales. But in Gurdjieff's narrative the story is not always fictitious. Some parts are historical and contemporary observation, as we may see in later chapters. We must have the ability to read parabolically, read the thought between the lines; but over the lines needs self-training.

Beelzebub's sixth descent and his last time on the planet, where he stayed fifty years. During that time three messengers, saints, appeared: Jesus, Mohammed, Lama. Why does he say that all three appeared during this short time? Each of the three left a doctrine but all three doctrines became so transformed that their authors would not recognize them. Their followers first split into sects. Then they introduced doctrines which had nothing to do with the original doctrine and were often contradictory. We see from our own personal experience that idea even when clearly stated is, due to our psyche, certain to be differently interpreted, split up and changed. This has always happened and will continue to happen so long as our psyche remains as it is. Thus it is impossible for truths to be generally spread.

Followers also imported certain ideas from the doctrine of St. Moses, ideas promulgated under different conditions and times. In each individual there is also a proper time for the reception of truth. If these ideas are met by a person not in the stage of effort to pass from "mi" to "sol" he may run down the scale. A certain running down may be necessary before he can become active. But the idea must be kept clear.

Shortly after the death of Christ there was a counter revolution, read of old Judaism which filtered into Christianity. Instead of the relation of an Old and a New Testament the old mixed with the new. Also the doctrine of Babylonian dualism, with paradise and hell introduced by savants and used by the fathers of the church to bolster up their power. The doctrine of heaven and hell occupied but little place in Christ's teaching but a large place in Christianity. Influence of theology on us.

Only a small brotherhood of Essenes still knows how to apply the principles of Christ to their own lives and strictly for the purpose of escaping from the properties of the organ kundabuffer. Religion on this planet is a special invention to get freedom from kundabuffer, but not so on "normal" planets. With us it is passed on by sociology and prevents the attainment of objective reason. None of us grow our planetary bodies. We take its growth for granted. Why do the other two bodies not grow in the same way? We are subjected from birth to sociological influences, resulting from the properties of the organ kundabuffer. If this suggestion could be lifted, emotional and mental bodies would begin to develop. Religion thus is not a permanent regimen but is a cure for a specific situation. This is why Jesus is often called "The Great Healer." The Essenes persevered and some actually succeeded in throwing off the influences of kundabuffer and thereafter developed normally. Beelzebub thinks that Christianity will not continue there much longer.

Beelzebub gets an etherogram from the Governor on Mars (the same young country man who once tried to inaugurate a reform on Atlantis). Recent etherogram speaks of opening a Jewish university in Jerusalem. In previous struggles of Christian countries to make Jerusalem Christian, many were killed. But now by common consent a Jewish university is formed. A university is a furnace in which everything acquired by previous generations is burned up. So that all that is left is a fire on which to cook the knowledge of the previous fifty years into soup. Destroy the old and prepare the new. On the spot where Jesus' body was buried will soon be all the equipment of mechanical society. With the discovery of the altar will go the possibility of certain worship within.

MOHAMMED

Hope of reconciliation but with it many such details such as the doctrine of paradise. This faith is also split, Sunnites and Shiites. The hostility between these sects was encouraged to prevent political union. This is the doctrine of all imperialist states such as England and will be that of the USA in the future. Divide your enemies—a method by which India was conquered.

ST. LAMA

Tibetanism is not a form of Buddhism but the religion of St. Lama who lived. For some time his discipline lasted. It is little known to us but was a cradle of religions like Christianity and Mohammedan. Its purpose was that of all religions: to free oneself from the properties of the organ kundabuffer. This spread less widely because of geography; but entered intimately into the lives of those there, especially a small group. Many of this group attained deliverance and others were on the way; but it was destroyed by war and the fulfillment of St. Lama's aim was delayed. There is a naive account of India's history, Younghusband's sounds much more realistic with its account of policies etc. But perhaps the truth is here. Only he who can penetrate to the motive can brush aside the rationalization. In this case the greed of England's governing classes. Heights of Tibet, perhaps when elevated places (science etc.) are attacked "by wrong motives" (greed) the results are as here.

All of intellectual mysticism may be an attempt to take by violence, heights which cannot be taken by these means. (Sermon on the Mount), a heightened state of consciousness also Jesus talked about in "an upper room."

The Tibetans were sad because they saw their own school in danger. The deliberated analogy between the pressure against these groups and threats which have been made against the institute because of dislike. The method of defense might be dropped rocks on troops in defiles. This was decided against because all beings have an objective value to their creator; that is they exist for a certain use. Our destruction of other beings is a destruction of other values. If it does not increase our objective value it incurs a debt. In Tibet the troops advanced further. A very holy man was sent down to the villages to see that there was no opposition from the villagers. Accidentally he was killed, he was the head of a very important group; his loss was a great disaster. Troops arrived at Lhasa, without opposition to find the government had left. What happened was not important then. After the death of the leader the doctrine became corrupted as in all other religions.

Hassein asks how did social organizations come to be on the earth? Family, clan, monarchy. Various methods: hereditary (essence), elective (educational). Heredity and essence are the continuity of values throughout the life of the individual. Elective means the intermittency of values. Gurdjieff is not interested in the history of social organization as such; but the analogy with what is important to us, that is, relations between essence and personality etc. Cf. Plato: "The state is the individual writ large." It is a manifestation in social organization of individual organization of the majority composing it.

The odd individuals may be very uncomfortable in it. They become pacifists, anarchist's etc., reformers of all types. The discord between essence and personality—"what is in his essence is not in his manifestations"—speech etc. and vice versa; a discrepancy between his real wishes and his conduct.

What we call the Last Supper and sacrament of the participation in the blood and flesh of Jesus Christ is explained hypothetically. In order to maintain a contact between the dead teacher and his succeeding pupils, there is something talismanic.

Before his crucifixion Christ shed blood, saturated a cloth and put it in a vessel—the holy grail. By contact with this, his surviving disciples in a certain state of consciousness established communication. It was often claimed that he was seen by certain people after his death. St. Lama had made no preparation. He was killed by accident, a fatal accident and his pupils had no way of referring to the original source.

Story of Judas: When it became known that Jesus was to be arrested, though he had power to abstract himself, he refused to use force. In order to give time to Jesus and the other apostles to prepare the sacrament and give instructions and learn how to accomplish it after the crucifixion, Judas undertook to gain time and entered into an intrigue with the Romans and promised to arrange for them to take Jesus quietly. He gained perhaps twenty-four or forty-eight hours with the knowledge of Jesus, from this narrative, Judas emerges as the most conscious of the disciples and the one who rendered the greatest service.

26 MARCH 1928

BEELZEBUB'S OPINION ON WAR

Hassein asks: Why, if beings on earth are mature in intelligence and sometimes can recognize laws of nature, does this red thread of war run through their history? Do they not feel the horror of it? Not stop it? Do they not think seriously about it? Beelzebub answered that they do think seriously and realize it all but there are no results from the thinking of a few; because these few are isolated and there is no planetary organization. There is no general result from the "serious thinking" of any one center.

Man can only do sincere thinking after his needs are fulfilled; and the few important and powerful who might (help) do nothing for other reasons. The young spend years, given for preparation for being responsible, in "self-calming" and such education as crystallizes the properties of the organ kundabuffer. The powerful are satiated and recline in a chair during digestion. They have developed mechanical reason and think from reflexes of their stomach and sexual organs. A few think sincerely but usually from external stimulus, as when someone near to them dies. But when hunger comes, they forget everything else.

League of Nations. Several preceding died without a struggle. Most fail on account of diverse interests, egoism and vanities. Due to the peculiarity of crystallized habit they would be unable to do anything in the way of uprooting the causes of war. Societies founded by a few beings after great upheavals, who have suffered by mechanical shock, because objective consciousness passes temporarily into their consciousness.

But other "important beings," simply because important, get in and not having resurrected consciences, the founders soon find themselves outside. No members with objective reason. It is impossible to achieve anything by rules and agreements. The universal disease of the mote and the beam. Necessity to teach others on the assumption that they themselves need nothing.

If others do not seem to wish to learn they become upset. If they seem to learn, the teachers are happy and only then can they speak of others without negative criticism. They are incapable of self-observation and are only agitated by the faults of others. By inner rage they increase the own misery; being uselessly concerned by what they consider the defects of others, in violent contrast with their own subjectively established standards—"Sad for the sins of the world." Occasionally we find some being whose inner life is under the thumb of someone who has penetrated to his chief feature, the mask usually built up by education, which had fallen before the owner of this thumb. Such people rage most and write books about government. Themselves they are being afraid of a mouse, but grow very indignant at those who are afraid of a tiger. They write books on what to do and what not to do on meeting tigers, or being themselves a walking museum of diseases, grow indignant at one who catches a cold. They want to teach their "wisdom" to individual victims and in some cases they are so brazen that they need to teach to masses. The disease of "having power within oneself" spreads especially among the intelligentsia. For a being who is perfected to such a degree that he has already the function of directing his planetary body at will this is possible; but the members of the intelligentsia are just the opposite of having power. They might be called the mechanigenzia.

They act and manifest in response to shocks from outside, become animated as long as "unrolling." "It" acts within them, independent of their own wish and will via objects that accidentally come in range of their retina or ears. They become bureaucrats with a limited repertory of experience; plutocrats and by artfully trapping more naive countrymen become owners of great wealth. Story of the origin of the name "plutocrat," mixture of Greek and Roman means in reality scoundrel-crats and though insulting, they swagger in the title as if in a top hat. Plutocrats play upon diseased trust and theocrats upon diseased faith. Democrats? Aristocrats? Cannot explain even in the words of Mullah Nasruddin, "How can a boat like that float?"

Change in organic life due, not to things within that species, but to the result of adaptation on the part of the planet to the cosmic trogo-auto-ego-crat. A story of the society whose motto was "the world must be free for all." The brotherhood was formed of those who have seen themselves. They had practiced self-observation to get rid of the consequences of the organ kundabuffer. They aimed to establish one religion in common, based on the Parsees but with change of nomenclature, from the fire to the sun, that is, from emotion to higher intellect. A common language, taking root in Asia—i.e. essence. A common government by a "council of saints." This broke up. The reason was the appearance of the philosopher Attarnach with his theory: Why wars appear on earth. His theory was based on an old

Sumerian scripture, well preserved because it was written with blood of a being on a skin of a being; i.e. incarnated. One statement: It is probable that a law exists of reciprocal maintenance of all that exists. That is, aside from subjective purposes or theories of existence, every being must have an objective value. Sheep have the objective value of mutton and wool. Similarly Attarnach argued, we, like all other beings, subserve an objective purpose. Changes in us are brought about by shepherds and butchers for our objective values. We must serve either by life or death.

Attarnach's theory was indeed near to the truth, near to trogo-auto-ego-crat, a reciprocal maintenance for something for which all this exists; certain chemical substances are necessary which can be formed and developed only in what we call "living beings." Now, chemicals go to maintenance etc., generally speaking after death. Whether of men or animals is indifferent. The society "Earth-must-be-free-for-all" invited him to come and expand his theory. Appointed a committee to examine details; but not of the experienced and disillusioned. They forgot their first effort and split, one group accepting, one opposing. Attarnach became president after several general sessions. "According to the laws of nature, wars and civil wars will continue." So they disbanded. Attarnach said why not sacrifice animals. This was current until a dervish abolished it. World War. Each being exists to furnish a certain form of radiation. Blood is also required from human beings' radiations for the Moon and Anulios. Two sets of radiations, involving two forms of activity.

When men functioned normally (conscious meditation) both forms of vibrations were derived from their lives. When they ceased to be normal there were substituted vibrations derived from essence after death. Corresponding deaths and births regulated by cosmic demand, that at times a certain number of deaths should take place. But Attarnach did not realize that the vibrations were necessary in quality and not in quantity. If the vein of ore is thin, more must be crushed. Attarnach did not know the details of what had happened under the regime of Ashiata. Both deaths and births were fewer.

Looisos told Beelzebub that both the Moon and Anulios must have askokin. Existence is never pure; only in admixture with abrustdonis (air) and helkdonis (impressions). Askokin can be released only if these two forms of food are consciously taken and digested. Thus, if honestly served, nature would also bring about the development of the other two bodies. But when the need to do this consciously ceased, the earth was forced to adapt herself and substitute quantity for quality in a very disadvantageous way. In World War, an excess of deaths, wolves appearing in the streets of Tiflis, rats and mice multiply.

Hassein asked: "Is it true they can never perfect themselves? Where is justice? Something is not right." Beelzebub sighed: "If Ashiata could do nothing, what can we do?"

- Time?
- Or a being of exceptional intelligence?
- Or a cosmic event?

2 APRIL 1928

"THE MOUNTAIN PASS OF IMPARTIAL MENTATION"

In this chapter a picture of a ritual taking place on a level just above our understanding. As if we were witnessing High Mass, an attitude of emotional wonder. On the ship, there was a pale blue light and much agitation. An Egolionopty appeared (only four in the universe); each made dependent on one of the four All-Quarters Maintainers. They have the ability to be anywhere, at anytime. There was an assembly of all passengers in the astral hall of the ship with myrtle and Devdelkascho. Archangels and angels from the cosmic Egolionopty bearing palms and a casket from which something radiated. They sang a psalm: Hymn to our Endlessness. While angels sing canticles an old archangel announces to Beelzebub that because of his connaissant life, his horns (conscious will) are to be restored to him. The old archangel has a rod in the casket from the All-Quarters Maintainer. The archangel addresses those of like nature with Beelzebub and invited each of them to surrender a part of the substance of his own horns. Those who freely desire should hold the rod by the handle, the length of time determining the amount of active substance passing from them to Beelzebub. A hubbub began; all desired to hold it a long time, so it was regulated by the captain of the ship. Horns appeared on Beelzebub's head, watching for the number of prongs. Four appeared. Beelzebub had the second degree of reason, short of the Holy Anklad. After the ceremony was over a fifth fork appeared. All fell on their knees for this meant Beelzebub had attained the Sacred Podkoolad, next to the Holy Anklad. The archangel speaks to all: "Let Beelzebub be an example for us, to renew our struggle and the doing of our part which alone can lead to our self-perfection." All sing a canticle: "I rejoice." Dr. Goldwater says that in Masonry, cassia is a symbol of eternal life.

The whole book represents the climb through various stages of reason. Beelzebub has made this climb and has at last reached the pass of impartiality. After turning this pass, a new order of life is possible. What motive could the others have for surrendering part of their development for the development of one of their kind? A passion for perfection is not necessarily a passion for perfection in oneself. It was not for Beelzebub's personal advantage but to carry out the objective duty of the maintenance of the cosmic machine. This could best be carried out if the scattered consciousnesses of all were concentrated in Beelzebub. In general the higher emotions are those in which personal ends are absent.

2 APRIL 1928

Last year I received a number of criticisms to the effect that, interesting as my comment on the text extracted from the book may be, it was not the book—so this year . . .

MOUNTAIN PASS OF IMPARTIAL INTELLECTION

It is a cartoon—a realistic ceremony—out of our reach—on a level just out of our ordinary understanding. We may perhaps have slight emotional understanding—wonder.

The whole region lit up with a pale blue light; and the speed of the ship diminished. One of the four great Egolionopti in the universe was approaching. An Egolionopti is an omnipresent moving platform—i.e. ability to be anywhere at any time. There are only four, each under one of the four all quarters maintainers. Presently, all on the ship began to assemble—each carrying in one hand myrtle and in the other a *devgelcishcho*. (Orage—I know not the meaning of either.) A procession began to enter through the side of the ship which had been slid aside. Each carrying a palm. An old archangel leads followed by two cherubim carrying a casket emanating an orange color. Beelzebub led his people. When these two parties of different race had met they joined in singing a Te Deum of his Endlessness, which is always and everywhere sung at such times. "By banishing the terrible heropass—thou has given us the opportunity to perfect ourselves to the degree of the Holy Anklad."

Heropass—passing of time. Time is that force that puts a limit on the forces in substance. Science confidently predicts that because of this, the universe will one day run down and vanish—but here it is said that by a process of reciprocal feeding the problem has been solved by his Endlessness.

When this Hymn had been sung—the old archangel approached Beelzebub and said that he was empowered and directed to restore to Beelzebub his horns on account of his conascent life spent in learning to know. Horns = will, hoofs = individuality, tail = consciousness.

Having said this, the old Archangel turned and reverently took from the casket the rod. Turning again to Beelzebub he spoke to the members of the same kind as Beelzebub and himself. The captain of the ship took charge—i.e. the determined the length of time each one should hold the rod by his hand.

The Holy Anklad is the highest order of any existing created being. It is third in order from the beginning of His Endlessness.

Cherubim and seraphim pre-existed creation—and their degree of reason cannot be reached by anything created. A son cannot, whatever he does become older than his father. One of the laws of objective reality is that all reasonable beings shall respect those of a higher degree of reason—and vice versa. Cassia in masonry is a symbol of everlasting life. Myrtle symbolizes love, laurel—fame.

These were contributed by various cockeyed verbalizers.

This chapter is the last part of the book. The whole book is a climb and one who passes this will find himself, so to speak, in a new country. What motive could those who surrendered part of their own will, consciousness and individuality have had?

Duliotherapy = therapy by slavery, i.e. treatment voluntarily taken by putting yourself into the position of a slave.

Gurdjieff took a position under a Russian Greek Duke on a two month voyage. He had to carry his food to him and most times it was thrown in his face. When he was through he could serve anyone. Incidentally, he was very anxious to make the trip for he wanted to get to Cairo.

The hymns imply an emotional understanding. Could you engage in such a procedure?

Horns = executive power according to his being.

Suggested—reappearance of sacrificing something or really sacrificing—that he might for example, spit in Larry's face and say, "Now you dirty little cur! Don't you dare interrupt again." Then call someone else to wipe his face and say: "You have no reason or being worthy of anyone's consideration—everyone knows this, yet you constantly put in these blithering interruptions."

We have no language to communicate feelings. Yet we have no difficulty for ourselves in distinguishing between an emotion and a thought. We don't confuse twelve by twelve with a feeling. And we have another form of experience—called movement. So, we have three primary colors which, when mixed produce a variety of colors. In any individual these will tend to mix in certain proportions. In women the element of thought is overlaid by a predominance of feeling, and in man vice versa.

We have various combinations of motor center, emotional center and intellectual center.

The problem of life is the problem of energy. Few of us have enough to become an outstanding success either in the physical, emotional or intellectual field. None but geniuses who are invariably pathological can succeed in one field. To succeed in two fields of life would be miraculous. Success in three fields has in the history of the world almost never, if ever, occurred.

The measure of our life is the amount of energy at our disposal. It is quite possible to grow old in one system while remaining young in the others. One may, and usually does reach senility at the age of twenty or twenty-one. Due to our education, one's brains are beaten into a state of rigid sterility that should never have been reached before a great age.

In another case, one's physical center may become old and the brain and feelings remain young.

Shaw's first book on Ibsen contains every idea you can find in every subsequent book that he has written. This is a little unfair; because it happens that he has some new ideas. But he will not write them for publication. At least not before his death, will they ever be published. We are all approaching death in these three forms, and tomorrow one of my centers may be dead—though, unless it is my physical center, it won't be apparent to me.

There is only one thing to be done that will prolong my life. A secret.

"Well," you will say, "if you can give me such a recipe, I'll pay ——."

"All right, here you are."

But you are by this time so tired and no doubt so sound asleep that you never will be able to undertake to understand what I say.

First—how does it occur that one center can deteriorate before the others or ——. We live by food. But it is not the quantity and quality of the food absorbed, but it is the quantity and quality assimilated that will determine the form, quantity and quality of energy we have.

We don't care at all what food is used. Eat any or all foods you like—but be sure you like it. If you are depressed, don't eat much for you won't be able to assimilate it. If you are elated, eat as much as you like—dine well.

Well, people grow old—not by use of energy—but by waste of energy. Every moment ticks off the life of each center.

My posture, for example, requires a certain number of muscles—but when I examine my body I find a number of muscles tensed and using energy uselessly, i.e. thereby wasting energy. So we live two days in one, i.e. use two days energy in one.

Every emotion about anything not of the present, we are pouring our emotional life blood into the sand. Either past, or to come, or absent things, should never bleed you emotionally. Never worry, never regret. But how? If you are aware simultaneously of your five forms of physical external behavior, you cannot either worry or regret. Your cup is full.

Intellectual waste occurs most of all in reading and in education and in "day dreaming." "Day dreaming" is thinking at the suggestion of outside stimuli. You get onto a bus, and because you have given yourself no definite problem, you react. "Not so many busses today . . . pretty girl . . . hm . . . he almost got run over . . . who's that getting on?—I think I know him—no I don't . . . is it going to rain? . . . nice enough now . . . good shop window, gee . . . I'll be late . . . well, I guess I'll read.

Well, give yourself any purposive problem.

9 APRIL 1928

Pondering an attempt to answer questions from their source. A process of stripping off the answers suggested by association and arriving at the essential personal answer.

The method can be applied to any question; e.g. where shall I spend the summer? What do I really want to do in the field of my potentialities? Only those who have pondered practical questions can be trusted to ponder practically on philosophical questions.

GOOD AND EVIL

Try to formulate your own definitions of good and evil. Good is that which fulfills the function for which a thing is created. "A good clock" subject to tests. Differ in understanding according to work and essence.

FORM AND SEQUENCE

After attaining impartial mentation, Beelzebub goes to his cabin for the rest he needed after an emotional experience. He found Hassein sobbing. The intensity of thought had established a tempo that was abnormal; afterwards, clash of tempos. Tears did not mean anything except that the three centers were at different tempos. A neurotic system is due to tempo intensification in one center, without others being raised to the same degree. The centers out of step were the cause, but the occasion was this: Hassein weeping over the beings on the earth, handicapped by kundabuffer. Hassein's objective conscience could suffer because beings, three-centered beings like himself, were shut out from the ineffable joy he had just experienced. Where is justice, that I should enjoy this?

Beelzebub is "actively pondering." A responsible being spends half his time in actively pondering (one-half of the energy developed in the body). Where is the center of gravity of your thought when you are at leisure? On the animal plane, food, rest, etc.? Where do your thoughts go? To be human one must spend one-half of one's energy on pondering. Make an objective analysis of your thoughts, where they naturally go. After pondering, you must cease and give chance for rest, for the planetary body is an independent thing, an auxiliary. Deal justly with it. Give it time for adjustment, help for your demands since it serves two masters. Biology and psychology may develop by leaps and bounds but the body only by degrees. When what we develop proves to have unbearable effects on the body, pause and give it time to adjust.

Otherwise, a part only of the total being (being and the planetary body) will acquire this accelerated tempo and will be lopsided. Silly saints, weak yogis and stupid ascetics are formed by indulging essential wish in one center at the expense of the rest.

Most of us are longing for, or asking to be whole. Change refuses to accommodate. Hassein's explanation is incomplete. Hassein would have been more correct if he had said he's sobbing because he had thought intensely, and after thinking, sobbing came from the emotional center. (Hassein had said out of tempo with the body.) If we think without feeling, at the end we become tired and go to sleep. If feeling had been in the thinking then emotional fatigue is the result and we are unable to control the body. Pondering in Beelzebub's sense included thinking and feeling elements. The body is manifesting materialization of intellection plus emotion. Dante is one of the rare Europeans capable of pondering. Read his "Inferno," a participation in intellection and feeling.

Beelzebub will explain to Hassein the difference between intellection and pondering. Thinking is according to knowledge. Understanding is according to essence. Essence is thinking and feeling. It is not emotional thinking but is a fusion. Beelzebub says let us go and sit, i.e. take a new posture—cf. drama.

The arrival of Ahoon—common sense: a personal practical application of ideas otherwise impersonal. The difference between understanding and knowledge. Beelzebub says: Let us compare the beings on the earth with normal three-centered beings throughout the universe—cf. average with normal. "Reason" on earth is the "reason of knowledge." That of normal beings is the "reason of understanding." Reason of understanding becomes an integral part of the being, while the reason of knowledge is alien and is merely acquired. Understanding is in one's bones and with it one cannot act contrary to essence. Reason of knowledge can understand clearly and yet act otherwise.

New knowledge acquired by a being with the reason of knowledge must be repeated or it is forgotten. Not so with reason of understanding. "Ah, I see the idea!"

We are engaged in trying to acquire the art of pondering. Pondering and being human are equivalent. Is my understanding of pondering according to knowledge or understanding? Simultaneity of thinking and feeling is a technique. Its effects are without injuring the wholeness. Gains according to understanding become inalienable parts of the being's essence.

Beelzebub adjusts the curls of his tail (change of planes). Hassein asks: What is the cause in your opinion of the molding of our psyche (chief cause) in this misshapen way, i.e. so little according to essence? Beelzebub replies: You are now at the beginning of real being and I determined to help you so that your intellection would go rightly.

If Hassein had asked him before, he could not have answered frankly because he had an aim in view in regard to Hassein. Why is it inadvisable for someone to tell you your chief feature? Beelzebub told facts in such order that Hassein would arrive inevitably at his own conclusions. There is an order of discoveries of self. Reason according to understanding (essence) depends on the presence of a chemical substance formed in the planetary body under the law of triamazikamno.

Beelzebub said to Hassein: Understanding cannot be acquired suddenly. It is generated and formed by a process. This is a most important fact but I did not tell it to you before. Three factors are necessary. Impressions already materialized as understanding in the three centers are either positive or negative. The new ones becomes neutralizing and become blended. Part affirms; new part denies, causing friction (clash between agreement and denial). Result—that the two are precipitated in a new understanding, either according to knowledge or essence. Part of the theory is transient; part of essence? What decides; whether at the time of the clash the individual makes effort (personal effort at resolving the clash?) Without this effort, understanding is deposited at random, according to the gravity of the words, verbal associations. No accretion of real understanding (Mullah Nasruddin's soup). By himself he must produce an effort to understand the directions involved in both affirmation and denial.

Had I first given you my conclusions and then the evidence, my conscience would have been clear but there would have been no effort on your part. That's why I told you these things in this order. I can give you my impersonal frank opinion and can tell you something about objective reason which had I known it earlier would have saved me many centuries of observation; but I can tell you only because you have made an effort up to this point. Without effort you would have only understanding according to knowledge, which is the greatest enemy of understanding according to understanding (essence).

[*At lunch.*]

The intellectual center of mental behavior is concerned with its own problems; speculation on the meaning and aim of existence. We have some disorganized material of mental behavior. Our three centers are embryonic.

QUESTION: Can a "germ" exercise?

ANSWER: Certainly. "Being" is developed by friction between "doing" and "thinking" on fundamental questions.

THE HOLY PLANET PURGATORY

Beelzebub asks: Do we know anything about the planet "Remorse of Conscience"? Hassein called it "the accursed planet," isolated and unique. Fundamental cosmic laws there proceed inversely and backward. We assume that experience teaches; but experiences do not occur in educational sequence but higgledy-piggledy, often too advanced for us. But sometimes we have "runs" and are surprised. If we were normal, these would be more frequent. "Remorse of conscience" is a state in which experiences occur without order, hence perhaps the feeling that we are out of joint, alone, on the edge of the universe. Hassein continues: his father had said that this state of discrepancy between inward growth and external experience will last until those beings have done away with certain substances ignorantly acquired. Every external event made possible by chemicals within; tragedy cannot happen to the untragical. We experience only ourselves. No arbitrary condemnation. Good and evil depend on chemical substances within. There are three means of taking in substances and each determines the nature of subsequent experience. Consequences are inherent in the chemicals, e.g. eat a bad oyster.

- Food determines the physiological.
- Air determines the moods.
- Perceptions.

Try to be aware of what we are doing every time we take a perception, i. e. to pass down Fifth Avenue and look at the shops with a little envy. Each such little perception builds up. Someday I will stop at one of these shops and buy something which I do not need.

Fable of the bank cashier. A series of unobserved perceptions at length necessitates an act. Similarly in self-observation. The souls on the planet "Remorse of Conscience" are not there because of any single crime. The long process can be undone only by another long process. A short cut is to make conscious perceptions.

STORY OF MACAREE

Macaree began as second generation of the Society of Akhaldans. All souls bear forever the name they bore on the planet where they began self-perfecting. Macaree acquired a state of reason entitling him to reside on the holy planet Purgatory. He continued his conscious labors on Purgatory until he was a candidate for the Sun Absolute. Earth beings transformed his "nearly correct" teaching into misinterpretations. A teacher is responsible for the effects of his teachings. The laws of justice are the laws of chemistry. Macaree, poor devil, meant well. He decided to share what he had learned with others. Among other things he had learned about positive and negative influences. All laws that govern the universe are exemplified in us—"the universe is our dream." Macaree's doctrine—positive and negative influences. Physicists say that outside in the universe is positive and negative electricity; the exemplified manifestations are proton and electron. What else is there in the universe? Nothing we know of.

Gurdjieff speaks of a neutralizing force. Consider the hydrogen atom. One proton and one electron; each moves in an orbit. What keeps them together? Not a substance, not a force. The forces are resident in the proton and electron. Nothing phenomenal, but the relationship is a third force, to which we are blind. Neither positive nor negative determines the totality within which we function as a whole. Earth beings are twisted. Macaree had said: we are formed by and consist of three forces:

1. Positive.
2. Negative.
3. Neutralizing.

1. May be called descending and good.

2. Is negative for it resists 1 and so in relation to 1 may be called evil. Electron may be considered as limiting the field of the positive and of the proton.

3. May be called spirit, only the relationship. But the stupid earth-beings identified themselves with 3 and instead of regarding 1 and 2 as equally necessary, thought of 1 as good (wishing their welfare) and 2 as evil (wishing harm). Now we have conception of only external

good and bad influences although good and bad influences are themselves and necessary. Philosophy is founded on this.

Some beings of Beelzebub's tribe lived on the planet earth and came to be considered as beings of the beyond. Beelzebub is not sure why and even after they left the earth the beings there formed a religion based on false ideas of good and evil in which beings of his tribe figured a tradition of invisible beings. They even gave traditional names to these supposed devils as well as fantastic attributes. These devils are supposed to suggest crimes. Whereas we do them because of habit; because we wish or have wished. If we have a nightmare we suppose the nightmare was "sent" instead of being produced by ourselves.

From failure to assume responsibility of majority we invent excuses, failing to realize the external experience as an objective dream. External events are subjectively determined. To change the dream we must change the dreamer. Superstitions only change the plane. We have superstitions in the objective field; earlier times in the subjective.

A sailor comes to announce that reflections of the sphere of Caritas are visible. (In preceding discussions we "saw" for an instant what Caritasian's are like. Awake to the subjective nature of objective experience—light.) Beelzebub continues: The results of abnormal existence on earth, not limited to earth, but were beginning to affect beings on other planets in the same solar system. Relatively conscious only of the planetary body; only a subjective consciousness of the other two. But the other two should become as objective and as usable as the first. Being unable to use them, we merely register the effects of their action in emotional and intellectual states. If the planetary body had no effect on the astral and mental it would not be so bad. But they interact. What the planetary body does, affects them even though I do not realize they exist. They may be deformed before we learn their use. Blossom, bud, seed. If the outer sheath is undisturbed all is well. But if . . . Beelzebub sighed deeply: "If only the reflections of the sphere of Caritas are visible, we still have much time to discuss the reactions on the astral and mental bodies of the planetary body. Beelzebub will explain to Hassein in detail.

CHAPTER ON ELECTRICITY

Beelzebub learned of his pardon while on Earth and went to Mars to prepare to return home. Must take the ship Occasion to Saturn where he would get the ship Omnipresent to Caritas. While waiting on Mars, he is in company with that Martian Tuf-Nef-Tef, the emperor, who had formerly been a "peacemaker" or "one who harmonizes his three centers." Then he was a candidate for emperor (sole ruler). We must harmonize before we can control. Those who help others to fulfill the totality of their duty—caricatures on earth: doctors, a merry tale.

The aged Tuf-Nef-Tef invites Beelzebub to call and makes a request: owing to his pardon, he can now become what he should become and in the future will meet people of his own reason—ask how to deal with inhabitants of Mars. It has been noticed lately on Mars that the abnormal conditions on the planet Earth had decreased the power of active intellection on the planet Mars. Inability to think objectively, the earth-beings call it a will-less-ness or neurosis. Present conditions practically ensure the spreading of neuroses. Neurosis is an exaggerated inability to think objectively or impartially. It is only due to the inhalation of certain substances that we can ponder at all. Beelzebub promises to bear the request in mind. (Why cannot we maintain a state of higher intellection for very long?)

Several days after, he left Mars forever and returned to Saturn. But the Omnipresent had not arrived; it was an inopportune time. Beelzebub visited Gornahoor Harharkh, who was interested in electricity. Gornahoor Harharkh said: "You remember the experiment of the lamp which proved that all life is electrical in origin?" Since proving this he had to unlearn not the fact, but the use of it, thanks to Gornahoor Harharkh's son (Beelzebub's godson). Saturnians are ravens in form and perch. They feel good only when after bowing, and supporting their weight on their own legs and when elevated, hence they put up perches. (Earth beings have a caricature, call perches, churches.)

Electricity, the source of biology. Electricity is of three kinds; the biology of any planet is limited by the electricity available for that planet. This earth has so much, within the solar system. If three-centered beings demand all three forms find themselves limited in one or two kinds, they are then limited in the possibility of becoming whole. An electrical age (ours is the second) involves an increase in neuroses, will-less-ness and biological degeneration. We spend the substance of life in mechanical aids. The difference between Beelzebub, Gornahoor Harharkh and his son shows the difference between those who hopefully began the development of electricity and those who later realize that this development has been at the expense of life.

15 APRIL 1928

There is a certain grammar of associations. A verbal thought is nothing more than a word pattern.

Formal thought can be reproduced in a suggestive way only in words. Formal thought is "thinking something," not "thinking about something."

Three modes of speech:

1. Expression of subjective state the speaker is in. It is instinctive speech.

2. Emotion (ex motion, i.e.—motion outward).

3. Evoke (ex voice—i.e.—voice outward). To produce or evoke in the mind of the hearer or reader a form which becomes for him a real experience.

The fluidity necessary for formal thought requires an emotional heat to attain formal thinking.

Beelzebub: If I had known what I now know it would have saved myself many years devoted to the study of the peculiar psyche of the earth beings.

Brain is our Sun Absolute.

Cells move up through emotions.

Karatas is a brain capable of impartial thinking, i.e. free from kundabuffer. Purgatory is heart. Such is the nature of our atmosphere that all things including sciences, ideas, knowledge, gold, etc., will "rust," as Plato put it.

One does not get rid of chief feature, only segregate it from influences and influencing.

Do you believe in astrology?

There is a certain implement for the manipulation of one's self. "As if." Seneca said "Even virtue."

(It is almost certain that questions of the moment aroused—incited—by what Mr. Orage says will be subversive rather than helpful. Considered questions are always stimulating.)

Whence, why, whither.

Have I lived before this life? Why am I here? Where may I go?

How is it that we know very well how to behave, yet we often behave quite contrarily to our common sense?

What is the difference between satisfaction and happiness?

If you accept behaviorist data, what do you say can be accomplished that will be extra behavioristic?

What is the harmonious development of man?

Questions need not be, and probably should not be, questions which you are not able to answer by yourself. Certainly, from my point of view, the best question proposed last week was—"Why are we here?" (It was the question I referred to when I said to Mr. Orage that there was in the lot one ideal question.) But I could have given the answer to that question three years ago—as everyone can verify by referring to an article I wrote which was published in England in January of 1925. We want to get at the root of the subject we discuss here.

We want to propose, seriously, questions, simply phrased which are near to the real final question of—how will you phrase it?

Make one's self drunk so that "I" can think, feel, talk, act?

Beelzebub, intent on his quest to know the nature of the human species faces the sixth descent. What profession shall he adopt in order to bring about for him the knowledge of the human species? Physician? Peculiarities of these human beings do not lie in the external and visible manifestations and are only to be discovered in the unconscious. Only with a physician or a priest is a human being frank, i.e. only with a religious or therapeutic motive will one confess himself.

Medicines administered by priests: opium, castor oil, quinine.

Termose—father of Moses—i.e. hygiene savior.

Especial respect is accorded to priests—especially if they are old.

Moses had very little truck with mysticism and was a hygienic law giver. He passed most of his time in some café or other where ordinarily no priests are to be found. His eldest son fell ill, and a physician gave him the entire contents of a bottle—the label read: Only three times each day of the week. But Termose said laughing—three kinds of medicine, of first you must be a little careful but bottle always have skull and crossbones so easily avoided. The other two kinds are always harmless out of the same barrel. (Skull and crossbones—don't do?) And the other medicine "do"—and this can all be lumped together under the word Sabbath. All advice is lumped together and taken on Sunday.

Pharmacists are practical psychologists, i.e., transmuters of energies. He came into his shop and went to the back of the place where he was engaged in pounding something in a mortar. The prescription was Dover's powder, but the pharmacists put in no opium. Said it was too expensive (i.e. no priest could put into his advice anything real—it is too rare). Beelzebub asks: "What about analysis?" "What is analysis? It would cost as much as a the whole shop."

Three bodies: mental, physical, emotional. An objective truth not realized is a theory for us.

What is an analyst? One who guarantees the prescription—religious doctrine.

If you have the idea that a doctrine is the same to emotional and intellectual as a doctor is to our physical body.

Priests are chemists for the emotional and intellectual bodies. Philosophers are the analysts. (Germans are the inheritors of the ancient Greeks—they are the present analysts.)

Describing now the sort of mind that takes up philosophy . . .

Pimples are very symbolic—complete education thanks to money if one reads all these German books on chemistry, compositions.

Sight, taste and fire—pragmatism.

Sometimes takes a little experimental work—in a slaughter house. Tough work.

So one takes a compound to this analyst who consults a book (the Bible). Copies out the description of Dover's powder varying the figures a little, of course.

Chemist still continues to make fake Dover's powder and says that they are all better because they at any rate contain no harmful ingredients, i.e. Christianity has been denatured. The general prescription contains a good deal of opium, so if one commenced to take the real prescription and later stopped taking the real opium, one would suffer a good deal.

Hypnotism is that property or quality in the earth beings from which all their trouble proceeds. It is this that distinguishes these beings from all the other beings in the universe. If they did not exist, this property would not anywhere exist. It is called their suggestibility—but when accelerated it is called hypnotism.

There are only three normal forms of consciousness. Sleep is the absence of the other two. Self-consciousness is a habitual awareness of the fact that we have a body. (Our state of sleep is chemically conditioned because we receive through inhaling atmosphere and through our senses.)

Kundabuffer has left its properties in the very air we breathe and in our very bodies—and thus we are never essential. Dimly aware at the back that we are not behaving individually. (Have you ever been aware that you have on occasion behaved as if you were hypnotized? Have your friends?)

If you show a flea to a man who is in this state and tell him it is a rhinoceros he will believe it. And always will believe it, i.e. a small irritation will appear to be a disaster. And a real rhinoceros, i.e. a danger on a large scale will appear to be nothing. (For example, self-observation is said to be a danger—that you will get to know something of yourself, but this is only a flea.)

Hypnosis is produced by "stroking"—i.e. idiocy by . . .

Man has two kinds of consciousness on that planet. First their real consciousness as beings—biological consciousness comparable to that of animals. Very natural, cats have it, i.e. they are not suggestible. The second is not due to biological nature—it is absolutely foreign to their real being. And even their very behavior is so adapted that it contains two independent regions where all impressions are deposited—one to the enhancement of our social consciousness and the other to our essential consciousness.

The first belongs to real being, to their essential being, and the second is only acquired during life. So they have side by side thoughts of their real being and thoughts that have nothing to do with this. "He was born a man and died as a sexton, a soldier, an English gentleman."

It may be marvelous, very admirable, but the person himself may be entirely worthless. He may be unspeakable in his private life.

Shaw's "Devil's Disciple" is an example of one who has preserved a portion of essence—i.e. he is devil to our ordinary routine. But his fellow officers, almost all of them said, he had acted so as to lose caste. He was human, humane, essential. Now in ourselves we can find the same thing, i.e. two forms of consciousness—essential and grafted. So we call essential consciousness our "sub-consciousness" and what we call our consciousness is something quite mortal—automatically and accidentally accumulated in a special part of our brain—and we then identify with it. Manchester was born—where? Parents—school—influences—sociological history (social history—real essence)—but not my history—i.e. subconscious history. I won't tell that—what I thought of my mother, sister, teachers, associates, etc. *No!* But that is my real history.

(Watson's behaviorism was not approved by Orage, which he considered "some far-fetched knowledge." And Bernie Shaw was too smart, said Orage.)

Watson said it is no matter what a child is born with, if he can control his infantile conditions. He can make one an artist, another a thinker, another a scientist. But he is right to say this. Yet only that he can graft onto any stock another chosen stock. Yet this is what has happened to each of us.

This so called cause—really only personality; a chance collection of prejudices segregated in a pseudo part of the brain, i.e.—in the formatory front part of the brain which is entirely separated from the back of the brain—the essential brain. These collected word associations begin to churn and "thoughts" and "opinions" having no contact with essence, continue to digest and change independently of essence and can be changed at any chance encounter with external circumstances, i.e. subjective or not related to essence. Objectivity is invariably connected with biological essence. Certain beings there have discovered this and are using it for healing. Émile Coué, Christian science. Anything that exempts a being from essential work is only a superficial cure, and can be uncured by a counter suggestion.

All the present day hypnotists employ one method, i.e., they all require the patient to concentrate or gaze upon on a bright object (Coué, so-called ideal meditation.) For there are literally two modes of blood circulation corresponding to these two modes of consciousness. One where the center of gravity is on one side of the blood vessels and vice-versa. (Where in your brain is the blood pressure greatest in different stages of yourself? I could spin off by associative means—and without a particle of thought—a very good lecture on almost any subject. But it would be of no value to me or anyone.) What is important is: "What is really the truth about that subject?" Plato said to one of his associates: "Aha! You think you are dizzy but you are only really thinking." In one case there is a tendency to go to the back of the head, and in the other, to the front of the head. Strictly speaking a being is only conscious when trying to ponder.

When fixedly regarding a bright object, certain muscular tensions bring about a change of blood circulation which affects a particular part of the brain. So reading this book sets up a certain muscular tension that makes the bloodstream affect, by conditioning, the word center only of the brain. So if one hears the book read—one has at least a better chance.

Beelzebub: I became proficient in hypnotism by stopping the blood-stream in certain habitual channels and so changed their consciousness. (The hysterical cannot observe themselves and a suggestion to do so will produce only a new novel churning—a new doctrine.)

Gurdjieff: I began my work in Central Asia (essence) where there was a great need of my service on account of many pernicious practices there. I collected certain data first, and gradually moved towards the West from center to center.

Question: What were the pulls that determined any given situation? (We have plenty of answers; need only questions—chemical formula.)

1. All situations answers—Doyle's emergency theory.

2. Concise, correct formulation is half the answer.

3. What is the difference between imagination and fancy? Knowledge and belief?

4. Suppose we think during the week and formulate questions for verification of our conclusions.

5. Questions should satisfy yourself, the others and Orage.

6. We ought not to want to formulate a question that we cannot answer—just look the question over and if it looks like a good starting point for a discussion—write it down.

7. Write down questions we wish someone else would ask.

8. Suppose we write down the three questions that interest us more than any others in the world.

9. What can Mr. Orage really do for us except to supply us with questions—or better, when possible to incite us to formulating our own questions? Being able to answer questions is easy compared to asking them.

10. Do we realize that we are going to die? Does this realization bring forth questions?

[*Daly King speaking?*]

The following statements may be judged for their clarity, truth and ponderance or weight. From my point of view some are false, some true, and some part false and part true. What is your natural attitude or reaction to them—if any?

1. God created the universe for the benefit of man on earth who is the only and original copy of God.

2. God is love. (a) God takes his rest and sleep like any man after a hard day's work.

3. God is omnipotent, never needing help—all loving, and wise. (a) God is a bearded patriarch, who rules the earth by a system of post-mortem reward for good boys and girls, and punishment for bad one's in everlasting heaven or hell.

4. Man is an automaton.

5. Man is an animal whose mind and emotions are limited to an apparatus only capable of providing adjustment for himself to varying circumstances.

6. Man is a sheep, the Lord is his shepherd.

7. Man is a natural animal discharging a natural function in the organic kingdom which at the same time has capacity for supernatural development.

8. Man is evolving into a cosmic butter and egg man.

9. Man's development of steam, gas and electricity power and its

application to labor saving devices will give man the time and opportunity to develop himself to the fullest extent. (Shaw.)

10. A non-productive aristocracy should be eliminated from society because its leisure and absence of necessity to work for its living makes it turn to wasteful and individually vicious and degenerate pursuits.

11. The universe is a rather bad jumble of planets and suns which up to the present time lacks the civilizing influence of man. Life is a gymnasium. (Before Orage came to Gurdjieff he was involved with the Shavians in Shaw and was later not proud of it.)

12. The universe is a perpetual motion machine.

13. The universe is an evasion of the weak man.

14. Pythagoras was a social climber, Jesus was a fool, Buddha was a word juggler, Confucius the first Rotarian.

15. Art is the science of evoking emotion. Art is an attempt to convey by a language other than a verbal one, something not expressible in words. It is preoccupation with art which makes the attainment of consciousness on the part of the contemporary artist practically impossible.

16. Art is the outward sign of the shining spirit within man.

17. Art is a result of frustrated desires.

18. Belief is the child of knowledge.

19. Knowledge is the child of belief. (God can be known through the heart alone.)

20. The intellect is the highest function of man and by concentrating on its development, man will become godlike.

21. Time is the fourth dimension.

22. Time is the source of our existence.

23. Man is more emotional than woman—woman is more intellectual than man.

24. Woman is the slave of man.

25. Man is the slave of woman.

26. Every man is personally responsible for all others on earth.

27. Every man is responsible for himself alone.

28. Marriage is God's most holy sacrament.

29. Marriage is a device of the devil.

30. Self-observation requires too much time and takes away my energy from useful and necessary work.

31. If self-observation requires any time or in any way diverts energy from our activities, it is not, in fact, self-observation.

32. Self-observation will make one a bigger and better automaton.

33. In order to do this work of self-observation one must give up all ordinary ambitions, all worldly ties and obligations, and all reliance upon one's own experience in life.

34. Non-identification with one's organism means that one will no longer feel, think or act.

35. This method for development implies identification with one's organism and the simultaneous development of one's soul.

23 APRIL 1928

BEELZEBUB: Do you happen to know anything about the planet "Remorse of Conscience"? "Yes, I know that it is remote and called the cursed planet, and there, all processes proceed backward or reverse!"

ORAGE: Here, for example, things proceed on certain occasions according to a rhythmic, developmental run of what we call coincidence. But on Karatas, for example, such a sequence of providential occurrences would be always in evidence and would in all cases proceed as life would in a good school.

The work of the institute is to make such a change in oneself that nothing can occur that does not agree with one's own qualities. The three means of taking substances into ourselves are food, air, and impressions. Now it must be realized that our experiences in life are determined by the food, air, and impressions which we take in—or are taken in. So with air, we can incur psychic indigestion, blood poisoning or what else. So with perceptions. If I go along Fifth Avenue and look with envy at the things I see, one day I shall walk into a shop to buy, for no apparent reason, something I by no means want.

Take a cashier who absconds. He has with complete (as he thought) innocence looked covetously on money not his, until one day he absconds. So a series of unobserved perceptions may result in any sort of unexpected acts. And it can only be undone after a long period of remorse. Or by a short cut, he may reduce it—by conscious observation.

By the way—this planet called earth is all these planets. A planet is a state of chemistry. There are on planet "Remorse of Conscience" thirty-nine souls and one Macarean. The laws that govern our bodies are exactly the same as the laws that govern our universe. There is in each of us a corresponding item—element, milky way, planet, sun, stars.

Gurdjieff speaks of a neutralizing force—and he speaks of it as a force. But there is no evidence of this third force. Take a hydrogen atom—one proton and one electron, which is to say positive and negative forces, but something holds them together. What is this? Good and evil are not ever outside one's self.

Positive is descending or "good," arising from the center. Negative is repelling or "evil" force since it is a limiting force acting on the positive force.

Men are small cosmoses in which there is always on this planet, a disproportionate quantity of three sorts of substances. Thus we have all our behavior explained, whether criminal or not. Dreams were until recently regarded as being sent—a sort of voodoo. We still speak of externally caused experience. But it is as subjective as a nocturnal dream. Assumption of responsibility for "external" behavior and experience is the first symptom that one has reached one's majority. Karatasians are beings like ourselves who have realized that all experience we now know is as subjective as a nocturnal dream.

We have three bodies but we are only objectively conscious of our physical bodies. But our astral and mental bodies should be as objective, and we should be able to use them as objectively as our physical body. At present it is almost possible to regard the possibilities of the emotional and intellectual bodies as being in the control of one's physical body.

The ruler of Mars—whereas on all planets he was selected from among the peacemakers—i.e. one who harmonizes his three centers, a doctor is merely a tranquilizer, if anything.

It might be that one would have a great wish to think clearly, but if lacking a substance necessary for active intellection, he cannot.

Beelzebub took the ship "Occasion" to the planet Saturn, to await there the interstellar ship "Omnipresence." There he asked Gornahoor Harharkh why the period on the planet Mars, during which it is not possible to engage in active intellection, was increasing. (On Saturn the beings are in the form of ravens.)

Electricity is the source of all biology—three forms—so men are composed of three forms of electricity. There is not an infinite amount of electricity available. During an electric age neurosis, willlessness and inability to engage in impartial intellection will increase.

Chapter entitled Termoses—Armenian for Moses, key to allegory in chapter.

Beelzebub on sixth descent chooses a profession which will enable him to understand the human psyche. It cannot be understood from external things, so he chose to be a physician because human beings are frank only to priests and physicians; that is, one can only tell the truth about oneself from religious or therapeutic reasons.

Physician: one who helps others to function.

All women, priests and spiritual healers have really only three methods:

1. Poppy seed.
2. Castor-oil.
3. Quinine.

Consider three forms of spiritual healing.

Beelzebub was first told of these three remedies by an Armenian priest. Consider that Moses appeared largely as an hygienic law-giver. Beelzebub was in search of an old manuscript. Helped by Termoses, a curious witty character. Custom on earth of honoring aged priests and asking their blessing. But Termoses always rebuffed those who asked blessing. If you have anything important, out with it. If not, off with you. Yet they all loved him. Gurdjieff has a liking for Moses, no mysticism. Termoses's son was sick. The doctor prescribed. Termoses gave his son the whole bottle instead of three spoonfuls a day. Beelzebub was surprised, but Termoses explained. One marked with skull and bones, containing a little poison. The others are all the same, from the same barrel. That evening Termoses's son had diarrhea and was purged; the next day he was cured due to two kinds of medicine:

1. Marked with skull and crossbones, prefaced by "don't."
2. Those marked "Do," prayers etc., three times daily.

Another man who was explained to Beelzebub as a pharmacist (dealt in substances), perhaps a practical psychologist, a Jew. Beelzebub found him in his laboratory crushing burnt sugar in a mortar for Dover's powder for coughs (impediment in air, reference to second food). But Beelzebub noticed the prescription called for opium and not sugar instead. Since opium was too costly the pharmacist used burned sugar for popular use. (Priests could not dispense the blessings in the quantity demanded if they included anything real.) So the pharmacist uses things that are cheap and easy to obtain and easy to take. He makes a powder of the same color and taste as the real thing. Beelzebub asks: But doesn't analysis expose you? The pharmacist answers that analysis would cost too much. Besides (Beelzebub) does not know how these analysts (priests) are trained. Because his mother omits to tell him certain things in his youth, he is pimpled and ignorant of his behavior (acts mechanically). He studies chemistry in books of German savants (gets a thorough theological training).

Suggestion here of a chemistry of the emotions and mind. A doctrine has substance like drugs. As drugs affect our planetary body, so we are constantly being exposed to treatment by quacks. Priests—chemists for the other two bodies. Philosophers are of the same order, standing as "experts" on the value of religions. "Germans" are spoken of as our authorities in chemistry—Gurdjieff perhaps thinking of Kant and Hegel. Gurdjieff is caricaturing the type of psychology in professional philosophers. A student learns formulae; having finished his training he becomes recognized as an analytical chemist. Now suppose our chemist is brought one of the Dover's powders. He consults a German textbook (Bible) and copies out the analysis. There are no complaints for our Dover's powders. They have sold it for thirty years. All this is needed if a remedy to be good should be so reported. And our imitations are really better because they contain no harmful elements. There are many dangerous things in the Bible but modern parsons give harmless inoculations. The genuine prescription calls for opium; but if opium is taken for a time it cannot be abandoned without bad effects. Beelzebub decided to become a "physician-hypnotist." Hassein asks, "What is hypnotism?" Beelzebub says, "A name given to that property of themselves from which all the peculiarities of the psyche proceed." This property of being subject to the hypnotism of others, distinguishes them from all other beings in the universe. Their whole life moves under the spell of suggestion. The only distinction between hypnotism and life is that life (a waking state of consciousness) suggests changes slowly. When changes come with absurd rapidity, they call it hypnotism.

There are only three normal states of consciousness:

1. Sleeping.
2. Self.
3. Cosmic.

Our "waking" state of consciousness is a pseudo form of sleep artificially induced under suggestion, thanks to substances we breathe and perceive during infancy. Chemically abnormal (air and perceptions) have been taken into our body, substances comparable to opium, hence we are never "essential." We go through life in a sort of somnambulism, dimly aware that we are not behaving individually. Are there any of us who cannot recall periods when we behaved with somnambulistic idiocy? When we ourselves feel as if we were behaving as if mad? Always a little doped; sometimes excessively. The only thing which prevents more openly idiotic conduct is the absence of necessary chemicals. You can tell anything to a person in this hypnotic state and if you happen to be the sort of person to whom he is sympathetic, he will believe you. If you show him a flea and say it is a rhinoceros he will believe. Trifles (fleas) that we know to be trifles are yet considered calamities. We are often commiserated with for calamities which we know to be trifles. (Think of such things in your experience.) Can induce rapid hypnotism; one of the methods, "stroking," can produce madness. But they do not know what hypnotism really is. The chief reason for possessing this peculiarity is that we have two kinds of consciousness:

1. Their real consciousness as beings. This is common to them as to all other beings, including those on their own planet, animals, birds, etc. Biological consciousness, native or essential or real. Some animals, e.g., cats we admire because they are not so easily suggestible.

2. A second kind not related to their structure but imparted to them. Every brain now has two separate regions in which every perception is simultaneously deposited. Enhances sociological consciousness, if it is at all a real consciousness.

1. Belongs to essence.

2. Segregated formatory part of the brain and associated chiefly with words, easily educated.

In the brains of these beings, two kinds of thoughts exist side by side, real and foreign. "He was born a man and died as a churchwarden." Consider the English officer. He is as if a second being had been grafted onto him. An extraordinary creation, in its way quite admirable, while essentially he may be worthless. Or consider the English officer and gentleman's idea of "honor"; to be counted on in public situations and not in private. Read Shaw's Devil's Disciple for a picture of Burgoyne at times showing essence through sociology. Read contemporary criticisms passed on Burgoyne for his humane conduct in America. What Shaw considers a virtue, his fellow officers consider as signs of having lost caste. This is the professional sense produced by special hypnotic training. They call their essential, real consciousness their subconscious, and what they call their consciousness is merely the totality of the perceptions they have accidentally and automatically accumulated in a certain part of the brain and with which they identify themselves. This consciousness is completely alien to their essence, as mortal as their body and environment. What is the history of Morris? (I say: born at such and such, went to such and such school, read such and such books etc.) Nothing but sociological history, events, perceptions etc., and we identify this with our name and call it our personality. We seldom speak of our real history, the history of our subconscious.

Watson says he can take the child of any heredity and train it in the belief that it is whatever "type" he wished it to be. Not touching here any essential development but guaranteeing to graft any desired personality through which essence will only appear at times in the subconscious. (But Watson imagines he is covering the whole field.)

Formatory center at the front of the brain instead of being controlled and regulated by the center at the back of the brain (the center of essence, the subconscious) is controlled by the instinctive and the emotional centers. Thoughts, opinions etc. emerge but have no contact with essence; they are merely the result of combinations and permutations of impressions accidentally received. And since opinions have been formed by personal contacts with no relation to essence, they are susceptible to being changed by similar forces to those that formed them. Hence the subjective is not related to the essence and hence not related to the objectivity that is biologically common. Hence: no will of their own.

Having discovered this, it is used for healing: doctor, hypnotist. (Coué, Christian scientist—anything which exempts one from all essential pondering.) Counter suggestion will undo what has been done. He has recently discovered certain new methods (refers to theosophists, Steiner etc.), one method consists in having patients look fixedly at a shining object. Allegory for gazing upon what we call an ideal. By this method some people cast their hypnotic state.

Since there are two organs of consciousness there are two forms of blood stream.

Not sufficiently expert in self-observation to distinguish such things. Can you tell where the center of gravity is in the head during different states of thinking?

[*Orage can tell the difference between association and thinking, though association may be very vivid and give the impression of thinking.*]

Contrast association with the effort to arrive at some personally understood truth. Must scrape down. "Don't lie, Morris. What do you really think about this? Out with some associated idea. Don't lie." One effect is likely to be a momentary light-headedness, a shift of center of gravity. Blood tends to go to the back of the head. Pondering is a method of giving the back of the head a blood-bath. There is a different circulation for associative and for real thinking. We are really conscious only when we are trying to ponder. But when gaze is fixed on a certain shining object the muscles are tensed and the state of consciousness is changed by muscular means in a trance. Suggestions then made will be accepted and afterwards carried out. The whole trick lies in the skill of changing the blood circulation. All the tricks of educators, artists etc., all who influence us are reduced to what muscles in us they employ.

The method Beelzebub used was the stopping of the flow of blood in certain familiar channels and the state of consciousness became different. Unfortunately this method cannot be used on those who are hysterical, they must be of certain normality; the hysterical cannot practice self-observation, merely take in new verbal associations and by churning, turn out new combinations of doctrine. Beelzebub began his career as a healer in Asia (essence) and gradually moved westward. He reached Russian Turkestan, affected by the gratitude of those he helped. He worked hard until he grew tired and went to Egypt to rest. He journeys back to Russia and sets up the first institute for the cure of hypnosis—suggestibility.

7 MAY 1928

REVIEW OF THE GURDJIEFF SYSTEM

Will require cooperation. Will realize how much you have heard. Will realize how little you have realized. Knowledge cannot be converted into real knowledge without effort.

E.g., the most illuminating statement in the doctrine: In essence, man is a passion for the understanding of the meaning and aim of existence. If Plato had made this statement it would have changed history source. But it means little to us. We have little experience of "passion," except instinctive. No passion of understanding, curiosity etc. We have little interest in man as a problem, except as individuals or for a two-for-a nickle-reform. Only one in a million has an interest in man as a being on this planet.

"The meaning and aim of existence"—this seems for most of us, only an academic question, beyond whether we are getting on well or not. We are children in regard to this. Yet these statements are directed to us. Are we prepared to pay the price of attempting to understand them by the method prescribed which seems so simple?

Self-awareness—few of us have made any serious effort to increase the continuity of awareness or to increase the field of self-observation. Yet raising the rate from 48 (intellectual understanding) to 24 (personal understanding) is the only way to make this of any value except as providing more dreams and fancies. Self-observation next year for assimilation.

[*For the next four weeks, instead of any ordered "survey," Orage has prepared a list of about one hundred topics. Each term has a definite meaning. He suggests that we keep such a list, and when we have spare time, purposively direct the mind to them with the purpose of being clear about them.*]

Man. Try to assemble under this heading, all that we have in mind concerning him; as if man were a proton and your essential understandings about him were electrons.

Sex.

Consciousness.

The world.

The universe.

Nature.

God. Is there a being? What is in the cosmological theory?

The three foods. Is air for you a real substance? Is breathing eating?

Can you correlate certain states with certain ways of breathing? Do you know you are incapable of clear thought if both nostrils are not clear? Does the statement that impressions are a food mean anything to you? Can you distinguish and experience between impressions taken unconsciously and consciously? If so, you would not need any stimulus to self-observation. Listening to the tone of voice is stimulus. The experience is necessary. Otherwise this is only theory. In the absence of the conscious taking in of impressions, the emotional and intellectual life cannot grow.

The three bodies. Have you a realization of the definite, concrete movements of the mental body as of the instinctive?

Hypnotism. Why are we, alone, of the three-centered beings, hypnotizable? We have no true waking state of consciousness—partial hypnosis.

The three centers. To be discriminated from the three brains, which are the physical organs of the three centers, which are simply focuses of attention.

The method. Can you clearly state what pseudo methods resemble? What misunderstandings always arise when first presented? What are the steps: self-observation; participation; experimentation? Second stage: voluntary suffering? Third: conscious labor. What do these mean to you? It has been said, the mind is a dragon. To come to terms with it, to give clear formulation of essential truth, is to slay it. The Greek legend of slaying the dragon of mind.

Religion and religions. We are all ashamed of being religious. Why? The paraphrases we are ignominiously driven to use with our neighbors to conceal that we are profoundly interested in anything; especially the aim and meaning of existence. Religions: Buddha, Christ, Pythagoras, Confucius. What was the serious purpose of these manly men? A psychological unknown with a great object.

Art. What does it mean, painting pictures? We might as well build sand castles on the shore awaiting the tide, if this is all there is to it. There is no immortal work of art but one art—which is making a complete being of oneself, transforming of chemicals to a higher order, to make a lasting work of art which would outlive the accidents of this planet.

Science. Are scientists merely trying to anatomize the corpse of this universe? This is of great value but those who wish to understand the living function as opposed to mechanics must approach from another angle.

Knowledge and belief. Try to discriminate in your own experience between saying: "I know this is so" and "I believe." Generally speaking—never say "I believe." Belief is a luxury for those who know. For the rest of us it is a matter of "plausible opinion."

The three forms of reason. Instinctive: we share with animals. Associative: depends mainly on words. Objective: must be acquired.

The law of the octave. The problem has practically no meaning for us. E.g. one stands in a certain relation to another person; goes over the case to familiarize oneself with the facts merely. Range or resonance of the situation *"do."* Until we have complete realization of the subject we can say nothing.

Next: *"re."* Attempt to discover on the part of the other person what they essentially wish (often different from what they think they wish).

Next: *"mi."* To see if the practical situation admits the gratification of the wish (for not all essential wishes can be gratified within our time; many, never).

It may be that at this point one can do something. If prepared to admit the impossibility of giving advice necessary at *"mi"* which means they must be prepared to take it themselves. (No one has a right to give advice who has not taken the same themselves and worse; and also to stand by and see the advice properly taken and carried out. This may take years.) After this, a person's individuality will direct.

Octave: Writing a book: realization at the beginning *"do."* Planning a vacation, a realization of what it should be, octave of light, color, minerals etc.

Law of three and law of seven. Essence and personality. Individuality, consciousness and will.

"I" and "it." We are not yet sufficiently conscious behaviorists. We research certain experiences from it for "I." Russell's criticism of Watson: that he is still prepared to think of entities. No organism in this room; no room. All that we call life is behavior. What behaves? Nothing. This is essence. "Essence is the field in which behavior occurs." Ultimately all our experiences will have to go into "it."

The three yoga's. Only of interest to those who have been interested in the occult. All can be reduced to three methods. Can defy any occultist or orientalist to displace his classification:

1. The saint.
2. The intellectualist.
3. The ascetic.

The fourth way of which there is no tradition, no school, no leaders. You do not get the fourth by adding the first three. Has anyone read the commentary by Proclus on Timaeus? A dialogue between three people, here there were to have been four; but the fourth did not come. Socrates: One, two, three, where is the fourth? Look at man; three centers. Where is "I"? Difficulty of speaking of "I" without referring to parts. Wholeness cannot be written about. Gurdjieff says the universe is made up of seven hydrogen's; each hydrogen is made of three parts: carbon—intellect; oxygen—instinctive; nitrogen—emotional. When the three are blended we have man. Number of the hydrogen in the universe is 24.

Force.
Matter.
Energy.
Radiation.
Emanation.

This glossary should take two forms:
1. As accurately recollected.
2. Personal significance.

Ouspensky said: When listening to these ideas, imagine two bowls. In one part, put the ideas as heard (competent reporting), in the other, what you understand. Keep these distinct. Can say "they say"; and "I understand."

Electricity. Fit in two forms: anode and cathode. But there is a third which is the field where these two are related. Lever, weight, what is the fulcrum? The emotional center is the neutralizing force of mind. Intellect is the positive; instinctive the negative. Emotional center, being is neutralizing. (Consider later in connection with knowing, doing, being. Being manifests only through knowing and doing.) We are electrical apparatuses. When thinking, we are positively charged; when doing, negatively. Our behavior is an electrical phenomenon. It is possible to consider man chemically, reduced to a few piles of chemicals, distributed in two and a half buckets of water. Or possibly to consider man physiologically; or biologically, or psychologically. If we consider him from these various aspects one gets an idea of the variety of uses man can be put to. One function is that of transformation of chemical energy: manure.

The Bible. Try to make up your mind as to what you think of the bible, it is certainly not history, except accidentally. All the so called sacred books, what was the purpose of the compilers?

Good and evil.

Time. What does the phrase "Time is the unique subjective mean?" Or "Time is the potentiality of experience."

Incarnation.

Reincarnation. Christianity has always stressed the mystery of incarnation, saying nothing of reincarnation. Becoming aware is merely surveying the body in which we intend to incarnate. Reincarnation can have no meaning to one who has not yet un-incarnated.

Spiritualism. A serious student comes to the conclusion that there is nothing in it except something dangerous (trivialities). Manifestations of one form or another of neuroses. This is not to say that the snakes a man sees in delirium have no reality for him. But to get the Delirium Tremens for the sake of investigating snakes?

Objective reason, objective conscience, objective art, objective science. E.g., a flock of sheep kept for their mutton and wool. They may gambol pleasantly on the hill unaware of their objective function, their raison d'être. Consider the experiences of a black sheep, who glimpsed their use. We are black sheep. We begin to suspect that our subjective values are not objective. By cooperating, we may cheat this.

Laws of association. Mental, emotional and instinctive. Merely physical laws of specific gravity. Thoughts and emotions have weight. As they are presented to us, they sort themselves out according to their weight. They sink to certain centers, and we find them thereafter associated. Our thinking, feeling and perceptions happen according to associations. The corresponding levels in each center are related. These interrelations make up the total associative psychology of man.

Go over the list, assembling all you can think about each. The more you think, roundabout, the more association ideas will form and give a richer substance in deeper levels. The material for essential understanding.

7 MAY 1928

SUNDAY AFTERNOON AT ROSETTA O'NEAL STUDIO

You remember I said that I would attempt to make a review of the ideas for your use. Try to realize how much you have heard and contrast it with what you have understood. Nothing in this world can convert knowledge into understanding, i.e. real knowledge. The most illuminating statement in the book is: "Man is an organism for understanding the aim and purpose of his existence. But we have no passion, except instinctive passion. We are defective in our realization even of "passion." Not more than one in a million has more than this. We are 99 percent animal, so this means for us, just the sum of instinctive advantages. Are we well-succeeding—pleasantly related to our associates? No, we are not on the plane where these things we speak of here have any meaning. Are we ready to pay the price, i.e. by the means of the method so simply prescribed—to gain a real understanding and knowledge, of the meaning and aim of existence? Very few have made much effort to increase the effort and the field of their awareness. A conversion of perceptions from 48 to 24, i.e. an octave of difference is necessary. And it can only can be gained by an increasing objectivity. You will have so much material in the next few weeks and a method guaranteed to enable you to assimilate it, that you will be able to go on for a year, if necessary, and by this time you will find, either in yourself or outside, an impulse that will carry you on.

I have prepared here a list of about a hundred different subjects and next week I will ask you to suggest headings of subjects I have omitted. I will comment on these briefly.

The word "centers" has for each of us a definite meaning—what does it mean to you? Is it, for me, an exact term?

Have a list such as this for use in "spare time" during which your mind will otherwise rot.

1. Man. Try to assemble under this word all you have heard said, and set it down very briefly—so that it will be a nucleus on which the statements will be as electrons—i.e. a solar system.

2. Sex.

3. Consciousness—get at your essential understanding of this word: sleep, waking , cosmic.

4. The world—do you mean planet, solar system, milky way?

5. The universe—(usually means two or three hundred white people).

6. Nature.

7. God. If you conceive of no God, what is your cosmological theory?

8. Three foods. Is air for you a food? Can you note changes of rhythm in breathing? Can you tell how you breathe when happy, depressed etc.? Can you note the corresponding change of breathing in respect of changes in emotional intellectual states? What do impressions really mean? We are taking them at the rate of 30,000 per second. Can you distinguish the difference between looking at a landscape when you aware of yourself and mechanically, i.e. unconsciously? If you did, you never would need any other stimulant to awareness. Listening to your own voice is more stimulating than any other that you could mechanically take. In the absence of the conscious taking in of air and impressions no growth is possible.

9. The three bodies. Do you, by experience, realize that an intellectual faculty is as definite an organ as any physical organ? As a body walking across this room, a mental body should proceed to a conclusion—as rhythmically and as definitely. Life in the physical body gives us movement, our emotional body emotions, our mental body thoughts.

10. Hypnotism. Why are we, of all three-centered beings, hypnotizable? The other two states of consciousness—self-consciousness and cosmic-consciousness are impossible because of hypnotism.

11. The three centers—merely focus of attention.

12. The method. Can you produce a clear statement of the method? What does it consist of? What pseudo methods resemble it? What misunderstandings are liable to occur in the first hearing of this method? What are the various steps of the method?

a. Self-observation, participation, experiment.

b. Voluntary suffering.

c. Conscious labor. It has been said in India that the mind is an octopus—and to slay this dragon you must give clear answers of essential truth to its questions. Watch how your mind shirks giving a clear yes or no.

13. Religion and religions. We are all ashamed of being thought religious—why? Why do we disguise from our neighbors that we are profoundly interested in anything—especially in the meaning and aim of existence? Buddha was not a highbrow—Jesus was not a

fool—Confucius not just a word thrower—Pythagoras not a climber. They were psychological workmen engaged in a eugenic labor.

14. Art. What does art really mean? The art of making a complete human being of oneself. The art of converting chemicals into an enduring work of art. (Perhaps the various forms of art are valuable in this art.)

15. Science. Engaged in making an anatomy of the universe—and so far as it goes it is of enormous value. But if you wish to understand life, you must approach it from an entirely different angle.

16. Knowledge and belief. Try to distinguish between the consciousness of knowledge and the consciousness of belief. If so, you will say generally: "never will say I believe." It is allowable only to those who really know—then it is a luxury—a plausible opinion.

17. The three forms of reason:

a. Instinctive—animal.

b. Associative—verbal.

c. Objective—to be acquired—to be pondered over.

18. The law of the octave. It has practically no meaning for us. For example—I stand in a certain relation to another person. I diagnose this. I at once say something a little intriguing to postpone a discussion. This is the note "do." A clear understanding of the facts of the case, you have not decided yet to do anything. You are merely acquainted with the resonance of the note "do." Suppose I have not completed my realization of the note "do"—I literally can say nothing. Then we go on to the note "re" which is an attempt to realize the essential wish of the other person. (Do, re, mi—then space, then fa.) Then next, "mi," to see if the practical situation allows of its gratification—within a time allowable. Perhaps it appears that it can never be gratified. Say a man and a woman are married—and the woman becomes ill or goes mad. The marriage should be ended—but perhaps due to children or other reasons this cannot be. Or a daughter with a bedridden mother—she is tied. Let her try to escape—she will not be able. Then it is to decide whether the essential wish can be gratified. "Mi" if it can, then you may, if you will, assume the responsibility to advise the person. But no one has the right to advise anyone unless he can take the same advice or something more difficult. And if he does, he must stand ready even for years to assist the carrying out of the suggestion. This method is a key for handling situations. Try to assemble all the regular phases through which a properly orchestrated symphony should pass.

19. The laws of three and seven.
20. Personality and essence.
21. Individuality, consciousness and will.
22. "I" and "it." To this day we subtract from "it" and give to "I." We are not yet sufficient behaviorists. Watson is still an incomplete behaviorist. (Read Bertrand Russell's philosophy.) Essence is the field within which behavior occurs.
23. The three yoga's:
    a. Hatha yoga—instinctive yogi.
    b. Bhakti yoga—emotional saint.
    c. Raja yoga—intellectual ascetic.

The fourth way. No school, no teachers. Gurdjieff = fourth way. But you can only arrive at it outside, yet including these, but not adding them together.

The wholeness—Father, Son, and Holy Ghost is not any of the parts—one, two, three, but where is four?

The whole of the universe consists of seven hydrogen's—i.e.—carbon (intellectual center)—oxygen (instinctive center) and nitrogen (emotional center) equally blended. Man is hydrogen 24. Build around this idea as a nucleus.

24. Force, matter, energy, radiation, emanation.

All this should be put into two formulations:
    a. What has been told to you.
    b. What you yourself have really proved.

Say you have two bowls—into one put all untried theory—into the other all that which you really understand.

25. Electricity. Anode and cathode—but there is also a third form—namely the field within which the positive and negative forms are related to each other. Any exhibition of electricity means a relationship such as that between the weight and the fulcrum and the lever. The emotional center, or essence, or being is the fulcrum in man. Knowing is positive, doing is negative, being is neutralizing. In the absence of knowing and doing, being does not exist. The state of being is that which we call feeling. One can regard man as an animal or as a collection of chemicals diluted in two buckets of H_2O. Biologically, psychologically, chemically. Consider the various uses of man from these points of view. Man is a medium for collecting chemicals

from the air too fine for the plants, animals, etc. So Gurdjieff calls us manure for the planet earth.

26. The Bible (and all the other so-called sacred books). What did its compilers intend?

27. Good and evil.

28. Time. Time is the unique subjective? Potentiality of experience?

29. Incarnation and reincarnation. The one thing that the Christian religion can be proud of, is that it emphasizes the mystery of incarnation and not reincarnation. To become aware of ourselves is simply surveying the body into which we are to incarnate. In our case, it is possible to survey before birth, the body which will be ours if we are born. Then we practice as if we were in control. Then experiment, wherein we commence to see what we can do with this body by changing its habits. This is the prime doctrine of Christianity. Such a revival or renaissance of the real Christianity would make a bishop of anyone.

We are like children who are given millions of money and we don't know what to do with it.

Reincarnation is a problem subsequent to incarnation.

Spiritualism, one or another form of neurosis.

Delirium Tremens. Drunks experience this for the purpose of studying snakes and is exactly comparable to spiritualism for the sake of studying ghosts. What do you understand by: objective reason, objective conscience, objective art, objective science?

For man it is mutton and wool. Try to imagine the experiencing of a black sheep brought up by the daughter of the butcher. He catches glimpses of the real functions of the kindly shepherd and butcher. Try to imagine how he would act, and how the other sheep would react, when he had grown up and was turned back to pasture. We can cheat this object by the method.

30. Laws of association. Mental and emotional and instinctive are simply the laws of specific gravity. All our thoughts, emotions and acts have their own specific gravity. As they occur to us, they sort themselves out and become grouped by identity of specific weight.

All our thinking is according to associative perceptions—so feeling—so instinctive perceptions. Deep answers to deep. So in the Gurdjieff-movements—each one stirs a corresponding thought and feeling. This interrelation of the three centers is a total associative psychology of man.

If you encounter this method and these ideas it is exactly analogous to putting a match to a pipe of tobacco—unless you huff and puff it will not burn more than an instant.

Pondering. Try to recall what in your experience, pondering implies as a process. Distance between pondering and thinking. Thinking is a comparison between likenesses and differences; but pondering is a weighing of values. It presupposes that thinking has already taken place and logical deductions have been made. Pondering weighs these.

Two kinds of pondering:

• Personal, directed to discovering one's essential relation to ideas, a situation, a person etc. Interrogating oneself as to one's deepest, most sincere, personal relation: e.g. where shall I spend a vacation? Or in regard to people, what is the weight of my liking? This is apart from any objective valuation and is subjective.

• Objective, more difficult, and is regardless of your personal relation, e.g. theory of behaviorism. What do you think it is? How do you weigh its value relatively to other theories? Irrespective of yourself. Or you set out to make a scale of values and the weight you attach to each. Pondering has as its aim to weigh as to value. To clarify is the aim of thought; to value, that of pondering. Normal man is expected to spend half his energy in pondering, getting the objective significance of ideas already defined—a function of normal man. The normal man is a measure of values.

Purposive thought (aim or goal). Where are you going? Aimless thought is by accident and is brain rot, day-dreaming. Purposive thought: to what end are you thinking? Are you trying to arrive at an answer to a question? Is the problem a specific one? Generally speaking the instinctive center is going somewhere definite; but the mind is strolling in the park, subject to accident. Do not learn to think. If you stroll, you will stroll in circles, do-re-mi describes an arc. Unless purpose is introduced at "mi," it will run down to "do" again, in a circle. The effort to make lives the only real exercise of the mind. Purposive thinking should take place during the whole of the waking life. It means using the mental body. Although it involves effort, it is less wasteful than day-dreaming. Nothing is more fatiguing than day-dreaming and nothing is more stimulating than purposive thinking.

A general law: directed energy is less wasteful than idling, in the smallest as well as the greatest things.

Experimentation is changing order in little habits, not to do better but to act purposively. Select the side of the street; observe people for a specific feature etc. Always with a plan. This brings about a more complete incarnation than drifting. Plot your day in advance; it will require a continual improvisation.

Playing Roles. What associations have you with this? Is there a distinction between playing roles and hypocrisy?

Arguments: We are always playing roles; but unfortunately we do this unconsciously. There is no such thing as sincerity. One is always an actor but our roles are determined by environment and chief feature. The same chief feature may under different circumstances play servile or bullying. Try to define the character which you essentially are; then watch yourself, especially in the presence of those whom you consider clearly inferior or clearly superior; those congenial and those uncongenial.

To the superior and uncongenial are you standoffish? To the superior and congenial do you toady? To inferiors both congenial and uncongenial are you patronizing?

Playing roles is to make what was unconscious become conscious. To carry out conduct you have planned. You will in general be inclined to play consciously, roles which are different from what you would essentially play unconsciously. By observing, learn more.

Being cast for roles unconsciously, the effort to play consciously is more likely to achieve a purpose; e.g. an important interview planned in cold blood. In presence the words may seem unsuitable but say them (with trepidation). You will be surprised to see how effective. (Orage tells the story of his interview where he was almost scared out of it by a man's beard.) You can devise a better play than you can improvise under pressure.

Next step: Suppose you play the role of an older brother i.e. change of attitude (ponder attitude). Cast yourself for a role and play it in private and public. Cast yourself in relation to the rest of humanity as older brother. (In England, surprising effect of promotion to the peerage, very often whole sets of likes and dislikes are changed. Why? Change of attitude. Why? More responsibilities.) Imagine that you have had conferred upon you in reality the title of older brother. Self-hypnosis.

Further step: Greek drama. Recall the chapter. No gods. Actors who cast themselves so completely in extraordinary roles, that it produced change in emotion and thought as well as in instinctive behavior. Try to conceive the being of a conscious man as if you were a playwright, a being who was always aware of what he was doing, feeling and thinking. This is relatively easy to conceive intellectually.

Having conceived, cast yourself. (Thomas à Kempis tried to conceive himself as Christ.) But you are advised not to model yourself on any well known figure but to make one's own conception of a conscious being. What would a completely conscious being do in this situation? Playing roles is the active alternative to hypnotic behavior. Our present behavior is the resultant of two forms of conditioning in essence and environment. Mechanical behavior is neither sincere nor insincere. Sincerity is possible only to the conscious. Playing roles is the beginning of sincerity.

Parables. E.g. Hymn of the Robe of Glory. Mental body. Acquiring the conscious use of the mind was winning the Robe of Glory.

Man—manners—mind.

We have three ways of meeting reality. Existence implies something we can sense or feel or think. Can you distinguish the three processes? If so, can you distinguish the three centers? When each one is developed and independent, each one meeting reality. Generally speaking, we make contact with the world through the senses. Artists are beginning to make contact with the world of emotions (only beginning; when developed the world of emotions is as varied and clearly defined as the world of objects). Intellectuals would be so, to the world of ideas. A complete parable is one which simultaneously presents a statement of identical content to the three different responses. Gurdjieff's book is a parable, using not events of ordinary life but of technical experience (machines, drugs, etc). An attempt to intertwine the dramatic with the parabolic. The characters in the book are like characters in a play, e.g. Ashiata Shiemash; but their words are parabolic (germs for the profoundest essays in years). How much work have you done in the past week?

Psychoanalysis. We will have to come to grips with this sooner or later. How would you epitomize your attitude towards the intellectual theory? Relatively clear. It assumes certain things as true which the Gurdjieff system disputes. Could you show that taking his own system as a base (not opposing any other system), his system is fallible? And secondly, could you then formulate another system?

Briefly summarizing—two major propositions of psychoanalysis:

1. Psychoanalysts have no clear concept as yet, as to the origin and contents of the subconscious. In regard to the contents, they are at a loss to explain how they came to be there (resulting in many speculations, such as Jung's "ancestral memory" etc). Gurdjieff opposes to these speculations the behaviorist point of view, with the addition

that our perceptions at the rate of 30,000 per second of which perhaps one is capable of being recalled. The surprise is not that our subconscious is so rich but etc.

2. The second proposition is that the most effective bringing to light of these perceptions is the direct analysis of manifestations. Examine forms of unconscious behavior, dreams etc. This is naive. Gurdjieff opposes: The shortest cut to the disclosure of the unconscious is the enlargement of the field of conscious perception and directed at those of current perception. While widening this field it deepens the awareness of the unconscious. If instead of being aware of 1 one can be aware of 2, one begins to recollect a buried perception one degree lower, etc. in proportion.

Mysticism, Occultism and words of that kind. Process of debunking these words. A mystic is a person who strives to attain an enlarged consciousness. Note I do not say: higher, deeper, cosmic etc. These poetic meanings are added by amateurs. As used by practical people—enlarged consciousness, enlarged of what? Of whatever you can be conscious of. Self-observation is the beginning of mysticism. Occultism is the technique of enlarging consciousness of which mysticism is the wish. Mysticism is the theory; occultism is the practice. Religion is the same thing: an attempt to increase consciousness. Keep these terms clear in your mind and do not let loose popular meanings confuse you.

Evolution and involution. Everything in the world occupies a certain place in a certain scale, or octave; and at any given moment any thing (being or object) is in the process of passing up or down the octave. If down: involving; if up: evolving. Intellectually considered there is no question of "superior" value, merely a change of form. For human pondering there is a question of value. Intellectually, there is no good nor evil, there is merely a difference of definition. There are two places in the octave where an external agency is required, which are not supplied. If evolving will involve; if involving will evolve: do-re-mi, mi-re-do, and over again. All objects, all beings. (Circular movement of day-dreaming.) The two intervals correspond to two conscious efforts, either from within or from without.

21 MAY 1928

Transmutation of substances. A cosmic chemistry. Transmutation of vibration. Strictly speaking, there are no substances; only our way of perceiving rates of vibration. Change of "key" which we perceive as sound, color, form etc. Evolution and involution are comparable to running up and down the scale. Changes in psychology due to either mechanical or conscious change of rates of vibration. This method attempts to raise the rate of vibration of certain master parts of the organism. Taken in connection with the octave there are only three points at which there is conscious effort: do, fa, si. Each brings about a mechanical change of the three notes under it.

Sun Absolute, suns, planets, moon. There are three orders of suns, or three octaves of vibration:

First octave: Sun Absolute—intelligence.

Second octave: Suns of the first degree (our sun).

Third octave: Suns of the second degree, planets on the way to becoming suns of the first degree. Just as suns of the first degree are on the way to become part of the Sun Absolute.

These three octaves are the three centers of the universe, which is a being with three centers corresponding to our own.

Center of gravity. In music, "absolute pitch" (striking pure, no wavering) is the center of gravity of that note. Anything "off" is abnormal. Every being has its own pitch or center of gravity (orchestral also each center). "Permanent dwelling place" or "habitual center."

One of the distinguishing marks of the chief feature. Within any of your centers, is your pitch absolute, or are they all a little off?

Every form of objective art would be an attempt to produce absolute pitch in consciously modeled forms.

Cosmic laws. According to Gurdjieff these are two:

Law of three. Every thing or being is composed of three forces: positive, negative and neutralizing. Nothing can otherwise exist. To the degree that the thing is developed, the three forces are specialized into three centers, differentiated and equipped with organs. The three forces are in a stone but are not differentiated. This law is confined to every existing thing.

Law of seven. The progression of things according to a series of seven. Every note is threefold; every series of notes is sevenfold.

Trogo-auto-ego-crat. Law of mutual feeding. Law by virtue of which all things, including beings, feed on each other. Trogo—I eat,

(Greek); auto (efto, Russian spelling), ego—myself, crat—system of government.

Law of fusion of similarities. Grouping within the centers of experiences. How does association of words take place? Attraction of similar rates of vibration. Effort of self-observation is an attempt to strike a certain rate of vibration; whatever by accident in past experience of the same rate attracted. A frequent experience of those really doing this is unexpected recollections of past reading, thinking, etc.

Law of Aeeioua. The highest rate of vibration in any given field tends to raise others in the same field. They are led to "aspire" to a higher rate. Psychological experiences: hope, aspiration; endeavor, making vows, etc., awareness of changes in chemical processes and other laws.

Birth.

Life.

Love.

Suffering.

Pain.

War.

Death.

These practically cover the sevenfold "tragedy" of life. Etymology of "tragedy" not traced to "goat" but connected with barley, wine, ecstasy. As originally played, tragedy was the contemplation of the sevenfold tragedy of life, seen from ecstasy. A distinction between the ancient classic drama and the drama we have. Ecstasy replaced by dream. Our drama opened period of dream.

Birth. Nature regulating the supply of machines for transmutation of cosmic substances. When the average efficiency is low, the birth rate is high.

Life. The expenditure of a charge of potential experience, potential experience we call time.

Suffering and Pain. Distinguish between these. Suffering is the conflict of centers. Nobody is recommended to incur pain; but it is encouraged to bring about the conscious conflict of centers. Putting oneself in situations where one or even two centers are attracted and two or one repelled. Overcoming of habits is the conquest of one center by others.

War. War is not a phenomenon within human control; it is regulated by nature in response to occasional special demands for special substances. Acting mechanically we find reasons for this, i.e. conversations between Churchill and other members of the British Cabinet in 1919.

Automatic or conscious. The only conscious act of which we are at first capable is self-observation. This is the letter "A" of a conscious alphabet. Everything else is the unwinding of potential experience. Because external events which are unwinding in us do not fall into easily intelligible order, we have the impression that life is an adventure or that we can control the order. This is why we do not learn from experience. We could learn only if there was order. How little would you learn of any technique if steps did not come to you in order?

Behaviorism. Come to some conclusions about this. The best critique is in Bertrand Russell's philosophy, but it does not go far enough. Be able to point out both to Watson and Russell where they fall into fallacy.

Inter-relations of centers. Physical movements. There is a jiujitsu of all three centers. This implies an ability to move each of the three bodies. This in turn implies an awareness of them. Any note struck in one octave tends to evoke a corresponding note (vibration) in other octaves. Physical movement of a note on the lowest of three octaves has overtones or echoes in others. This principle can be used. If one can establish relations between posture, gesture, etc. you can aid the production of emotional or mental states which are desired, and vice versa. This is a subject for experiment.

Positive forces, negative forces, neutralizing forces. The neutralizing is the field within which the positive and negative act. In one sense it can be said not to exist. The difficulty in defining consciousness is that it is this field. All the contents of consciousness can be defined objectively.

Sociological influences. Some of the external stimuli that unwind the potential experience.

Astrology. Subject included here to recall serious treatment in chapter on ancient ——. At the moment of conception, precipitation (as being, not different at this moment from a seed at the moment of conception only morphologically) is actualizing certain potentialities. Elements contained in that seed, said to be the "fate" of that being. But astrology has not developed any science for predicting the order of actualizing. It is impossible to arrive at a certainty on this little planet in a corner of the milky way.

Psychological exercises. Devices for obtaining freedom of movement for the emotional and mental body. Efforts of a baby to crawl are instinctive but the astral body does not crawl instinctively. Collect these and try them.

Potential.

Actual.

Real.

Ideal.

There is an indefinable thing called potential: that which because of given external or internal conditions can change a potential into an actual. We are actualized because of certain potentials of the seed. But what others were present? We are visibly recorded records of tunes played up to date. But our number of potentialities is limited. Nothing could have made that seed develop into an oak or a crocodile. The "idealizer" contradicts the limitation of potentialities. We entertain two kinds of wishes: actualizable and unactualizable. The latter sap the life energies that might actualize the former. Every "ideal" entertained prevents the actualization of a potentiality. A parasite like mistletoe, think of the Druidic ritual of cutting away the mistletoe. List your wishes and classify whether actualizable or not.

Sleeping consciousness, waking consciousness, self-consciousness, cosmic-consciousness. Our "waking" state is abnormal; "when the sleeper awakens." Self-consciousness is consciousness of self. Self is that part of the seed that has been actualized, i.e. the body. Cosmic-consciousness is nothing mystical but is an awareness of other planets, suns etc.; and that they are centers of a being. Consciousness of the body of God.

Chief feature. Try to discover the chief feature of others not by elaborate arrangement of centers but by offhand happy phrase. St. John Ervine's remark on G. B. Shaw: "His brains have gone to his head." Intellectual conceit; preoccupation with values of the intellectual center determines all his relations. Or Napoleon's ambition, to which he would sacrifice anything or anybody. He certainly loved Josephine and suffered at the divorce, but sacrificed her to ambition. Each of us has such a deity to which in a pinch, we would sacrifice anything else; but it is unfortunately an unknown deity. Picture a stage with a procession of historic figures and assign to them a single word or phrase. Then suddenly add yourself to the parade. Maybe their momentum will help you. A psychological trick, like the trick to remember self-observation by an emotional need for it. "I wish to remember myself"; with your most vivid memories associated with each word. After making associations you have definite experiences linked artificially together, producing force. This is a mantra and is useless if mechanical repeated.

Horse—emotional.

Carriage—instinctive.

Driver—intellect.

Passenger—"I."

In a normal man the driver drives at the behest of the passenger. The passenger does not drive but is not merely contemplative (the aesthetic point of view). In the average man, the passenger is asleep; and the driver is drunk, with the reins fallen from his hands. He sits on the box and dreams that he is driving. The horse is timid and knows nothing of the cart; starts at every stimulus, dashes first one way and then another (fancy, likes, dislikes, etc). The cart is soon dashed to pieces. The driver can always say that where the cart goes is where he wanted to go (rationalization). How to wake the passenger? Any rate of vibration (thought) intercepted by driver. Find something neither driver, cart nor horse can do. Passenger wakes and does it. Driver becomes aware that he should be driving somewhere; then learns to control the horse. Behavior is the stepping down of energy through octaves driver; horse; cart (behavior).

21 MAY 1928

Black sheep. Mutton, wool; objective standards—subjective standards. Sheep—attitude to sheep and their objective use to men.

The sheep's subjective standards are useless without mutton and wool. These are the last thing the sheep is likely to be aware of. Take our classical standards, intellectual distinctions between us, in view of a superior species. Man to sheep, and moon to us. Perhaps what we despise for value, what we value is despised. A chemical purpose for which we are raised and bred. The lamb that becomes aware of the shepherd and the butcher. Black sheep—but a little nearer the truth. Perhaps this justifies our interest in the devil, the rebel; because he had an inkling of mutton and wool values. He had incidentally arrived at objective values.

Succession and simultaneity. Only these two, for there is no word for the third dimension. Time is the potentiality of experience. Succession is the experience of one potentiality. Carrying out three functions in succession, simultaneity, you approach a surface. (Succession of lines = plane.) If realizing all potentialities, third dimension is a solid. The universe is the third dimension of time.

Meaning and aim of existence. The preoccupation of normal man. If only occupation, philosophy, art etc. Active pondering continuously carried on; in the back of the head while the three centers carry on. What is our cosmic view? We implicitly act on one which is the chief pattern of our intellectual center; this is implicit in our standards etc. It is infantile and it is secret in its influence, bring it out and let it grow up.

Conditional immortality. Contrast with natural immortality; and immortality as an impossibility. Most people are in one camp or the other of these two. The neutralizing view is that it is potential but not actual, dependent on effort. Potentiality and responsibility are conditioned. What part of man's potentiality is immortal? Only his third body, within the period of the manifestation of this universe; capable of maintaining itself. It is said that diamonds are immortal on this planet for they can survive all natural heats; but on other planets it is not so. No same substances nor rates of vibration.

Various definitions of man. Man is hydrogen 24; man is the mind of God; man is a passion for the understanding of the meaning and aim of existence.

Purgatory, hell, paradise. These can only apply to souls which survive the death of the planetary body. Only such souls can survive that have an astral body sufficiently developed. Mental body cannot experience being etc., hence words apply only to the astral body and are of no immediate concern to us.

Doing (instinctive), being (emotional), knowing (intellectual). Being is merely the resultant of the conflict between doing and knowing. Must try to know and to do, in order to be. Conflict raises the scale of being. Why is man a superior species? Knowing and doing at higher intensity and hence a higher being. Same as in individual men.

Being; that which feels, gradation of being according to range and intensity of feeling, which are determined by quantitative factors of knowing and doing. Must aim at being, not directly, but through knowing and doing. Error of usual schools of mystics, occultism etc. resulting in psychic development and imaginary feelings; whereas true feelings are the result of positive and negative. The psychic body is like an umbilical cord between the planetary body and the two higher bodies, visually confused in theosophy and literature with the true astral body. Spiritualism, clairvoyance and audience are functions of the psychic or etheric body. But since it is merely an umbilical cord it is the most perishable of bodies. All the psychic arts and exercises, breath, clairvoyance, exercises for direction of "higher faculties" are both futile and dangerous. Special significance of word "emotion." Three fundamental emotions : faith, hope and love. Gradations of beings when faith, hope and love are objective (growth of).

Language. Each word we use has only the meaning we give it, by accidents of our experience. Anthology of our associations.

What a word means "in itself" is impossible for us; it is so conditioned by associations. One aim of a school is to establish a language. In the prayer book there is one Anglo-Saxon and one Latin word "When we assemble and meet together." This is common in Elizabethan writing. When pondering there is need for exactitude, e.g. "emotion"—faith, hope and love; the growing ends of essence. Pass through three stages (two subjective, one objective)—Ouspensky. "Fragments of a Faith Forgotten." How to discriminate between faith, hope and love.

Sphinx:

Head—represented love.

Wings—hope.

Legs of Lion—confidence or faith.

Confidence is not belief. Many of our negative emotions are from weak legs; ability to walk. Hope is not a wish that it may be so but effort. Love is subjective in love of self or of self in others. Love is subjective in love of others and of oneself in them. Love which is objective makes love of oneself and of others a by-product of love, the purpose for which we were created. Nietzsche: "Myself I sacrifice to my love and my neighbor as myself." Individuality is consciousness of possession of will and is an intellectual distinction; but faith, hope and love are essential distinctions of emotions.

Objective critique of man. This is the subtitle of Gurdjieff's book. Effort to look at man as a biological species, subserving functions of all species; but specially adapted to one function would bring about a momentum which if suddenly turned on itself would bring about an objective attitude. (Physics; momentum toward something objective; then turn on self). Parade of character etc. Exercise of seeing planet from a distance where two thousand million beings crawl. Continue this for ten minutes which may give you ten seconds of non-identification; a feeling of shame when you discover your chief feature, indicates that you are still identified. Ability to say the truth about oneself without emotion. Can one say unemotionally: "He (planetary body) is not the sort of person I like"? Only if we are unidentified can we begin to change. Plain intellectual effort to state the truth about man as a species helps one to come to the individual case. Hugh asks, "If one is amused?" Amusement is not true emotion. Emotion leads to action. Humor is a chance combination of emotion and ideas, corresponding in emotion to intuition in thought.

Kundabuffer. How to express this idea? Compare the difficulty of expressing an idea of relativity in popular terms. We must learn to express these ideas without using technical terms. (When people in London made propaganda in technical terms, Ouspensky said: "How provincial. This is a pedant's habit. But the intelligent man, who uses the vernacular, conceals his pedantry, by his very exactitude.") What is the reason for our touchiness, etc? What nipped us in the cradle?

Harmonious development of man. An all-around man must be equally at home in all three centers. This rules out all the specialized yoga's; and all the monstrous geniuses of one center or another. How to sum up the contribution of Gurdjieff to life in these centers? Ouspensky suggests: "Attempt to make objective what has been subjective"—impartiality. Only when impartial to the planetary body can the judgment be trusted on any opinion. Introduction of this one idea into the arts and science would cause a renaissance (e.g. psychology, the observations of the psyche are already colored). Or take art. Objective art (applies to any object) produces the same effect on the subject as self-observation. Consider the reports of those who have observed the pyramids, Taj Mahal, certain cathedrals. These are identical responses to those from the desert, Himalayas etc. "I felt my nothingness"—a moment of non-identification. Objective art is designed to produce by artificial means a moment of non-identification. Objective—because it produces objectivity; conscious—because it can be produced only by a conscious being.

Being, existence, non-being. Being and non-being are the two opposites with existence moving between. Evolution and involution. All beings are graded between these two absolutes. Scale of beings, lowest metal. Man is third from the highest, hydrogen 24. Highest vibratory rate is 6—solar gods, next octave 12 (a chemical form of matter; beings whose bodies are composed of planetary gods, 24) 48—monkey; 96—vertebrate; 192—invertebrate. (Our astral body is in the invertebrate stage, air, hydrogen 192) 384, 768, 1536, 3072. Scale of beings in relation to the scale of hydrogen. Biological scale in relation to physical.

Difference between effort and relaxation. Reduce to personal experience. Lifting heavy weight and then relaxing. Ought to know whether making effort by this comparison. Effort: trying to comprehend simultaneously one's own behavior and the behavior of the external world. Making effort where you are "pressing against the collar" (team of horses) like a horse dragging a load uphill, trying to drag the unconscious up into consciousness. Not by sudden jerks. Life consists in sustained effort to include in consciousness more and more phenomena (including a greater number of phenomena than the natural).

Standard of values. What distinguishes man from man? Quantity and range of consciousness. All our judgments are implicitly based on this.

[*End of series. Orage goes West.*]

4 DECEMBER 1928

The seed shares the fate of the plant—i.e. if the plant dies before that seed is separated from the plant, that seed will die too. "I" is like that seed, in that it will share the fate of you—if you die before "I" is separable.

Dual consciousness, i.e. through yourself, you are conscious of other things while also conscious of yourself, i.e. your body (or a skin full of chemicals). It is disgraceful that no one can say what he really wishes . . . that he grows prematurely old, not only in the body but in emotional and intellectual ability—and he cannot perform the one human function—that of keeping in one's consciousness both that behavior of the external world and of oneself.

Never be absorbed in any external object. While regarding this room be also aware of your posture, gestures, facial expression and movement. Any aesthetic emotion you may derive from a work of art will be ten times as great if you are simultaneously aware of your own five forms of external behavior.

14 JANUARY 1929

RECEPTION, BLANCHE GRANT

Nothing is to be said to the musicians about Gurdjieff's music or his connection with Gurdjieff.

Rhythm—phrase—discord—consonants—concord vowels.

If you hear the book in music you will understand it emotionally—then having understood it also with the mind—we shall have real understanding of it.

Approaches to the world are:

Mind—Eddington.

Emotions—art or religion, beauty or love.

Then through senses—i.e. common sense.

The book and the music plus observation taken together will bring about a forth center. Understanding of the worlds. De Hartmann. Know how music is related to the book.

Law of the octave.

Now is man at the note C (?)

Now, have animals the potentiality of developing fully the first two bodies, i.e. the octaves, in the absence of a third center or octave?

(Some animals have already developed a second body, said Orage.)

Man is a three-centered being etc.

Man is a being that can do—all other beings are "done."

Man is potentially a three-centered being, but the man of today has only one fully actualized center, one less than half-actualized and the third hardly at all actualized.

Astronomy and cosmogony by Jean.

Man is a representation of the universe, as a "still" cosmos is representative of the universe as a movie.

Instinctive center—nature is on the moon.

Emotions on the earth.

Intellect on the sun—Man is H24.

The world consists of a series of graded hydrogens in extinction, that actively neutral state wherein it can be actualized.

An atom of will—an atom of individuality—an atom of consciousness.

H3 is His Endlessness.

Man will be used for the universal aim—but if he passively serves, he will degenerate in the process; if actively, he will develop.

Man is mechanical because he lives only in his instinctive center. The other two are unconscious. It is as if our two higher centers were communal possessions and that these two are controlled not by us, yet the instinctive center is controlled by these two. Now our object is to take the control of our first two centers over from nature.

Even in sex, our entire behavior is controlled by nature—our two higher centers are not yet individualized.

Observation—first bridge.

Voluntary suffering—second bridge.

Conscious effort—third bridge.

When proper "distance," "attitude," and "endeavor" have been established, then the first bridge is finished and voluntary suffering may be begun.

The physical body is an unfailing representation of one's entire history. Intellectual, emotional and instinctive . . . The necessity of observing the instinctive center alone.

Positive emotional equals agreeable, equals promise of more being. Negative emotional equals disagreeable, equals threat less.

All impressions which we cannot avoid—eyes open—must see hand on table—must touch and so forth are no good. But even if it is the same sense we use, say hearing with ear one's own voice—this will be yours forever if:

Reception= passive impressions.

Perception= impressions attended to.

Concept = mental image to be recalled at absence of object.

Apperception = impression of body during these three.

4 FEBRUARY 1930

PARABLES

The meanings for all the words in this system have their orientation.

For us, all the words have a meaning relative to consciousness connected with them.

A parable is a verbal form intended to produce a certain effect.

The parable as used in this system is not to establish analogy. It is to establish a truth in at least two centers and generally in three. It is not just the same thing as the moving center producing repercussions in the other two centers, the parable strikes the centers simultaneously.

"There is an organic relationship started between the centers by a parable." (Mike Robinson.)

The figures in the book are mythological and their language is parabolical.

[*Someone asked a question about "The Odyssey." Answer: "The Odyssey" is written in fable, not parables.*]

The language of these being-created figures cannot be ordinary, the parable is their language. The mythological figure is credited with the consciousness of a three-centered being. (Jesus, a mythological figure, spoke in parables because he had a three-centered development.)

The developed conscious being puts more into his speech than a mechanical being and so more is read into what he has to say. Three meanings, one for each center. Example: the text of John, it is said, can be read in seven forms by a conscious being. It can be read as an allegory, a parable; the third, fourth, fifth and sixth ways are not given; and the seventh can be, transcendentally. It may be read in its simplest form allegorically and so on till it becomes an oracle.

QUESTION: Can parable be unconscious?

ORAGE: Yes, the parable has not only the line of the story but the state of the psyche of the writer. It is not a work of art unless done consciously. Gurdjieff's Beelzebub is a mythological character with parabolic utterances.

In the story of the history of the races in the book, Gurdjieff does not always purport to put down facts. What he has in mind is three centers in talking of races. He says: "I don't claim it is right but you can't prove it is wrong. Why was the king's name in ancient Atlantis Appolis? We can't prove that it wasn't.

Jesus took very familiar experiences as illustrations. In the gospels these became more complex. A miracle is not to be taken as fact, but as plausible. Five loaves and two fishes might have meant five diagrams and two statements. The truth was put into simple stories and words because a story is more likely to be handed down and its meaning may be kept intact, while less simple words would be documents which would lose more quickly their meaning and probably be tucked away in archives.

Meanings in the old fairy tales: Hop-o'-My-Thumb was the seventh son, the most despised, the smallest, but saved all the other six.

Little Boy Blue, full of meaning, was told to propagate safely the truth it carries—the truth was the running downhill of the three centers. Much the same meaning as the story of the sleeping passenger in the story of horse, coach, driver and sleeping passenger.

The magnetic center of young children begins to be filled by fairy tales. The new fairy tales do not do that. Perhaps Alice in Wonderland is the one exception. There are no good modern fairy tales as no one has the development to write one with meaning. Also the reading of a Story with inner significance has no meaning without understanding in the reader. Reading a parable is an act of understanding.

The passages in the book about Bolshevism taken literally are crude, but they are to be taken as analogies of revolting centers. The meaning of these passages and indeed the entire book is not to be arrived at by the mind but by a species of new understanding. A mind which ponders is capable of understanding more meaning. Kingdom of heaven, bread, upper room etc., all had a technical meaning at the time of their use. Some current words of science used in the book such as anode and cathode may be no more understandable in a few hundred years than the words like elixir of life or philosopher's stone used by the alchemists of the past are understandable by chemists today.

It is not safe to take literally the meaning of the book. The words are used only as platforms for the content that is to be understood.

QUESTION: How does one go about getting the key to a parable?

ANSWER: The supposition is that something must be known of a method back of it. The key to the Bible was entirely lost or swallowed up by the church.

The Bible: The Old Testament—do, re, mi. The two triads of the octave. The New Testament—sol, la, si.

The interval between (fa) was the history of Jesus and the history of his becoming Christ. Christ was born between the two triads, the interval.

The interval is the incarnation of the universe. See the universe in a grain of sand. The dewdrop does not slip into the sea, but the sea into the dewdrop.

Christ was a conscious creature.

In the Old Testament—the development of man; do, re, mi; parabolic history of man with three lower centers.

In the New Testament—the development of man; sol, la, si; parabolic history of man when he begins self-consciously to change in his psyche, or it might be when his psyche begins to develop.

St. Paul takes certain stories from the Old Testament and translates them into the New Testament: he calls these stories allegories.

"Promise" used in the Bible has the same meaning as "potentialities" in the book.

"Beings with promise" meant beings on the road to the development of the higher centers. Very seldom in the Old Testament is a being spoken of as a "being of promise." It was with Abram that the process began. Abram changed to Abraham. "Ham" was the masculine for the Egyptian god Ra. Isaac, the female god of the Babylonians.

The exodus of the Jews, the crossing of the red sea, are not substantiated in history. There may never have been such occurrences but certain facts might be true and the stories were used parabolically.

Just as the Bible must be regarded as parabolical so must Gurdjieff's be taken as a kind of Bible.

The disciples astonished those about them by the things they did. He will practice this method, will himself bring out of his treasury things both old and new.

QUESTION: Why is the method given in parable and not in fact?

One reason can be found in the parable of the sower. We may give a story that may be remembered and carried down even though the hearer did not understand. Its form would be carried, ready for understanding in the future. (Allan Brown.) If written down as fact it would lead to verbalization and intellectualizing and would not lead to formulation and understanding. (B. B. G.)

ORAGE: "I bury the bone for the dog to smell and dig it out." Until you have dug out the meaning, you have not acquired the ability for understanding. By use of the method your senses become more keen.

Gurdjieff is afraid he has given too many keys to the book. He has put a key for every lock but he has not placed the key by the lock.

The organic reason for using stories as parables is that there is no language for the emotional center nor the instinctive center.

The book makes neither sense nor nonsense but something neutralizing.

ALLAN BROWN: A third reason for using parables is found in the fact that a substantiated truth is three dimensional, it can't be expressed literally in explicit language, its presence can only be indicated by a figure.

ORAGE: Your mind must drive the horse but not be concerned with the horse, the horse must pull the cart but not be interested in the cart.

We should be able to read through the images in parables to get the content, but we are like children, if the rhyme jingles, they do not look for meaning.

We are just as incapable of writing a parable as we are of writing a fairy tale.

Allegories are parables and speak to the mind. Illustration—Swift's Tale of a Tub.

Tolstoy's stories are accepted as having spiritual value, they have only psychological.

Fables are distortions of facts.

Parables are disintegrating to the ordinary paths of association as they speak to three centers.

A parable has as its content a cosmic truth.

The old definition: "An earthly story with a heavenly meaning." It would be truer to say, "A heavenly story with no earthly meaning."

[*This brought a laugh.*]

20 JANUARY

Conversations may be reported according either to the gist or according to the exact. If you make a suggestion in a weak way, you lose caste—and it tends to set up a habitual tendency to reject your suggestions.

We cannot remember ourselves because it is only with the mind that we try—the two other centers have no interest in it but they must change. For total change is possible only through the emotional and instinctive centers—yet those two centers must be changed, but they have no language (i.e. mind cannot address these even though it wishes). Yet mind alone is not a human being—any more than a driver alone is a whole equipage.

The center of gravity of change is in the emotional and instinctive centers—but these are concerned only with the present. Mind looks ahead but the desire to change must be in our emotional center and the ability to change must be in our body. Yet reason is not a total stranger to the feelings and the body, but it must learn their language. This is the work of self-observation.

25 MARCH

THE FIRST ADVANTAGE

The first advantage of self-remembering is that one makes fewer mistakes in life. To complete self-remembering, three centers are necessary and all must be artificially stimulated. The intellectual from outside, the other two from inside. Distinguish between sensation, emotion and thought. Thereafter say to each sensation, emotion and thought, remind me to remember you.

Human work is with three centers, any other is subhuman. For this reason, it is thousands of times more precious to the human soul to scrub a floor consciously than to write a hundred masterpieces unconsciously. Combined three-centered work is impossible until each center has been taught to work by itself.

FOURTH LECTURE

Freedom is the ultimate goal of all schools—consciously or unconsciously. There are two freedoms, the greater freedom—from outside influences and the lesser freedom—from inner influences.

The chief obstacles to the lesser freedom are self-pride and vanity. Vanity refers to the body, self-pride refers to intellectual accomplishments. Self-pride of the real kind begins with the work of "I." He who has real self-pride is already half-free.

FIFTH LECTURE — CHRISTIANITY

Until a man separates himself from himself, he can neither do anything himself nor be helped. We have two aims—to separate "I" from "it" and thereafter to govern it unaided (freely). An adult is one who seriously wishes to separate himself. Mind and essence live separate lives. Essence is always changing with food, people, weather, etc. At present, mind submits to serving this changing essence.

Mind is governed by a devil (by a changing essence). Do not let your mind be a slave for your essence. The thinking center is Christian—the emotional center is pre-Christian—the body is pagan. Emotional center with body make the devil, which the thinking center must learn to control.

1. Parentage—birth.

2. Infancy.
3. Childhood, youth, maturity, old age, death.

Trying to do consciously what psychoanalysis does attempt:
1. How we came to be—what we were born. Loci.
2. What people were around you?
3. Schools, companions, family, etc., the kind of wishes you had—whom did you like—dislike?

Daily Review:
1. Pictorially.
2. Sensually—(seven senses, re-sense previous sensations).
3. Emotional review—emotional history during the day.
4. Try to review what you have thought during the day.
5. Try to judge the day from a standpoint of your aim (i.e. development of will, individuality and consciousness).

Formulate the varieties of world views, cosmologies. Collect as many views as possible from others.

Begin to think of the jujitsu—always insure that your opponent should use his strength against himself. But carry this along from the physical to the emotional and intellectual. Every variety of negative emotional attack can be turned so that it will attack the attacker—and so with an impertinent or other kind of intellectual attack. Say a person comes to you angry—say: "Oh, come off it. Let's go have a drink." (Perhaps it doesn't work—this means you have used the wrong jujitsu.) Probably you could have over agreed and succeeded. If you use the right words your adversary will react against himself or his idea or purpose.

Preface—conversation on ship.
1. Story of Beelzebub's exile and pardon.
2. Descriptions of souls and other planets.
3. Captain discusses ships.
4. Hassein asks what he can do. On conscience.
5. Genesis of moon.
6. Why men are not men.
7. Descent to Atlantis.
8. Relative understanding of time. Arch-absurd. All events. Reading figures.

October 1st—resume.

Sundays—October and November—series of public lectures: behaviorism, fundamentalism, religion, can science tell us anything?

Mondays—discussions of problems which have hitherto been better discussed only in private with me—personal problems. Our discussions will be serious—must be private—this will eliminate certain types.

Tuesdays—for new members only and for those who are not admitted to Mondays.

Wednesdays—class for those who wish to develop the art of expression, eventually to be used in education.

Wednesday, Thursday, Friday, Saturday—classes in music, movements, pantomime, modeling, painting, jewelry, etc.

The sun may be lacking in heat and light. Still the three-brained beings on earth they call scientists explain night and day, .heat and cold, and all other phenomena arising on their planet as being already made.

In reality, the sun may be covered with ice.

Oskiano means education.

Everything in the universe exists and is maintained by the cosmic autoaftoegocratic process.

The universe is actualized on two laws of the first order: eptaparashinoch and triamazikamno.

Before the creation of the megalocosmos there existed these two sacred laws.

Eptaparashinoch is the law of seven—the course of a straight line breaks seven times and deflects and reunites. These points of deflection are called stopinders, and are centers of gravitation. This is the law on which all manifests.

Triamazikamno is the law of three. Everywhere all that manifests in three aspects. Holy affirming, holy denying, holy reconciling. This law always flows into a consequence. The new arising mixes with okidanokh—electricity. Okidanokh owes its arising to the Sun Absolute, is an active element, and is omnipresent.

Scientists say we have two forms of electricity. Gurdjieff says there are three forms, and to make the distinction, calls electricity okidanokh.

The new arising is called harnelmiatznel. The cosmic law *aieioiuoa* (meaning remorse) is the process of one part which has become, entering another, part of its whole. This proceeds in harnelmiatznel okidanokh.

Ethernokrilno is the prime source of cosmic substance. Cosmic substance is the foundation of all arisings and maintaining. (See chapter 18.)

"Always guard against such perceptions as may impair your three brains." First brain is found in head—the holy affirming. Second brain is spinal column—holy denying. Third brain—holy reconciling. The place of this brain in man is not localized in a mass but is localized in different places of the planetary body. Earth beings call them nerve nodes and they are largely localized in their breasts and called the solar plexus.

CHAPTER 18—THE ARCH-PREPOSTEROUS

The purpose of the chapter—to understand the three parts of electricity and that they cannot be sensed.

Tirzikiano: a huge electric lamp—glass walls which are impervious to all rays. A table and two chairs inside; over the table an electrical lamp; underneath, three exactly alike; "momonodooars" and other unknown instruments. Outside are two special appliances called "lifechakhans" or dynamos or "khrikhirkhis."

Another especial appliance—a vacuum pump begins to work when touched by the left wing, while the right wing starts the dynamo. This dynamo draws the separate parts of electricity later to be collected in the generator. (Cerebellum.)

It then flows into another dynamo, where it is separated and each part concentrated in an "accumulator" from containers; of the second order, he takes each active part of electricity.

Sacred inkotsarno:	Birth.
Sacred rascooarno:	Death.
Harakhrakhrookhry:	Head of government on Saturn.
Gornahoor Harharkh:	Name of Beelzebub's friend.
Teskooano:	Instrument for observation.
Khrkh:	A workshop.
Lifechakhans:	Circulation of magnetic currents around life center (solar plexus).
Solookhnorakhoona:	Vacuum-pump (heart).
Prana:	Life fluid (electricity in its different aspects).
Parijrahatnatius:	Pari = equality of nature. Rahbat = prana (breath). Nation = to be born.
Harhrinhrah:	Heart.

Physiological description of the action of circulatory system as given by Sir Arthur Thompson.

Two pumps—ventricles side by side. Right pump drives impure blood to the lungs. Pure blood returns to the left auricle. Purified blood passes from left auricle to left ventricle. Left ventricle drives it to arteries and capillaries. Then into venous capillaries, veins, right auricle.

Left pump also drives pure blood to heart itself, stomach, intestines kidneys and head, trunk and limbs.

Impure blood comes to right auricle from head by superior vena cava, from posterior body by inferior vena cava. Also into the posterior vein passes (by the renal vein), blood filtered by kidney, by hepatic vein from liver and from heart itself.

All veins carry impure blood except pulmonary veins from lungs which bring purified blood from lungs into left auricle.

PARTIAL VOCABULARY, CHAPTERS 1 TO 20

Merciless Heropass:	Flow of time.
All Planets:	Moods.
Mars:	Mood of overcoming.
Beelzebub:	A normal man (with objective conscience).
One-centered beings:	Plants.
Two-centered beings:	Animals.
Three-centered beings:	Man.
Ors:	Our solar system.
Moon and Anulios:	Split from the earth by a comet.
Teskooano:	An observatory.
St. Venoma (phenomena?):	A scientist.
Elekilpomagtistzen:	Psychic force.
Comets:	Sex urge.
Ethernokrilno:	Ether.
Okidanokh:	Electricity.
Purgatory:	Is the state in which you wish to apply the technique which you have not acquired.
Karatas:	A special fourth dimensional planet.
Trogoautoegocrat:	I-feed-myself—reciprocal feeding.
Triamazikamno:	Law of three noumenal world.
Eptaparabarshinoch:	Law of seven, phenomenal, octave.
Theomertmalogos:	Emanation of the Most Holy Sun Absolute.
Holy Sun Absolute:	Dwelling of His Endlessness, the center of the universe.
Djartklom:	Shock which scatters okidanokh into its three component parts.

Aieioiuoa:	Remorse. "Such a process when any part which has arisen from any one holy source of the sacred triamazikamno revolts, as it were, and criticizes the former unbecoming perceptions and contemporary manifestations of another part of the whole, a part obtained from the results of another holy source of the same fundamental sacred cosmic law triamazikamno.
Three being-foods:	Ordinary food for the planetary body. Air for the astral or emotional body, impressions for the potential mental body.
Partkdolgduty:	Duty in three languages; i.e. duty in each center.
Triamazikamno:	Holy affirming, positive, father. Holy denying, negative, mother. Holy reconciling, child, neutralizing.

Radiation is a vibration of the ether. Emanation is an outflow of particles.

* * *

Beelzebub finds an essence friend.

Ethernokrilno is the prime source of all substances sub-ether-potential matter-mother of matter.

Ethernokrilno was converted into activity by the force okidanokh—three forms of electricity. This was the first work of the Sun Absolute.

Ethernokrilno is not destroyed when played upon by okidanokh. Okidanokh forms the connecting tissues of the prime ordeal. Ethernokrilno in each unit formed, from an atom to the more evolved forms, up to man; organs begin to be formed from these three forms of okidanokh. These three organs or localizations are called the three brains. Impulses correspond to volts in electric currents. The voltage of two of our accumulators is determined by heredity and environment. Only one accumulator ever actually accumulates; the other two spend. The third accumulator, instinctive center, has an external dynamo and can go on; the dynamo of this is nature. The result is that instinctively man goes on developing. Our bodies go through youth, middle life and old age. We never ripen emotionally nor intellectually. The instinctive center can still be stimulated by society after the other two centers have ceased to be stimulated. Life is then producing morons. There is simply superimposed culture, as there is no more power of initiative in emotional and intellectual centers.

This chapter has significance and suggestion in both physics and psychology. In certain circumstances a vacuum can be produced in which "I" is so isolated that literally nothing of the sensible universe appears to exist. This is the state of "I-am-ness," it means God before the world manifested. God's fear was of going into this state and never again being. This is one of the emotional high spots of the book.

The aim of this chapter is to produce in the reader the effects of the experiments described. It must be read with both the physical and the psychological interpretations. Realization of this fear of non-being, of having burned all one's bridges behind one, is comparable to the fear of loss of life, but from the other side of nothingness. That is, there is always fear of non-being. The difference between existence and being: to exist is to depend on the outside. To be is to be without.

JOHN RIORDAN: An individual in the state of I-am-ness would still be subject to time.

ORAGE: Yes, that was God's state when he warded off the wearing away of I-am-ness by time, by means of re-establishing contact with existence—by manifesting the world.

There is no relation between the feeling people have of being essentially alone, we are all essentially alone, and the realization of aloneness in nothingness. In I-am-ness there is not even memory.

The group, I fear, is on the wrong track when it tries to divine the significance of the use of Armenian in the book by looking up the language in the encyclopedia. Didn't Orage make some suggestions in the notes you have as to the possible meaning of the different languages referred to? His guess, as I recall, was that Gurdjieff had in mind the different forms of language we all continually use besides words; such as our postures and gestures, etc.—in short, our behavior. For our outward expressions of behavior, like our thoughts and feelings and our verbal languages, begin early in life to be so corrupted by the sociological influence of custom (i.e. what Gurdjieff calls the "bon ton" language, or the language of the grammarians, which has no relation to our real natures) that it becomes impossible to express anything essential in them. I think Gurdjieff set the period of corruption of Armenian at forty years—i.e. the period from birth to middle age, with the implication that by the time a man has lived that long he is hopelessly entangled in the artificial language of sociology. And when Gurdjieff said that if he wrote in his "native" tongue Greek, there would be no one to translate his words, he was certainly not thinking of dictionary meanings.

The Sunday night Orage was at Pelham, we talked a little about the book, and Orage reminded us that he had often suggested looking at it as one looks at a political cartoon. When a cartoonist draws a grotesque picture of an elephant, he is not interested in the anatomy of that group of mammals known as the Proboscidea: the implication he has in mind is something about the Republican Party. He is gaily indifferent to his drawing, from the ordinary point of view, and quite willing to stick the trunk on the wrong end if doing so will emphasize his meaning. Similarly, Gurdjieff's drawing, if you like, is terrible; he will not only put the trunk on the wrong end but put two or three of them there if he thinks it will add zest to the cartoon. He doesn't expect his reader to examine the details of the elephant, but to divine ("smell" is the word he constantly uses in that connection) the implication, about the Republican Party. Orage added that he was still in the position of the child examining the elephant curiously, and missing the Republican Party.

Gurdjieff's own attitude towards the book seems to be, like the cartoonist's, both serious and gay. At heart he is apparently so convinced of its importance that he lets nothing in its way: people, money, time and his own strength have been poured into it like water, and he asserts that its publication is going to strike existing values like a cyclone. But when any part of it is read aloud in his presence, he frequently chuckles and his eyes roam over the solemn faces of the listeners with a twinkle to see who is getting the malicious implications about the Republican Party.

I think I've quoted to you before his remark that he "has buried certain bones in the book for dogs to dig at, and that the curious thing is that in digging they become men."

The only thing that appears certain about the whole performance is that he is no more interested in the comparative study of language or, say, water closets, than in the elephant's trunk. The key to that passage about water closets, and perhaps to the whole revolting "America" chapter, seems to me to be that phrase repeated several times in connection with the water closets, "without being-effort." You made the natural mistake, which every intelligent reader will make, from the cheap horse-play about prohibition, etc., that he was concerned, like Siegfried or Keyserling, with social conditions. But all through that part of the book, Gurdjieff put the names of countries in quotation marks, to indicate that he means something different from their literal meaning (though why he doesn't put quotes around every other word in the book I don't know), from his references to the "Germans," whom he calls the modern descendants of the Greeks. I think he means by them our intellectual ingenuity in metaphysics. (What Milton in speaking of the philosophical debates of the damned calls "pleasing sorcery.") And my guess is that "America" means in general, our modern, highly sociological, propaganda-filled and materialistic civilization, wealthy and magnificent to look at, "but hollow within." The fruits, which are the largest and most highly colored in the world but without savor, being our innumerable religions, with their beautiful buildings, expensive plants, etc. . . . The implication in the canned foods, which are not taken fresh but long after they have been separated from the living stalk, is probably to be found by remembering that impressions are a food. The clue to the high buildings, where the air is too rarefied for human use, is given by the reference to Christian science.

The stress on water closets etc. appears to be because Gurdjieff considers that, whereas some civilizations have petered off in intellectual or emotional corruption, modern civilization is killing itself in its belly and sex organs. He has said that the "America" chapter is intended to leave the reader with a feeling of disgust for our current civilization.

I can only say that, however estimable an intention, the chapter never seems to have that effect. It strikes everybody as a crude and clumsy attempt to be witty.

SELECTED BIBLIOGRAPHY

Nott, C. S.
Teachings of Gurdjieff: A Pupil's Journal. Routledge & K. Paul, 1961.

Bennett, John Godolphin
Talks on Beelzebub's Tales. Coombe Springs Press, 1977.

Taylor, Paul Beekman
Gurdjieff and Orage: Brothers in Elysium. Weiser Books, 2001.

Welch, Louise
Orage with Gurdjieff in America. Routledge, Chapman & Hall, Incorporated, 1982.

Gurdjieff, G. I.
The Struggle of the Magicians. The Stourton Press, 1957.
Views from the Real World: Early Talks of Gurdjieff. Arkana, 1984.
Beelzebub's Tales to His Grandson. Harcourt, Brace & Company; Routledge & Kegan Paul, 1950.
Meetings with Remarkable Men. E. P. Dutton, 1963.
Life is real only then, when "I am." E. P. Dutton, 1978.
The Herald of Coming Good. La Société Anonyme des Éditions de l'Ouest, 1933.
Transcripts of Gurdjieff's Meetings 1941–1946. Book Studio, 2009.

BOOK STUDIO

Solano, Solita, and Kathryn Hulme.
Gurdjieff and the Women of the Rope: Notes of Meetings in Paris and New York 1935–1939 and 1948–1949. Book Studio, 2012.

Hulme, Kathryn.
Undiscovered Country: A Spiritual Adventure. Book Studio, 2012.

Leblanc, Georgette.
The Courage Machine: A New Life in a New World. Book Studio, 2012.

Cosgrave, John O'Hara.
The Academy for Souls. Book Studio, 2013.

INDEX

www.ingramcontent.com/pod-product-compliance
Lightning Source LLC
Chambersburg PA
CBHW020351100426
42812CB00001B/27